D1549667

WORLD WAR — COLD WAR
Selections from
War Commentary and *Freedom*
1939-1950

FREEDOM PRESS CENTENARY SERIES
Volume 3 WORLD WAR — COLD WAR 1939-1945

FREEDOM PRESS CENTENARY SERIES
1886-1986

TO COMMEMORATE the Centenary of FREEDOM and the
FREEDOM PRESS in 1986 the editors produced a special issue of
FREEDOM which is available as a FREEDOM PRESS title:
FREEDOM A HUNDRED YEARS October 1886 to October 1986
8 pages (A4 11¾" x 8¼") ISBN 0 900384 35 2

This volume is one of six FREEDOM PRESS are producing to cover
a century of Periodical publishing:
    Volume 1* Selections from FREEDOM 1886-1936
    Volume 2* Selections from SPAIN & THE WORLD 1936-1939
    Volume 3* Selections from WAR COMMENTARY & FREEDOM
               1939-1950
    Volume 4   Selections from FREEDOM 1951-1964
    Volume 5   Selections from ANARCHY 1961-1970
    Volume 6   Selections from FREEDOM 1965-1986

* Indicates that there are also supplementary volumes. Full
particulars from FREEDOM PRESS

This ambitious project has been made financially possible firstly
by a major contribution from the FRIENDS OF FREEDOM PRESS Ltd
for FREEDOM's Centenary issue, and for the six volumes by the
generosity of a long-standing friend of FREEDOM PRESS: Hans
Deichmann.

WORLD WAR — COLD WAR

Selections from
WAR COMMENTARY and FREEDOM
1939-1950

FREEDOM PRESS
London
1989

Published by
FREEDOM PRESS
84B Whitechapel High St
London E1 7QX

1989

© FREEDOM PRESS

ISBN 0 900384 48 4

PRINTED IN GT. BRITAIN BY ALDGATE PRESS LONDON E.1.

CONTENTS

PART 1
WORLD WAR
1939-1945

PART 2
COLD WAR
1945-1950

Cartoons by Philip Sansom

Editor's Note

On this 50th anniversary of the declaration of war on Germany by Britain there will be no shortage of commemorative meetings and religious services, and a shoal of books extolling the gallantry of our fighting men and women who gave their lives in the struggle against "the evil forces of Nazifascism". The present volume will be the odd man out in that it consists of articles selected from a journal which opposed from the beginning that fratricidal struggle which cost the lives of some 50 million men women and children (for this was the first war which did not discriminate between the armed forces and civilian populations). In the first issue published in December 1939 the editors wrote:

That many sincere anti-fascists believe in the "righteousness" of this war, quite independently of the propaganda served up by the Conservative and so called Radical Press, is not surprising. They say: "We, who have always shouted that Fascism must be crushed should, now that an opportunity presents itself, act in accordance with our principles". Their actions are, therefore, governed not by reason but their desire to prove to themselves and to others that they are consistent both in speech and in action.

There are others calling themselves Revolutionaries who believe that war creates a Revolution. The tragic consequences of the last war have apparently not taught them anything. To-day the "strategists" are in good company with the British Government which has been doing its utmost to convince the British people that there will be a revolution in Germany before long. They omit to add that in the event of a revolution in Germany they will crush it with the same ruthlessness that they propose to crush Nazism. Mr. Churchill, with his past experience, will see to that.

Finally, there is that vast mass of people with no opinions; who are fed exclusively by the poisoned pens of the Capitalist Press, and the noble words uttered by their political leaders through that most effective channel of propaganda, the BBC.

All these categories of "anti-fascists", referred to above, are either mistaken or misguided, for in no circumstances can this war be justified; in no circumstances can this war be justified; in no circumstances can it bring peace.

* * *

The first issue of *War Commentary* consisted of 16 duplicated pages reflecting, one imagines, the four editors' pessimism as to the reception it would receive. There was justification for this pessimism since earlier that year with the final collapse of the revolutionary struggle in Spain the journal which had supported our Spanish comrades for more than two years, *Spain & the World*, folded and though a successor in *Revolt!* followed, it quietly faded out in June 1939 after six issues, and with it most of the editorial group. However the pessimism was ill-founded, for the second issue had to be printed and appeared as a monthly until 1941 when six supplements were issued, and from 1942 *War Commentary* appeared twice a month, increasing its format in 1944 and changing its title to FREEDOM the following year. In 1942 because of growing difficulties with printers, we took over an abandoned printing works where nearly a quarter of a million F.P. books and pamphlets were printed and sold through bookshops and at regular open air meetings in London, Glasgow, Bristol etc. as well as at the weekly lectures and public meetings organised by the anarchists or by the political parties.

Between 1939 and 1950 248 issues of *War Commentary* and *Freedom* appeared which in terms of printed pages of a book would have filled some 7,000. This volume of Selections and the four supplements take up less than 900 pages none of which reveals that that original group of four had much expanded, had attracted many active sympathisers; that *War Commentary* was regularly reporting the imprisonment of comrades either for conscientious objection to military service or for 'obstruction' when selling the paper or holding street meetings or public protests. Nor does it include interesting debates and historical material. I regret the omission of the former; most of the historical material has been reprinted in pamphlet or volume form and has therefore not been lost. However regular features such as Through the Press, Red & Black Notebook, Anarchist Commentary, have been lost except to the researcher (since all our journals from 1886 are available on micro film).

*   *   *

In my Introduction to the 1988 edition of *Neither East nor West* I pointed out that though the selection of 51 of Marie Louise Berneri's articles from 1939-1948 was made with a view to providing a comprehensive picture of the war years and the phoney cold war that followed, it had to be read in conjunction with this volume. Inevitably I must now recommend you the reader of *World War — Cold War* to the first supplement *Neither East nor West*!

We were fortunate in the late 1930s to have made contact with Reginald Reynolds who was deeply involved in the anti-colonial struggle. Much of the second supplement on *British Imperialism: Background to the Palestine Crisis 1938-1948* consists of articles he contributed in the decade preceding the creation of the State of Israel in 1948. Few people now realise that Palestine was once a British Mandate and that many of the Arab-Israeli problems of today stem from a British policy which, as Reginald Reynolds put it "used Jews as colonists in a British scheme to create an 'Ulster' in Palestine".

As one observes the antics of the political parties, the media and the public over the nuclear 'deterrent' that never was, one would like to hope that some lessons might be learned from the third Supplement on *The Left & World War II 1939-1945*.

The fourth Supplement: *Neither Nationalisation nor Privatisation 1945-1950* is more than topical as the Thatcher government "sells off the family silver at any price". It was the Labour government from 1945-1950 which nationalised major industries and services such the railways, mines and steel, and introduced the National Health Service.

PART 1

Self Confession

The Freethinker, referring to the British White Paper, writes:

"But the following criticism of the mentality of our Berlin Ambassador is also worth noting: In paragraph 5, Sir Neville [Henderson] refers to 'the great achievement of Hitler who restored to the German nation its self respect and its disciplined orderliness' and in the next sentence writes: 'The tyrannical methods which were employed within Germany itself to obtain this result were detestable, but were Germany's own concern'. This does not make sense. How can it be a 'great achievement' to restore 'disciplined orderliness' by 'detestable tyrannical methods'? . . . Sir Neville continues: 'Many of Herr Hitler's social reforms, in spite of their complete disregard of personal liberty of thought, word or deed, were on highly advanced democratic lines'. Many contradictions are packed into these few words. It must obviously have been very hard for Sir Neville to find that after all Hitler, as a champion of advanced democracy, in the end overstepped the mark. What a hero he would have been to the Ambassador if only Hitler had confined his 'advanced' ideas to such trifles as the monstrous persecution of the Jews, or the horrors of a concentration camp."   *War Commentary*, December 1939

"Crusade for Freedom and Against Fascism"?

"What caused the Second World War? There can be many answers: German grievances against the peace settlement of 1919 and the failure to redress them; failure to agree on a system of general controlled disarmament; failure to accept the principles of collective security and to operate them; fear of communism . . . at the end, perhaps only mutual bluff. The question of its immediate outbreak is easier to answer. The house of commons forced war on a reluctant British government, and that government dragged an even more reluctant French government in their train. The British people accepted the decision of parliament and government without complaint. It is impossible to tell whether they welcomed it or whether they would have preferred some other outcome. Argument was almost stilled once the war had started, and, if doubts existed, they were kept in the shadows.

There was much talk later of a world crusade for freedom and against fascism. France, Great Britain and the Dominions were, however, the only powers who declared war on Germany. All other countries which took part in the war waited until Hitler chose to attack them, the two world powers — Soviet Russia and the United States — as supinely as the rest. Perhaps the difference was no more than technical."

(A. J. P. Taylor, *English History 1914-1945*, Oxford University Press 1965, page 453)

"God is with us" — "Gott mit uns!"

That is the history of all religions; that is the effect of all divine inspirations and legislations. In history the name of God is the terrible club with which all divinely inspired men, the great 'virtuous geniuses', have beaten down liberty, dignity, reason, and prosperity of man. — MIKHAIL BAKUNIN

The British Government

"Now may God defend you all and may God be with the right" — **Chamberlain** (3/3/39)
". . . and we reverently commit our cause to God." — **King George** (3/9/39).

His Majesty's 'Opposition'

"May God be with you" — **Greenwood (for the Labour 'Opposition')** ". . . with a firm reliance on the protection of Divine Providence . . ." — **Sir Archibald Sinclair (for the Liberal 'Opposition')**

The German Government

"We only wish that God Almighty, who has blessed our arms, may enlighten other nations . . ." — **Hitler (Danzig speech).**

The Polish Government

". . . the blessing of the Almighty rests on our fight." — **President Moscicki**

The Church

"May God help us in the great ordeal which now awaits us." — **Archbishop of Canterbury and other dignitaries of the Church.**

"When you come to think of it, it is a great honour to be chosen by God to be his ally in so great a contest." — **Canon C. Morgan Smith**.

"We thank God that He gave us a speedy victory to our arms. . . . We thank Him that injustice, centuries old, has been broken down through his grace . . ." — **The German Evangelical 'Opposition' in the Spiritual Councils Proclamation on the capture of Poland.**

Bedlam Politics[1]

Speaking at the Royal Institution yesterday, the Soviet Ambassador invited us never to forget that good English expression, *first things first*.

An admirable sentiment which we can all approve.

But what are the first things which we should put first?

The first thing, according to Mr Maisky, is to crush Hitlerite Germany — not, be it observed, to crush *fascism* — that might bring the mailed fist down on the heads of some of our friends — on Admiral Darlan's head, on General Franco's head, on Comrade Stalin's head — and on heads still nearer home.

No! Our politicians no longer revile fascism; they have invented an historical abstraction called 'Hitlerite Germany', something which is neither Hitler nor Germany, neither fascism nor totalitarianism.

Is that putting things first? Is it not rather an evasion of the real issue, which is now as it has always been the issue between freedom and tyranny.

When our leaders speak in unequivocal voices about political realities; when they admit that fascism is not confined to Italy or to Germany, but is a disease which has invaded every country in the world — Spain and France, Japan and the United States, Soviet Russia and the British Empire — then and only then shall we believe that they are putting first things first.

The reality is far otherwise. Our politicians are grotesque. They only need a bladder on the end of a stick to complete their clown-like appearance; an appearance which is nevertheless very deceptive; consider them:

Clown-politicians who hand out contracts with one hand and receive them with the other;

Clown-politicians who are patriotically inspired to defend their class interests with Swinton Committees and anti-comintern funds;

Clown-politicians who do their buying in the Black Market; and their cooking in Whitehall;

1. Text of Herbert Read's address to the inaugural meeting of the Friends of Freedom Press in the Conway Hall on 28th September 1941.

Clown-politicians who launch their chartered platitudes on the deep Atlantic of their hypocrisy.

Now, the hypocrite is nearly related to the lunatic. The definition of one kind of lunatic is a man with a split mind.

Our leaders are mostly of this kind. With one half of their mind they admire this fellow Hitler. He has abolished unemployment, which they could never succeed in doing; he has created the most efficient army in the world, which they envy; he has liquidated these troublesome trade unions; above all, he is now doing the best job of all — ridding the world of the Bolshevik menace. One side of the mind of our leaders finds fascism very very attractive.

But the other side of this split mind realises that this fellow Hitler does not play the game. He is not a gentleman. He not only breaks the rules of what is curiously called 'civilised' warfare, drops bombs on private property, and on innocent civilians; he actually wants to pinch our markets, our shipping, our empire!

One could almost pity such tortured consciences, but then we realise that it is these idiots with a split mind who rule the demented world of today. A world in which the mad lead the mad.

For we have to admit that it is not our rulers alone who are mad. They have infected whole nations.

The extension of the war to Russia has achieved what the press calls the final unity of the British nation. From the Tory right to the Communist left, we fight in one unbroken line.

Similarly, according to the same press, the virtual extension of the war to the United States has achieved a world-wide unity of the democratic nations: they fight in one unbroken line.

Now when you find such an appearance of unity in the world, history leads us to suspect the most complete form of suppression and persecution.

Man is various. He divides into various psychological types, and according to his type, his feelings and opinions will differ.

It is natural that men should suffer, and progress consists in the discussion and reconciliation of differences. That is the dialectical principle of life itself, and is a process that has no finality. The only finality is death, or biological extinction.

When two men cannot reconcile their difference by reason and discussion, and cannot agree to differ, then they resort to fighting. Their neighbours pull them apart and the state of our civilisation or social morality is exalted enough to make such men feel ashamed of their behaviour.

When a few score men lose their reason and threaten to fight, then it is called a riot, and these men are restrained by their neighbours through professional keepers-of-the-peace called police. But the men who lost their reason are no longer so ashamed of themselves.

When a large part of a nation loses its reason and threatens to fight, then it is called a rebellion. Police are no longer adequate and the two halves of the nation must fight it out. Nowadays the side that can command the greatest number of tanks and aeroplanes suppresses the other side and that is called a victory for order and justice.

When two nations lose their reason and begin a fight, it is called war, and there is now no longer the slightest trace of shame. To fight becomes a high moral duty, blessed by the churches. Each nation is united. It is a mass renunciation of reason, it is mass insanity. And there is no limit to what D. H. Lawrence called "the abysmal insanity of the normal masses".

This abysmal insanity is now world-wide. It engulfs Europe and Asia, Africa and Australia, and now spreads to America.

When bedlam is universal it is the sane man who is accused of being abnormal. A sane man in an asylum has not much chance of being taken seriously. And if the lunatics are violent and break out of bonds, he is powerless to restrain them.

I wish this was a metaphor. I wish I were speaking to you in parables. But it is a strictly scientific description of the world we are now living in. We are living in a world seized with mass insanity. And it requires an almost superhuman effort to remain sane in such a world.

But assuming we retain our whole minds, our sanity, what then can we do?

Frankly, I do not think we can do anything spectacular. We are helpless. We have no tanks, we have no aeroplanes. We are a handful of peaceful men and women caught in the mad rush of millions of madmen.

Willy-nilly we are carried in the irresistible swirl of military and industrial conscription, of crushing taxation and poverty, of death and destruction. We are condemned to live in an epoch of physical misery and social degradation.

But one thing we retain, which all other people have lost: our spiritual calmness, the still voice of reason.

It is a precious possession which we have to carry through this dark age, and this we can do in the immemorial way in which truth has always survived tyranny, neglect and persecution.

The true believers in freedom are being driven to the catacombs again, and it was from the catacombs that a faith which was to transform the world once emerged.

That faith, in all its social and ethical implications, has long since been abandoned by the Church which is its official embodiment.

We here are nearer to the spirit of the catacombs than any other group of men in the world.

Let us act in the spirit of the catacombs, forming our cells, sending out our preachers, striving to throw out the evil spirits which possess the masses.

But the modern evangelist must work mainly through the printed word, and that is why we must establish and maintain a press, a press from which the Friends of Freedom can pour out an endless stream of pamphlets and periodicals, all testifying to this truth: *that man is born equal, to share equally the fruits of the earth, and to live in mutual friendship with all his kind.*
November 1941   HERBERT READ

Contradictions Exposed

"The definition of one kind of lunatic is a man with a split mind. Our leaders are mostly of this kind," says Herbert Read elsewhere in this issue. This seems to be particularly true of our 'leaders' in connection with their attitude to Russia and the Communist Party. While Beaverbrook and other prominent politicians praise Stalin and Russia to the skies, Herbert Morrison calls the Communists "miserable people" and "semi-Nazi". This would be understandable if the Communist Party in this country and the Russian Government were not bound together by the closest connections. But the argument used to justify the suppression of the Communist Party in France and other countries and of the *Daily Worker* in this country (though unofficially) was that the Communists take their orders from Moscow.

Malayan Communists Gaoled
While Beaverbrook and Stalin were drinking toasts to the Friends

of Soviet Russia, a Singapore magistrate was sentencing two Chinese to 18 months rigorous imprisonment for assisting in the management of the Communist Party. The magistrate accepted "the police submission that the Malayan Communist Party was not pro-British".

More Stalinist than Stalin

Stalin has been able to obtain all the help he wanted from Beaverbrook and Co.; why then has he not put in a good word for the *Daily Worker*? Have not the Communists in this country pledged themselves to give their full support to Churchill? Is not Harry Pollitt encouraging the workers to go to it? If Stalin has not used his influence to restore to the Communist Party in this country the right to have a newspaper, it is probably because he does not consider the matter very important. If he does not think so, the Communists in this country should stop trying to get the support of influential people and spending money on advertisements.

Tory-Communist Coalition

That *Strike Now in the West* is an empty slogan, and nothing more than that has been further shown by the attitude of the Communist Party at the Lancaster by-election.

Instead of supporting the Independent Liberal candidate, Colonel Ross, who advocated the creation of a second front in the West, the Communist Party sent a deputation to the Conservative headquarters and offered to work for the return of Second-Lieutenant Maclean, the National Government candidate. Maclean was backed by Churchill, who, so far, seems to be completely opposed to the opening of a new front. He proved this by defending Halifax after he had declared that it was impossible for Britain to attack in the West now. And has not Churchill defended Colonel Moore-Brabazon against all his critics?

Why should the Communist Party urge workers to sign petitions asking the Government to send an expeditionary force on the continent, while, at the same time, it supports Tories completely opposed to that tactic or even openly hostile to Russia? Another case of split minds.

Revolution in Europe Another Slogan

We have often said in these columns that the British Government was not seriously concerned with the creation of revolutionary movements on the Continent. This view has been confirmed by the attitude taken by General De Gaulle regarding the assassination of Germans by French people. As the (self-appointed) leader of the French people he gave his orders. *French people must not shoot Germans.* Did he give this order to stop, as he said, the spilling of blood in an unequal struggle? Such sentimental considerations are unlikely to sway the minds of people who rub their hands at the news that hundreds of thousands of Germans are blown to bits or burned alive. De Gaulle has no objections to British bombs killing French people, as most probably happens when the RAF bombs French ports. He has no objections to quixotic expeditions to the colonies where French people are involved.

We shall not discuss here if the shooting of German soldiers can have a revolutionary effect or not from our point of view, but we want to ask the people who have for months past glibly advocated a revolution on the continent what they meant by it. When Churchill and lesser politicians advocate sabotage and make splendid calls to revolt, do they imagine that the people under Hitler's domination will carry on these revolutions without having to do any killing? The Beaverbrook Press will perhaps now initiate the French workers into Gandhi's tactics. Up to now there has been only talk of revolt and sabotage which cannot be carried out without a tremendous sacrifice of human lives. The British Government and their stooges like De Gaulle would not hesitate to sacrifice the lives of hundreds and thousands of French people if they thought it served their ends. But as we have pointed out before, they are afraid of a revolution. They know that the people who will take part in it will not be well-bred reactionaries à la De Gaulle. They know that when revolutions start they would be unable to control them. They prefer to wait to fight the Germans when the French people will not be left to their own initiative, but will be fighting under the orders of bourgeois generals who will see that the victory remains *theirs*.

The newspapers reported that Chile was the only country on the American continent that lodged a protest with the German Government regarding the shooting of the French hostages. It is needless to point out that the protest of such a weak country as Chile will not have the slightest effect. But it is significant that the US has not thought it worthwhile to add its protest. It offers another indication of the indifference of the 'democracies' towards the attempts of the French people to revolt.

November 1941

M.L.B.

Women, War and Conscription

The last war ended just in time to save women from conscription; this time it has overtaken them,[1] and it is going to be interesting to see how it operates and to watch feminine reaction to it. We are assured there is to be no class distinction; women of all classes, married and single, will register and will be set to work where they are likely to be most useful. We have already seen the hosiery factory and mill workers transferred to munitions' factories; one may perhaps be forgiven a little scepticism as to whether we shall see a similarly wholesale transference of middle-class girls and women — many of whom have never earned their livings in their lives, having been supported by their fathers until they married and then by the husbands they secured in the marriage market — to such work. As the majority of middle class women workers are employed in offices, and office work is apparently a reserved occupation — the burden of the industrial conscription of women falls where it might have been expected to fall — on the working class.

According to a Ministry of Labour statement the question of any conscientious objection on the part of women conscripts "does not arise" as women may be drafted to other occupations than munitions making. That a woman might object to being conscripted for any war work at all does not seem to have occurred to the Ministry. Such a phenomenon as an out-and-out female objector to any kind of participation in what is popularly called "our war effort" is apparently unthinkable to the official mind. What is the position of such a women? The Appeal Board is not prepared to consider any 'frivolous' appeal — such as disinclination to participate in the national war effort; it will presumably consider only cases of hardship, domestic difficulties, unsuitability for the appointed work, etc. In the opinion of the Central Board for Conscientious Objectors the out-and-out female objector has no choice but to refuse to register . . . and "non-compliance with any regulations will, in the absence of specific penalties, be those laid down for general offences under the Defence Regulations". That is to say imprisonment or a fine or both. The Appeal Board would no doubt take into consideration

1. Three hundred thousand women registered for war work in April 1941 — Editor.

any pacifist objection to the manufacture of munitions, though such an objection *would not be a specific ground for exemption.*

The industrial conscript, in short, both male and female, is in the same position precisely as the military conscript, except that the industrial conscript is not to be allowed to "make known conscientious scruples" at the time of registering — in case these should "turn out to be quite irrelevant". But "it is not the Minister's intention *so far as it can be avoided* to direct persons to perform services against which they have genuine conscientious objections."

The emphasis is mine. It is all very vague, as will be seen, and somewhat contradictory and the Minister seemed to overlook the fact that you can send a mare to the water . . .

Crêches are to be provided for the children under school age of conscripted mothers, and the children, we are assured, are to be properly cared for. It seems odd to recollect the outcry there was in this country a score of years ago over the alleged wicked Bolshevik break-up of home life by sending the mothers to work in factories and leaving their children to be cared for by the State in nursery-schools and crêches. Where now is all that fine sentiment about the sacredness of motherhood? Mothers now are asked — nay more, compelled — to do their bit in co-operating in the murder of other mothers and their children in German and Italian towns. As I write this, how the women will take it remains to be seen. Complaint is likely on two scores — the class distinction operating, securing the better jobs for the 'better' class women, the assumption that a factory girl is only fit for factory work; and on the score of relegating the children under school age to crêches. The conscientious objectors are likely to be a mere handful, because the mass of women are still no more than grumblers over the criminal insanity of war. They grumble about the nuisance of it, the black-out, the difficulty of getting different things from the shops, the increased cost of living, but the mass of them never ask themselves whether war is the only solution of international problems — still less what causes those problems. The majority, even of women who are opposed to war, are deplorably lacking in any realisation of the *causes* of war innate in the State system of society. Their opposition to war is purely pacifist, nothing to do with any anti-capitalist, anti-imperialist attitude, still less anything so profoundly revolutionary as the realisation that the State, by its very nature, is the source of all evil. The conscription of women may assist the slow process of thinking. The mass of women who support war can have no logical objection to their own conscription — though they may and should object to sex differentiation in the rates of pay in the trades to which they are conscripted. In spite of all the talk of sex equality — and the bland general assumption that it is a fact — the fact still remains that woman labour is cheap labour. It is up to women to see that they are not exploited in their forced labour — but more importantly it is up to women to begin to *think*, instead of merely acquiescing into everything the capitalist press tells them in its rôle of mouthpiece of 'democracy's' dictators, or at most grumbling. War is a man-made affair, but the conscription of women brings it into the very heart of the home; women are no longer to be allowed merely to acquiesce — or to volunteer their services; they no longer have any choice but to become part of the war-machine along with the men — or go to prison for resistance. Forced out of their homes and out of jobs of their own choosing — or idleness and parasitism according to class — resentment may smoulder into a spark of revolt which might well express itself in a stubborn, sullen incompetence Mr Bevin had not bargained for. So long as women acquiesce and co-operate in wars they sanction wars and have no right to complain either over the horror and stupidity of it, or the inconvenience and disruptiveness of it where ordinary living is concerned. If instead of acquiescing and co-operating on the side of war they gave their support to the opposition to it, to the exposure of it as a capitalist-imperialist racket from which the common people may expect to gain precisely nothing — despite the hot-air of the press and the glib assurances of politicians — what immense potentialities for peace would the vast 'regiment of women' represent.

"If it were left to women I am sure there would be no wars", a woman whose husband was in France wrote to me early on in the war. The trouble is that the women have always left it to the men — and in doing so have given them a free hand to wreck their world.

The conscription of women gives them a chance to protest — beyond mere grumbling — at the man-made folly they have sanctioned for so long. It is a woman's opportunity to range herself on the side of sanity and peace, and instead of encouraging men in their madness begin a long overdue process of bringing them to their senses.

April 1941   ETHEL MANNIN

War Aims at Last!

"Less than two years after 'Cameronian' fired the first shot in
Reynolds News of 10th September 1939, the campaign for a
statement of war aims has been won." In this jubilant fashion
Reynolds News of August 24th acclaims the joint declaration of
Churchill and Roosevelt which Attlee broadcast to the world on
August 14th. Drawing attention to the similar declaration of
President Wilson's Fourteen Points in the last war, *Reynolds News*
goes on to point the similarity of the Eight Points to Attlee's Six
Points of November 1939. But 'Cameronian' himself, in the same
issue, quotes with approval the remark of a war minister that "we
have still to learn many of the lessons of the last war." *Reynolds
News* premature jubilation makes it clear that the lesson of the
origin and fate of the Fourteen Points has been wholly lost on
them. On the other hand, the Eight Points make it equally clear
that Churchill and Roosevelt, representing the ruling class, have
learnt it only too well!

The recent declaration indeed bears a striking resemblance to
Wilson's ill-fated Points — 1 merely repeats Balfour's declaration
to the effect that we did not wish to add one square inch to our
colonial burden; 2 and 3 repeat Points 6 and 13 in Wilson's list; 4, 5
and 6 cover his third; 7 is Wilson's second; 8 is a modification of his
fourth and nineteenth. Two of the Fourteen Points are omitted
altogether; there is no reference to secret treaties being
abandoned in favour of 'open diplomacy' (hardly surprising in
view of the embarrassment which this question has raised in the
past — in regard to the mutually contradictory Palestine pledges
given to Jews and Arabs, and the National government's several
'gentlemen's agreements' with Mussolini, for the partition of
Abyssinia, and the assistance of Franco, for example). More
significant is the other omission — the absence of any reference to
the colonies — an omission which has doubtless been the subject
of considerable colonial discussion. But the colonies, especially
India, are too voluble about their 'rights' themselves, for Churchill
and Roosevelt to reopen this delicate subject!

Peace Aims and the Trade Unions in the last war
But we are less concerned with the content of the Eight Points
than with their possible effect in clearing away working-class
doubts about the purity of the Tories' war motives. When Wilson

advanced his Fourteen Points, he was conscious of a "vital need
. . . for a 'revision' of what some termed the Imperialist
aspirations of the Entente. . . . The Allies must make it plain that
they were waging their battle on behalf of permanent peace and
not for the sake of territorial annexations. Only thus could the
enthusiasm of liberal and labour elements be maintained."
(*Intimate Papers of Colonel House*, Vol III, pp. 172-3, 176-7). He
believed that "it was important also to pledge, if possible, the
Allied Governments to the principles of a settlement which would
justify the sacrifice of the war and maintain the enthusiasm of the
liberal and labour circles in Great Britain and France." (Idem., p.
326). Wilson was evidently fully aware of the propaganda value of
his peace programme.

Lloyd George was no less alive to the need for clearing away
doubts on the home front. "There was . . . an advantage," he
writes in his *War Memoirs*, "in having a Government at the head
of affairs which had the support of Labour. This secured the
adhesion of the great Labour organisations whose action and
sympathetic aid was essential to its vigorous prosecution. Had
Labour been hostile the war could not have been carried on
effectively. Had Labour been lukewarm victory would have been
secured with increased and increasing difficulty. The most
prominent and influential leaders of trade unionism worked for
victory throughout the war. Without their help it could not have
been achieved." (page 220). (One may be pardoned for asking
whose victory the prominent and influential leaders of trade
unionism worked? Certainly not the victory of the British
workers!)

Yet just as in this war, the declaration of war aims was deferred
as long as possible. Wilson had to resort to threats of a public
exposure to the American Congress before his special emissary,
Colonel House, received any sympathetic hearing at all from the
Allies. By the end of 1917, however, Lloyd George reports that
"amongst the workmen there was an unrest that was disturbing
and might at any time become dangerous. The efforts we were
making to comb out more men for the army were meeting with
resistance amongst the Trade Unions whose loyalty and patriotism
had been above reproach" (page 486). Conscription and the
dilution of skilled labour had created "difficulties with our
manpower" which "had almost produced a deadlock with the
Trade Unions. Without their goodwill and co-operation we could
not have secured further recruits from amongst the exempted —

certainly without a resistance which might have alienated organised labour throughout the land. . . . It therefore became necessary to open negotiations with them." As a result of all this Lloyd George summoned the Trades Union leaders to a meeting in the Caxton Hall on January 5th, 1918, and there decided that the Government's peace proposals were essentially the same as those put forward by the Labour party in December 1917. "I made it clear that our one object of the war was to defend the violated public law of Europe, to defend Treaty obligations and to secure the restoration of Belgium" (page 2486). The Labour Party replied with a manifesto on the *War Aims of the British People*, adding a special "Note on the Prime Minister's Statement" declaring that "The great speech made by Mr Lloyd George to a Congress of Trade Union delegates on 5th January 1918, is by far the most important which any statesman has made during the war." (Similar claims have been made for the Churchill-Roosevelt declaration!) "It makes plain the essential unity of purpose that now animates the British people. It reveals a Government and a people seeking no predatory aims of any kind, pursuing with one unchanging mind, one unchanging purpose: to obtain justice for others so that we thereby secure for ourselves a lasting peace. We desire neither to destroy Germany nor diminish her boundaries: we seek neither to exalt ourselves nor to enlarge our Empire." If the Labour leaders of that time were sincere (and from the conduct of their successors in this war, one may doubt it), one hopes that they received a jolt at finding the Empire which they so curiously describe as 'theirs' increased by one million four hundred thousand square miles, Germany's boundaries heavily curtailed, and lasting peace a mirage. But the point to grasp is that Lloyd George succeeded, with the help of the Fourteen Points, in fooling the Trades Unions into acting once more as recruiting sergeants for the bosses.

When, in the last war, H. G. Wells' great slogan — "The War to End War" — had worn a bit thin in the face of unequal sacrifices of the workers and the soaring profits of the employers, Wilson's Fourteen Points came as a godsend to the Coalition Government. We have tried briefly to indicate the actual role they played and to recall their fate in the waste paper baskets of Versailles. Now, as then, the course of the war is marked by increasing pressure on the workers of the belligerent (and, indirectly, of the 'neutral' nations). Now, as then, the denial of precise statements of what they are fighting and sacrificing for has produced apathy and unrest among the workers. Lloyd George's remarks, quoted above, apply with equal, if not greater, force to the present war. As before, the same method of injecting further doses of ideological 'democratic' content into the war has been applied. This is the real content of the Eight Point declaration, and it has no other purpose.

It only remains to see if a further study of the propaganda history of the last war can help us further to analyse the moves of politicians desperately seeking for means of maintaining the support of the workers' organisations. The trade union leaders are easy enough to fool, from the point of view of their parliamentary colleagues; but there is beneath them the discontent of the workers. The Eight Points are really directed at them. The final shot in the last war which showed up at the last minute of the tottering morale of the Allies, was the League of Nations. There are still those who would try to breathe a semblance of life into that smug old corpse, the "thieves' kitchen" as Lenin called it. But they will be only voices crying unregarded in the wilderness of Geneva. Yet it is not to be supposed that a substitute is lacking.

'Federal Union' raises its ugly head

The League of Nations was conceived — I believe by H. N. Brailsford — quite early on in the first Imperialist War. It sank into obscurity until finance capital needed it for its own purpose — to revive the again-flagging war-enthusiasm of the workers in the Allied countries. Federal Union was conceived by the ingenious Clarence Streit even before the present war had broken out. Yet in spite of its wealthy and philanthropic backers, and the enthusiasm of intellectuals of the Left like G. D. H. Cole, it too was laid by in the bottom drawer, ready to be brought out again when it could usefully serve the turn of British ruling class interests. It has been stirring recently, and one may safely bet that Federal Union will figure in the next propaganda push thrust by the Ministry of Information on the war-weary British workers. It is a fossil well suited to the musty propaganda department of Whitehall! Nevertheless the Eight Point declaration of those two stalwarts of Democracy, Sidney-Street-Churchill and strike-breaker-Roosevelt, must not be underestimated. The jubilation of *Reynolds News* indicates how easily the Labour leaders, with their vast organs of propaganda, are fooled even in the teeth of the most glaring lessons of history.

September 1941   J.H.

For What?

The whole world is at war. Even the few countries not directly engaged in the struggle are suffering an economic crisis and political repression which makes their fate just as bad as those of the belligerent countries.

In Eastern Europe, the Pacific and North Africa, total war is carried on with all it implies in the sacrifice of human lives and natural riches. The myth which was born in 1939 of an easy war where Maginot lines and blockades would replace tank battles and bayonet charges seems far away. With it has died the confidence in a short war in which fascism would be completely crushed and democracy triumph not only in Europe but in the whole world.

The progressive 'democratisation' of Britain and of the Empire has not taken place. At home, as in the Dominions and Colonies the ruling class remains all powerful and the greatest sacrifices have been borne by the workers.

The aim of the war which seemed to many people extraordinarily obvious becomes more and more difficult to define. Democracy becomes an empty word when countries with a long record of feudal oppression like Poland take part in it. Democracy becomes an obviously hypocritical excuse when countries like India are forced to fight for it. How can we fight for democracy when we have on our side a Roman Catholic, anti-semitic country like Canada, when we seek the alliance of South American governments with more resemblance to Franco's than to democratic ones, when Burma is refused independence?

The excuse may be put forward that the means justify the ends, that socialist measures must wait and alliance with reactionary governments be sought so that the war can be won more quickly. This excuse can convince only those who do not grasp the nature of the forces in conflict. But even if we stop considering for a moment the means to be used we find that the *end* for which concessions and compromises are advocated has not yet been defined. Are we fighting for the Europe of the Polish foreign minister Count Edward Raczynski who, in the *Sunday Times*, talks of restoring the balance of power in Europe by giving to Poland the place previously occupied by France and by carving up Germany?

Are we fighting for the preservation of an Empire which will not even be given the privileges of the Atlantic Charter?

Are we fighting for the Britain of the probable future Archbishop of Canterbury, the Archbishop of York who stands for "a heavily armed Britain and conscription for the next two generations?"

Are we fighting for Stalin's order in Europe which will strengthen Poland, *allow* a certain amount of independence to Europe and leave Britain's ambitions in the Mediterranean and North Africa a completely free rein?

This is the end which the head of the Russian State, the Church of England and mighty politicians want us to achieve, while they talk of fighting for democracy!

The war becomes more and more clearly an imperialist war. While people may believe that in Britain and France they were defending democracy they have no excuse for thinking that they will die in the Far East for the same cause. What has taken the place of the 'fight for democracy' humbug? For many a faith in Russia, in Stalin's order in Europe! But is it because Russia represents democracy? or socialism? No, Finland is not forgotten yet and Stalin has been a 'red Tsar' too long to become a second President Roosevelt. Russia arouses a certain amount of confidence and admiration because she is the first country to resist Hitler with any success. People are not interested to know how the Russians are defending their country. If they use means similar or worse than those used by the Nazis; if in order to wage the war successfully Stalin has to decree that black marketeers should be shot and people imprisoned if they absent themselves from work. The people are not in the least perturbed in their admiration for Stalin when he uses exactly the same methods which they condemn in Hitler. They are supposed to fight totalitarianism and they put their trust in exactly the same kind of totalitarian regime!

The people of Britain and of the Allied countries have been so doped by high sounding pretexts to their struggles and sacrifices that they do not realise that they are only unthinking pawns in the hands of their exploiters and that they are fighting for interests which are not theirs.

February 1942

Darlan's Assassination and the Press

An unauthorised squabble among the dolls is an embarrassing situation for any ventriloquist to face and De Gaulle's intransigent screams of anger at the favours shown to his scab rival Darlan caused something of a hot spot for the British authorities and their sly American partners, especially as the row was taken up by all the pseudo-Left element who wished to divert attention from their support of the attack on the workers in England itself.

Christmas, however, brought a pleasant surprise (or was it a surprise?) in the Government's political stocking, with the sudden exit of Darlan from the Punch and Judy show. It also did the Communists and the Labour scabs a bad turn by forcing them to find a new red herring to drag across the factory floors for the next few months.

Of the event itself there is little one can say, as the secrecy of the hurried trial and execution have allowed little information of any value to emerge. This very secrecy ('for reasons of security') does, however, tend to increase one's suspicions. There are a number of possible explanations, any of which might well be true. The assassin might have been a German or an Italian or a British or a De Gaullist agent, or he might have been a revolutionary terrorist or even a freelance enthusiast. The Germans, naturally announce that he was a British agent, but produce no evidence. The Allies content themselves with oblique suggestion, by remarking that the man's mother is an Italian, living in Italy. Supported by no other evidence, this is meaningless. Louis Levy, writing in *Reynolds News*, states that "it is rumoured that he was a member of the Parti Populaire Francais the super-Fascist and pro-Nazi party of Jacques Doriot". This, again, is a possible explanation supported by no facts whatsoever.

STALIN PLEASE COPY

"The relief felt by everyone in consequence of the air of North Africa having become suddenly purer must not be allowed to obscure the fact that the assassination of Darlan does not settle the problem that he represented. History teaches that such isolated acts of violence never accomplish a liberating object, and all too often provide a pretext for perpetuating the systems against which they may be a protest."

Daily Worker 28th December 1942.

There is a fairly wide divergence in opinion between the politicians and press in America and those in Britain. The Americans on the whole regard the assassination of the protegé with indignation. Roosevelt, for instance, remarked.

"The cowardly assassination of Admiral Darlan is murder in the first degree. All leaders of all the United Nations will agree with that statement. Nazism and Fascism and military despotism will hold otherwise. I hope speedy justice will overtake the murderer of Admiral Darlan."

And Cordell Hull described the assassination as "an odious and cowardly act". (It is a little difficult to realise the cowardice of a man who must have known that his own death would be the almost inevitable consequence of his act!)

The American press, in general, followed the lead of the politicians. The *New York Times* remarked:

"It is only the ignorant and the thoughtless who will assume that such a murder at such a moment solves a peculiarly difficult problem. The arrangement with Darlan clearly saved many British and American lives."

The same line was followed by most of the leading American papers, except for the *New York Post*, which implied satisfaction by referring to Darlan as "a man who has no support anywhere in the world except in Washington."

In England, significantly, there were no immediate expressions of indignation on the part of government leaders, and up to the time of going to press (three days after the killing) we have seen no statement either from Whitehall or from the Fighting French. The early reports on the BBC were bald and unsympathetic, and seemed to imply a hidden pleasure.

It is significant that the papers most violent in their condemnation are the right-wing sheets which have always supported the reactionary elements of Europe and which before

ON THE WAY TO MARTYRDOM

"Before his death by the odious method of assassination Admiral Darlan had renounced his earlier claims, and his friends will be glad that his last statement before his death was an appeal for French unity and that one of his latest speeches was an assurance that he would not let any personal ambition stand in its way."
Manchester Guardian 28th December 1942.

the war condemned revolutionary attempts on the life of Mussolini. The *Observer*, while remarking in its diplomatic column that "The assassination of Admiral Darlan has opened a way out of one of the worst tangles of the war", states in its editorial, "Murder in any case is vile. In this case the murderer rendered a great service to Hitler and Mussolini." The *Sunday Times* spoke in a similar vein. "Whatever views one takes on Admiral Darlan's career, there can be nothing but regret at the manner of its ending. Assassination is a weapon which everyone ought to reprobate who has regard either to decency or to democracy."

These statements of the semi-official press make interesting reading when one compares them with the almost universal approbation which greeted the assassination of Heydrich (an act which had tragic repercussions on the lives of hundreds of innocent Czechs) and the attempts on the lives of Laval and Déat. Whether or not murder is vile and assassination worthy of reprobation, these people are willing to encourage them when they are far enough away and seem to be in their interests. If murder is objectively vile, then it could not have been good to assassinate Heydrich. Or one might remark that if Darlan had been at Versailles with Laval and Déat, his assassination would have been praiseworthy in the eyes of these gentlemen, while his present fate at another time and place is the subject of reprobation.

January 1943   G. W.

Fascists at work in Algeria

The latest political moves in North Africa have been greeted with something approaching delight by certain sections of the English 'Left', and their press, from the *Manchester Guardian* to the *Daily Worker*, has praised the new set-up resulting from the latest reshuffle of reactionary bigwigs. The *Daily Worker* (8th February 1943) describes the developments as a "blow to Vichy men," and remarks that "under the pressure of public opinion, Giraud has been enabled to make considerable headway against the Vichyites, but the Vichyites have by no means as yet exhausted their ammunition or their power to prevent a much bigger extension of unity under the banner of Fighting French." A significant characteristic of their commentary is the way in which the Communists are trying to present Giraud as an angelic liberal struggling against the reactionary tendencies of his associates, whom even the *Daily Worker* cannot claim as enthusiastic anti-Fascists. The *Manchester Guardian* (8th February 1943) appears to share this illusion of Giraud as the gallant democrat, for in its editorial remarks it says "General Giraud has taken further measures to give a broader authority to his administration and a more liberal character to his policy."

Let us examine the measures taken by General Giraud, in an attempt to discover the liberalism on which his admirers are so emphatic, and also to elucidate the manner in which democratic principles are applied in the liberation of countries formerly subjected to Fascist tyranny.

To begin with, let us admire the democratic way in which General Giraud achieved his position. In fact, he was elected to it by himself and the few associates who formed Darlan's Imperial Council and now form Giraud's War Committee. These associates — Peyrouton, Boisson and Generals Nogues and Bergeret — are all supporters of Vichy and admirers, avowed or otherwise, of Fascist methods, which they have been applying in Africa for the last two years since the fall of France. Giraud, having been elected by the Imperial Council to the position of Civil and Military Commander-in-Chief, issued a proclamation saying that he had 'assumed' this position and that the new War Committee would consist of Governors and "other persons who were being or might be invited by General Giraud."

This assumption of power was not preceded even by the pretence of an accord between the various French parties and movements. General de Gaulle was not consulted, and the appointments do not appear to have been discussed even during the much-publicised conversation between Churchill, Roosevelt, de Gaulle and Giraud.

General Giraud also invested himself with the right to name governors, magistrates, university heads, etc. He has, moreover, the right to dispose of the "legal and political status of any person," whether French or foreign, in Algeria. If this is democracy, then one wonders why Hitler should put his democrats in concentration camps. But perhaps the democrats in the concentration camps of North Africa think a little differently!

It is estimated that these concentration camps contain at least 65,000 prisoners, held in some seventeen camps, eight in Algeria and nine in Morocco. It is further believed that a number of new camps have been established, and that since the arrival of the liberators in North Africa a number of prisoners of revolutionary or de Gaullist sympathies have been added to those already incarcerated. The new measures have included the release of a number of these internees, but it is significant to see how the released men have been chosen.

After the Communist deputy Grenier had pledged the official support of the Communist Party to the War Committee, some 27 Communist deputies who had been kept in prison in Algiers for more than two years were released. The propaganda value of this move is obvious, and is further significant that there has been no general release of rank-and-file Communists or of revolutionaries or democrats.

Men of military age and fitness are to be released; whether they are Fascists or not. In this connection Giraud remarked: "When I see a member of the SOL [a French Fascist organisation] and I hear that he is imprisoned, I look at his record. I may find he is a good fighter. I release him." Men not fit for military service, on the other hand, whether they are democrats or not, must await an investigation commission of mixed French and American representatives. The commission, however, has no power to release them. This can only be done by the French authorities, and as these are mostly Vichy men it will be seen how much this provision is worth.

Almost all members of the War Committee have shown anti-semitic tendencies in the past, and Peyrouton was the originator of a number of laws against the Jews in Vichy, France, and one of the prime instigators of the persecutions of French Jews. It is therefore not suprising that Giraud should have announced that he was going to solve the Jewish problem gradually, and not "by a stroke of a pen or a stroke of the sword." The Jews have been given back their property, and Jewish children can attend schools, while a limited number of Jews are to be admitted to the professions. The Jews are still, however, deprived of their political rights, in spite of the fact that since 1871 all inhabitants of North Africa have been regarded as having equal rights to those of French citizens.

The right of association has not been restored, so that workers, whether French or native, are not allowed to revive their trade unions or syndicates. A number of syndicalists who took advantage of their liberation in this way have been placed in concentration camps.

From these facts it would appear that the measures taken by General Giraud are in fact intended purely as propaganda to nourish the illusion in England and America that the new French regime in North Africa is really democratic. In fact, it remains a dictatorial regime whose Fascist characteristics have been mitigated only to the least degree required for the purposes of the deception.

The Nazis are now celebrating the tenth anniversary of their acquisition of power in Germany. In that acquisition of power they were assisted materially by the reactionary interests of England and America. Later, when the German aeroplanes and tanks were destroying the Spanish Revolution, they were again assisted by British and American conservative interests, while the representatives of the British government outclassed Pontious Pilate at the washing of hands. Now, after Britain has been nominally at war with Fascism for more than three years and America for two years, we find the same people aiding and abetting the perpetuation of fascist government, under men like Peyrouton with recent records of close collaboration with Hitler, in the very few countries to which their troops are supposed to have come as liberators. This was shown very clearly in the House of Commons on the 4th February, when Eden defended the Anglo-American position by saying that "Both Governments wished to see that traditional freedom which flourished on French soil once more re-established both in North Africa and in France itself, and for this reason both were agreed that nothing must be allowed to distract for the first and imperative duty of developing the maximum military effort upon which all depended." (*News Chronicle*, 4th February 1943). The old story of pie in the sky!

mid-February 1943

BEHIND THE SLOGANS

'Humanising the War'

As war becomes a more destructive science so are attempts made apparently to restrict the action of certain weapons of destruction. To clear-thinking people 'humanising the war' can hardly ring true, for apart from the fact that war in every respect is brutal, and cannot therefore be humanised unless abolished altogether, their 'International rules of warfare' are just agreements which, as all international agreements go, are adhered to or broken at will when convenient to any of the belligerents. Already certain sections of the British press are preparing public opinion for 'unrestricted warfare'. The *Evening News* (18th December) states in its editorial that

"International law to be just should benefit or restrict both belligerents equally. Unless it succeeds in doing this, international law may one day become a dead letter. No country at war can be bound indefinitely by the letter of rules which an enemy ignores and breaks daily."

The same paper writes "The Nazis will obey no laws unless they gain by them", which also explains Britain's eagerness to abide by the 'laws' restricting submarine warfare and mine laying. Submarine warfare plays no important role in Britain's naval warfare, for it has been openly stated that there are no German merchant ships on the high seas to capture! Nor does she require to sink neutral shipping for perfidious Albion by her geographical position effectively blocks the channels leading to the Baltic. Most neutral ships proceeding to the Baltic are obliged to call at a British port to be searched for contraband. Germany is less conveniently situated geographically to escort neutral ships proceeding to Britain from her own ports for inspection and consequently ignores all these so-called 'international laws' and her submarines sink both neutral and British ships and sows the much publicised 'magnetic mines' around the coast of Britain. She is adopting inhuman methods, for many lives of unarmed seamen have been lost, but no less inhuman than these methods are the British Government's gentlemanly methods of starving 80,000,000 Germans against whom, we are told, we bear no grudge! Apart from these considerations, the following report of a speech delivered by Vice-Admiral Usborne to the Anglo-American Press Association in Paris (reported in the press, 7th December) confirms the main thesis of this article.

"The Allies had mastered the magnetic mine, which was no novelty because during the last war they had a big field in the Dover Roads over which no submarine could pass without being blown up."

Again it may be remembered, a few years ago it was proposed to abolish the bombing aeroplane as a weapon of warfare. Objections were raised by the British representative Lord Londonderry on the grounds that this instrument of death was needed for policing the Empire. Clearly, in this case it was not convenient to 'humanise' war!

And the same people who shout the loudest for the respecting of these laws of warfare in order to save human life are those who, recently, attacked with the greatest vehemence the captain of the 'Graf Spee' who scuttled his ship and saved every man on board rather than send them to certain death. The *Evening News* in the article quoted above, considered that the Captain of the Graf Spee might have sent her not to a tragic, but splendid death in battle. How much easier it is to go to a "tragic but splendid death in battle" from a comfortable armchair in the editor's office a few thousand miles from the scene of battle!

Such irresponsible people can only inspire pity and shame that they should be allowed to handle such a delicate instrument as the press. Another of these gentlemen who have the word 'honour' ever on their lips, Mr Churchill, thought that by "coming out to fight and going down in battle like the Rawalpindi, would have been honourable to her."

Compared with the relatively few lives lost by this 'indiscriminate mine warfare' carried on by Germany there have been other 'laws of war', for instance, which instead of saving lives have resulted in the death and maiming of millions. These 'laws' however were not made public until after the Great War, and whilst the facts may be known to the last generation, it is imperative that those of the new generation who are being coerced and herded into another war, should also be acquainted with these facts of Capitalist wars. A book published in 1937 on the armaments firm of Krupp recounts certain incidents of the last war in which an interesting feature is the efficient production of arms both in German and French territory.[1]

"If the working of war industries could proceed so brilliantly and smoothly, the war itself might go on. The smoothness of their working was certainly surprising. War histories, crammed with accounts of deeds and valour, have little to relate about the operations directed against industrial establishments belonging to the enemy. The very aviators who bombed schools and processions of children behind the enemy lines appeared to make a point of avoiding attacks on certain industrial centres. In so far as these establishments of Essen and Le Creusot were concerned, their distance from the front and the relatively limited radius of action of contemporary aircraft, may account for their immunity from air attack, but just behind the lines of allied and German trenches in North France were important industrial centres which were of particular value to the respective combatants as sources of supply for raw materials. These centres were the iron-ore mines of Briey on the German side and the Pas-de-Calais coalfields on that of the allies. It is astounding to note that though the Briey mines and iron-works were less than 20 miles behind the German lines and therefore well within the range of French bombing aircraft, they remained immune throughout the whole war from any vigorous and systematic effort to destroy them. Right up to the autumn of 1918 Germany was permitted to raise, smelt and ship millions of tons of Briey ore to the Ruhr whence it returned in the form of Krupp guns or shells.

The question as to how this was possible effects one of the darkest chapters of the history of the World War. It is to asking for what purpose millions of soldiers of all nations who lost their lives after 1917 were sacrificed.

Enquiries into this astonishing 'negligence' of the French Army 'brought to light irrefutable evidence that repeated attempts had already been made to deal with those responsible for it.' All these attempts had proved fruitless. General Sarrail, who prepared a plan for the capture or destruction of the industrial zone as early as 1914, was promptly replaced by General Gerard. Was this quite accidental? Doubtless it was, just like the refusal to adopt the suggestions made by the Deputy Engerand in the following year by an expert of the General Staff — who was a member of

1. *Krupp* by Bernhard Menne, published by Hodge.

the Comité des Forges! When Henry Berenger made a report on the Briey scandal to the Army Committee of the Senate he was violently attacked by the most influential organs of the press, including *Le Temps*.

. . . In the course of one of the debates on the matter in 1919 one of the owners of the Briey mines replied: 'If it was so easy to achieve the desired results by bombing why did the Germans, who were perfectly well aware of our acute shortage of coal, not destroy the pitheads of the Pas-de-Calais collieries which were not 17 to 20 miles distant from the front line like Briey, but only 10 to 12 miles away?

The reason was given by Deputy Barthe in 1919 when in the Chamber of Deputies he said that the order to spare Briey emanated from the military authorities . . . This prohibition seems to have been due to an argument between the opposing combatants."

The *Matin* of that period sadly wrote, "War is a matter of conventions . . ."

All the 'humane' rules of war made in time of peace are just scraps of paper in time of war. Their only purpose is to give a sense of security to the civilian population (if such exists in modern wars), and to make war appear less bestial. When will the workers call their bluff?

February 1940   LIBERTARIAN

'Not at war with the German people'

For the past few weeks the British public has been entertained to a number of broadcasts explaining the propaganda methods adopted by the Nazi Party in its rise to power during the past six years. The methods which have been used, the barefaced lies which have been told to the German people, have been exposed by the genuine anti-fascists long ago. During the Spanish War, for instance, all sections of radical opinion pointed to Germany's and Italy's armed intervention in that country, but at that time Mr Chamberlain preferred to believe Dr Goebbels. It was convenient, in the same way as it is convenient nowadays for Mr Chamberlain and the controlled press to label as lies everything emanating from Berlin.

However, in view of the fact that the BBC will not broadcast a programme on British propaganda methods, the following extracts should prove useful in gauging the sincerity behind those idealistic and even sentimental declarations made by those in power.

The first is from a book by H. G. Wells published in 1914.[1]

"We began to fight because our honour and our pledges obliged us; but so soon as we are embarked upon the fighting we have to ask ourselves what is the end at which our fighting aims. We cannot simply put the Germans back over the Belgian border and tell them not to do it again. We find ourselves at war with that huge military empire with which we have been doing our best to keep the peace since it first rose upon the ruins of French Imperialism in 1871. And war is mortal conflict. We have now either to destroy or be destroyed. We have not sought this reckoning, we have done our utmost to avoid it; but now that it has been forced upon us it is imperative that it should be a thorough reckoning. This is a war that touches every man and every home in each of the combatant countries. . . .

We are fighting Germany. But we are fighting without any hatred of the German people. We do not intend to destroy either their freedom or their unity. But we have to destroy an evil system of government and the mental and material corruption that has got hold of the German imagination and taken possession of German life. We have to smash the Prussian Imperialism as thoroughly as Germany in 1871 smashed the rotten Imperialism of Napoleon III. And also we have to learn from the failure of that victory to avoid a vindictive triumph.

This Prussian Imperialism has been for forty years an intolerable nuisance in the earth. Ever since the crushing of the French in 1871 the evil thing has grown and cast its spreading shadow over Europe. Germany has preached a propaganda of ruthless force and political materialism to the whole uneasy world. 'Blood and iron', she boasted, was the uncanny cement of her unity, and almost as openly the little, mean, aggressive statesmen and professors who have guided her destinies to this present conflict have professed cynicism and an utter disregard of any ends but nationally selfish ends, as though it were religion. . . ." (pages 7-9)

The same phrases are being used today by war apologists, with the only difference that one reads Hitlerism instead of Kaiserism. But what makes the above extracts more interesting is the fact that some 25 years later, the same H. G. Wells wrote:

"I was in control of the propaganda against the German Government by the British Ministry of Propaganda from Crewe House (in the last war). . . .

The work I did was done in absolute good faith and the gist of the

---

1. *The War That Will End War* by H. G. Wells, published by Frank & Cecil Palmer, 1914.

business is that we, who lent ourselves to propaganda, were made fools of and ultimately let down by the traditional tricks of the Foreign Office.

We were kept in the dark about all sorts of secret entanglements to which these gentry had committed the country, and we were allowed to hold out hopes to the German people of a liberal post-war settlement our masters had no intention of making. We were tricked, and through us the German liberals were cheated."[2]

As Wells further explains, the liberal propaganda was simply used to weaken the resistance of the German liberals behind the Kaiser, while the Northcliffe 'hymn of hate' was directed at the British public. The pious platitudes to the German people ('We are fighting the Kaiser, not you!') were ignored at Versailles, but the *Daily Mail* policies were carried out.

As Wells admits (despite his implied support of the present war, which conflicts with his determination not to be fooled again) the gentlemen of the British Foreign Office and the Quai d'Orsay are of no different calibre to their predecessors: "little, purblind, mean chaps".

The democratic sentimentalists are going to be fooled again, and so (if they do really listen to the Chamberlain propaganda) are their colleagues in Germany. The people who will get their own way are not the Attlees but the Milnes, not those hoping to 'defend democracy and destroy Hitlerism' but those determined to destroy Germany for imperialist reasons. This means: no chances of Hitler being overthrown from within (at least by the democrats) and certainly no lasting peace.

January 1940

'The Fifth Column'

Consciences are bad in Fleet Street. Our press lords, who boosted Hitler to the skies when Hitler only did things one attacks him for but had not come into competition with the City of London, are now in opposition to him. Consciences are bad in the homes of the

---

2. *In Search of Hot Water* (Penguin Series, 1939).

aristocracy and the politicians: the Friends of Hitler in Mayfair and Westminster have to change their tactics.

Lord Redesdale declares that he has no longer any sympathy with the Hitler regime (despite daughter Unity Mitford's antics and son-in-law Oswald Mosley's convulsions) for now "the enemies of the King are the enemies of every honest man". George Robey left for a trip to Australia and told the *Daily Express* how much he admired Hitler — by the time he came back he had to say "it was only a joke". Lord Londonderry indignantly denies canards about his being interned as a spy (because he had entertained Ribbentrop in the old days) — an analogous position with Prince Louis of Battenberg in the last war. The Page-Crofts and the Arnold Wilsons, the friends of fascism in Germany, Italy and Spain in the old days (still, so far as the last two go), the Lennox Boyds, and the others — all have to swallow their words, and all do their bit with patriotism.

Hannen Swaffer mentions Tory MPs such as this — and forgets his own idol, Winston Churchill: "Had I been in Italy at the time, I should have been a fascist," "I have always declared that if Britain were defeated in a war, we should need a Hitler to lead us back to our rightful place amongst the nations."

This was what we once called the Fifth Column. In Spain, Franco had four columns converging on Madrid, and boasted of a fifth of provocateurs, spies and fascists within it. The reference was clear. All the friends of fascism were the enemies within the gates: so they were called in revolutionary Spain.

The Communist Party took up the slogan parrot-fashion, and urged purges of the 'Fifth Column' everywhere — until its master, Stalin, about-faced and they were forced to join it.

But our Fifth Column, also reversed when war was declared. They supported Hitler, Mussolini, etc., because they wanted to preserve Capitalism-Imperialism. This war against Hitler (which poor dupes of workers are kidded is *against* fascism) is *for* the preservation of Capitalist-Imperialism. Excited patriotism took the place of fervent fascism. Sudden 'sympathy' for fishermen killed by Nazi machine-gunners (not a new development in totalitarian warfare) became one of the 'excuses' for this reversal.

Now what? Our Fifth Column has a bad conscience. It must save its face: for previous admiration for Herr Hitler is now at a discount. So it looks for a scapegoat.

Norway provides for it. Major Quisling, at the head of the Nazi party, led a movement to help the Nazis.

To put it bluntly (but don't tell Mr Lennox-Boyd or the Friends of Nationalist Spain), Quisling did a Franco. Not a very effective Franco, but certainly Quisling had the support of an important section of the Norwegian ruling-class, e.g. the head of the Oslo police, the Bishop of Oslo, and many officers. (The Norwegian ruling-class has always had pro-German, and recently pro-Nazi, influences: largely as a result of the strength of social revolution.)

Now the Nazis have other movements, too: the German-American Bund, the Dutch, Rumanian, Swedish, etc., Nazi 'culture' and 'sports' movements: all of which could emulate Franco, Quisling or Kuusinen. Similarly, any Communist Party would help Russia (e.g. the Finnish Communist Party, although it did not exist outside Moscow) if it were the opposing force.

One might say, perhaps, that such movements represented (to the ruling classes of the Allied powers in a capitalist war) the new 'Fifth Column'. Our ex-Fifth Column, and still fascistic, ruling class might perhaps term these the new 'Fifth Column'.

Oh no. They have a better trick. With these they deliberately confuse the genuine anti-war (anti-Hitler's and anti-Stalin's, as well as anti-Chamberlain's, war) elements — socialists, pacifists and anarchists.

The *Sunday Dispatch* has a flaming article: 'Where Britain Must Strike Next'. Freedom of speech does not mean freedom of speech for 'defeatists' and anarchists, it declares. The Peace Pledge Union it denounces as a 'revolutionary' organisation. It insists on dictatorial measures in the French manner. All this from a Rothermere paper — Rothermere, the backer of Hitler and Mussolini in days gone by, the man who introduced Fascism to Britain by his support of Mosley, and the man who was recently dragged through the police courts on that case about the Princess and the royal heads of Europe and Hitler.

Hannen Swaffer, cynical Fleet Street scribbler, writes in the 'Labour' *Daily Herald* as though he didn't know of the huge numbers of local Labour parties opposing the war and affiliated to the No Conscription League, or of trade union rank-and-file opposition to the war, by writing as though only fascists, plus a few communists, opposed the war — with the possible exception, perhaps, of one or two 'sentimental pacifists'.

Careful propaganda, 'public opinion made to order', biased reporting, unscrupulous misrepresentation; gradually it is worked up to insist to suppress all revolutionary, peace yes, and labour movements. Churchill may not be able to 'control' all the seas all the time, on his statement, but he 'controlled' the General Strike very efficiently. Chamberlain, Rothermere, Beaverbrook: we all know what even the ordinary trade unionist thinks of them.

Is the working class going to allow its movements to be broken by action, following careful propaganda? Let us know in advance the technique:

1. Ex-boosters of Hitler clamour for imprisonment of all Germans, as potential spies, including those who risked their lives fighting Hitler underground while these gentlemen wrote letters to *The Times* in their clubs, saying what good Hitler was doing for Germany.

2. The demand for dissolution of all communist, fascist 'defeatist' and *similar* organisations (the term *similar* to include trade unions, Labour Parties and co-ops opposing the war; ILP, NCL, Peace Pledge Union, anarchists, educational and civil liberties bodies).

3. The creation, gradually, of the power of the executive to dissolve anything they choose.

4. The strengthening of the executive power as the dictatorial body controlling the country.

5. Hitlerism, and not even with the social programme that was used to delude the German people.

May 1941   ALBERT MELTZER

'Ministerial Inefficiency'

The inefficiency of Ministers used as a slogan for victory? It sounds almost incredible, and maybe it would be in another country, but it is a fact today in Britain. The Tory leaders are thoroughly discredited: Chamberlain has been an omen of disaster to the Conservative Party, and his followers, local Tory MPs who were full of praise for Hitler and Mussolini, would have no chance in the country if — as is not now possible — a General Election came. The man-in-the-street would be very likely to agree now with the statement of one Conservative MP some years ago: "The Blackshirts have what the Conservatives need" — not dictatorship but Brixton!

This is shown by the phenomenal success of the book *Guilty*

Men. It had a very good send-off by being unofficially banned, but it created a sensation apart from that. *Guilty Men* tells the familiar tale of a complacent Chamberlain leading a Hitler-loving Conservative solid majority in the days of Munichism. More and more people are coming to recognise this fact: yet, conversely, the Government does not lose in popularity. The antidote to all criticism is: 'But now it is all different'. A Chamberlain is out, a Churchill is in. Apart from Mr Churchill looking more like a bulldog than his colleague and the more important fact that his support and warmhearted defence of fascism under Signor Mussolini has had a chance to be forgotten while Mr Chamberlain's visits to Munich are too fresh in the public mind, there is little difference. But the man-in-the-street is fooled: he is led to believe we have suffered some defeats because of inefficient Mr Chamberlain, and now we are to be led to victory, via the change of Prime Minister, by Mr Churchill.

Even now, with the change of Ministry to 'efficient' Ministers, criticism of them has to continue. Mr Duff Cooper went into office in a blaze of glory, having made a brilliant speech crying out to Chamberlain, "Go, go, in heaven's name, go!" It was a dangerous speech, though, for now everyone is crying that at Mr Duff Cooper. True Mr Cooper has to defend the ridiculous methods of the Ministry of Information, sure Minister-breaker, since the Ministry can only give official policy, while the nation wants the soothing syrup of Transport House variety, the 'better land after the war' type, which the rulers may promise but cannot specify too closely. Also, he has had to tread on the corns of newspapermen by censorship of news — always a risky business! But apart from that, what significance has Mr Duff Cooper's inefficiency? True, propaganda could be a great force in the war, and he is retarding it; but no more than any other member of his class would.

The reason seems clear: the Cabinet may be likened to the proverbial Russian sledge, after which the wolves of public opinion run. The mother on the sledge has to throw off her babies one by one: a hard parting, but inevitable, anything to allay the wolves. And this mother is distinctly hard-hearted and will throw them all off if she can maintain her position on the sledge. Some of the babies, though, are lusty brats and run after the sledge crying, 'Shame!' — e.g. Mr Hore-Belisha!

The ruling class can well afford one or two Ministers as a burnt-offering if it can stop the public from thinking and acting thereby.

At the moment, there is some denunciation of Sir John Anderson, and a demand that he should resign, because of the suppression of liberty underneath him, and also because of the internment of so many refugees either anti-Nazi or friendly to the allied cause. But we are not concerned with whether Sir John would resign or not: the question is whether such practices would stop if we had a new Home Secretary. The agitation must be against the offence, not the individual acting as figure-head or held responsible.

In the trade unions, it is the same: agitation against any particular person sometimes leads to their being replaced by better men, who in turn, because of the method of trade union bureaucracy, become equally reactionary. The introduction of Labour leaders into the Government has not altered the character of the war: Mr Attlee, who before had led the demand for a statement of peace aims, once Lord Privy Seal, had to declare that the time for stating peace aims was 'inopportune'. Labour MPs led the demand for such things as nationalisation of mines; now a Labour Minister of Mines has to state that this cannot be done. So it seems that change of Ministers does not lead to a change of methods. But the agitation against inefficiency leads to a lessening of the struggle against the system, and that, of course, is what the ruling class want.

It might be stated that there is an interesting exception to the rule that inefficiency against individual Ministers is largely inspired by a desire to avoid essential criticism rather than to face actual criticism. That is the widespread belief in this country that Britain is inefficient, too lenient, too humane, etc. which is, of course, fostered with the intention of making the people believe that we must be less lenient, less humane, etc. If it were stated bluntly — 'we must be intolerant, we must be inhumane', etc. — it is doubtful if the British people would agree. But they are told that we are notoriously lenient, ridiculously humane, and are likely to remain so, and the result is support for the reverse action to be adopted. Then, when the news comes out, the reaction is, 'Well, it's about time too!', or the like.

It is, by the way, a remarkable illusion that inefficiency does not exist in Germany — a thing which all good patriots here believe. Why this illusion I cannot fathom: it may have arisen as a means of exhorting people to do their bit, but it has never been very true.

In the last war the myth of German efficiency rose to an alarming extent, but was grossly exaggerated. Hasek has portrayed the corrupt and decaying Austro-Hungarian Army for ever in the the *Good Soldier Schweik*, while as to the German Army in the last war, Bernard Shaw — who has written on everything — pronounced the truest words, in the mouth of a member of the ruling class, who says "if the British public knew that I had said it, I should be at once hounded down as a pro-German". It is:

"Our people have for some reason made up their minds that the German War Office is everything that our War Office is not . . . my own view . . . is that the German War Office is no better than any other War Office.

I found that opinion on my observation of the character of my brother-in-law; one of whom, by the way, is on the German General Staff." (*Augustus Does His Bit*, 1917)

Today, of course, the Nazis have got rid of the aristocratic Junkers: whereas we retain the aristocratic junk. Nevertheless, today in Germany the State is in control: and the State, in its totalitarian stage, though it eliminates capitalist waste and oligarchic inefficiency, creates bureaucracy and its attendant 'red tape'. When we get much better information on how Germany wages this war (which will only, perhaps, be afterwards), we shall very probably see that Germany has not been winning victories because of the superior efficiency of Nazism, but because the bourgeoisie of the west are fearful, and therefore timid. They fear that a major war of destruction will ruin their property, and expedite social revolution: the Nazis, representatives of a 'have not' nation against the 'have' imperialisms, and who have deluded at least themselves that revolution is impossible, for they are the revolution, have no such trepidations, and so take the initiative and the drive. They err in underrating social revolution, for it is becoming ever more of an imminence, and will sweep away both them and their bourgeois 'sisters under their skins'.

October 1940   A. M.

'The only good German is a dead German'

We do not want to gain support for our cause by pretending the path is an easy one. We could quite easily gain a certain amount of support for our demands for the struggle for a European and a world revolution by claiming that the revolution in Germany had already begun, and publish reports 'smuggled past the Gestapo' showing Germany on the brink of revolution that would, in the end, prove to be written by German emigrés, and have been smuggled from Hampstead to the City. There is a certain amount of revolutionary feeling in Germany, probably chiefly expressed as disillusionment and cynicism, just as there is in Britain. There is in all probability no more of an active revolutionary movement there than there is here. That movement will grow in both countries, but only those anxious to seek office in a 'British Quisling' or Stalin government of Germany will pretend that they represent from abroad an active movement there.

So far as *deeds* are concerned, there is no doubt that the German masses are actively or passively pro-Hitler, just as much as the British masses are pro-Churchill. This leads our Churchillians to ask the question: 'Must we destroy Hitlerism or the German nation itself?' Chamberlain, who was of the typical British bourgeois school that couldn't possibly imagine anyone doubting the righteousness of its cause, stated that we were not fighting the German people. Mostly, that statement was accepted in the early months of the war, when everyone was waiting for the German revolution that was going to pull Britain's chestnuts out of the fire. Since it has failed to appear, they now believe that we are not fighting one man, but the nation. The German nation is the cause of every war: 'the only good German is a dead German'. Typical comments come from men of the last war who, finding themselves once more at war, imagine the reason is that 'the job wasn't done properly last time' — that, in short, Germany should have been absolutely and completely destroyed, which, in fact, was done in 1918 so far as it was possible economically and politically. They believe it should have been done humanely as well.

But what we must ask is this: what do they expect of the German masses? Do they want the Germans to be so much braver than they are, to do all that they themselves would never dare do? Unfortunately, if they are no worse, they are no better. If our patriots at home dread revolution as meaning a possible victory for a foreign power, they cannot blame patriots abroad for having the same views. If our patriots stand for their country, right or wrong, they cannot wonder at others with the same doctrines. If they hold that however valid criticism of the government may be, it must be withheld until after the war, they cannot blame the Germans for not facing graver consequences than they would for withholding criticism of Hitler.

We are told of the 'delight' the pilots of the Luftwaffe take in 'bombing women and children'. It is no doubt as easy to distinguish delight on a pilot's face from the ground as it is to distinguish women and children from men when looking down on them from the air. But have our patriots of the calibre of Sir Robert Vansittart ever suggested an alternative for men conscripted for the Luftwaffe? Perhaps it is because they are frightened that men conscripted for the RAF might do the same thing when bombing Berlin, but the fact remains that, whether Germans are sadists or ordinary men, the 'anti-Hun' patriots have never suggested anything they could do when told to bomb open towns.

Perhaps they hold that it is a good thing for Germans to be conscientious objectors (CO), and to adopt the course of the CO in either facing death or the concentration camp (as German pacifists and Christian sects such as the Jehovah's Witnesses have done) in refusing to join the armed forces, or to sabotage instructions and the war effort, such as German revolutionaries who have joined the armed forces have done. But if this is what our patriots hold, we have yet to hear them say it. They attack disobedience as such: they 'explain' to pacifist COs that refusal to take up arms is no protection against high explosives and invading armies, and ask them what they are doing to protect their homes and families, they 'explain' to revolutionaries, COs and others that their views are simply treason. Never have we heard a patriot explain that such conduct is perfectly permissible, and that the only objection to it is its being used against British imperialism.

In short, our 'Hun-haters' cannot really object to their own opinions being translated into German. They would not raise their voices against Britain invading a smaller or a weaker country — they certainly did not in the past. 'My country — right or wrong'. The menace of patriotism should be clear enough to them when adopted by someone else.

It must be realised once and for all that the German and the

British masses are no better and no worse that one another. Neither of them is at the moment prepared to overthrow their government: either may do so in the future. The futile argument that the Germans accepted Hitler without fight and the British resisted Hitler is answered quite easily. The Germans, like the British, were trained in obedience to the State, in patriotism, in not resisting the legal government, and they certainly did not change their minds just because the penalties for disobedience and resistance became stronger. The British were trained in the same way. They resisted Hitler only because the government told them they had to. Had they resisted a British Hitler it might have been different. The only other factor is that humanitarian sentiment in Britain was shocked by Nazi atrocities, and therefore supported the war with more zest than they would have done if it had been another government.

August 1941   A. M.

'V' for Victory

The campaign for V for Victory is in full swing. The idea originally behind the campaign was from the point of view of military strategy not a bad one. The Government hoped by a declaration in favour of the Allied cause, by the peoples of Europe themselves, to arouse opposition to German rule.

At first the campaign was a great success, because the peoples of Europe are so war-weary and disillusioned that they are prepared to support, in the main, any campaign directed against the Nazi masters of Europe. This has been manifested by a series of pin-pricking attacks on Nazism — such as V signs everywhere, chalked inscriptions on the walls (propaganda, which one may mention, the capitalist Press here has sneered at for years), and finally that campaign of tapping, coughing, whistling, laughing, etc., the V rhythm in morse code.

What the Government did not take into account, apparently, was that their scheme for a V campaign would founder not in Europe, but in Britain and America. Precisely where it has failed dismally to arouse a victory psychosis is in the very countries whose victory it is supposed to herald, and not because of its neglect, but because of its being taken up. The 'V' campaign which might have been a symbol of resistance on the continent, is just another rage of sophisticated London and New York. Milliners' shops, cough-lozenge advertisements, slapstick comedians, schoolboys scribbling the morse code rhythm on the wall in a sense of derring-do, the smart ladies who paint their finger-nails with a V for Victory, the novelist who follows his 'W Plan' of the last war with a 'V' Plan of this war — the V's, in short, that one sees everywhere — obviously these are not symbols of victory, but symbols of self-advertisement. V is just a rage of the hour, like mah-jongg once was, and yo-yo once was.

So far as Britain and America are concerned, V is quite clearly a symbol of capitalism. It illustrates, as the current rage of the hour, both the immense need for distraction from the real problems of the day, and the immense need for advertisement in a competitive system, wherein not the most meritable, but the most advertised, is the most popular. No doubt from a serious point of view it is not at all inappropriate that the sign of Victory should be a symbol of capitalism, but our propaganda leaders did not intend this. Unfortunately there was no avoiding it.

On the Continent, it has perhaps had more success, so far as propaganda is concerned.

So much indeed did the Nazi hierarchy dread the effectiveness of the V campaign that they simply adopted it for themselves, on an old-established Hitler plan of trying to steal his opponents' thunder. V stood for Viktoria, they declared. Everywhere Europe was celebrating the victory of Germany that was to come. The correct German for victory is, of course, Sieg. This did not deter the Nazis, of course, in their claims, and they have simply hoisted their own V signs when they couldn't obliterate the V signs that others had set up. And what is important to a study of propaganda as a use in warfare is that the Nazis have got away with it. Obviously it is no use chalking V's on the trees in Paris if there is an enormous one stuck up at the Eiffel Tower. Moreover, if V does not stand for Sieg in German it does stand for Victoire in French, and a Frenchman celebrating Victory might just as well be a Darlaniste celebrating a Hitler Victory as a De Gaulliste celebrating a British Victory.

It is just there that the British propaganda comes unstuck. Since, as responsible statesmen have echoed since the beginning of the war, 'We have one aim — Victory.' 'Our war aim is to win the war,' etc., we are bound to fall into this morass of misunderstanding. We believe in one thing — victory; obviously, so do the Germans.

And in the last analysis, even if people realise whose victory the victory campaign stands for, what then? For a German or a Bulgarian or a Norwegian to read that Britain wants Victory is nothing sensational. (The only people who might consider it sensational would be people seeing the procrastinations of our bureaucratic officials at first hand.)

And even if Britain's victory were to become to the oppressed peoples of Europe a symbol of liberation, which it is far from being, there is still no indication of how to achieve it. The German wishy-washy reformist anti-Nazi paper *Die Zeitung* published in London, did, indeed, suggest following the V campaign with an S campaign — S for sabotage. The government has studiously refrained from encouraging large acts of sabotage in Europe. Such a policy, carried much beyond the limits suggested by *Die Zeitung* would be best calculated to bring Hitler to his knees. It would involve radio and 'plane-leaflet instructions on the methods of sabotage and silent striking; on the means of ca'canny strikes and obstructive tactics. Finally, it would work up to explaining how revolutionary tactics could be employed to oust the ruling classes of Europe from their positions.

Obviously this cannot be done by the Government. Nor is it likely that the masses abroad would respond to such an appeal from a ruling class obviously resorting to such measures merely to save its own skin, and not from any belief in them itself.

Only a revolutionary Britain could offer such assistance to working-class Europe. Which country it will be that makes its revolution first and offers such assistance to the world revolution remains to be seen. One thing is certain, the defeat of Hitler by **revolutionary** means could not be done by **capitalist** Britain.

September 1941   A. M.

'Strike Now in the West'

The Communist Party and some others are demanding immediate and complete aid for Russia, and it is indeed obvious enough on a superficial view that the fullest collaboration between the enemies of German Imperialism is an urgent necessity for their successful prosecution of the war. When it comes to the question of how to aid Russia, however, the strangest hot air emerges. Nowhere have we yet seen any discussion of the realities of the problem.

The 'obvious' course is the Communist battle cry of 'Strike Now in the West'. Elsewhere in this issue, F. A. Ridley has touched on this slogan and has indicated its absurdity. It therefore merely suffices here to point out that the Germans only just pulled off the invasion of Crete, a small island with (as Eden subsequently divulged) inadequate garrison and supplies of arms, and 400 miles from the nearest British air base. The defenders of German occupied Europe do not labour under these disadvantages, quite apart from the obvious fact that whereas Germany is a powerful land power, Britain is primarily a sea power, and does not possess the sheer weight of numbers necessary to maintain a forced landing. Memories of the Dardanelles, of Narvik, Dunkirk, Greece, etc., are by no means reassuring in this connection either.

Nevertheless the fact remains that if it were possible, the best way to aid Russia in a military sense, would be to face Hitler with a land war on two fronts. With this in mind, Stalin's past foreign policy may well be reviewed. If 'Strike in the West' is the right policy now (although as we have seen, a somewhat 'Utopian' one), 'Strike in the East' was clearly the best policy two years ago, when there still was a Western front to strike on. But Stalin's blows were reserved for Poland and Finland, Estonia and the rest. Except in collaboration with a strongly armed continental land power, Britain cannot strike in the West; yet Stalin stood by and supplied Russian materials to help Hitler to smash France, and thereby crush the danger of the war on two fronts. It is ironical that French materials and resources are now being used to smash at Russia!

Hitler, it is clear, had foreseen all along the danger of two fronts — German strategists have always been preoccupied with the avoidance of this cardinal source of weakness. In retrospect, it becomes obvious that the Soviet-Nazi pact of August, 1939, was the essential step in safeguarding Germany's eastern frontier. With that achieved, the full weight of the military machine was turned on France: France crushed, the danger from the east could then be dealt with. The 'wise all-seeing Stalin' was completely fooled because Hitler had cleverly played on his fear of war, with its consequent threat to the unstable bureaucratic regime. He even handed over to Hitler the means which were to be used against him.

We used to be served up with stuff about the USSR being strong enough militarily to resist any power or combination of powers. From this fact, it was claimed, derived Stalin's 'wise policy' of neutrality, of peace. It now appears that the USSR is in desperate need of aeroplanes, tanks, etc., in which case it becomes clear that Stalin's peace policy was, in reality, dictated by a fear of war. And Hitler has thoroughly exploited this fear to the point of completely isolating Russia from all effective allies. The boasted 'Soviet power' has not stood up to Nazi efficiency, in spite of the tremendous natural resources, the almost limitless reserve of man-power, and the twenty years of preparation for war which has characterized the Bolshevik regime. The 'Soviet power' crumbles because the initiative of the Russian workers and peasants, which has proved itself in three revolutions (1905, and February and October, 1917), is everywhere crushed and regimented by the corrupt and brutal Stalinist bureaucracy by its unparalleled and unlimited use of police terrorism, mass assassinations and transportations, and deliberate economic pressure to the point of mass starvation.

An interesting sidelight on the Anglo-Russian alliance was provided by the incident in the House of Commons between Communist MP Gallacher and Churchill. To an attack by Gallacher asserting that the Government was not sending full aid to Russia, Churchill replied with a sneering reference to the Communist Party taking its orders from a foreign power. The incensed Gallacher immediately shouted out abuses . . . but later made a full and abject apology, reminiscent of the Pollitt-Campbell recantation of autumn, 1939, and the Moscow trials. Trivial in itself, the incident shows who 'wears the trousers'. The Communist Party have played so completely into the hands of the Tories, and Churchill's help is so necessary to Russia, that the Conservatives don't even pretend to be gracious to their new allies. From Stalin's point of view, Churchill and Roosevelt are incomparably more useful than Pollitt and Gallacher (the American Communist leader Earl Browder is reported to be still in gaol), so the latter have to dance to the conservatives' tune — by giving pep-talks in the factories, and by gracefully swallowing Churchill's insults in Parliament! The parties of the Third International have once more to play second fiddle to the needs of the Russian Foreign Office and its alliances with the capitalist 'democracies'.

Tied hand and foot to the Tories, the Communist Party has to try and retain such influence as it still has over the masses. Having closed up even a semblance of waging the class struggle in favour of 'national unity' and 'maximum production', it has to fall back on its reputation for being go-ahead, for getting things done. This is the real explanation behind the ridiculous demand for 'Strike now in the West'. Such a ludicrous strategical blunder is hardly likely to be made by even the Churchill Government, so the Communist Party are probably quite safe in demanding it. The slogan's chief merit for them is its demagogue's appeal of being the 'obvious thing to do', the course of 'action'.

'Strike Now in the West' would provide a more plausible policy against Fascism, if it were put forward by revolutionaries, and accompanied by revolutionary slogans of the class war. But neither Stalin nor Churchill (or therefore their dutiful stooges of the Communist Party and its fellow-travellers) is anxious to foment revolution on the continent — a fact of which Hitler has shown himself fully aware, and of which he has made the fullest use. Nor is it possible, as some would-be revolutionaries seem to think, to beat Germany by inciting the German workers to revolt, while advancing reformist policies here. Revolution, as has been remarked before, is not an article which can be reserved for export only! Finally, even if military action in the west were undertaken to the accompaniment of revolutionary actions and slogans, it would merely be to repeat the Bolsheviks' mistake in Poland, of trying to impose socialism at the point of the bayonet. It cannot be too often stated and emphasised: only the social revolution can defeat Fascism; and social revolution can only be achieved by unremitting adherence to the class struggle, waged by the workers themselves at their places of work. It will never come from the twisting shifts of politicians like Gallacher and Pollitt, Churchill and Stalin. Never from support for national wars, but only from the international working class, acting in international solidarity.

October 1941

'Food for Starving Europe'

You cannot help the people by playing the government's game, for the interests of rulers are fundamentally opposed to those of the people. Socialists and Pacifists only perpetuate starvation by advocating reformist half measures.

A great deal of propaganda is being put out at the moment in favour of petitions and what-not to 'compel' the government to send food to starving Europe, especially France and Greece. While we respect the humanitarian motives of those who devote energy to this 'campaign', we consider it dangerous in that it provides another red herring drawn across the track of those who are trying to see through the tissue of propaganda falsehoods which conceal the real nature of war and government.

Help for Hitler
In many cases Hitler is just as anxious to avoid starvation among subject peoples — and the Germans themselves for that matter — as the humanitarians. For Britain and America to feed these peoples would be indeed humane. But since it would manifestly interfere with the prosecution of the war — and Churchill and Roosevelt are hardly going to assist Hitler in his difficulties — it is necessary for these propagandists to face the fact that they are playing Hitler's game. Or rather, that they would be, if it were possible for petitions and 'demands' to influence the policy of the ruling class in this matter. And all history shows that it is impossible by constitutional means to make them do something against their interests.

That food ships may be sent from the 'democracies' to the unfortunate peoples whom they forced into the war and then deserted, is not entirely ruled out, however. Such acts would be a powerful propaganda weapon, not so much among the peoples to whom the food is delivered by the Red Cross or the Quakers, but among the workers in the democracies themselves. Clearly the task of *adequately* feeding a starving population would be a gigantic one. And since the food would have to be provided free, it is difficult to see how this could be achieved under an economic regime such as the present one, which is based on production for sale rather than for use. (Permission for the free distribution of an apple surplus which could not be exported from Canada, was refused recently; instead the apples were rolled down a hillside. When the local population began to pick them up, they were warned off, and the apples were then sprayed with kerosene to make them unfit for eating.)

Starvation not new, but chronic

Starvation is a chronic condition for the workers in almost all countries. It is only when the government-controlled press, for its own propaganda needs, draws attention to the sufferings of peoples under Nazi domination, that the liberal humanitarian sections of the bourgeoisie begin to take these wholly inadequate steps to try and mitigate the conditions. In effect, they are unpaid propagandists for the government. The socialist press (at least the left elements of it) have for years been drawing attention to the gross malnutrition in India, which lowers the average expectation of life for the Indian to 26 years. But the humanitarians have never suggested sending food ships — and there would have to be a hell of a lot of them — to the starving three hundred and seventy millions of India, to mention only one of the British colonies who have for years been in the same plight as the Greeks are to-day.

Pacifists and others are never tired of reminding us that the British government kept up the blockade of Germany for two whole years after the armistice of 1918. What they do not realise is that the Hoover commission and the Quakers who sent food parcels to Germany with government permission throughout the period wholly failed to make any significant difference to the conditions inside Germany. What they did do was to give humane people the illusion that 'something was being done', and so enabled the government to carry out its inhuman and beastly policy of starving the Germans to keep them slaves. As now, they were, in fact, playing the government's game, by drawing attention away from the fact that governments are never in the slightest degree concerned with the sufferings of men, women, and children of the workers anywhere, but only in retaining their power and in advancing the interests of the class they represent.

This is not to say that we are indifferent to the sufferings of the starving workers on the continent, *or anywhere else*. As Anarchists we fight against all injustice and cruelty. What we also have to fight against are methods of struggle against these things that are wholly ineffective and totally misleading. Such methods only delay the application of radical cures, and so, in effect, assist reaction to maintain the hideous status quo.

Real Cause of Starvation
Starvation is omnipresent in a world of potential plenty in peace as well as in war. With modern methods every country could feed its own population from its own soil: They fed their smaller populations in the past with undeveloped methods of cultivation, and with the application of modern methods — prevented everywhere by various forms of vested interests — they could also feed their much larger populations to-day. The idea that British soil *cannot* supply its population is merely capitalist propaganda though it is often echoed by the Marxists. When most of the capital and labour power in all countries is mainly devoted to production of non-consumable war products, instead of to essential needs, it is not surprising that people starve. Hitler tells the German people that they starve because of the blockade; Churchill declares that we go short because of the U-boats. The real cause of starvation everywhere, however, is the misapplication of labour and capital and technical resources in order to suit the capitalist method of production for profit, instead of for need. By spouting about the blockade, these well-intentioned people are only helping the governments to delude their slaves, and divert their attention from the real means of throwing off the yoke which condemns them to misery and relative or absolute starvation.

When they say that 'that is all very well but that we can do something, even a very little, to relieve suffering', we reply: for every ton of food that Britain and American propaganda departments send to Greece or France, Hitler will take a compensating ton out of those countries. Humane but reformist attempts may help Hitler, but they won't help the Greeks. Indeed they will only make them imagine that the British government are somehow different from all other governments, and cherish humane feelings towards them, thereby enabling the British financiers once more to enslave Greece for the benefit of British imperialism.

Lay the Axe to the Root
You cannot help the people by playing the government's game, for the interests of governments are fundamentally opposed to those of the people. The desire to relieve suffering and distress is universal — it is a manifestation of the principle of Mutual Aid —

yet poverty and misery have always been the lot of the masses of mankind who are shuffled about by their governments. We appeal to all those who are moved by considerations of humanity and justice, not to spend their energies on efforts which can only be ineffective within the status quo. Let them rather devote their strength towards the overthrow of the authoritarian system whereby the few rule the many; whereby the minority enjoy luxury and security while the masses live precariously or starve outright. Where men are free, their impulses of mutual aid can build a life of plenty for all. Where governments monopolize the organization of the people's lives misery will always be universal.

As with all other social questions, the lesson of wartime starvation is that reformist methods are quite useless, however well-intentioned. And they assist reaction by once more deferring the application of radical revolutionary methods. They help to perpetuate suffering, and divert human energies that the revolutionary movement can ill-spare. Capitalist reality must be faced; our solutions may seem harsh to the sentimental; but until they are applied the workers and peasants of the world will continue to suffer miserable and slavish lives so that the few can carry out a pointless and vulgar existence of luxury and power.

February 1942   J. H.

'End Inefficiency'

End inefficiency, and tighten up the war effort, demand the critics of the government. This seems a fairly safe slogan. After all, no one can defend inefficiency (at any rate, admitting it to be such). Surely there could be nothing more estimable at the present time than demanding an end to all the inefficiency, waste and corruption. It may be said that in doing the job a bit too enthusiastically the critics give nations abroad a wrong impression of Britain today, but it cannot be denied that it would be better to correct inefficiency and give the wrong impression than remain inefficient and give a favourable impression. Not even Mr Churchill could alter that opinion that many people hold.

Left-wing propaganda seems to concentrate more on exposing

the weaknesses and inefficiencies of the war effort, which are corrected or not as the case may be, than on fighting the cause of the working class.

We do not uphold any case for strengthening the war effort or for ending any particular governmental inefficiency as such. The ruling class will, if it sees the need, strengthen its war effort by placing additional burdens on the workers, and should the position be desperate might even make a few sacrifices itself. If it sees the need, it will equally perform the feat of Vichy. Neutrality, war, peace, strong war effort, weak war effort — this is decided by those in power. We would no more interfere in such matters as domestic policy of the ruling class than we troubled about the domestic affairs of Edward VIII.

The point at issue is the vigilance by the working class to see that its own liberties are not still further curtailed, that the sacrifices it has made are not still further demanded, that it retains some independence, thinks and acts for itself and comes round to a consciously libertarian way of action.

How does this 'inefficiency' witch-hunt help us? Do the critics want more of us than the government or less? Frankly, they want more. Are men conscripted? They raise an outcry at older men, younger men, or reserved men, being left at liberty. Is the age limit lowered and raised, are men de-reserved? They demand that women shall be conscripted. Men and women are conscripted. They demand wealth should be conscripted. Even, it is said that conscription of wealth is a means of making the money of the rich fight the same as the lives of the poor, but it is forgotten that when the wealth of the rich is used to fight it is only in order that it may be preserved after the war. It will be seen that as the government introduces conscription of wealth the magnates' power will be increased, not weakened. (But this is leading us to the case against nationalisation.)

The critics sometimes complain about soldiers' pay being small. True. But do they want it to be raised? No, they want to pay the men outside the forces less. Very acceptable to the ruling class, and perhaps easier to achieve than the demand for the raising of soldiers' pay. Is there a shortage of coal? The miners are blamed for absenteeism, and mine-owning MPs cry out for attacks on the miners — not for acceding to their small demands, or for the curtailment of coal profits, or for supplementary parties of mine-owners to work in the pits with them to make up the numbers. . . .

Criticism of the government goes on from all quarters now. Some critics are easily silenced, by the simple device of taking them in the government. Others tone down before public opinion, or up again as the occasion demands. Whether the criticism comes from those who profess to speak in the workers' name, or from those who speak in the name of sections of the ruling class, we repeat: our criterion is not that of efficiency or inefficiency so far as it affects the interests that are not those of the masses. Accordingly, our criticisms are not made with the object of effecting some Cabinet changes, but in order that they may contribute to the masses' understanding for the need of independent action.

Mid-April 1942   A. M.

'Lend to defend'

Since the beginning of the war, this country has been deluged with posters and leaflets calling on all citizens to 'Lend to defend the right to be free', etc. Savings Groups, Warship Weeks, Tanks for Russia, Spitfire Funds — a whole gamut of clever stunts have been arranged periodically by the government in order to extract from the masses the 'millions of pounds necessary to pay for the war'. According to posters, etc., lavished upon the British public, the purchasing of Defence Bonds, Savings Certificates and other official issues is a vital part of the war effort, as it enables ships, tanks, guns and planes to be produced.

But Oscar R. Hobson, City Editor of the *News Chronicle*, stated on 21 May the brutal death of the whole question of money, and the part it plays in society.

"An East Finchley reader, whose letter was printed in Tuesday's *News Chronicle*, referred to the recent purchase by the National Gallery for £3,250 of a Hogarth picture, and said that he read 'with disgust' of such a transaction at a time when our Russian allies were in dire need of our help, when the Red Cross was crying out for funds and the Greeks were starving. I make no apology for saying a word on this letter, because by implication it opens up an issue of very wide importance — the issue of 'money' and 'real things'.

On the one hand the National Gallery has acquired a certain work of art. On the other the Russians need munitions, the Red Cross needs medical stores and the Greeks need bread. Stated thus it is obvious that there is no real relation between these various needs. By no process of alchemy can the Hogarth picture be transmuted into munitions or medicaments or bread. Our reader would be the last to suppose that it can, yet by his mention of a sum of money he has subtly contrived to suggest to himself and, I doubt not, many thousands of others, that just this miracle could be performed.

In normal times, it is true, the possessor of £3,250 might well be able to choose between these four classes of 'real things'. But these are not normal times and no munition worker, chemist, farmer or miller will work the less hard because the nation has acquired from X, its previous owner, a picture by Hogarth or any other great master."

Now it is obvious from this article that money does not create any single commodity in society whatever, and it is obviously useless, therefore, for producing munitions of war.

Then why is the ever-gullible public induced to part with its hard earned wages, believing that by doing so, it is keeping the war going? Why these elaborate arrangements by the government for collecting all this money?

It is a means whereby the purchasing power of the people is cut down, thus reducing the *real* wage of the masses. Since this cut is made voluntarily everyone feels quite happy about it, whereas a direct heavy income tax deduction would arouse a storm of protest and raise some doubts about this 'war for democracy'.

It was this same City Editor who endorsed the remarks of Dr Funk, the German economist, on the same problem. Dr Funk stated that "surplus money is liable to lead to a lowering of the will to work. The State must at all costs re-absorb the surplus money by taxation *or saving drives*, lest the expansions of war production and social discontent arise!" And Hobson thought that a good point!

Thus stands revealed the true reason for the activities of our financial experts. It is in order to keep the workers under control, forcing their noses nearer the grindstone, that such appeals for money are made. The wage-slaves, having given up their surplus cash, have to return to work continually, in order to meet the enormously high cost of living. The 'will to work' is kept as high as possible by such methods. The workers should ignore all such patriotic appeals for their money.

June 1942

T. W. BROWN

'National Independence'

Hope, it has been said, is a good breakfast but a poor supper. So is the struggle for national independence. Since most oppressor nations force on subject nations the loss of political and social freedom as well as national freedom, which means little by itself, the original struggle for national freedom becomes linked with the struggle for political and social freedom, and is therefore progressive and even revolutionary. Scotland, when she lost her national freedom, did not become politically unfree as separate from England, and so Scottish nationalism has never become a reality, though the demand for social freedom persists there as in every capitalist country. India, when she became part of a foreign empire, lost any chances of political freedom, and the demand for political and social freedom is linked up in a progressive movement.

Above all we see this illustrated in the struggles of the European countries against imperialism in the nineteenth century. Hungary, Finland, Italy, Bulgaria, Greece, Czechoslovakia, Macedonia, Armenia, Albania, Poland. The sympathy for these subjugated nationals was intense in the Western World, and in spite of many bloody struggles and suppressions, liberal republicanism did its best to achieve national independence from the ruling powers of Europe — Russian, Austrian and Turkish.

Each of these empires was destroyed — the Czarist, the Hapsburg, and the Ottoman. Excepting Macedonia and Armenia, each of the oppressed nations of Europe became free in a national sense following the great split-up that followed the First World War. National independence, the goal of the nineteenth century, became a snare and a delusion. Poland, that had suffered under three despotisms (Austrian, Prussian and Russian) simultaneously, suffered the ignominy of seeing a fourth despotism arise, that of the native Polish landlords. All the blood that had flowed to make Hungary free flowed again beneath its rising fascist dictatorship. The last of the independent nations to retain forms of liberal democracy were Finland and Czechoslovakia; the latter to lose it in the Munich share-out, and the former to suffer beneath the two-pronged drive of Germany and Russia in this war.

National independence cannot be said to have been a boon to the suppressed nations of Europe, now once again suppressed beneath newest imperialism. Since it retains today the Western sympathy it enjoyed in the last century, let us see how genuine much of that sympathy is.

The sympathies of the British Government inclined of course to the balance of power. It supported Italian freedom when the Austrian oppressor was a rival. Under Disraeli and the Tories it supported Turkish Imperialism, though Gladstone denounced its massacre and its possible rivalry to the British Empire. It attacked Austrian Imperialism always, and when Russia became a rival and a menace to the Indian Empire, Russian Imperialism too. That British ruling class 'sympathy for national independence' was hypocritical was shown in the answer by foreign diplomats: "What about your Irish?" At that time, the Irish question was at least as burning as, say, the Finnish. Another ironical — and true — answer came from Nasir Pasha, general of the Sultan, who replied to hostile English critics that he was going to do what the British had just done in the Transvaal (Boer War), before he massacred the Albanians, Bulgarians and Macedonians, after the Monastir rising.

Whenever British policy inclined to a nation, that nation was helped; when it inclined to its ruler, that nation was forgotten. Such was the 'balance of power'. Ruling class sentiment always inclines to its own interests. Today, Germany attacks British Imperialism for its colonial policy — not because her colonial policy is any different; British Imperialism attacks German occupation, not because she was not its tutor; they are neither of them concerned with national independence *as such* but only as a means of attacking their rivals.

The Allies did not pick Poland's cause because they supported Poland, but because (admittedly) at some time they had to stop Hitler's Imperialism before it directly attacked British Imperialism. Wars are not caused through the defence of national independence, or through any 'St George and the Dragon' motive, but through economic causes and for purposes of aggrandisement or retention of aggrandisement. Let us therefore make an end to all the nonsense current that the major powers are moved by feelings of sympathy towards the minor powers.

Also, let us finish with the nonsense that certain nations are responsible for wars, insofar as they cause wars between major nations, e.g. Alsace-Lorraine, the Balkan countries, etc. The peoples of those countries can, when unaggravated by senseless national distinctions and deliberate attempts to foster separatism between peoples, live together peacefully. Interests not their own cause trouble between them. Hostile prejudices and inculcated teachings foster dissension, but taking away power politics one takes away those prejudices and teachings. In the future there must be no more of this petty disruption that has so long served a privileged few, but a united Europe and a united world.

Certainly we must take up the struggle for national independence when it becomes a struggle against an imperialism. But that struggle for national independence must be waged by the workers and peasants, and we must dissociate ourselves from any bourgeois leaders — for instance, the exiled governments in London, the bourgeois leaders of the Indian Congress, etc. — and associate ourselves instead with the masses who alone carry out that struggle. And independence must not be a goal, but a lever to oust imperialism; and when that imperialism is ousted, we aim not for an independent bourgeois government, but a revolutionary movement that is going to struggle with other revolutionary movements in other countries for a FREE WORLD.

December 1942   A. M.

'Atrocities'

Certain far-seeing statesmen thought, in the heyday of Liberal Party pacifism (post-Gladstonian: a legacy that was abandoned when the war of 1914 internationally drove the bourgeois politicians into their natural home — the imperialist camps) not so much to abolish war, which was never with them more than a pious hope, but to restrict and 'legalise' it, so that modern war, with its horrors even worse in the contemplation, might not finally destroy civilisation in its growing vindictiveness. Hence the somewhat contradictory 'legalisation' of war: the drawing up of 'humane rules of warfare' and the like, which are inevitably forgotten in the heat of battle, and which have served only to ease consciences.

We have seen this particularly with regard to the conventions drawn up regarding prisoners-of-war. It is an entirely callous doctrine to inflict punishment on men taken prisoner, and to treat them as hostages. It is not, of course, any the less callous to slaughter wholesale in total warfare; but limits must somewhere be defined, and civilised nations have generally refrained from the system of hostages.

All that is today going by the board. *Total war* is regardless of conventions, limits and legalisations. War is no longer to be restrained by platitudes. Most people were shocked at the recent feud between the British and Canadian Governments on the one hand, and the German Government on the other concerning the shackling of prisoners-of-war. Following the binding of prisoners in the heat of battle by commando troops (who are, incontestably, specially trained for warfare in which 'rules' are disregarded), the Nazis shackled British and Canadian prisoners-of-war taken at Dieppe. Retaliation upon retaliation followed; and prisoners-of-war looked like being generally in irons. Today we read that the British and Canadian Governments are unshackling their prisoners-of-war, while the Nazis may or may not do likewise.

The system of putting men in irons is detestable. We could wish that some of those who are vociferous in their protests against prisoners-of-war being shackled were consistent enough to protest against the putting of men into irons at all, whether they are military, political or criminal prisoners, but we are glad that general feeling has led to some unshackling, at all events.

We cannot, however, admire the standpoint taken by the Allied Governments in this matter, much as we detest the Nazi mentality that originated it. The Nazis' attitude has been despicable: in retaliating on prisoners-of-war for deeds committed in battle they open the field to wholesale slaughter of the defenceless on both sides. On the other hand, what of the British-Canadian Governments' attitude? If deeds committed by Nazis are to receive retaliation, is it not a palpable lack of principle, and a display of, to say the least, narrow partisanship, merely to retaliate when their own subjects are concerned? On their own evidence, they would give to the world proof of the most abominable atrocities committed by the Nazis on the soldiers and even more the civilians (particularly the civilians fighting at home), who happen to belong to the nationality of its Allied Governments, yet these apparently call for no retaliation on prisoners-of-war: the only interests to be protected — if retaliation is to be considered protection — are those of the larger powers![1]

---

1. I take the following at random from the Press: "Although the chains of German prisoners in Britain and Canada have been removed, Germany is still

This is the main case against retaliation, other than the humane
one, which is not likely to weigh with Governments. Humanity is
apt to get pigeon-holed in the offices of the ruling classes. The
considerations most likely to weigh with governments, perhaps, is
that to ill-treat prisoners-of-war is to discourage desertion from the
rival army. In Africa, it has been shown quite clearly that the
general anti-war feeling in Italy (just at the moment being
deliberately confused by British Right-Wingers with the pro-war,
pro-fascist Catholic and Royalist circles which in every country —
witness above all France — stands in with the victors and readily
changes sides and double-crosses at will, but always with the big
battalions) has shown itself not, in avoidance of military service (as
it did in peace-time) but in desertion from the army. A policy of
shackling Italian prisoners would have given a new lease of life to
Mussolini.

Unfortunately, the question of expediency fades away, and the
arguments that weigh with Governments concerning military
prisoners disappear, when the issue of brutality of treatment
concerns nationals or subject-nationals. We are all familiar with
atrocity stories: they do not appertain to any one war — many of
the same stories are handed down through the ages. But while
journalists of the world concoct obviously fake atrocity yarns, the
grim fact remains that the truth is too often far worse. The
inhumanities of this epoch far out-do the best efforts of the
newspapers. The atrocious crimes committed in the world today
cannot be equalled in history.

People have asked us our attitude in view of this. Do we, like,
say, the Vichyite Duke of Bedford, wish to gloss over Nazi
atrocities, yet stress the atrocities of war; or do we, like, say, the
up-and-coming Lord Vansittart, wish to stress Nazi atrocities

---

considering her decision. 'The affair is in the stage of diplomatic handling,' the
Wilhelmstrasse declared to Reuter.
    Britain unshackled the prisoners as from 10am yesterday.
    In Canada . . . unshackling took place on Friday night." (*The People*, 13th
December 1943)

"The Germans, it is reported from Sofia, have shot more than 300 Greeks at
Lamia as a reprisal for the blowing up of the vital railway bridge at
Gorgopotamos, near Lamia . . .
    The Greeks are said to have been shot for sheltering the guerrillas who
destroyed the bridge. It is reported the Germans are taking further vicious
reprisals." (*The People*, 13th December 1942)

towards the subject peoples, yet gloss over Nazi atrocities towards the Germans? Do we, like the Finnish social-democrats, wish to stress the brutality of Stalinism, and forget about Hitlerism for the time being; or, like the Dean of Canterbury, give a blessing to Stalinism, and forget its identity with Hitlerism? Do we, like the Minister of Information, wish to proclaim Nazi atrocities and apologise for British Imperialism; or, like Goebels, uncover British Imperialism and blandly apologise for Nazism? Or, like the bourgeois Americans of the former isolationist school, attack British, Russian and German Imperialism, while still waving the Stars and Stripes and forgetting Uncle Sam's own record.

None of these attitudes are ours. We recognise the truth of what most of the imperialisms say about each other. Every government is forced to descend to rousing the worst passions in man when it is a question of maintaining its own rights. That is our case against governmentalism. The fascists are extreme examples of this, and products of decaying capitalism: that is why we are anti-fascist, and why we want capitalism to be destroyed before it produces more such. When we are confronted with proof of atrocities in war, *that is our case against militarism*. When we are confronted with proof of atrocities in peace-time or non-belligerent conditions, *that is our case against capitalism and fascism*.

And, since our case is not merely on those grounds, and since our study of social conditions shows us that militarism, capitalism and fascism are inter-linked in this age, the proof adduced by all governments on the horrors inflicted on mankind by other governments, only strengthens us, and all thinking workers today, in our determination to *end all domination*.

January 1943

A. M.

'Jail Mosley!'

Sir Oswald Mosley has been released from detention on medical grounds, following reports submitted by Lord Dawson of Penn, the King's physician, and Dr Geoffrey Evans, as well as the prison medical authorities. On two occasions, at least, Mosley was allowed to leave prison in order to consult West End specialists.

Mosley's release brings up a number of questions. He has not changed his political ideas, and was released on medical grounds alone. But will Herbert Morrison accordingly sanction the release (on 'medical grounds') of other prisoners who may be in equally bad health, though perhaps, with fewer friends among the ruling class? There are hundreds, maybe thousands, imprisoned under wartime, basically political offences — Conscientious Objectors, deserters, absentees, and those who have infringed the industrial as well as military code, by leaving their jobs without permission.

And since British Fascists are being let out, how about releasing Indian Democrats? Old Gandhi may die in detention at his age.

Fascism thrives on notoriety. If it can't get publicity, it remains an insignificant growth. Hitler deliberately went out of his way in the years before 1933, to court opposition.

Mosley, after a prolonged visit to Berlin, copied these tactics in London, He, too, began an aggressive propaganda which invited attack. The Communists, who also thrive on the same kind of publicity, of course played up to him, and very soon Mosley's party began to grow, and attracted wide attention. This was just what he wanted.

The present outcry about the release of a few Fascist leaders,

fanned chiefly once more by the Communist Party, also serves the
ends of Fascism. The holding of counter-demonstrations is once
more represented as 'militant anti-fascism', while the revolutionary organising of the workers is never mentioned. Just when the
Second Front is at a pretty low ebb, and the Stalinists are
beginning to feel the comeback from their reactionary strike-
breaking policy, Morrison has supplied them with a programme —
attack Mosley! They do not mind playing over again their pre-1933
policy of assisting the Fascists to keep themselves in the public eye
— their own policy is not essentially different from the Fascists.

While Pollitt and the *Daily Blackleg* squawk against Mosley, the
ruling class, with their politicians who backed Hitler and Mussolini
without a second thought, include in the government Lennox-
Boyd, who was so prominent a Franco supporter while the Spanish
Anarchists were giving their lives in the revolutionary struggle
against Fascism in Spain.

December 1943

THE INDUSTRIAL SCENE

Back to the Brass Collar

'There is nothing new under the sun' said the ancient maker of proverbs, and modern legislators seem unable to develop any new ideas. The Labour Decrees of Bevin are curiously like the Statute of Labourers and other laws of the fourteenth century. Before Bevin became Minister of Labour many workers were taking advantage of a shortage of labour to change their employment, to hire out their labour power to the highest bidder. Against this rising wage tendency the Minister of Labour introduced his Essential Works Order and other measures. Workers in certain industries were forbidden to change their employment at their own will, but may have jobs chosen for them by the Minister of Labour; and employers were forbidden to 'poach' labour — that is, advertise enticing wages.

Now let us look back 600 years to England after the Black Death. Shortage of labour created a kind of demand that had hardly existed before this time.

"It became worthwhile to leave one's district to seek work elsewhere. A royal proclamation of 1349 tried to deal with this novel situation. It commanded everyone, free or villein, to remain with their masters until their contracts of service had expired, and to work for the accustomed wages. When Parliament met in 1351, complaints were made that the provisions of this proclamation had not been observed. The labourers were demanding much higher wages, and going where they could obtain them. The Statute of Labourers was therefore passed in order more effectively to enforce the principles of the proclamation. Men were to accept work when it was offered to them at rates of wages prescribed in detail for labourers and artisans. . . . The government attempted rigorously to enforce this law by appointing local justices with power to punish offenders." (H. de B. Gibbins: *Industrial History of England*)

Not very different from English labour laws today. Gibbins shrewdly adds "The first experiment in controlling labour conditions by governmental intervention was inspired by the desire to prevent workers from securing for themselves the advantages of the free play of the principle of supply and demand." Exactly. The first experiment and the latest.

The complaints of the Parliament of 1351 are echoed in 1941. The select committee on National Expenditure, publishing its report at the end of May, laments the high competitive wages being received by many workers. "But" adds the sub-committee, "it had had evidence of firms in the aircraft industry deliberately paying their operatives more than the agreed district rates, and by doing so disturbing other firms in that district. . . . The Ministry should do everything in its power to ensure that factories working for it, either commercially or on a management basis, observe strict federation wage rates and keep their bonus percentages in line with those of their neighbours" (*Financial Times*, 29th May 1941). Look out, aircraft workers! Its your wages they are after.

It may be necessary to explain the bonus system spoken of by the select committee's sub-committee. This bonus is a form of piece-work, or payment by result. In its most common form a worker is given a certain time, let us say ten hours, to do a job. If he finished this job in eight hours he is credited with two hours bonus. This is spoken of as time-and-a-quarter (note: the extra hours are not paid for at the usual rate of wages. Usually the bonus hours are underpaid by sevenpence-farthing per hour).

Now the standard bonus rates referred to by the sub-committee are trade union rates, rates long since outstripped by individual and group bargaining outside of the union apparatus. The customary standard aimed at is double time (or much higher), one hour extra for each hour worked, but the trade union agreement fixes bonus rates at time-and-a-quarter. If the worker is reduced to the trade union standard he must sweat, worry and run about like a mad horse for a few pence per hour extra. Wherever a misguided operative appeals to the union agreement (as in demonstration of bonus times) he is defeated, for the trade union rates are below the prevailing wage rates.

The ruling class employment of labour leaders to subdue labour is not new. It has gone on almost continuously since over thirty years ago a French Socialist Minister used soldiers to break the railwaymen's strike. We must not think of the Minister of Labour (Ernie Bevin) as the solitary trade union official in the service of the State, though he gets most of the publicity. Hordes of trade union officials have obtained leave of absence to take up positions in the Ministry of Labour. The new bosses have nothing further to learn to become efficient taskmasters. Here is Trevor Evans of the *Daily Express* writing on the Merseyside dockers' dispute, a dispute of food, wage rates and workmens' buses.

"A plot in the Merseyside ports to smash the Bevin scheme for dockers has been smashed. It was wrecked by the firmness of one man — Mr Harry Pugh, who, after being a trade union official for 30 years, is now Port Labour Director for the North West region. Last night it was reported, after practically the whole of Manchester's dockers had been suspended by Mr Pugh, that the majority either had resumed work or had agreed to start work again tomorrow under Bevin's scheme rules. There are still 500 men undecided, and Mr Pugh announces that any man who does not re-start tomorrow will be suspended and subsequently dismissed. 'And' he (Mr Pugh) added, 'if we are forced to do it, we will not hesitate to bring in the Pioneer Corps to discharge our cargoes'. At the docks there will be 'cages' with gates in which the dockers will await their duty. Gates will be closed punctually at 8am. Malingerers and those persistently unpunctual will be punished (*Daily Express*, 13th June 1941).

Cages for discontented dockers! Bring 'em back alive! Call in the military, forbidden to change employers, prison to tame the unsubdued! All that is left is to reintroduce the brass collar of the mediaeval serf, stamped with the employers' name and address. But this is a democratic regime and Labour will insist the collar bears a union label — 'made throughout by trade union labour'.
July 1941   TOM BROWN

Morrison's Spring Offensive

The government seems to be only able to launch offensives and show initiative in the suppression of the workers' rights and the liberty of the press. Mr Morrison has stated his spring offensive by warning the *Daily Mirror* that if it goes on with its criticism it would be suppressed. Under Defence Regulation 2D Morrison is able to suppress any paper without any form of trial. He does not even have to warn the paper he intends to suppress.

In this case the excuse for the warning is peculiarly feeble. The cartoon for which the *Daily Mirror* is attacked suggested — according to the Home Secretary — that merchant seaman died to protect the interests of oil companies. (The *News Chronicle* pointed out, incidentally, that it could equally be interpreted in an entirely patriotic sense.) Mr Morrison's anxiety to protect the susceptibility of the capitalists is not very well suited to a Labour minister. He is on the way to becoming one of the most unpopular men in the government. In spite of the fact that he goes out of his way to assure the House that the Prime Minister and the whole government entirely approve of the measures he takes, he is nevertheless held to be responsible. He does the dirty work for the government and is covered with insults by the whole press. Such is the fate of lackeys and traitors; no one will pity them.

The case of the *Daily Mirror* has aroused much comment and provoked a great deal of indignation all over the country. While we are very pleased to see these protests we suspect that all this talk about liberty of the press means something entirely different in the mouths of liberal MPs, in the editorials of the capitalist press, or at communist meetings; what they mean by the liberty of the press is the right to criticise the conduct of the war. All of them are opposed to maintaining the right to criticise the war itself. This is made clear by the editorial in the *Manchester Guardian* for 21 March.

"It is therefore unhappy that so early in the new start there should come an onslaught on the press, *not on the little pacifist or defeatist sheets (which go on unrebuked)* but on a newspaper which differs from others only in the violence and asperity of its pursuit of what it conceives to be shortcomings in carrying on the war."

If the government suppressed papers which criticised governments and wars (i.e. those that the *Manchester Guardian* calls "pacifist and defeatist") no one would protest. When the House and the press accepted the regulations they thought they would only be used against revolutionist elements. They raised no objections to that. Now that they themselves feel threatened and see the instruments they had hoped to use being used against themselves they raise their voices.

The kind of liberty we want, the freedom the workers should work for, is not a mere right to criticise within certain regulations and limits defined by people in power, but the right to attack the causes of war and injustice.
April 1942

Railways: Shares and Wages

George Ridley's pamphlet putting the case for the nationalisation of railways by showing that it would be cheaper for the government to buy the railways rather than to hire them as it is doing at present, has caused a certain amount of comment in the press. These are the arguments used by Ridley in favour of nationalisation:

"The State is hiring the controlled undertakings (that is, the four Group Companies and the LPTB) for £43,000,000 per annum. I hold that it would be cheaper to buy them and I explain my contention as it applies to the four Group Companies. Their hiring figure is about £38,000,000. Their Stock Exchange value is about £750,000,000. If for the purpose of purchase a loan was raised at three per cent, the interest charges would be £22,500,000, instead of the hiring charge of £38,000,000.

This would leave a balance of £15,500,000 a year for capital redemption, plant modernisation, or whatever else may be thought to be desirable."

This shows very clearly the ridiculous position in which the government finds itself with regard to the railways. The nationalisation proposed by certain members of the government at the beginning of the war was so strongly opposed by the Tories that a compromise had to be sought which would give satisfaction to vested interests. The arbiter in these matters was the Minister of War Transport, Lord Leathers, who like so many of his colleagues in similar positions, is a director of many companies and a City man.

The Labour party case for the nationalisation of railways may seem convincing but it is difficult to see in what way it is a socialist scheme. If the State has to purchase a loan at three per cent, who is going to pay the interest if not the already heavily exploited workers? But people with money to invest will be able to put it in a government loan at three per cent, instead of railway shares which, at their best, pay two per cent interest.

Railway workers are now asking for a minimum wage of £3 per week. Agricultural workers, who have always been the lowest paid workers in Britain, are now in a better position than railway workers and yet railway workers generally live in towns and have more expenses than people living in the country. J. Marchbank, NUR General Secretary declared recently that:

"The lowest rated employee was today, with 47s. a week plus his war bonus, still 3s. 1d. below what was necessary to preserve his inadequate standard. The 48s. employee was 3s. 5d. the worse off, while the 50s. worker was 4s. below the standard.

Nearly 200 grades, including women, were receiving, excluding war bonus, less than £3 a week. About 195,000 employees were affected in the traffic grades, some 3,500 class V clerks and 100,000 female staff. As any change in the basic minimum was bound to have repercussions on grades earning over £3 per week, about 320,000 workers were on the traffic side alone would be affected."

The wages of railway workers are ridiculously low and action should be taken for an immediate rise. Railways are of primary necessity in wartime and railway workers should, just like agricultural workers, take this opportunity to demand and force from the railway companies a rise in wages.

Railway workers will have been pleased, however, to see that their sacrifices are not in vain. The railway companies have this year paid the highest dividend since 1930.

"The London Midland and Scottish Railway Company has declared a dividend of two per cent on its £95,000,000 of ordinary stock for 1941. For each of the previous two years holders had received 1½ per cent, and not since 1930 has 2 per cent been paid. That is a clear sign of how the agreement of last August, with its still unpublished arrangements about war damage, is working out." (*Manchester Guardian* 19th February 1942)

Two per cent dividend may not seem very high as compared with the eight per cent and more paid by rubber, steel and oil shares, but it comes all the same out of workers, thousands of them, who get less than £3 per week, a bare minimum to live on. It is also worthwhile mentioning that while railway shareholders safely put their dividends in their pockets every year, retired railway workers get as little as 3s. 6d. a week (in many cases they have worked for railway companies for 20 years or more!). When Pick retired, however, he got £5,000 a year and Lord Ashfield the LPTB chairman will get something in relation to his salary of £15,000 a year!

The refusal of the government to take over the railways glaringly proves the hypocrisy of the 'sacrifice for all' and 'conscription of wealth' empty declarations. While soldiers are sent abroad to sacrifice themselves for the defence of the Empire, while children are put in uniform, women ordered to leave their homes according to the whims of the Minister of Labour, the rights of shareholders remain sacrosanct.

Nationalisation offers no solution to this question. Those who will have to pay for the 'buying of railways' will be the workers and when the railways will be owned by the State their conditions will not improve. We have many examples of State owned industries or institutions where the conditions of the workers are similar or worse than in privately owned industries.

Railway workers cannot rely on Labour Party MPs to better their conditions. They have to organise the struggle for their interests by relying on themselves and on their fellow workers.

March 1942

Direct Action by Kent Miners

Leaders gaoled

It is customary nowadays to deplore strikes and automatically dismiss strikers as 'slackers' or even 'quislings'. The reactionary press has fostered this attitude, but so also have the so-called 'Left' papers. Thus the Co-op paper Reynolds News *in its leader on 25th January states that: "There is little to be said in defence of the Betteshanger strikers, except that miners do not deny the community coal nor their families bread merely for the fun of the thing . . ." Even in the daily press, however, the manifest justice of the striking miners' case has had to be grudgingly admitted, especially after the high-handed gaoling of their leaders and the imposition of fines on the remainder of the men.*

In view of the unsatisfactory nature of the press reports of the strike, it was decided to obtain first-hand information. At first the miners, on account of the unfair treatment of their case by other papers, were reluctant to talk, but they were soon convinced by our comrade that WAR COMMENTARY *was concerned only with the truth of the whole matter, and volunteered the following information. The facts given below are vouched for by the miners, who are prepared to challenge contradiction.*

In November a number of men were transferred from the East Side, where the face was comparatively easy to work and where earnings were about 10/- a day, to No. 2 face which is a very hard one to work, so that 'earnings dropped very considerably. A

Government arbitrator (Sir Charles Doughty) came down when a dispute arose over this sudden drop in wages, and decided that certain allowances should be made as from 10th December. It should be pointed out that Sir Charles required to be advised "upon all mining technicalities and customs." He collapsed in the pit whilst on inspection, and in his condition it is very doubtful whether he could have made an accurate examination of the face concerned. In any case, Sir Charles' conclusions are challenged by miners who consider several of them to be innaccurate and misleading. To take one example, he states that one shift produced an average of six tubs per man hour, and another only one tub per man — entirely failing to mention that in the first case the men were 'heading' the coal (which can be done at a vastly greater speed) and in the second case working on a face in an abnormal seam. Incidentally, Sir Charles Doughty swallowed whole the excuse given by the management for the transfer to the more difficult seam, which was that there were insufficient boys to do the haulage work on the East Side. This, however, fails to hold water since there was a shortage also on No. 2, to which colliers had to be transferred to do the haulage work.

The miners, however, made an effort to carry on in accordance with the arbitration decision, but when only 7/- per shift was paid for week-ending 2nd January negotiations were opened with the colliery management in view of the fact that under the Minimum Wage Regulation and the Kent County Agreement *the minimum rate per shift is 10/4½d.* The atittude of the management was seen at the end of the following week — 9th January — when the miners on No. 2 found they had been paid at the rate of *6/9d per shift* (a war bonus of 4/6d per shift over and above all the rates quoted above is paid by the Government and is not the concern of the owners). *This state of affairs aroused the men to action, and by a unanimous decision of the whole 1,600 men working at the colliery they came out in defence of their minimum wage.*

At the end of the following week the management issued summonses against the miners for breach of contract damages, but these were later withdrawn. The men then received summonses from the Ministry of Labour, charges being made under the Defence Regulations, and at Canterbury on 23rd January three of the strike leaders were gaoled. William Powell, Branch Secretary of the Kent Miners' Association, got two months; Tudor Davies, JP (President Betteshanger Branch KMA) and Isaac Methuen (member of the Branch Committee) both of them Deal Town

Councillors, got one month each, all of them with hard labour. The rest of the strikers were ordered to pay fines amounting to over £1,000.

Company breaks wage agreement

The company had broken the wage agreement without a word to the miners' representatives, and the charge of ca'canny is much resented by the men — men who, after 'staying put' during air raids and invasion warnings, were congratulated by the Prime Minister and the Minister for Mines, saying "The country will never forget the debt it owes to the Kent miners." It is not surprising that they are feeling a little bitter! The miners say they are ready to return to work when the £35 due under the Minimum Wage Agreement is paid to the men on No. 2 face, and their leaders are released from gaol.

The attitude of Magee, the agent for the colliery owners (Pearson and Dorman Long) has aroused considerable resentment among the miners. He has been at Betteshanger since 1938, but had acquired an unpopular reputation before that at the Nunnery Colliery, Sheffield, and at Featherstone Colliery. He is regarded as an enemy of Trades Unionism and workers' rights.

Solidarity throughout the mine

At a recent meeting of 800-1,000 of the miners, Mr J. Elks, General Secretary of the KMA, and Mr E. Lawther, the Financial Secretary of the KMA, proposed that the men should return to work (whilst their representatives were still in gaol). *The miners spontaneously rejected this proposal and their hostility to such a compromise was not left in doubt.*

When our comrade left the miners today (Tuesday) they were adamant and determined to stand out for their rights, whatever happens. One view expressed was that rather than go down the pit before their demands are met and their comrades released from gaol, they would go back where they came from — to Wales, Scotland, Cumberland, Yorkshire, etc. There was no sign of the "frayed nerves" referred to in the *Daily Express* of 27th January.

There can be no doubt of the justice of the demands of the miners working on No. 2 face — to be paid 6/9d per shift instead of the minimum of 10/4½d — amounts to open robbery. *But it must be made clear that this gross injustice directly affects only the 40 men on the face referred to. The rest of the 1,600 miners are out in solidarity with them.*

On top of the injury of 6/9d a shift, the men have been subjected to insults in the shape of allegations that they are 'slackers' unconcerned with national need. The men's attitude to this sort of calumny is clear. The 40 men demand £35 from the owners, to make up their wages to the agreed minimum. The management has preferred to lose three weeks' work from 1,600 men (about 25,000 tons of coal at £3 per ton while £320 was expended on summonses which were later withdrawn). The men have lost so far over £7,000 in wages. Clearly the management is more intent upon repressing these militant workers than on assisting the 'national effort'. They merely use this as a stick with which to beat the men.

Legal juggling

Strikes being illegal, the strikers themselves get no relief whatsoever. Those with dependents get 12/6d a week for a wife, and 4/- for a child, from the Public Assistance Committee. The question at issue is one of elementary justice, and to claim, as the press generally have done, that it is 'only' a question of miners demanding 'more money', is to belittle their cause, especially as the overwhelming majority are out in sympathy with an injured minority.

Regarding the legal proceedings, it is significant that the claim on the miners for '"breach of contract damages"' was withdrawn by the firm, thus leaving only the charge under the Defence Regulations, i.e. that the miners did not give the required 21 days' notice of the strike. This left the miners dealing with the Government, in the form of the Ministry of Labour, so that representations regarding the conduct of the colliery owners were ruled 'out of court'.

In this strike the militancy comes from the men themselves. The KMA, as our report shows, has acted in a conciliatory capacity. The decision to strike was a spontaneous demonstration against the continued refusal of the owners to pay the minimum rates after representations had been made by the men the week before. The gaoling of the three men was carried out on the excuse that statutory 21 days' notice of the strike had not been given. Of course, as is realised by the miners, this clause in the Defence Regulations was inserted in order to allow employers to organise their defence and so deprive the strike of most of its effectiveness.

The key to victory

If they are compelled to continue on strike much longer, economic necessity will force the Betteshanger men back to work, otherwise they will starve.

The action taken against the miners clearly demonstrates that in spite of the flagrant injustice to the men, the Government, through Bevin, Minister of Labour, immediately came to the support of the owners. It must never be forgotten that it was the Minister of Labour who summoned the miners, fined them and gaoled their leaders.

Such success as the miners have had so far comes from the spirit of solidarity which brought the other miners out in defence of their comrades on No. 2 face. But to ensure rapid victory, the solidarity should also have been extended to them from miners all over the country.

If the miners were organised throughout the whole industry on the syndicalist principle that 'an injury to one is the concern of all', there would be no fear that injustices such as this would fail to be met with effective action on the part of miners throughout the country, resulting in speedy removal of the injustices. Workers as a whole should be suspicious of appeals to them to accept wage cuts 'in the national interest' extended to them by employers who show no disposition to consider the national good, but only their own profits.

All who work for the freedom and emancipation of the workers will extend fraternal greetings to the Betteshangar miners in their struggle: but they must also be prepared to back them up with action.
February 1942

Postscript

The strike ended with the colliery owners, Pearson and Dorman Long, agreeing to pay the amount by which the miners' money fell short of the Minimum Wage — although it should be pointed out that it was paid 'ex gratia' and 'without prejudice'; presumably in order that this should not jeopardise any action by the company in the future. Also, it should be pointed out (contrary to the impression given in some papers) — no money was paid for the time the men were on strike.

The decision to return to work was made after several hours discussion, during which D. Grenfell, Minister for Mines, urged that by returning the miners would strengthen his hand when proposing the release of their three leaders by the Home Secretary.

Now that the leaders have been released, this must automatically lead to a cancellation of the fines imposed on the men, as both gaol sentences and the fines were imposed under the same Defence Regulation. No mention of the fines has, however, so far appeared in the national press.

Although the miners are to be congratulated on the result (apart from the fact that they lost a considerable amount in wages) they should not lose sight of the fact that the Government was in this case no doubt concerned with the loss of output during the strike, and for that reason adopted a conciliatory attitude. When there is no 'national emergency' to consider, as has been found in the past, the clash of interests between the owners and employees became sharper. Whilst they are able to do so, let all workers consider how they may best organise in order to not only so safeguard their day to day interests, but to seize the earliest opportunity of gaining their freedom from all exploitation — by taking control of the means of life themselves and using them for the common need of all.

Mid-February 1942

Don't Go Down the Mine, Harry!

Workers are becoming a little tired of being given slogans when they ask for the loaves of improved conditions. For many months now the resentment of the miners, at bad working conditions and unjust treatment by the State, has been growing and demonstrating itself in strikes and in the universal working slow which lowered the per man output in almost every coalfield in the country.

The miners have many grievances, besides the usual ones concerning poor pay. Owing to the withdrawal of miners to the forces, the average age of miners has increased from 33 to 38, so that fewer and older men are expected to bear the burden of heavier work. In many pits the good seams are being left and the difficult ones worked, so as to get the high wartime price for the coal which is most costly in labour. The condition of the pits and pit machinery has deteriorated since the beginning of the war owing to the lack of men and materials for its maintenance. In addition there are many men in the mines with individual grievances because they have been dragged away from better jobs outside the mines which they had obtained in the days when the mine owners had no use for them.

The miners have been subjected to bullying of various kinds, but this has had little effect on the most independent section of the British workers. Now persuasion is being tried, and the miners have been confronted with new machinery for the settlement of disputes arising out of the running of the industry. The machinery is very much like any other negotiating machinery, i.e. a National Negotiating Committee with 11 members from each side, and a National Reference Tribunal of three independent members appointed by the Master of Rolls. The only important difference is that wage negotiations will once again be on a national rather than on a district basis.

Surely it is time the workers learnt from experience that 'machinery' of this kind is always only a drag upon their activity and is, indeed, intended as such. This Will Lawther admitted when he said, "It is a serious attempt to prevent on either side any drastic upheaval either in peace or war". This kind of trickery should always be treated with the contempt it deserves. Only by their own direct action will the workers ever get the conditions they desire. From negotiating committees and 'independent' tribunals they can expect nothing beyond such mean sops as it is convenient for the capitalist to give them when his prosperity allows it.

As was to be expected, the Communists are full of sycophantic praise for the new machinery and hearty 'congratulations to the Mineworkers' Federation'. They choose the opportunity to demand that the federal organisation of the MFGB should be replaced by a highly centralised union, in which, no doubt, they hope to carry on their own activity to greater advantage.

Communist Party General Secretary Harry Pollitt also speaks his mind to the miners in a pompous little pep-talk pamphlet entitled 'Miner's Target'. Just as he is anxious for a second front on which he is unlikely to get the chance of dying, so Harry is anxious to speed up production on the coal face he himself will never work. He starts with a little bland flattery, and then goes on to pleading for just another 3 cwts a shift, comrade! Next he demands co-operation with the State and the bosses in the Coal Control Scheme, and then waxes stern on absenteeism.

'How can any decent man voluntarily lose work at a time like this! To do so is a crime.'

Avoidable absenteeism, lockouts, or strike stoppages do not damage vested interests.'

This sounds very much like the voice of Ramsay Macdonald.

The pamphlet continues in this vein. The workers have to put up with inadequate equipment, to endure transference, and so forth. At every barricade Harry stands stalwartly beside the bosses. Appropriately, the concluding paragraphs contain a flattering reference to the 'excellent proposals of the Beveridge report'. That the 'revolutionary' Mr. Pollitt should come down to supporting such a manifest fraud is sufficient comment on him and his pamphlet.

The other section of the workers who are showing their desire to have some proof of the good world for which they are fighting are the locomotive drivers, It is impossible at this juncture to predict what will happen, for the union executive are obviously not enthusiastic about the strike and are merely following the belligerent attitude of their rank-and-file members.

While, as in all cases, we support the day-to-day struggle for the immediate demands of the workers, there are several points in which the present railway situation calls for criticism. These points arise from the difference in nature between the trade unionist and the syndicalist conceptions of action and organisation. For instance, one of the most unfortunate tactical errors of the locomotive drivers is the long delay in taking action, a delay which the government have no doubt already used to prepare for the dispute. This arises from the bureaucratic and reformist nature of the trade unions, where action is in reality vested in the permanent officials and dominated by the conception of the trade union as a part of the capitalist social order. To the trade unionist negotiation is desirable. To the syndicalist action is necessary, because in the last resort only the direct action of the workers can force the hand of the exploiters.

Again, as syndicalists we oppose the craft union form to which the ASLE & F adheres. In the present situation the position of the locomotive men is palpably weaker because they are only 10% of the men in their industry, striking without the support of the remaining 90% of the workers. Only when all the workers on the railways are united in one syndicalist and federalist organisation, only when they can present a single and integrated front to the

State and the capitalist will they be able to act efficiently, either in
the daily struggle or in the revolutionary struggle for a free society.
February 1943.

Clydeside Invasion

Daily Worker Fears Militant Glasgow

There descended upon the Clydeside last week a strong man from
the staff of the *Daily Worker*. The *Daily Worker* is not convinced
that the Clydeside worker is being exploited to a sufficient degree;
so in order to alter this condition of things, it sent down Jack
Owen, well known Communist Party boss, to psycho-analyse the
Clydeside worker and to prescribe and administer the corrective
treatment for the ailment commonly known as discontent. Jack
Owen is a turner who has forsaken his lathe, and in preference to
turning a crankshaft, he now turns the handle of a barrel organ
which monotonously grinds out the Communist Party theme-song-
of the day — Increased Production.

In the *Daily Worker* of 17th March he declares (or should one
say, laments) that "pervading the every thought of the Scottish
worker is the age long struggle". And he goes on, "They suffered
on the Clyde in the days of the engineering depression. That
suffering is now, mistakenly, used as a guide to action to-day."

Scared of Anarchism
He professes a sympathetic approach — so also does the
undertaker. The guile of the politician is immediately apparent in
his correct characterisation of the Clydeside worker — "heroic
fighters for their class, possessing a vitality invaluable to us, if we
can guide it into the correct channels". But he betrays the fears
which made the Communist Party send him up to Glasgow, when
he says, "In such soil the fungoid growth of Anarchism, ILPism
and all such theories of the mentally inert find root to grow."

The attitude of hostility and suspicion to the boss-class, which
Owen depicts as his 'problem' — "It can and must be dealt with",

he declares — is as natural to the class struggle as sunshine in summer, and the Communist Party, when they ordered the suspension of the class struggle, should have remembered the old story about King Canute. Besides examples of fine skill and craftsmanship, the Clyde has produced men like John McLean; and in the atmosphere of Political Dictatorship, such as prevails to-day, with all its trappings, regional Gauleiters, total negation of representation, total conscription of labour, with their resultant starvation wages, the Clydeside worker is taking to Anarchism, the road to freedom, just like water fills the hollows of a plain. If Owen and other Communist clack-talkers cannot (or do not choose to) distinguish between 'fungoid growths' and the healthy growth of the revolutionary struggle, the Glasgow workers can, and they also have a wonderful capacity for smelling out renegades.

No doubt it will be painful to remind Owen (and some Clydeside MPs) of the Clyde Workers' Committee, but the very fact that such a movement, only on a much higher revolutionary plane, is today slowly taking shape, even though it has not yet taken a concrete general expression, is undoubtedly the reason for his unwholesome presence on the Clyde.

The Bosses' Man

Howling to high heaven for unity, Owen proceeds forthwith, using the disruptive tactics of the Communist Party to try to split the class unity of the workers by pointing out that "there is a tendency, easily explainable, for the semi-skilled man to draw, through the medium of bonus, a much higher wage than the skilled engineer". So far as his constructive proposals go, as a solution of course to *his* problem, he quotes an instance in John Brown's yard of nine men contracting to do a job in the same time and for the same price as eleven men previously did. Perhaps this is Stakhanovism; if so the workers are painfully acquainted with this method here, and know it generally as payment by result. The result always being an intensification of labour and an exhausting fight in debilitated conditions for payment.

Note that he never once suggests that the boss should disgorge some of his enormous profits, only that the worker should work harder and longer for the same cost to the owning class.

This is employer craft, and the worker can nowhere any longer be fooled by it, neither is he fooled by sleight-of-hand adjustments to wages which he is told will be 'worth £1 a week after the war'. It is strangely reminiscent of 'Pie in the Sky'. The Clydeside worker is beginning to recognise Fascism as a Hydra-headed monster which grows nine heads for every one lopped off, and today is in the birth throes of organising as a class for the total kill. The preliminary skirmishes are already being fought, and he will forge his necessary new weapons in the struggle itself.

Revolutionary Syndicalism
Yes, the undergrowth is already being cleared and so also will the overhead foliage which obscures the workers' clarity of vision. The Craft Unions to-day stand clearly exposed as being unable to act for the working class; the Communist Party will bite the dust singing its swan song of increased production. In the not-very-distant future the workers will organise as a class in their Industrial Syndicates, and emulate their Spanish comrades who knew how to fight Fascism — by the method of the Social Revolution. Although there are many barriers still to overcome and a difficult path as yet to tread, the signs of awakening are unmistakable (as Jack Owen) and the Clydeside worker will remain loyal to his tradition of class solidarity and be in the vanguard of the struggle to abolish the class-rule of authority once and for all.
April 1943   CLYDESIDE WORKER

WAR IN THE FAR EAST

Our Rulers and Japan

We have already had occasion to point out in the case of America the now familiar spectacle of a nation's capitalists arming the enemy whom to-morrow they send the workers to fight against. The press cries of 'Japan's treachery', 'violations of treaty rights' etc., come home to roost if one recalls American connivance. *"Despite our revulsion at Japan's conduct and our numerous protests against Japan's violations of America's rights and treaties, we have been allowing Japan unlimited access to our markets and materials. We are the unofficial but indispensible partners in Japan's guilt."* (Dr Walter H. Judd in *Readers' Digest*, February 1940.) Similarly the *New York Times* on March 1st 1940 reported a deal between the British and Japanese governments, involving the sale of about 1,000,000 barrels of crude oil produced by British companies in Iran to Japan.

These are recent transactions. It might be thought from the British government's new-found sympathy with China, that they have always considered Japan as a 'gangster'. The record of the government's spokesmen is not a happy one in this respect. And the quotation from Churchill shows that the blame cannot be fastened on to those useful scapegoats, the 'Men of Munich'.

When Japanese political leaders have, or are believed to have, betrayed their country, they either commit hara-kiri, or are assassinated by Japanese patriots. Britain, being a civilised country, reserves a different fate for her politicians. Thus Sir Samuel Hoare in spite of his actions in regard to Japan and that unfortunate affair with Laval, is now in receipt of a splendid allowance as ambassador to the 'Christian Gentleman', Franco. Sir John Simon, far from having to make a hasty disappearance from world politics after his odious behaviour in 1931, is now Lord

Chancellor, in receipt of £10,000 a year, and a guaranteed pension of £5,000 a year for life.

Manchukuo

In 1931 the National government came to power just after Japan had annexed Manchuria. Sir John Simon, then Foreign Secretary, successfully temporised at the League of Nations, for 15 months. He then made a speech at Geneva, which made Matsuoka, the Japanese delegate, remark that Sir John Simon had said in half an hour what he had been trying to tell the Assembly for weeks! The whole transaction bore out Lenin's apt stigmatisation of the League as a 'thieves' kitchen'.

Although Sir John Simon has borne most of the criticism he was by no means alone in his attitude. Mr. Amery, the present Secretary of State for India, on 27th February 1933 said: "*I confess I see no reason whatever why, either in act, or in word, or in sympathy, we should go individually, or internationally against Japan in this matter. Japan has got a very powerful case based on fundamental realities . . . when you look at the fact that Japan needs markets and that it is imperative for her, in the world in which she lives, that there should be some sort of peace and order, then who is there among us to cast the first stone and to say that Japan ought not to have acted with the object of creating peace and order in Manchuria and defending herself against the continual aggression of vigorous Chinese nationalism? Our whole policy in India, our whole policy in Egypt, stand condemned if we condemn Japan.*"

Japanese 'peace and order' has meant, in fact, almost continuous war for ten years in China. But we can agree with Mr Amery's last sentence entirely!

Just to make it quite clear where the Conservatives stood, we will quote Sir Nairn Stuart Sandeman speaking on the same day: "*I am frankly pro-Japanese, entirely pro-Japanese, because I believe that the Japanese will settle the question in Manchuria and settle it quickly, and the less time that is spent in settling the row in Manchuria, the sooner we shall get to doing trade in China. Frankly, I wish we were in close touch with Japan and were prepared to say that we are going into the Yangtse Valley.*"

The renewal of the Anglo-Japanese Naval Alliance was constantly advocated at the time by Conservative MP's like Sir Roger Keyes, who is so vocal now about Japan's perfidy. No wonder that a writer in the *Japan Chronicle* of 4th February 1933 in seeking the naval alliance stated "I am confident that Mr

88   [1942]

Churchill and the British Naval officers will endorse my view. So
will the *Daily Mail* and the *Daily Telegraph."*

Sir Samuel Hoare, now at Madrid, continued Sir John Simon's
policy.

In the summer of 1937 it was Mr Eden's job to parry awkward
questions by equivocal replies justifying Japan's renewed
aggression in China. Neville Chamberlain was another vigorous
defender of Japan. (It is perhaps worth while to note that in their
report of 28 April 1932 ICI record that Sir John Simon holds 1,512
of their shares, while Neville Chamberlain had 11,747 shares
[quoted in *Le Monde* 8th July 1933]. ICI are said to have supplied
poison gas to both Japan and China).

WHAT WE SAID IN 1937 . . .

*The most truly important happening of the week has been the
determined action of the Southampton dockers in refusing to land
Japanese goods from the Canadian liner 'Duchess of Richmond'
last Saturday, not only for the intrinsic value, small though that
may be, but as an example of direct action and solidarity.The
News Chronicle of* Monday the 6th reports that the legality of the
dockers' action may be called into question, since this may be
described as a strike with a political motive. Fortunately, the
rejected cargo is on its way back to Canada, and we hope that
the dockers have learnt the lesson that nothing succeeds like
success!

SPAIN AND THE WORLD, 10th December 1937

WHAT CHURCHILL SAID IN 1933 . . .

*"British interests required us to keep out of the quarrel which
has broken out in the Far East and not wantonly throw away our
old and valued friendship with Japan. It was the interest of the
whole world that law and order should be established in the
northern part of China . . . The condition of China, plunged in a
strange combination of anarchy and Communism was the cause
of boundless and inexpressible misery to her industrious people.
China was in the same state that India would fall into if the guiding
hand of England was withdrawn."*

(24th February 1933)

Bevin Does his Bit
But the Conservatives were not alone. Bevin also did his bit. When in February 1938 dockers in London and Middlesbrough refused to load scrap iron on to the Japanese ship 'Hararra Maruh', Bevin, as secretary of the Transport and General Workers Union disowned them. This may be regarded as the official attitude of the Labour leaders towards effective intervention on the part of the workers.

Chinese 'Democrats'
The government's new found sympathy for China will no doubt win it some popularity, among those who have forgotten its many declarations on the lines of those quoted above. We have always declared our sympathy for and solidarity with the Chinese workers and peasants, fighting against multiple Imperialist exploitation and Japanese aggression. But we are not deluded into thinking that the Chinese Government is democratic. A recent writer states that *"Indeed the Second Revolution of 1926-7 which established General Chiang and the Nanking Government in power might be compared to the Nazi revolution in Germany"* (Pringle *China Struggles for Unity* 1939). Chiang-Kai Shek has killed his political opponents and rivals, and massacred sections of the Chinese workers on almost as grand a scale as Stalin in Russia. But the 'aggressive Chinese nationalism' of Mr Amery in 1933 has now become a democratic partner in the firm of ABCD powers. A junior partner we fancy.

Stalin and Asia
We have already seen Matsuoka hand in hand with Simon at Geneva in 1932, where he warned against the danger of 'Sovietism' in China. It remains to recall him on a similar footing of friendship with Stalin in May 1941 — eight months ago. After the conclusion of the Soviet-Japanese Non-Aggression pact, the journalists at the Moscow station were astonished when Stalin came down to see Matsuoka off. Embracing the Japanese warmly, the all-wise leader of the USSR declared eternal friendship with the Japanese. *"After all"* he said *"we are both Asiatics"*.

"The Soviet Far Eastern Armies are intact. This superbly trained and magnificently equipped body of armies, far from having been drawn on since the German assault began in the west has actually been augmented" (Phillip Jordan's cable to *News Chronicle*, 11th December 1941). In spite of this however, and in spite of Litvinov's tactful speeches in America, the USSR has already

expressed the view that the most useful contribution they can make in the Pacific contest is to engage the Germans on the Eastern Front. General Tojo also stated on 16th December that *"there is no change in the attitude of Japan towards the Soviet Union which has repeatedly declared that she considers herself bound to the neutrality pact with Japan"* (*News Chronicle*, 17th December 1941).

Russia has refused to open a second front against Japan and has made no declaration of war. That these have not been immediately forthcoming as soon as the war with Japan began, is an indication that the motives behind the war are not so simple as our propagandists would like us to believe. For if the issue were really one of 'Democracy' versus 'Fascism', such concerted action would be immediately undertaken. Even if the 'Democratic' powers had not, on their own showing, armed Japan to the point where they are able to take on both America and Britain at once, the hesitations and equivocations of those vociferous protagonists of 'Freedom' would be enough to discredit their propaganda.

To Hell with Politics!
Of course the attitude displayed by Amery, Simon and Hoare towards Japan, was also displayed by the same group, representing the capitalist interest of the ruling class, in regard to Italy over the Abyssinian war, General Franco in Spain, and throughout the whole pre-war period, Hitler himself. For those who remember these indications, the falsity of the 'righteous claims' of the whole crew of war-makers, from Churchill and Stalin, Hitler and Tojo, Roosevelt and the Labour leaders, is apparent. It is impossible for the conscious workers to associate themselves or their movements with such self-confessed reactionaries and hypocrites. The workers must steer clear of all such intrigues and leaders and the brutal wars their power-politics and self-seeking produce. For the working class there is only one struggle and that is the class struggle, against all exploiters whether at home or in other lands. That is the only struggle in which the ideals of Justice and Freedom are not besmirched and have any true meaning.
January 1942

J. H.

Imperial Twilight in the Far East

The Social Significance of Singapore

The rapid retreat of the British forces in Malay and around Singapore has brought out the usual excuses, chief of which is 'lack of preparation'. Even the most newspaper-sterile mind finds that story difficult to swallow, for we have had Singapore preparedness hammered into us for more than twenty years. Military works on the island, carried on for several generations, were intensified in the early twenties and in 1938 there was completed "*the largest, the most powerful and most modern naval and military base in the world*". It would be as well for a fire brigade to declare it was not prepared for fires. Few will remember how the financing of further Singapore defences entered into the election disputes of 1923, becoming, in some constituencies, almost a major issue.

Although those electoral disputes often caused a great deal of heat, the present danger of Singapore arouses among the general public less emotion than a football match or an outbreak of hiccups in the royal family. We do not seem to be an imperial people by inclination so much as by accident. I have always suspected the imperial fervour of the British people since I discovered schoolchildren waving Japanese-made Union Jacks on Empire Day (the Japanese-made flags were bigger and *cheaper* than the British articles).

Situation Well in Hand

Fresh news of retreat and loss in Malay arouses only cynical smiles. Official assurances of imminent victory and good news tomorrow turns the smiles into hard laughter. The public is not helped by the apologists of the Government. Defending Air Marshall Sir R. Brooke-Popham against the attacks of Lord Addison, Lord Trenchard (himself an ex-brass hat), said in the House of Lords, "*What does Lord Addison expect of a commanding officer in his speeches? Is a commanding officer to say, 'Hong Kong will fall and must be evacuated'? Is he to say that Malaya cannot defend itself?*"

Well, if he cannot say that he could keep silent, but that would not occur to a brass-hat. You cannot stop a general making speeches. But next time you read official statements of "*Air supremacy in three days, Hong Kong is impregnable or the situation is well in hand,"* remember Trenchard, *"What does one expect of a commanding officer in his speeches".* We expect a horizontal champion to state, on the eve of his big fight "I'll murder him in one round", but we do not pay any attention to him.

Dilemma Down Under

Singapore is of the greatest possible significance to the British Empire. With this great base in the hands of the Japanese, where else can the British and US navies be based, refitted and refuelled? Singapore is the key to Burma, India, the East Indies, New Zealand and Australia. It is little wonder that Australia is alarmed, her best troops scattered in military gambles, or in the care of 'titled nincompoops', the enemy likely to approach her northern shores, with a vast continent to defend and a population of 7,000,000 against that of Japan's 100,000,000. It is not surprising she should look around for assistance. In these circumstances we are not surprised by the statement of the Leader of the Australian Labour Party that Australia will look to America rather than to Britain for military aid.

Nor are we surprised by Menzies' attack on this statement. The economic conflict between Britain and the USA has been, since the last war, carried into all the British dominions. In Australia this has led to an ever-increasing American share of capital investment. War accentuates the economic conflicts of other times and the economic war of the two 'Anglo-Saxon' powers will, from time to time, be reflected in the line up of Australian political parties. So far the Labour Party looks like becoming the champion of yankee capital.

It must be of little comfort to the Australians to learn that Malay is short of tanks and aircraft because Britain has sent so many to Russia. It is hardly complimentary to Australia to say that Germany and not Japan is the enemy, for the German military might is embedded in Russia, while Japan is approaching the gates of the southern continent. As little comfort as that of the relatives of the crews of the Prince of Wales and the Repulse on learning that they lacked air support because the planes had been sent to Russia. 'Save Bolshevism and lose the Empire' seems a queer slogan for the Conservative Party.

Misalliance

One might here turn aside to comment on the ramshackle character of the Anglo-Russian alliance. While Russia and Britain are allies against Germany, Russia remains on terms of treatied friendship with Japan while, according to pro-Russian reports large Soviet forces are idle in the far east. Says Ivor Montague in 'The Red Army', *"In the East, near Vladivostock, there must be a fleet strong enough to keep off the Japanese or anyone else on the Pacific"*. (It is possible that a large part of the Russian navy is there, that part which is in the Baltic is of little use). And further, *"Not long ago Kuznetsov declared that USSR had more submarines than Germany, Italy and Japan put together"*. Of the army Montague says, *"The Far Eastern Army, which would have to face the Japanese, is entirely separate from the rest of the forces, with separate tanks and air force, separate war industry, separate food reserves and supply"*.

Above all it is Russia alone which holds the territory from which Japan might be attacked. In the present case, while any combination might turn up, it seems that Stalin is very reluctant to become the ally of Britain in the East. Perhaps the communists may persuade him to open a second front in the East.

White Niggers

The general effect of the retreat in Malay must be to weaken the imperial bonds and system of alliances. Chief of the problems will be that of continuing to hold down the 'coloured races' of the Empire. How often have we heard that British forces must be in India, or Burma, or Africa because the 'coloured races' cannot protect themselves. The carefully built up legend of 'white superiority' is receiving a severe hammering. As it declines, the confidence of the colonial subjects will increase. It may be that we are at the beginning of a severe contraction of the Empire.

As the Eastern empire shrinks there will arrive in Britain increasing numbers of colonial administrators, planters and slave drivers; those whom even the capitalist press speaks of as ignorant, selfish whisky swillers. Their arrival here can only mean the further depression of the metropolitan working class. The white sahibs have been used to a very high living standard, a standard wrenched from a starving native population. With the loss of imperial possessions that high standard can only be maintained by lowering that of the British workers.

Further, the sahibs have been used to power. Who has not heard them boasting while on a year's leave, of 'jumping on a nigger's feet', or 'kicking a Chinese in the ribs'. Often it is just the whisky talking but it reveals the mind of this type.

They will not quickly lose this habit of power, they will ask to exercise it on the British workers. We only become the home coolies, the white niggers. A poetic fate for an imperial people. With the increasing surliness and rebellion which the workers will develop on the prolongation of the war, some sort of 'black and tan' force is likely to arise. What better candidate for the job than an out-of-work sahib? When these gentlemen arrive home in increasing numbers we shall learn the meaning of fascism.

Such a social phenomenon is not new; it happened in Spain after the decline of the Spanish Empire. At the height of that empire a vast parasitic class had developed in Spain. The loss of the fruits of overseas possessions led to an intensification of exploitation at home. Even to-day the ruling class of Spain is faced by an insoluble problem, how to maintain an imperialistic parasitic growth without an empire.

It seems we are beginning that historical process in Britain. It may take a long time or it may come swifter than any of us dream, but come it will. In these stormy days to come, talk of the restoration of British parliamentary democracy will be sadly out of place. Britain will become the most fascist or the most revolutionary country. It is up to us.

February 1942   TOM BROWN

Two Fronts in Malaya

I still have fresh divisions. I intend to keep them to maintain order."
General Weygand in June 1940.

Now that Singapore also has fallen the capitalist press is busy conducting post-mortems on the strategy employed, lack of supplies and a hundred and one other factors. We do not expect Imperialist blimps to be efficient where sacrifices in property are required, nor do we doubt that supplies were inadequate. But all these 'explanations' really serve the ruling class (they are put out, after all, by the capitalists' press) by concealing the fundamental problem that confronts any imperialist power fighting a military action on colonial territory.

Capitalist Imperialism Fights on Two Fronts

While the British Sahibs were fighting against the Japanese imperialists, they still had to carry on their bitter class fight against their oppressed colonial slaves. In war between rival imperialist 'mother-countries' such as Germany, Britain or France, the fundamental class war can be glossed over by stressing patriotism, 'union-sacrée', love for the Fatherland etc., — of course to the advantage of the dominant class. Such a method of side-tracking class antagonisms is however not open to colonial rulers. Calls to 'patriotism' could hardly be expected to muster the Malayans to solidarity with their imperialist oppressors — the opposite result of arousing Malayan nationalism would be far more likely!

Thus Japan's most powerful weapon in the Pacific war is the resentment with which the victims of Imperialism view their British and American oppressors. History — particularly the history of the working class — is full of instances where men labouring under a tyrant's yoke have preferred 'the devil they don't know' — in this case Japanese imperialism — to the 'devil they know'. For to them it appears that no change could worsen their position.

It is said that the British were *"unprepared for a land attack on Singapore — having always expected a Japanese attack by sea"*. But we find that Mr P. C. Spender KC, a member of the Australian Parliament already envisaged such an event when he said in *May 1939* "Sometimes I wonder what would happen if Singapore were attacked from behind."

Reynolds News of 14th January declared *"Singapore must be held . . . and for that, the co-operation of all the peoples of Malaya, Singapore, and the East Indies is essential . . . otherwise the roar of Singapore's big guns may do no more than echo the greatest Empire crash in history"*. Of course "the co-operation of all the peoples of Malaya, Singapore, and East Indies" is just what imperialist tyrants cannot manage to obtain. So far from being 'stupid' about it, as most of the socialist press describe them, the British Sahibs seem to have realised this from the start, for they made no serious attempt to enlist the co-operation of the Malay and Chinese coolies in the Peninsula. They knew they wouldn't get it. But *Reynolds*, in the article already cited, complains *"we forgot to make allies of the Malayans and Chinese who make up the mass of the population, not only of the Malayan Peninsula but of the surrounding islands on which the Japanese are now tightening their grip"*. The nature of Imperialism being what it is, we would like to know how one makes 'allies' of a subject people? Even the ingenious Nazis are finding it a difficult job in occupied Europe!

Better the Japs than Malayan Insurrection

But the British masters were not only unable to make 'Allies' of their slaves, they actually feared them. How else can we explain the failure to arm and equip the population, or understand the fact that "*Chinese troops went into the battle for Singapore armed with nothing more than shot guns*". (*Evening Standard* 17th February 1942)?

While Mussolini was defending Abyssinia against the British the Press was full of reports about the imminent revolts of Abyssinian 'patriots' against the italian Imperialist tyranny. But when the British troops marched into Addis Ababa they found the Italian Army had remained on duty, 'to maintain order'.

The *News Chronicle* for 16th February 1942 reported that "*1000 armed British soldiers will be left in Singapore City to maintain order until Japanese Army completes occupation*". The *Evening Standard*, later in the same day, added "that it was in the interests of the population that the British troops who were there should maintain order *rather than allow any trouble to grow and be dealt with by the Japanese* . . .". There are 1,000,000 inhabitants still in Singapore, including 100,000 British (i.e. 10 per cent). It is the old nightmare of every ruling class — "We are many, they are few".

Scared of a revolt against themselves — they would rather not 'allow any trouble to grow and be dealt with by the Japanese' — it now only remains for the Empire propagandists to broadcast radio appeals to the Singapore and Malayan coolies 'groaning under Japanese oppression' to 'rise up and throw off the invader's yoke' etc., etc.

March 1942

WAR & PUBLIC HEALTH

The War and Public Health

In an article in the last issue of *War Commentary* evidence was presented to show the degree of ill health which was prevalent in this country in the years preceding the war. It was made clear that malnutrition played the major role in the production of ill health, and that this malnutrition was itself directly dependent on poverty — the income available for food after 'fixed' payments, such as rent, insurance, etc., had been paid, was insufficient to provide enough food, more especially of the 'protective ' foods. In the words of Sir John Orr, "a diet completely adequate for health, according to modern standards, *is reached at an income level above that of 50 per cent of the population.*" It was pointed out that reformist measures, where they were not actually harmful, were inadequate to do more than touch the fringe of this formidable degree of ill health. As the PEP report said: "the most effective means of improving nutrition *is unquestionably a rise in the real wages of the workers, with a consequent increase in the amount the housewife can spend on food.*" One may say that "a rise in real wages" forms the *only* way of improving health under an economic system based on wages and production for sale. The question arises: how does the war affect the situation?

It is only possible within the scope of one article to outline in general terms the changes brought about by the war in the main factors bearing on health. We have seen that wages are at the very heart of the problem; have wages risen? and if so, is it possible under wartime conditions for the housewife to spend any such increase on food?

The enormous increase in productive output demanded by the needs of the war has created a relative shortage of labour in industry and on the land. Inevitably, therefore, wages have shown a tendency to rise. But on all sides the government has introduced measures to check this tendency. The Essential Works Order, for example, by preventing a man from leaving his job, deprives him of the ability to bargain with an employer about wages by threatening to take his labour elsewhere. The determination to prevent wage increases was however officially indicated in the Government's White Paper of July 1941 on Price Stabilisation and Industrial Policy. After declaring that prices must be stabilised in order to prevent the 'vicious spiral' of inflation it quotes the Chancellor of the Exchequer as pointing out that "it is clear that persistence of the tendency toward rising wage-rates, which necessarily increased costs of production at every stage of the productive process, would compel the abandonment of the stabilisation policy." Since the government is committed to the latter, it must necessarily take steps to prevent a rise in wages.

It seems likely, therefore, that real wages will not rise. Have measures then been taken to ensure that in spite of that, adequate amounts of the protective foods, milk, eggs, meat, and vegetables are available at prices which the working class families with children can pay? According, once more, to Sir John Orr "the present system of rationing and price fixing will not do that. The protective foods are already more vigorously rationed by prices than by the present system of coupons. The coupons provided in March for 4 oz. of bacon and 8 oz. of butter. *One third of the population cannot buy these amounts. Some households are so poor that they never have butter at all. These households will not purchase the rationed amounts.*" (Sir John Boyd Orr: *Nutrition and War*, Fabian Tract, No. 251, April, 1940). The situation has probably not improved since this was written. One is justified in assuming that the standard of nutrition has not improved during the war years, but if anything has tended to fall.

The Last War and Tuberculosis
In the last war, of course, the privations undergone by the civil populations undermined resistance to disease and rendered them particularly susceptible to the influenza epidemics which swept over the world. Influenza, according to most authorities, caused more deaths than the whole of the actual fighting. Let us, however, consider another disease — Tuberculosis — which is more directly affected by social conditions and has not an epidemic character. According to a Committee of the Socialist Medical Association (June 1941) "Food shortage was the other important social factor incriminated officially (i.e. by Chief Medical Officer to the Ministry of Health; 1920 Report) in the last war, a shortage that was accentuated by reason of the increased energy output necessary for the lengthened hours of work. In Germany and Austria, of course, this factor played an even greater part with appalling results. Indeed it has been estimated that as a result of

the war and subsequent economic depression (1914-27) Germany lost an extra 280,000 civilian lives from tuberculosis." The report states that in England "there were 25,000 more deaths from TB during the war of 1914-18 than would have occurred had the 1913 death-rate continued. This excess is increased if, as is reasonable, it be assumed that the pre-war decline would have continued had there been no war."

The Ministry of Health's report recently published states that "Non-respiratory tuberculosis accounted for 4,077 deaths in 1939 and 4,484 in 1940 . . . The increase in respiratory tuberculosis has been most noticeably among young women between the ages of 15 and 25." Hence, tuberculosis is on the increase in this war too. (According to the *Manchester Guardian* for 17th March 1942 the same thing is happening in Germany; "the statistics show that while there were 69,000 cases of tuberculosis in the first forty-eight weeks of 1939 the figure for the first 48 weeks of 1941 was over 88,000".)

In some instances the capitalist press has tried to gloss over these facts. *The Times* of 29th December 1941 wrote in a leading article: "Fears have been expressed recently that the incidence of respiratory tuberculosis among young women is increasing. Such facts and figures, however, as have been cited or as are available do not appear to furnish a sufficient basis for conclusions and cannot certainly be accepted as a statistical warning." Under the headline "It's Taken a War to Make Us Healthy," the *Star* (17th March 1942) seeks to suggest that the increase in tuberculosis is unexpected. "For an *unknown reason*, tuberculosis deaths in 1940 were 9·7 per cent higher than in 1939." In spite of this apparent surprise, nevertheless, a similar increase in the death rate, especially evident among young women, occurred in the last war. Hart and Wright analysed the question at some length, and concluded that this increase was associated with the markedly increased employment of young women in factories during the last war (*Tuberculosis and Social Conditions in England* 1939) and it was pointed out by Collis and Greenwood that the rise was directly proportional to the extent that women were employed in munitions. The present increase should therefore cause no astonishment.

The question of Tuberculosis in wartime has been dwelt on in some detail because it is a disease which is closely associated with the standard of living. In other words, the control of tuberculosis is dependent on the solution of social questions. Like the question of malnutrition, it is linked directly with wage levels and with hours of work. In the April issue of *War Commentary*, Tom Brown wrote of the "struggle the British workers have waged for one hundred years; the fight to keep women out of certain jobs. . . . The workers then felt such labour to be degrading to women and most harmful to their health." The experience of this and the last war shows that the instincts of the worker were very well founded.

Under a system dependent on the control of the means of life by the few, wages are always at the lowest point compatible with subsistence for the majority who are compelled to sell their labour in order to live. With all the productive resources now available, an economic system based on production for sale instead of for need, allows those resources to remain idle while under nourishment is universal. And this situation is so much a part of the daily lives of all people, especially in industrial countries, that the incredibly low level of health is accepted as 'normal'. We have tried to show that it is certainly not surprising under conditions in which workers have to work themselves to exhaustion for wages which are inadequate to maintain even the simplest nutritional needs.

The last hundred years has of course seen enormous advances in the treatment of disease. Many which formerly gave rise to high mortality have been eliminated or controlled, by better treatment or preventive methods. Improvement has undeniably taken place — though it is noteworthy that the general upward trend was interrupted by the last war, and replaced by a deterioration in health standards. The danger lies in the fact that this gradual improvement *within capitalism* is regarded by devotees of gradualism and reformism as grounds for general satisfaction. Sir George Newman, for instance, who was Chief Medical Officer to the Ministry of Health from 1919 to 1935, and of the Board of Education from 1907 to 1935, wrote as recently as January of this year: "But if we take the long and correct view of our own social history we shall find good ground for saying that, as a whole, the English people are today better housed, better clothed, better fed, better educated and enjoy better health, than at any other period of our national history of which we have record." He added that "their life is *longer* and larger than ever before. They receive, as a rule, higher wages than before, though they work shorter hours . . ." (*Britain Today*, January 1942). These remarks are probably quite justified. But in view of the facts regarding health and nutrition summarised in our article in the last issue, satisfaction at the present position is simply grotesque. It does not help the ills of the present to say, in effect, that the situation was much worse, forty, fifty, or a hundred years ago.

The intimate connection between Poverty, Nutrition, and Ill health which the work of the last ten years has conclusively demonstrated allows of only one conclusion: general improvement in health standards will always be limited by the factor of widespread poverty: there is therefore a limit to the effective elimination of ill-health by purely palliative means which do not take the factor of poverty into serious account. The great bulk of ill health, such as existed in this country before the war, and will almost certainly be increased by the war itself, is directly linked with the continuance of capitalism, of the wage system. What then is the prospect?

Neither in peace nor in war, does capitalism show itself capable of improving this revoltingly low level of 'health' in any radical way. But this is seen to be inevitable where the conditions described have their root and cause in the very structure of capitalist society itself — in the wage system and production for the market rather than for use. Obviously to seek amelioration of the present ill-health within the frame work which directly gives rise to it is foredoomed to failure. Attempts at reform are useless, and worse than useless. A healthy and expanding life will only be made possible when men are free to secure for themselves and their fellows the abundance which is now arbitrarily witheld from them. The social revolution must place the means of life — and therefore of health — in the hands of the workers themselves and under their direct control. The immense natural riches of the world will then be open to all, and the economy will be organised on the principle of 'from each according to his ability, to each according to his need'. The drudgery of wage-slavery is the root-cause of ill-health; only the abolition of the wage system and of all kinds of domination of man over man can bring freedom of access to the means of life. And freedom will bring health.

Mid-April 1942   JOHN HEWETSON

Venereal Diseases

33b Solves Nothing

The war has enormously increased the amount of Venereal Disease in England, provoking a considerable outcry. The question is an extremely complex one; but it provides an interesting example of the way in which such social matters are 'tackled' under class-society.

Venereal Diseases are to a large extent both preventable and curable; yet in actual fact they are responsible for an untold amount of physical suffering and misery. They cause a great deal of insanity, paralysis, disorders of the nervous system, of the heart and blood-vessels, and about half the total cases of blindness. In addition they are responsible for a high proportion of the still births, of infantile mortality, mental deficiency and physical deformity in children, besides a great deal of sterility and chronic invalidism in young women.

Because of the social stigma which surrounds them, statistics regarding these diseases are hard to get, and cannot be entirely relied on. Their victims tend to hide their complaint and in many cases are deterred from seeking treatment in spite of the seductive posters placed by local authorities in public lavatories. Some years ago it was estimated that there were 122,500 new cases of venereal disease each year in London, and 800,000 new cases in the United Kingdom as a whole. Up till the beginning of the war, the position was thought to be improving but a recent (1939) estimate stated that "in England there are about half a million people suffering, or who have suffered from syphilis, and about another million and a half who have gonorrhoea". These figures are not intended to be regarded as entirely accurate, but they give some idea of the extent of these diseases in peace-time. Since the war, according to the Chief Medical Officer to the Ministry of Health, there has been a 50 per cent increase among the civilian population, and if the Services are included, of nearly 70 per cent. Hence the outcry.

The prevalence of these diseases in peace-time caused a number of Anti-Venereal Disease Societies to spring up, and these invariably reported the opposition of the State as the chief factor in preventing a rational approach to these problems. When, therefore, the Government tries to give the impression that it is undertaking a vigorous campaign against VD, we have a right to be sceptical.

Were it not for the concealment which the general secretiveness about VD imposes, it should be possible to know the exact time of exposure to infection, and therefore to take immediate precautions. One authority writes: "The micro-organisms causing these diseases are very frail, and are at once destroyed by any antiseptic that can reach them, but they soon dig themselves in, and once they have got below the surface and beyond the reach of antiseptics they will multiply rapidly and a lengthy course of treatment will be necessary to assure cure, that is, the destruction of every single microbe . . . . *These diseases are therefore easy to prevent, but difficult to cure . . . . The distribution of prophylactics and instruction in their use was attended with considerable success in the regular army. In the wartime army however, this method of stamping out these diseases is to some extent hampered by the sense of shame which still prevents the immediate application of preventative measures. The main problem is therefore the breaking down of this veil of secrecy, and the dissemination of knowledge. Dr. R. A. Lyster, the Chairman of the National Society for Preventing VD, wrote in a letter to the News Chronicle* for 22nd November 1942,

"During the last war, as part of my military duties — I was VD officer over a considerable military area — I succeeded in securing among the troops a widespread knowledge and adoption of practical preventative measures with the result that venereal disease diminished as if by a magic wand".

But, he adds these significant words,

"Over all these years (i.e. from 1907 onwards) the strongest opposition has arisen from the Ministry of Health which must be held primarily responsible for preventing the prevention of venereal disease".

In 1917, a VD Act was passed, but a clause was inserted making it a punishable offence to expose disinfectants for sale for the prevention of VD or even sell them on demand accompanied by written instructions for use.

As now, the rapid increase in VD during the last war scared the government into 'doing something'. In 1922 a Committee of Enquiry was set up under the chairmanship of Lord Trevethin, to advise on methods of dealing with the problem. Evidence was given by all the leading authorities, and in 1923 the Committee issued its report. In Clause 14 it recommended that "the law be altered so as to permit properly qualified chemists to sell *ad hoc* disinfectants provided such disinfectants are sold in a form approved and with instructions for use approved by some competent authority". Subsequently attempts to get various Ministers of Health to give effect to this clause have failed.

In 1926 a bill introduced by Sir Basil Peto, President of the Society for Preventing VD, endeavoured to get Clause 14 legally enacted, and was supported by every medical MP except one. It passed two readings, but Neville Chamberlain refused to give Government support or facilities for a third reading.

In 1937 the Ministry of Health sent a Commission of experts to study conditions regarding VD in Holland and Scandinavia, where these diseases had been practically eliminated, ostensibly by compulsory notification and treatment. The Committee doubted whether methods of compulsion were suited to this country, but the Ministry took no alternative steps.

The present Defence Regulation 33b is a facing-both-ways measure, well designed to allay immediate fears, and so tide over the present crisis. The Minister of Health is definite in declaring that "it leaves the voluntary basis unchanged," thereby keeping on the right side of the laissez faire people; but he also insists that if the voluntary system fails, he will not hesitate to apply compulsion. This satisfies the devotees of a 'strong line'. All that 33b actually does is to provide "that persons named by two separate patients under treatment as the suspected source of their infection, can be required, by notice served on them by the Medical Officer of Health of the County or County Borough in which they live, to attend for examination and, if necessary, treatment by a 'special practitioner' and to continue treatment in accordance with his directions until they are certified as free from Venereal Disease in a communicable form". It is neither one thing nor t'other.

The "voluntary system" as it is understood in this country has already proved a failure, as the rise in VD shows. But it is unlikely that compulsion would prove much better. Where there is such a powerful social stigma as attaches to these diseases in England, compulsion will merely drive the disease still further underground and make still more difficult the task of prevention or early treatment. In Scandinavia, VD is regarded in much the same way as any other disease, the sexual act not being treated with the same odium as it officially receives over here. This is probably the reason why VD has so markedly diminished there; the compulsion is not felt as an imposition on individual liberty, any more than the compulsory notification of, say, typhoid is here. The Chief Medical Officer to the Ministry of Health, Sir William Jameson, may bombinate over the BBC about treating VD as a disease like any other, but he is neglecting the powerful forces which seek to keep them as diseases apart, and is wholly forgetting the role which the Ministry itself has played in the past in obstructing the efforts of the anti-VD societies to get a rational attitude adopted.

In the past the Church has taught that venereal diseases were the punishment of God for sin. They are not interested in the effects of VD with the hideous misery which follow in its train but solely in repressing sexuality. A Committee of the Free Church of Scotland, (*Manchester Guardian* 13th May 1942) stated in a report that

"promiscuity is being condoned and even encouraged among the armed forces by the gratuitous provision of facilities by which it is designed that the more direct consequences of vicious relaxations may be escaped".

They are referring to the provision of condoms which, in the Army, are intended not only as a contraceptive measure, but also as a protection against VD. It is rather difficult at the present juncture for the Church to say openly that attempts to reduce VD amount to interfering with God's divine justice. The Archbishop of York is reported as saying in the House of Lords that he approached

"the problem from the religious rather than the medical point of view, but as he pointed out there need be no inconsistency between the two. The Churches would support a bold and enlightened policy of education *provided that prevention and avoidance of promiscuity was urged as the best safeguard of all.* There should be more treatment clinics and local authorities should be encouraged to employ more women police",

Keep down sex at all costs!

It will be seen that in all this, there is no attempt to provide people with the knowledge and means whereby they can avoid contracting these diseases themselves. To do so would be to imply that a man or woman's sexual life was their own business, and that would never do. Rather than appear to condone 'vice', the State will go on tinkering at these problems, evading them most of the time, and merely being content to give an appearance of 'doing something' when the situation becomes serious enough to evoke a public outcry.

It is obvious that the problem of eradicating VD is bound up with the extirpation of sex obscurantism. It is also obvious that much of the mental suffering associated with these diseases is produced *solely* by the social stigma attached. The retention of these cruel and obscene taboos is the principal barrier to progress, and as such is inevitably supported by the State, the Church and the reactionary bodies. A free people would clear out VD in no time!

January 1943   J. H.

WAR COMMENTARY

For Anarchism

Vol. 4 No. 22.   MID–SEPTEMBER 1943.   TWOPENCE

'LIBERATORS' AT WORK

THE REACTIONARY POLICY of the Allies has led Italy to a catastrophic situation. Her towns are shattered, her population starves. While in the North and Centre the Germans are trying to establish their rule and to put Mussolini on his feet again, the "liberated" Italy is expected to accept the King and Badoglio as her saviours.

Ruins, starvation, Quisling generals and AMGOT politicians, this is what the Allies have brought to the Italian people. The Italians' efforts to destroy Fascism have been frustrated. They had, by their refusal to fight, by their strikes and demonstrations brought about Mussolini's fall. They were not going to stop there. The King-Emperor and his Addis-Ababa Duke were just as hated as the

Duce himself and the Italian people intended to get rid of them as well. But the revolutionary movement which would have cleansed Italy of all vestiges of Fascism was immediately crushed by the Allies. They started negotiations with Badoglio thereby recognizing his authority. They carried out the systematic bombing of all the big towns thereby making it impossible for the Italian workers to organise their own resistance. How could the Italian workers organise strikes, occupation of the factories, the taking over of transport and industry under a rain of bombs, in cities filled with ruins and the stench of corpses, devastated by epidemics, with people crushed by fear and sufferings?

It is clear that British and American imperialists did not want the Italian people to raise their heads and to take their lives into their own hands. As soon as Mussolini fell they found a man as corrupt and brutal as him to hold a whip over the Italian masses. General Badoglio, the man who

ALLIES'
COUNTER REVOLUTIONARY
ROLE

People in Arms

The situation in France demands the closest attention from the working class everywhere. Before the Allied invasion, the country was held down by the military power of the German occupation. *War Commentary* has already pointed out that the slackening of the Nazi grip in France would provide an opportunity for the French working class, would provide in fact, a revolutionary situation. But we added that the significant problem would remain for solution — that of preventing the successful imposition of another centralised State power. Events are now clothing these theoretical problems of the revolution in actuality.

Dual Power
The French workers seized the opportunity presented by the Allied landings. A general strike was declared in Paris, while the armed bands of the maquis seized control in the provinces from the failing grasp of the armies of occupation. The armed population became the source of initiative, the centralised governmental control vanished, at least for the time being. It has been said that the only guarantee of freedom is the people in arms, and although the general property relations in the country remained fundamentally untouched, it only required a spark to set alight the fires which would consume the basis of the old economic order. Such a spark could easily be generated by the deplorable economic state in France. Unemployment is increasing, and in Paris alone there are 300,000 on the dole. Nor does the wage increase of 40 per cent do much to offset a rise in the cost of living of between 300 and 400 per cent.

The government of de Gaulle has set about reducing this dangerous position to one of 'order'. In effect, there exists to-day in France a dual power, such as existed in Russia between February and October 1917. On the one hand the armed populace,

on the other the central government. This is the background of the
struggle of de Gaulle to disarm the popular militias.

Accordingly, on November 1st, the cabinet confirmed its
decision of some days earlier to disarm the Militia. Members of the
Resistance Movement could join the regular army, while everyone
in possession of arms must report to the police and surrender their
weapons within fifteen days. The French government is in a weak
position; it consists of many who remained in comparatively
comfortable exile, and did not endure the years of occupation,
while the resistance groups, by contrast, bore all the danger of the
underground fight, and took the main part in the final
disorganisation of the Nazi occupation forces. In the circumstances, de Gaulle has to rely once more on persuasion and
propaganda rather than on force. He has withdrawn his original
intention to dissolve the militia, and has insisted simply on the
surrender of weapons. But troops sent to carry out this disarmament are already reported to have withdrawn on seeing that they
would be resisted

All the Leaders Oppose Arms
In this situation, the fundamental position of the government is
being greatly assisted by those political sections who appear as its
most vocal opposition. The guarantee of freedom is the people in
arms. For the government to establish its central authority
therefore, the main problem is the disarming of the people. But
the communists and other leaders of the Resistance movement
have shifted the emphasis on to the question of prestige. They
make much of the fact that the original intention to dissolve the
militia has been 'reduced' to the order for disarming them. The
National Council of Resistance "remains an unquestionably *moral*
force" says Emmanuel D'Astier, one of its leading members.
These men are not opposed to the government, much less to the
principle of government. "We have no intention", says another of
their spokesmen, "of endangering the nation's unity or of
questioning the Government's authority. We want order." Nor do
they like to see the workers armed. The *Daily Worker* reported
(2nd November 1944) that M Saillant, the president of the
National Resistance Council, had stated "that it did not envisage
individual possession of arms. These would be kept at a central
depot, and issued as required." Now it is reported that the Council
have proposed "the creation of Republican Civil Guards to replace
the militias. They would be under the control of the mayor of each

town and of the local liberation committee, and would be armed by the municipality only when they are carrying out a specific task."

Of course the de Gaullists will jump at these proposals which will save faces all round, and at the same time place the militias at a hopeless disadvantage compared with the armed forces of the State. The government will have solved its main problem, and the potentially revolutionary situation will have passed, if they succeed in taking the weapons out of the hands of the individual men and women whose courage and initiative give to the maquis their immense power and influence.

Similar Conditions Elsewhere

This situation is not by any means peculiar to France. In Greece also the disarming of the resistance forces is one of the first pre-occupations of the 'liberators'. So also has it been the case for months in Italy. But perhaps the most striking display of governmental hostility towards those popular forces who have borne the brunt of resistance to the German occupation comes from Belgium.

Ten thousand members of the Belgian underground movement rallied in Brussels on Sunday, November 5th, from all parts of the country. They were then informed by the Burgomaster that they could not use the town hall, and public speeches were forbidden.The demonstrators therefore printed their demand and distributed them in the streets.

These situations are symptomatic of the revolutionary potentialities inherent in the closing period of the war. It is the duty of anarchists to urge the workers everywhere, as Connolly did the Irish workers of the Citizen Army, to "hold on to your arms". While the people have weapons in their hands, Governments are weak. They will use every blandishment, every treacherous promise, to wheedle arms out of the workers; but when they have done so they will ruthlessly crush every remaining bulwark of free initiative.

11th November 1944

CID Raid Freedom Press Offices

At 6pm on Tuesday, December 12th, Inspector Whitehead of Scotland Yard accompanied by some eight officers raided Freedom Press offices. His search warrant was issued under Defence Regulation 88A and the suspected offence was 39A, which refers to disaffection. The three persons working in the office at the time were searched and literally no book was left unturned in the search that took place in the offices. The homes of two comrades were also searched and papers and other articles removed.

We bring the above to the notice of all readers and comrades to make whatever use they choose of the information, but in particular we would like those readers who still persist in thinking that democracy exists to consider the implications of the case. Too often it is imagined that the police of this country are only used for controlling traffic and for helping schoolchildren across the roads. But the police is also there to maintain the *status quo*. Is there so much difference between a group of police raiding newspaper offices in Germany and the same thing happening in this country? There may be a difference in tactics. Inspector Whitehead might try to explain that he is raiding our premises to save us from some dangerous elements, whilst the German police might not feel so paternal. But the underlying principle is the same: THAT WHEN IT SUITS THE CONVENIENCE OF THE RULING CLASS THEY WILL ATTEMPT TO TRAMPLE ON ALL LIBER-TIES. That is not real freedom and the sooner people get this into their head the sooner will they come to despise *all* governments since all governments are maintained in power by force, intrigues, spying systems and all the other lowest forms of human behaviour. Only in a society based on co-operation and mutual trust will such institutions as the police, the armed forces, prisons and concentration camps be abolished once for all.

30th December 1944

Churchill Saving Greece from the Greeks

Fascists Hail Allied Intervention

The general facts about the intervention of British troops in Greece is clear enough: although accounts differ in some respects, and varying interpretations are placed on these accounts, there is no doubt about the feeling which the events in themselves have aroused. All over the world, with the exception of the most shameless reactionaries, there has been an outcry against British Imperialist policy. Not all the whitewashing of the Tories undertaken by Ernest Bevin, and his colleagues among the Labour Party bosses, can sweeten the bitterness, although it has provided a screen behind which cowards can shelter. Churchill has attempted to justify his class's action in Greece by vilifying the EAM and ELAS members, but he cannot obscure the real facts which form the background of the present struggle. Greece was one of the first countries to be occupied by the German armies. The Greeks were among the first in Europe to feel the horrors of the man-made famines which have characterised the war. Nevertheless, the Resistance movement in Greece fought hard and well against the Italian and German occupation. Nearly two years ago, in March 1943, their strength was such that they organised a General Strike which frustrated the Nazis' attempt to conscript Greek labour to the full. They had driven the German authorities out of large tracts of Greece long before the Allied armies landed. These are the people whom Churchill refers to as "bandits from the mountains", "murder gangs", and "ruffians".

But the present intervention was foreshadowed nine months ago. The Greek resistance movement, during the time when it was struggling against the occupation (of the Germans), had expressed itself in definite terms against King George and the Greek reaction. Greek troops had booed him when he reviewed them, and in April 1944 they mutinied in solidarity with the resistance movement inside Greece. This mutiny was suppressed in Cairo with the assistance of British troops. All news of it was kept out of the press for several weeks after it occurred.

The attitude of the Greek troops and of the Resistance movement towards the reactionary circles represented by the King is not unnatural. In 1936, King George had set up the dictatorship of General Metaxas, and begun a systematic repression of all opposition groupings. It was, in effect, a Fascist administration. This is the Government which Churchill refers to as the "Constitutional Government of Greece"; it is the Fascist régime which British bayonets are being used to re-instal. "Stability" and the "defence of order" means dictatorship. In the present struggle, the Greek Government have been supported not only by the British units in Greece but also by the security police which did the Gestapo's work for Metaxas before the war, and collaborated with the Nazis during the German occupation.

Provocation and Bloodshed

The Papandreou government owes its existence to the support of the British Cabinet. So unpopular was it in Greece, that the resistance organisation arranged a demonstration and a general strike against it. The immediate cause of this demonstration was the attempt of the Papandreou Government (doubtless acting under orders from the British Government) to disarm the resistance groups while permitting the reactionary armed organisations to retain their weapons.

According to the *Times* correspondent and many other correspondents in Athens, the demonstration was unarmed and contained many women and children. It is important to stress this early testimony because Churchill has tried to suggest that the demonstrators were armed to the teeth and drove women and children before them as protection. No reports of this type appeared till after the storm of indignation over Greece had arisen, however. The Greek police were evidently well prepared for the demonstration (forbidden, of course, by the democratic Papandreou administration), for under the shadow of non-interfering British tanks, they opened fire on the crowd with Tommy guns. Newspapers the next day showed British soldiers carrying wounded children to places of shelter.

A police reign of terror then ensued with arbitrary arrests of anyone suspected of 'left' sympathies. Barricades were hastily erected and the fight was on. Before long the resistance forces had organised themselves and occupied the greater part of the police stations in Athens. The Nazis had capitulated in the face of a Greek general strike, and the Greek Premier, Papandreou, faced with this formidable demonstration of opposition on the part of the Greeks, resigned in favour of Sophoulis, the senile liberal leader. But where the Nazis had quailed the British cabinet simply dug its heels in — at the expense of Greek and British workers' blood. Churchill refused to accept Papandreou's resignation, and British troops were ordered to intervene on the side of law and order.

Since then the Greek people's resistance has stiffened. It was not to be expected that those who had thrown out the Nazis would tolerate the instalment — by force of British occupation bayonets — of the circles which had ruled under Metaxas' fascist administration. The strength of the resistance may be gauged from the fact that British reinforcements from Italy, and Indian troops, have been rushed to Greece. Class considerations must take first place in Churchill's strategy; it matters little that the lives of the Italian resisters behind the German lines depend on the rapid advance of General Alexander's armies in Northern Italy. The troops which might relieve them have to be rushed to prop up Fascism in Greece.

The use of Indian troops suggests that there is considerable — and natural — reluctance on the part of the British units to play out the dirty role assigned to them by their Tory leaders. In such circumstances as astute government does not hesitate to exploit colour hostility to carry out the worst jobs. The French Government used the same tactics when they sent Senegalese troops to occupy the Ruhr after the last war. French troops would have refused, from solidarity with the German miners and industrial workers of the Ruhr.

Birds of a Feather
Churchill's action in Greece (besides the support of Bevin) has been acclaimed in significant quarters — by Franco in Spain, Salazar in Portugal, and by the Hearst Press in America. Not even the *Times* had given full approval in this country, adopting instead a critical tone. There is no doubt that the British Imperialist policy is one of naked intervention against the very people in Greece who fought against the Nazis.

Such intervention has been supported by appropriate methods. The Greeks have been starving for three years. Even under the German occupation the International Red Cross was able to distribute some supplies. Now however the British have intimated that they cannot distribute supplies because of difficulties in unloading. But reports contradict this exuse in the next breath, for at Salonika, food shipments which had been unloaded were reloaded on to the ships. Another excuse advanced is the brazen one that they cannot be sure that distribution will go to the 'right people'. It is fairly clear that those who are fighting against the re-imposition of native Greek Fascism, are not regarded by British Interventionist authorities as 'right people'.

What is the Resistance?
It is clear that the leadership of the EAM and ELAS resistance comprises differing political trends. Some assistance has been given to it (according to some reports) by the Stalinist Tito. But it seems likely that it is by no means a Stalinist set-up, and that the main body of the arms have come from the British, and disarmed Italian and German troops, rather than from Stalin. The Greek Communists are unlikely therefore to possess the same disproportionate influence which their counterparts in Spain secured through monopoly control of arms distribution.

The leadership of EAM was not apparently opposed to the disarming of the people (implying the strengthening of the Government) in itself, but only to unilateral Left disarmament.

Some leaders are apparently in favour of capitulation, others in favour of fighting to a finish. Whatever the tendency of the leaders, however, there seems no doubt about the solid popular basis of the present resistance to British Intervention. That the resistance is backed by the Greek workers and peasants is also shown by the reports (if true) that the socialisation of land has already started in some parts of Greece. The fury of the Churchillian intervention itself suggests that class issues of some depth are involved, especially since the events in Greece show the same general tendency as the British policy towards the workers in Italy, France and Belgium, and the eulogies which the Prime Minister showers on such men as Franco and Salazar and now King George 'of the Hellenes'.

The forces of popular insurrection, of the social revolution, can hardly stand outside the present conflict in Greece. They will be the inspiration behind the ranks of Greek working-class opposition. For them the terrible struggle against the overwhelmingly strong armament of the British troops and reinforcements is the main consideration of the moment. But they will also have to assess their position towards the politicians in the ranks of EAM, the yes-men of Moscow, and those who aspire to government posts. The Greek rank-and-file resistance will have noted the (reported) situation in Salonika, where EAM is said to be the effective authority, and therefore the British are collaborating with them. Collaborationism with British occupation forces is hardly to be distinguished from collaboration with the German authorities, and this situation may be a sinister straw in the wind.

Such matters, nevertheless, are to some extent speculative. What is certain is the fact of the reactionary and murderous intervention sponsored by Churchill.

30th December 1944

J. H.

Greece

"We shall not hesitate to use the considerable British Army now in Greece, and being reinforced, to see that law and order are maintained."

CHURCHILL

After four years the 'liberation' of Greece has begun. Not much time for celebrations is allowed the Greeks, before the iron heel of the new conquerors stamps down resistance as the former conquerors had done before them.

On Sunday 3rd December the Greek Government police fired on thousands of unarmed demonstrators, wounding and killing. British tanks patrolled the streets to keep order, and RAF Spitfires and bombers flew over Athens in 'demonstration flights'. It is only too evident what they were demonstrating.

General Scobie, GOC in Greece, proclaimed martial law in Athens and the Piraeus. He declared:

"I reiterate that with the vast majority of Greeks I stand firmly behind the Constitutional Government and shall aid them to the limit of my resources and until the Greek State can be established with lawful armed force behind it and free elections can be held."

He backs the monarchist semi-fascist government of George of the Hellenes and Papandreou, and intends to restore it by 'lawful armed force'. 'Unlawful armed force' is always, of course, what the other side uses. We must remember that the pre-Hitler Greek State was a dictatorship since the 'Constitutional Government' ruled autocratically and did not permit even the pretence of 'free elections'. Hence the fine phrase of standing 'firmly behind the Constitutional Government' simply means to force a dictatorship upon the Greeks who have for so long fought against the Nazi dictatorship.

9th December 1944

Stop Intervention in Greece!

The revolutionary upsurge of the workers on the continent is being crushed between the democratic bayonets of the United Nations and the fascist bayonets of the Axis powers.

The events of 1917-21, the years of the interventionist wars in Russia and the blockade of revolutionary Germany are being re-enacted. As then Winston Churchill, erstwhile admirer of Hitler and Mussolini and friend of Franco, is openly organising the slaughter of the working-class. He is backed by the Labour leaders who, like Bevin, boast that the decision to massacre the workers of Greece was taken with the knowledge and approval of His Majesty's Labour ministers.

The British ruling-class are demonstrating that their aim is to subject the workers of Europe to reaction. The only difference from September 1939 is to be that governments of Europe will now dance to the tune called by the capitalist Allies.

The policy of Stalin in Poland and Churchill in Greece is identical. Stalin withheld aid from Warsaw during the insurrection so that the voice of the independent working-class movement in Warsaw could be silenced by the guns of the Nazis. The British authorities in Greece are using the army — allegedly fighting for freedom and democracy — to crush the working-class forces.

As soon as the threat of social revolution develops, the governments of the so-called 'freedom-loving' nations are determined to prevent revolutionary action from spreading. As in 1917 their fear is that the workers will turn their arms against their real enemies and unite across the artificially created frontiers which serve only the interests of the exploiting class.

Let the issue be quite clear. It is our responsibility to see that the workers in Europe, at the moment in particular in Greece, are not crushed by the pro-fascist policy of the British ruling-class. It is our job to stop British arms being used to bolster up the rule of the Pierlots and Papandreous — the mouthpieces of international capitalist reaction.

The only weapon which the ruling class understand is direct action. Clydeside workers have staged demonstrations to protest against our fellow-workers in uniform being used to massacre the people of Greece. Churchill states that the government's policy is to be continued.

Reaction is on the march. The only way in which it can be stopped is by our concerted action in the factories, shipyards, mines and docks.

Lobbying MP's and sending telegrams of protest to Churchill is so much futility. The hypocritical Communist Party, who advocate this 'militant' method of 'struggle' know this only too well. If any practical steps are to be taken in support of the revolutionary workers in Greece and elsewhere, we must be prepared not to talk but to act.

Time is getting short. Already the old gang are back in power in France and Belgium, supported, when necessary, by the armed force of the Allies, who are 'liberating' only the vested interests of European capitalism.

In 1917 we betrayed the Russian workers by our apathy. Similarly in 1918-19 with the German revolution. In Spain one of the main factors in the defeat of the libertarian revolution of the anarchist-inspired workers was the almost complete lack of support displayed by the workers throughout the world. *And now Greece!*

Workers! Organise support for your Greek comrades! Take action on the job! Force the Churchill-Bevin gang to stop intervention!

30th December 1944

WHAT'S THE DIFFERENCE?

An RAF escort drew his revolver and shot an airman who tried to escape near Aldershot railway station this afternoon while he was being taken to detention barracks.

The man, who was taken to hospital with serious injuries, was one of several prisoners who had arrived under escort at the railway station.

The party had walked about 500 yards when he broke away and dashed across the road. *The Star*, 29th September 1944

When the Germans shot British officers trying to escape from a prisoners' camp there was an uproar about it. When a British airman is shot by an RAF escort it is merely a news item.

Churchill Confirms Reactionary Policy

The House of Commons was privileged to hear the British fuehrer again on January 18th. Mr Churchill spoke for nearly two hours. When all the fine phrases and tricks of oratory are whittled away all that is left is a restatement in perhaps more emphatic terms of the age-old British policy of supporting reaction wherever it shows itself, and at all costs opposing movements which show any likelihood of upsetting the capitalist order of society. The old campaign of atrocity stories, half truths and insinuations is being directed against the Greek ELAS in order to discredit it, while tanks and aeroplanes carry out the policy originated by the Germans and Italians in Spain and continued by the British in Italy in 1943.

ELAS is represented as being much more interested in fighting the British than it was in fighting the Germans, despite the fact that one of their enemies, and one of Britain's allies is the Security Police formed by the Germans to keep the Greeks down. ELAS is condemned for asking that the Right wing armed forces and the Security Police should be disarmed at the same time as themselves. It is not the purpose of this article to discover whether ELAS is a bunch of crooks or not, perhaps they are, but even if they are not it is obvious that Churchill will spare no efforts to paint them as black as he painted the Russian revolutionaries at the end of the last war; and remember that at that time Lenin and Trotsky were also accused of accepting German gold.

The slimy trail of British power politics is extended all over Europe. Greece, Italy, France, Belgium, in all these countries the most reactionary forces have been those favoured to take over the administration, because they are the ones who will be the most ruthless and cunning in putting down any move towards freedom on the part of the workers. But it would be quite unfair to single out Britain as the only country guilty of this crime. It may be that she is being used as a convenient stooge by American capital as well; it is far better to get someone else to do the dirty work so long as it is done. However, the article reproduced from *Politics* elsewhere in this issue demonstrates clearly the attitude of America towards 'liberated' Europe. In effect it means that the two American officers concluded a pact with the German General *against the French people*. As *Politics* points out, there is nothing unusual about this sort of thing, it has happened in the past and will continue to happen so long as power politics are the order of the day.

Russia Supports Reaction

The record of the great ally demonstrates exactly the same principle, *viz*, deal with who ever will best be able to control the country in your own interests. Hungary, Rumania, Bulgaria and Poland demonstrate how Stalin will use anyone who will keep the 'peace' for him. In Hungary the Russians are promoting a new government which it is intended will turn that country into a 'co-belligerent'. The leaders of this government are Conservative-Nationalists, the party of the ex-Regent Admiral Horthy, and they are supported by so-called democratic groups. Significantly the Premier in this government is a General named Bela Miklos. No doubt the Russians realise that a militarist is probably better able to control the population than any of the Left wing parties.

The new Bulgarian government likewise is a coalition, this time of the Military League, Agrarians, Socialists and Communists. The government is known as the Patriotic Front and the key positions are held by members of the Right Wing Military League. This ensures that the Bulgarian military forces will be co-operating with the Red Army.

The same kind of government is favoured by Russia for Rumania, here again the leader is a General and the government is composed of Right wing and Left wing elements.

Although superficially Stalin's stooge government for Poland looks different, yet the Lublin Committee will play the same part as the militarists are doing for Stalin in the Balkans. Russia wants to control and direct the policy of those countries which are close to herself, Stalin trusts the Lublin boys and not the 'legal' Polish government in London. That's all there is at issue.

The Future of Germany

Rumours are about concerning the kind of government which Russia will set up in Austria when that country is occupied, and that it will consist of Conservative-Catholics, Social-Democrats and Communists. Already there is the Free German Committee in existence in Moscow, with two ex-Nazi generals as members — von Paulus and Seydlitz. There is to be no possibility of a German workers' revolution after this war if Stalin and Churchill have their way. The grip of reaction on Europe is not at any cost to be relaxed, the workers are to pass from the yoke of the Nazi or

German-quisling dictatorship to the yoke of a military dictatorship, Patriotic Front, or whatever is favoured by the allies. But even though the future of Europe may look black for the workers, yet the combined efforts of all the Allied powers will not be able to suppress the movement towards freedom that the workers are already beginning to make.

War Criminals

The British Foreign Office has suggested to the War Crimes Commission that Hitler should not be treated as a war criminal, and the *Daily Express* has pointed out that Hitler "has technically committed few crimes known to the vague code of international law, and on a purely *legal* basis might even be acquitted".

That does not surprise us at all, we know quite well that the biggest crooks never see the inside of a jail because all their crimes are sanctioned by the law. But the writer of the *Express* article suggests that perhaps Hitler could be tried by the Russian legal system, since says the article: "The Russian legal system is a remarkable one. It is universal. That is to say, according to Soviet jurists, theoretically it applies to every individual in every land."

One of the biggest reasons for the British having nothing to do with the trial of Hitler is the very obvious support and praise which he has been given in the past by our present leaders. We could start off by quoting Churchill's hope that if ever Britain was down and out she would find a man like Hitler "to lead her back to her rightful place among the nations". We could quote statements by all sorts of other politicians on the greatness of Germany and Italy under Fascism, and we could show how British financiers helped Hitler to gain power. But all these things are being continually re-enacted by the allied policy in Europe today. They might still condemn the Hitler gang but they would find a German Badoglio to take his place. One thing is certain, we know that wars are not caused by Hitlers or Churchills, but by the capitalist system of society. And so long as capitalism remains it will be personified by the so-called 'great' men. The replacement of capitalism by workers control is the only way in which war and with it war criminals can be abolished.

27th January 1945

The Stilwell Episode

The recall of General Stilwell from the Burmese theatre of war has unloosed a flood of press 'revelations' about Chiang Kai-shek and the Kuomintang government. The *New York Times*, for example described the Chinese Government as "a moribund anti-democratic régime, more concerned with maintaining its political supremacy than in driving the Japanese from China". The *Daily Mail* (2nd November 1944) declares: "The present Chinese Government, according to all observers, is becoming increasingly unpopular and distrusted. It maintains three secret police services, and concentration camps for political prisoners. It stifles free speech and resists democratic forces. Most of its armies are poorly fed and badly treated."

Hitherto, China has been represented as the most heroic, the most progressive and democratic of Allies in the fight for freedom. Why then do the press make these 'revelations' now? The capitalist papers affect to be very shocked at the 'news' that China is still trading with Japan. Yet almost a year ago, *War Commentary* drew attention to the fact that imports to occupied areas from free China during the last six months of 1943, *according to a Governmental spokesman*, were to the value of £1,250,000 sterling on Government account, and £25,000,000 through commercial channels. For anarchists, the military dictatorship of Chiang Kai-shek has never seemed like a democratic free republic. We have known for years that massacres of Chinese workers and peasants brought Chiang to power.

Needless to say, these facts are well enough known to the capitalist press also. It is too transparent for them to claim that the facts about China have been concealed because of the 'iron censorship', for there is nothing to prevent returned correspondents from telling the facts, provided, of course, their papers will print them! The indignation of the leader-writers is so much hypocrisy.

11th November 1944

Allies Fight for Old Order in Europe

Since the German armies lost the initiative in the war and were placed on the defensive, the events in Europe have been increasingly disillusioning to those who saw the conflict as one between progressive and reactionary forces. Ever since they gained the initiative the Allied High Command have had repeated opportunities of acting in a way which might feed the hopes of those who support the war on anti-Fascist grounds. Yet on every occasion, so far from acting on these opportunities, they have shown themselves to be the mainstay of reaction.

Such behaviour comes as no surprise to us. Before the war, and from its start, we have frequently reiterated what should be a self-evident truth: that Governments represent ruling class interests only, and can therefore only behave in a reactionary direction. Ruling classes everywhere have a record of friendliness with, or appeasement of, Fascist administrations. *War Commentary* saw from the outset that the leopards do not change their spots, and has proclaimed the fact in and out of season since.

The recent events in Europe strikingly bear out the anarchist view of the war. It was not we who acclaimed Churchill as a progressive, determined anti-Fascist. Rather sourly (as our critics thought) we harped on his past record of friendliness with Mussolini, admiration for Hitler, and hatred for revolutionary workers, whether in Russia in 1918 to 1921, or in this country in 1926. And Churchill merely reflected the attitude of the ruling class of the British Empire. Their attitude in Manchukuo in 1931, in Abyssinia in 1935, in Spain in 1936, remained unchanged in Italy in 1943, and in France, Belgium, and Greece at the present moment. Elsewhere in this issue the events in Europe are reported. It is important that the significance of their general trend be fully appreciated.

In Italy, in France, in Greece, and in Belgium, the path of the Allied Armies has been made smooth by the spontaneous activity of resistance movements. These groups have shown the truth of the anarchist contention that the way to freedom lies through insurrectionary movements against the ruling power. The truth of this is certainly recognised by the Allied leaders. Now that the

Nazi administrations have been overthrown mainly by these insurrectionary movements, the Allies are anxious to secure to themselves or their puppets, de Gaulle, Pierlot, Papandreou and the rest, the effective reins of power. Their first move therefore has been to try and deprive the resistance movements of their arms lest they should themselves be overthrown. Moreover, since the economic stability (in a class sense) of 'liberated' territories depends on the owners of industry, they have also supported them and protected their interests and property. And they have done this regardless of whether the employers have collaborated with the German forces of occupation. Of course, most of them have collaborated; the Nazis needed them in order to keep the workers in subjection; and they needed the Nazi government, just as they now need the Allied governments, in order to maintain their positions of power and privilege.

The Italians do not want Bonomi, and did not want Badoglio or Umberto. The French Maquis bitterly resented de Gaulle's disarmament decree. The Greeks have many times expressed their views about the Greek puppet government. The riots and demonstrations in Brussels and elsewhere in Belgium leave no doubt as to the attitude of the Belgian workers towards Pierlot. Yet all these unwanted rulers owe their continued existence in power to the support given to them by Allied arms. None the less, the phenomenon is not new. The German people did not want Hitler, yet his régime was assisted and maintained by financiers and politicians who are now vociferously (though not very convincingly) in the 'Anti-fascist' camp. Franco was unequivocally rejected by the Spanish people; yet Franco is only able to hang on in Spain because he is supported by Churchill and the interests Churchill represents.

The Allied Government support reaction on the Continent, just as they have always supported it. Their actions give the lie to the high sounding slogans of the early years of the war — the war for freedom, the people's war, and the rest. *War Commentary* came into existence to point out the course which the war was bound to take. The present position is not fortuitous; it was inevitable, for Government is an instrument of reaction, and cannot act otherwise than in a reactionary manner.

But *War Commentary* in its first number, more than five years ago, also pointed the way whereby the war could be ended, and Fascism and reaction wiped away for ever. Anarchists held then, and hold now, that the anti-Fascist struggle must be a revolutionary struggle. The overthrow of existing property relations, and the destruction of the monopoly of power in the hands of the State will bring the war rapidly to an end. Beginning in one country, the social revolution will quickly spread all over Europe, perhaps all over the world.

At the present moment in Europe the Social Revolution is a possibility. The Resistance movements are not however animated by any clear intentions as regards property relations. Moreover, the most vocal sections in them are devoted to the reaction. Communists and other political groupings within the movement of the workers constantly urge collaboration with the government even when they appear to be in opposition. They have supported the principle of disarming the militias, limiting their opposition to technicalities.

Despite this the situation is a critical one. Because of the part they have played in the underground resistance large sections of the workers possess arms. And the disarming which has gone on with the aid of the Allied soldiers has been far from complete even according to reformist sources. An armed population is difficult for a government to coerce. And with arms in their hands workers are less respectful of the 'rights' of property. Moreover, the food situation is one which makes the populations very impatient of the private control of the economy. On the other hand, governments have learned to use food supplies as a means of coercion. (German civilians are not forced to work for the Allied Occupation Forces; but they are not given ration cards if they don't). The important fact about the situation is that, faced with an armed population the governments are weak, even though they are backed by the Allied Armies.

In such circumstances, if the workers took the initiative; if they disregarded the politicians and took over the factories, mines, transport and farms; they would have put their hand to the central problem of food supply and economy. It is true that they would instantly provoke open opposition from the Allied Governments; they would have to be prepared for intervention. But British and American soldiers are, like them, workers. They hate Fascism, and are increasingly disgusted by the rôle their reactionary rulers ask them to play. Direct revolutionary action will win their sympathy far more effectively than timid half measures.

Delay always favours the ruling class; every day they are perfecting their counter-revolutionary preparations, strengthening their feeble puppets. The working class should occupy the means of production and thereby secure to themselves the means of life while they yet have arms in their possession. Soon it may be too late. The ruling classes in Europe are scared, and will therefore be ruthless. If they succeed, with Allied help, in re-establishing their power, they will not hesitate to use starvation and the most brutal instruments of oppression to secure themselves once more. The signs are clear enough. Decisive action on the economic field provides the only hope for the future of millions of working class men, women and children throughout Europe — perhaps, throughout the world.

9th December 1944

1944: A Year of Courage and of Betrayals

Fascists replace Fascists in 'Liberated' Europe

Wars seldom end in a way which is expected by the powers which initiate them. One has only to glance back at the great wars of the last century to notice how popular feeling intervenes towards the close and introduces a new factor into the interplay of ruling class interests which had governed the main outlines of the earlier stages. The Napoleonic wars drew to their close with the determined attempts of the machine-breaking Luddites to stem the increasing unemployment and fall in wages. They were followed by many years of active and bitter struggle on the part of the English workers. The Franco-Prussian war of 1870 ended in the class war — with Thiers and the French ruling class joining hands with Bismarck and the Prussian armies to stamp out the Paris Commune of 1871. The Russo-Japanese war of 1904 brought on the first Russian Revolution of 1905, and the last war (1914-18) saw the imperialist rivalries of the Allies and the Central powers seriously modified by a whole series of working class uprisings. In 1916 the Irish Rebellion; in 1917, the February and October Revolutions in Russia, and in 1918, the German and Hungarian Revolutions, and serious unrest in France and Britain.

The present war has dragged on for five and a half years without such dramatic intervention, and a pessimist might conclude that the ruling classes of to-day, fortified by the counter-revolutionary technique of the past twenty-five years, are able to do whatever they like with a docile working class. 1944, however, gave certain indications that made such defeatism in the camp of those who struggle for freedom and justice seem unjustified. It will perhaps be as well to consider the last twelve months from this standpoint, for the pace of history is now so rapid that events of the greatest importance to the workers are easily forgotten.

Mutiny in the Greek Navy

The present struggles in Greece give added significance to the mutiny in the Greek Forces at Cairo last spring. Already then the emigré Greek Government sponsored by the British Cabinet was looked upon with so much suspicion that the Greek armed forces outside Greece mutinied as a protest against them, acting in solidarity with the indignation of the partisans on the mainland of Greece. The British Government foreshadowed its contempt for the voice of the Greeks who were resisting the German occupation by employing the British Navy to crush their fellows in the Greek Navy. This event showed on the one hand the feelings of justice and the ideal of freedom which animated the Greek people both in and outside Greece; and on the other, the hostility of the British Government of Churchill and Bevin for any manifestation of popular feeling which does not chime in with the imperialist aims of the Allies. (Did not Bevin justify British intervention on the grounds that the Government could not permit the Greek events to throw the British Empire in jeopardy?)

Already therefore the suppression of the Greek mutiny and its implied disregard of the opinion of the Greek working class resistance movement shows the class war between the rulers and the ruled breaking through the thin ideological veil of the 'war for freedom'. As the year developed the rift between class forces came more and more to the front to culminate in the naked interventionist war at present raging against the Greek resistance movement.

India: Famine Smothers Unrest

In the background must not be forgotten the smouldering continent of India. The unrest felt by the Indians and their indignation at the savage irony of their being conscripted into the 'war for freedom' waged by their imperialist gaolers has been checked in the most gruesome way. The horrors of the still continuing Indian famine paralyses for the moment the struggle for Indian freedom. But it also underlines the rift between the population of India and their British rulers, and tears to shreds the myth of the 'benefits' which British rule brings to the stricken country. 1944 brought no dramatic events in India, perhaps, but India remains the cornerstone of the British Empire, a cornerstone composed of four hundred millions whose hatred of Imperialism has been seared into their starved bodies by the past two years.

The Deadly Farce in Italy

Italy, too, provides a deadly indictment of the war aims of the Allies. While the Italian working class in the North conducted the most militant struggle against the occupying German armies — they forced the Nazis to negotiate with a strike committee for the first time since their access to power twelve years ago — their fellows in the South were enduring the 'liberation' brought by British and American bayonets. Famine, with its attendants, epidemic disease and massive prostitution, have followed the footsteps of the liberators. And, despite the opposition of the entire Italian people, the Allies have everywhere kept in office the Fascist Prefects who thereby dominate every aspect of local affairs.

Success of the Maquis

The early summer saw working class forces everywhere gathering to oust the German occupation forces. In Denmark and Norway tremendous strikes taxed to the utmost the Nazi and Quisling ruling powers. But the most dramatic developments came in France where the Maquis everywhere deposed the German and Vichy authorities, and cleared the road before the invasion forces of D-day in June. The continuity of working class struggle was provided by the thousands of Spanish militants in the South of France who wholeheartedly joined the liberating movement of the Maquis. What a contrast to the early rapprochement with General Franco established by the Government of General de Gaulle — established moreover at a time when reports were rife of unrest, even insurrection, in Spain itself! The spirit of the workers who freely and spontaneously entered the Maquis, and without regard for self, waged the bitter and, in supply of arms, unequal fight against the armies of Hitler and Vichy — their spirit typifies the free initiative of insurrectionary movements against tyranny. It is the generous spirit of the revolution.

Warsaw: the Betrayal

Before calling to mind the miserable manoeuvrings of the emigré politicians to disarm these popular militias — it is necessary to turn

to one of the most brutal betrayals of human heroism in history —
the second martyrdom of Warsaw. The people of Poland, groaning
under the tyranny of the Nazis, listened to the propaganda over
the Soviet radio urging them to revolt. With the rapid advance of
the Red Armies across eastern Poland, they thought the time had
come, never dreaming that the promised aid would be deliberately
withheld from them. Accordingly the people of Warsaw raised the
standard of revolt as the Russians approached the eastern suburbs.
They overpowered the German garrison and controlled the city,
and their action was everywhere acclaimed. Everywhere that is,
except in Moscow. The radio which but a few days back had been
urging a rising, now condemned their action as 'criminal'. The Red
Army's rapid and virtually unchecked advance was diverted to the
south of Warsaw, and Stalinist apologists everywhere began
explaining the check in terms of military necessity, strategy and
what not. The inhabitants of Warsaw held out for sixty-three days.
Scant supplies were dropped by the British and American Air
Forces — flying from Britain, for the Soviet Government had
refused to accord them landing facilities for this purpose. Finally
they were overwhelmed and virtually exterminated by the German
armies. Never was the contrast between working class heroism and
the treachery and callousness of the ruling class exhibited more
nakedly.

The disillusionment of the people of Warsaw when they realised
their betrayal by the Kremlin can be imagined. But what an
inspiration to the workers everywhere is their determined
continuance of the fight against overwhelming odds for no less
than sixty-three days. Betrayed, their refusal to capitulate even
though the issue was hopeless, is simply heroic. There is no ground
for pessimism in the workers' struggle here.

Disarming the Partisans
The closing months of the year saw the attempts made by the
puppet governments set up by the Allies in Belgium, France and
Greece to disarm the men and women who had successfully fought
against the German Occupation. By their arms these partisans had
freed themselves; unless they were disarmed their subjection to
new rulers would be impossible. That is the ruling class logic of the
disarmament and disbandment decrees. And the working class
logic was resistance. Needless to say, the political parties, from the
right to the Socialist and Communist parties, saw no objection in
principle to the disarming (law and order must be preserved), but

only tried to sidetrack the matter with face-saving outcries for purges. When the collaborationists were safely gaoled they would gladly offer up their arms. Politicians could not proclaim the people in arms as the safeguard against the State, for they themselves sought positions in the State machinery. Once more the cleavage between the ruling class (and their hangers on, the politicians of all shades) and the resisting workers was underlined. In Greece open conflict developed. In Belgium, the partisans had hardly been disarmed, when the Germans invaded the country again, this time to find a population disarmed by their own emigré rulers.

Throughout 1944 therefore we see workers in active revolt against their rulers, whether Axis or Allied. So far the ruling class has managed to maintain its power, not without the valuable aid of that shady Fifth Column, the working class political leaders. But the significant fact remains that the working class have begun to make themselves felt as a factor in the shaping of events.

A dangerous trend

It remains to point out a dangerous trend. The beginning of the end of Nazism would be decisively initiated by a revolt of the German people against their rulers. Such a revolt would be received with sympathy and acclamation by workers the world over. But such a revolt would be disaster and a menace to the ruling class; it would stimulate the fires of revolt everywhere; and it would end the war — while the war is necessary as a means of keeping the anti-fascist workers in the Allied countries in subjection. The Allies therefore are preparing in advance for such a revolt on the part of the German people. On every possible occasion they claim that the whole German people must bear the guilt of the Nazi party (and they are faithfully echoed by the bosses of the TUC). They fill the press with atrocity stories. They stop at nothing to alienate the sympathy of the British workers from their fellow workers in Germany who for twelve long years have been oppressed by the Totalitarian Nazi State. But the lessons are clear. Ruling class tyranny is international. Freedom from that tyranny can only be achieved by international working class solidarity. 1944 has shown the issue to lie between working class resistance and rulers whether German or Quisling or Allied. The present war will not be the last war unless the tyranny of rulers and the State is obliterated for ever in the free solidarity of workers of all lands.

13th January 1945

Big Three — Workers Must Pay

It is as good as certain that the most important topics discussed by Churchill, Roosevelt and Stalin at the Crimea Conference did not figure in the declaration. The Conference took place behind locked doors, and one may fairly guess that what was said by the world's most powerful politicians was not the sort of thing they would like to see broadcast. These conferences are really to discuss programmes of action. And the actions embarked upon by the Allied powers — in Italy, in Greece, in Poland, for examples — actions which were clearly thought out beforehand, do not cut very democratic patterns. Plan the next steps in the great struggle of the ruling groups against the people; and then issue some fairly acceptable sort of declaration to draw wool over their eyes. That is roughly the formula adopted at these gatherings of the powerful.

Yet it is probably possible to draw some valid conclusions from the Crimea Declaration. For example, the laying down of the Curzon line as the Russian border of Poland indicates that Stalin had to accept the propositions of Roosevelt and Churchill, despite the much greater territorial control now exercised over Poland by the Red Army. Furthermore the tentative preparations for a new League of Nations — the 'International Organisation' — shows that the same old methods are again to be tried out. But with this difference; that the new 'International Organisation' will be a joint body organised by ruling groups for the purpose of destroying jointly any revolutionary attempts by the international working class. It will be the same 'Thieves Kitchen' as the old League, but with added counter-revolutionary experience.

German Workers Must Pay

Much the most interesting part of the declaration relates to the treatment of defeated Germany, however. And we must here point out that the interests of the workers are international. What happens to the German workers will inevitably affect their fellow workers in other — Allied — lands. The Crimea Declaration makes no attempt to mince matters. "It is not our purpose", it states, "to destroy the people of Germany . . ." But it then goes on to outline measures which, in the class rule framework envisaged (and bitterly defended) by all three leaders, will in fact mean the virtual destruction of the German workers' standards of life, low though these have already been under Nazism.

How is this to be done? Let us disregard all the fancy talk about "wiping out the Nazi party, Nazi laws, organisations and institutions". We heard all that sort of thing after Mussolini fell, but the Allies insist on keeping Fascist Party officials in key administrative posts in Italy. The Allied Military authorities have adopted much the same methods of maintaining order in occupied Germany as the Germans did in France and elsewhere. We may be quite sure that the main political problem for the Allies will be how to keep the German people down, and they will have no scruples at all about using the ready made machinery of oppression perfected by the Nazis. Did they scruple, in Greece, to use the Security police organised by the Nazis, when it came to quelling unarmed demonstrators on December 3rd? No, we may treat all the talk about destroying the Nazi party as so much . . . talk. The leaders may be made to walk the plank, but the Nazi governmental machinery will be kept intact.

Let us turn instead to the economic proposals of the Big Three. First "German industry that could be used for military production" is to be eliminated or controlled. If eliminated, the unemployment amongst German wage earners will be astronomical, and they will starve. If controlled, they will be controlled at such low rates as will also starve them. But it will also starve their fellow workers in heavy industry elsewhere in the world by providing low cost competition. Heavy industry is organised in world wide cartels; production will be carried on first in these areas where maximal profits can be extracted, that is to say, those areas where *labour is cheapest*. Workers the world over must realise that wherever poor wages are paid, they help to lower wages everywhere.

This same lesson is to be learned in regard to the other great economic pronouncement of the Conference, that regarding reparations, "Germany will be obliged to make compensation for the damage *in kind* to the greatest extent possible". To-day, production is maintained and full employment kept up, only because of the war. Already with the change over to peacetime production in some industries, workers have been paid off. Everywhere workers are thinking uncomfortably about post-war unemployment. But the German workers are to make reparations in kind. They are going to be kept producing — at very low wages, of course — in order to repair the damage of war. That means, in effect, that they will be compelled to do work which will throw out of work their fellows in Allied countries. That is what reparations mean.

After the last war, the confiscation of German shipping by the victorious Allies, completely disorganised the shipbuilding industry in this country. The same principle will be applied again, and with the same results. If the British workers permit their own ruling class masters to trample on the German working class, they will simply be cutting their own throats. In international affairs, no less than inside a single country, "an injury to one is the concern of all", for the class interests of the workers are the same all over the world.

The Appeal to Justice
In the foregoing section, we appeal to workers to use their heads and consider their own interests before letting the German workers be trodden down. But, in our opinion as anarchists, there is far more strength in the appeal to justice and international comradeship. For twelve weary years the German workers have suffered under Hitler. Protests, demonstrations, revolts have been crushed by Panzer Divisions, by Gestapo tortures, by concentration camps. When their enemies the Nazi ruling clique were weak, they were strengthened by loans from the City of London or from Wall Street; or by the alliance with Stalin. The German workers have looked for help in vain not only from the governments of the democracies, and from that of the USSR; they have also received no flicker of practical support *at any time* from the official trade union movements in those countries. Socialists used at one time to distinguish between workers and their reactionary governments. But even this lip service to socialism has been denied to the German workers by the TUC in this country. Led by the delegation of Soviet trade unionists, they passed the Vansittartist resolutions about the German people bearing responsibility for their government's crimes. The plain truth is that the German people have had to fight against one of the most ruthless and efficient tyrannies of all time, and they have had Vansittartist insults added by smug allied reformists to the injuries and tortures and murders meted out to their militants in concentration camps.

Starvation
This is what the Allies are planning for the German workers and their wives and children — many of them born since 1933, even since the outbreak of war. Here is Lieut.-Col. Joseph M. Canby, Civil Affairs Officer of General Patch's Seventh Army:

"In Italy we had a sympathetic interest in the local inhabitants, but we have no such interest in the German nation. If their rations get too low, it will be just too bad. No rations will be brought into Germany until their food reserves are so low that the starving population becomes a menace. We will make no effort to restore industry, and we do not care if the banks are open or shut — we are not going to help them.

The 3,000,000 displaced personnel of the Allied nations who are now in Germany will be requested to be supervised and controlled by Allied personnel, but will be fed and clothed from Germany. 'The policy will be', said Colonel Canby, 'to force Germans to denude themselves of what they need to feed themselves for the sake of displaced people'."

(*Evening News*, 17th February 1945)

It is difficult to imagine anything more savage. Our 'sympathetic interest' in the people of Italy has allowed us to let starvation, disease and prostitution be the order of the day in that tortured (though liberated) country. What then is in store for the Germans? They could hardly be degraded further than our leaders have degraded the Italian people.

In this policy of starvation, moreover, the children will suffer most. In the hospitals in Vienna at the end of the last war, out of every hundred children born, ninety died of starvation. So those who do not even remember peacetime will be the first victims of the Big Three . . .

If the British workers permit this monstrous ruling class vindictiveness to be visited on their fellow workers of Germany and their families, they will not only be cutting their own throats; they will be passively assisting at the most colossal injustice of a war already heavy with brutality and cruelty and treachery.

Hopeful Signs

But there are signs of hope. Signs which indicate that mutual solidarity is not lost among workers, signs that the ruling class are yet afraid of the spectre of fraternisation. From Germany come reports that the Nazi Government has issued strict prohibitions against German workers making contact with foreign workers in Germany. Nazi officials have been perturbed about the sympathy between German and foreign workers. At the very same moment Eisenhower's edict against British and American soldiers fraternising with German civilians is requiring increasingly severe punishment for its effective enforcement. Soldiers are prohibited from asking the way, or even from playing wth German children! Where there is contact there is human sympathy and kindliness.

The Big Three have said their vindictive piece. We anarchists declare once again; we are uncompromisingly for the international solidarity of the working class across all frontiers. We denounce the attempt to crush the German workers. We supported them against Hitler; we support them equally against our own ruling class!

24th February 1945

Four London Anarchists Arrested

Our comrades Marie Louise Berneri, John Hewetson and V. Richards, were arrested at their homes at 7.30 am on Thursday, 22nd February and taken to West Hampstead Police Station where they were charged with a number of offences under Defence Regulation 39a. They were later taken to Marylebone Police Court where they were joined by comrade Philip Sansom (who, as reported in this issue, is at present serving a two month sentence at Brixton). He was charged under the same Defence Regulation.

All four comrades appeared before the magistrate Mr Ivan Snell. The charges were read out and we reprint them from the *Evening News* report of the same day:

"Charges against all of them alleged that between November 1943, and December 1944, at Belsize-road, Hampstead and elsewhere, they were concerned together with other persons unknown in endeavouring to seduce from their duties persons in the Forces and to cause among such persons disaffection likely to lead to breaches of their duty.

Circular Letter
Vernon and Marie Richards were also charged that on 12th December 1944, at Belsize-road, with intent to contravene the Defence Regulations they had in their possession or under their control a circular letter dated 25th October 1944, which was of such a nature that the dissemination of copies among persons in His Majesty's Services would constitute such a contravention.

Hewetson was similarly charged with having in his possession or under his control documents dated 2nd October 1944, at Willow-road, on 12th December.

Sansom was charged with reference to a similar circular at his studios, dated 30th December.

Richards and Hewetson were also charged with endeavouring to cause disaffection among persons in the Services on about 11th November 1944.

No Reply

Detective-Inspector Whitehead, of Scotland Yard, told the magistrate, Mr Ivan Snell, that when, at 7.30am today, he told Vernon Richards and Mrs Richards that he was going to arrest them they made no reply.

At 8am he saw Dr Hewetson at Willow-road, Hampstead. He made no reply when told he would be arrested.

Sansom was charged at Marylebone, and replied: 'I have nothing to say'.

In reply to Mr Gerald F. Rutledge, defending, Inspector Whitehead said that Hewetson was the casualty officer at Paddington Hospital.

Inspector Whitehead asked that the case should be remanded until March 9th and bail of £100 with sureties of £100 was granted to the three first named comrades. Comrade Sansom was taken back to Brixton to complete his two months' sentence.

It has been decided to form immediately a Defence Committee and comrades will be shortly notified of its composition, and address. Helpers will be required and we are confident of the response from our comrades and sympathisers everywhere.

24th February 1945

[The four anarchists were committed for trial at the Old Bailey where, after a four-day trial which was given wide press coverage worldwide and intro-duced many new readers and sympathisers, the three men were given nine months prison sentences — Editor]

Fraternisation means 'Workers of the World Unite'

It is impossible to justify modern war with its indiscriminate destruction of combatants and non-combatants, of women as well as men, of the old as well as the young. But fighting itself can be justified — for to be inert in the face of injustice and cruelty and oppression is simply base. One must struggle against it, just as the unarmed Spanish people did against Franco's attempted coup d'état in July 1936, just as the anti-Nazis and anti-Fascists of the underground movements of revolt have done for years. Workers everywhere realise the injustice of such a struggle and instinctively support it — it is also *their* struggle — it is only rulers who are indifferent to it, and concern themselves solely with preserving their own power.

Yet our rulers recognised the hatred of workers in this country for Nazism, and have used this feeling for their own ends in the present war — 'the fight against Nazi oppression'. Anarchists do not forget, however, that the first victims of Nazi oppression were the German workers. If the war had any meaning for the working class, it must secure the liberation of the German workers who have suffered under Hitler's rule for twelve years.

Ideology wearing thin

But the excuses of the former friends of Nazism are wearing thin indeed. It becomes clearer and clearer that the war of nation against nation covers the war of rulers against the ruled. The latter are only just beginning to realise this, and they may yet be duped. The rulers, on the other hand, have realised it all along, and have sought many ways to cover it. But their deeds betray their aims. Faced with concrete situations — for instance in Italy and Greece — our rulers have not hesitated to side with reaction, have not scrupled to shoot down workers and protect native fascists.

Now the same thing is happening in Germany. Stanley Baron describes in the *News Chronicle* of 21st March 1945, how well-to-do Germans have escaped the privation which war has inflicted on the German workers. He describes how they have been able to seek relative safety in such places as Bad Godesburg.

"To come into Bad Godesburg after spending hours among the bomb-shattered people of Cologne, or even from the plain where German men and boys in droves are shovelling stones and earth, working side by side with American soldiers to widen the roads, *is to realise profoundly the falsity of the myth that for all social classes in Germany the war has been total.*"

These privileged social classes in Germany, like their counterparts among the Allied countries, are chiefly afraid of the working class in their own country. "What will be their fate?" asks Stanley Baron. "They look to the Allies in the hope that it will be a not too uncomfortable one. They hope that in the struggle which they know must come within the German social classes *our presence will throw the weight to the Right, not to the Left.*" Experience in Italy and Greece shows that their hopes are probably well founded. But if the Allies do in fact 'throw the weight to the Right', the Right which supported Hitler, if they act against the German working class (and, of course we know this is exactly what they *will* do) then what becomes of the justification for the war with all its ghastliness and accumulation of suffering?

German workers against Hitler

"There is no doubt" declares the commentator Howard K. Smith, "that the vast majority of the German people are deathly sick of war, and, if the present slice of Germany we hold is an index, there is little doubt that most of them are pretty sick too of Nazism." The Stockholm correspondent of the *Manchester Guardian* reports increasing numbers of desertions from the German army, such that the Nazi press has to issue instructions openly for their apprehension. Clearly, therefore, anti-Nazi forces entering Germany would receive help and support from these anti-Nazi forces inside the country. But the Allied forces entering Germany — at least as far as the commanders go — are *not* anti-Nazi. They are concerned with the war of nation against nation, that is to say, the war of one imperialist interest against another. They are concerned to see that the fundamental war, the war of rulers and ruled, does *not* come out into the open. And that is what would happen if rank-and-file allied anti-Nazis linked up with German anti-Nazis, for our rulers for years supported and subsidised Hitler, and at this moment are supporting Franco and Plastiras.

Such is the background for the most important issue of the war in Europe at the moment: the question of fraternisation. For months now the Allied High Command has been issuing orders against fraternisation and even imprisoning soldiers who play with German children or smoke with German girls. Now Montgomery has issued yet another order to try and impress British soldiers with the untouchability of their German fellows. For twelve years the German workers have been held down by the Nazi Party; now they are kicked by the British ruling class as well. Monty's order is evidently needed, for according to S. L. Solon, the *News Chronicle's* reporter, on 16th March 1945, "the issue of fraternisation is rapidly becoming the most urgent disciplinary problem on the Western front."

Soldiers chafe

Solon describes how uncomfortable the soldiers feel under the No Fraternisation order. Further, they are not slow to notice that the Allied appoint upper class German officials to run the occupied towns, sometimes appointing Nazis for the job; while, on the other hand, German workers are made to do the hard manual labour. One soldier said: "It seems to me that we pick on the same Germans the Nazis kicked around to do the dirty work." They see the contrast. "Local officials appointed by the Allies *are treated with official respect and courtesy.* In order to make the Germans respect them we must treat these officials correctly, one Military Governor told me. At the same time this creates certain problems in the mind of those Germans *who now see men they knew as Nazis playing a role under Allied control in the new administration.*" Thus 'No Fraternisation' is the order for the rank and file, while the high-ups fraternise with one-time Nazi officials.

The rulers fear of fraternisation is even more clearly shown in the case of the Russians. There the memories of 1917 and 1918 may recur. For fraternisation between the German and Russian soldiers was a decisive factor in the February revolution, and again in frustrating the full force of the German Army's counter-revolutionary attacks on the Russian Revolution. The Russian rulers of today can certainly not afford to see a repetition of that working class solidarity on which their revolution originally founded itself.

So the Russian press pours out hysterical filth about the 'obsequiousness', the 'servility' and so on, of the Germans. Their women are all cruel, their girls all treacherous. *Soviet War News* describes the men as 'bloodstained clowns'. Yet this repulsive abuse — directed, be it noted, against German workers — emanates from the same government which contracted a pact with the Nazi leaders. Compare this ultra-vansittartist stuff with Molotov's declaration on 31st October 1939 that this was "not only

senseless but criminal to wage such a war as a war for the
'destruction of Hitlerism' camouflaged as a fight for 'democracy'
... We have always held that a strong Germany is an
indispensible condition for durable peace in Europe. It would be
ridiculous to think that Germany could be 'simply put out of
commission' and struck off the books." Once again, fraternisation
between high-ups like Molotov and Ribbentrop was all in order;
but for a Russian soldier to extend a courtesy to a German would
be a serious crime.

Difficulties
The enforcing of the order nevertheless presents certain
difficulties. An Allied soldier, if he has any feeling for the war, has
a conception of anti-Fascism, of liberating oppressed populations.
Inside Germany he comes in contact with men and women who
have been oppressed by Hitler longer than any other people — the
German workers. Now he sees them continue to be oppressed by
Allied-sponsored Quislings as well, and it is natural — and proper
— that his sympathies should lie with the German workers. But
the No Fraternisation order demands that he should not respond
when a German does him a small courtesy, when a German girl
smiles at him, when a child waves. It is not in human nature to
adopt the frigid attitude demanded by authority. "If the
regulations insist that they are to be punished for behaving like
human beings, then the regulations had better be revised."
(*Manchester Guardian Weekly*, 23rd March 1945).

The very absurdity of the No Fraternisation order exposes the
nature of the Allied rulers' war. The continued attempt to enforce
it will merely bring the well merited contempt of the common
soldier.
7th April 1945

Churchill snubs TUC

The relationship of the TUC to the Tory bosses was once again illuminated this week over the question of amending the Trade Disputes Act. Citrine asked to be allowed to come and discuss the matter with Churchill on behalf of the TUC. Churchill told him — in a letter — that "although I am always glad to see you, I do not think that there would be sufficient reason to put you to the trouble of coming to see me on this matter." A not over-polite way of saying 'don't waste *my* time!'

This reply of Churchill's is especially interesting because it comes a very few weeks after Citrine had shown how faithful he is to the interests of the ruling class by that masterpiece of one-sided reporting, his report on Greece. He acts like a servile lackey and Churchill treats him as such.

This is all the more interesting in the light of Chamberlain's promise at the beginning of the war that if the trade unions played their part in the national effort (i.e. the interests of the bosses) the question of amending the Trade Disputes Act would be very favourably considered by the Government when the war ended. The very terms of this promise are so slighting that one wonders that the TUC could swallow the insult. But now Churchill comes forward to tell them that even though they have been good boys they aren't going to get the prize!

The Conservatives have got the Trade Union officials sized up. At the Conservative Conference one member declared that "the trade union movement has grown into a vested interest", and added that "the trouble with the Trade Unions is that they are looked upon as stepping stones for ambitious politicians to get into parliament." The Tories realise — how could they fail to, in view of the attitude of the Trade Union officials to strikes and compulsory labour measures — that the interests of the Trade Union leadership are bound up with the interests of the employers and the State. Hence the TUC cannot really oppose the ruling class, and their attitude to the Trade Disputes Act shows it. The Tories naturally treat such half-hearted 'opponents' with contempt.

In the autumn of 1943 the Civil Service Clerical Association, the Inland Revenue Staffs Association and the Union of Postal Workers — all unions of government employees — decided to defy the ban which the Trade Disputes Act imposes on them, by applying for affiliation with the TUC. The TUC decided to make an issue out of it and accepted the affiliation. But when the Government showed itself ready to take up the challenge and fight it out, the TUC withdrew its affiliation of these unions on a promise that the matter would be discussed with the Prime Minister. Since then Churchill has not found time, however, for such a discussion, and has now kicked Citrine in the face when he asks for the promise (of discussion only, be it remembered) to be redeemed.

The very next year the Government arrested four Trotskyists and charged them with offences under this same Trades Disputes Act. Did the TUC protest, or support the four accused? Of course not. Instead they obediently sanctioned the Government's new Defence Regulations IAA, which actually goes further than the no-strike clauses in the Trade Disputes Act. The TUC thus showed that they by no means want the Act repealed — they only want certain clauses amended. The anti-strike clauses actually strengthen the hands of the Trade Union official as far as controlling the rank and file goes, and they are all in favour of these. (D. N. Pritt, the Stalinist lawyer, also argued that there was no need for IAA because the Trades Disputes Act already adequately covered the ground!) What the TUC want eliminated are the clauses which forbid government employees to affiliate to the TUC. With the present prospect of an ever increasing number of government employees and petty bureaucrats, the TUC looks hungrily at these employees and is most anxious that they should receive dues from them. They are anxious to completely monopolise the dues-paying capacity of the workers, and at the same time entrench themselves still further in the State machinery.

The Tories on the other hand want to retain these clauses as a bargaining counter, and also to keep the TUC in the servile position which they voluntarily adopted at the beginning of the war. They have no scruples about repudiating promises made to their Trade Union stooges, and openly rebuff them.

Yet the TUC invited Churchill to address the World Trade Union Conference. Well, well . . .

24th March 1945

Starvation in Europe

If we stress the sufferings of civil populations in this war, it is
because, as anarchists, we place ourselves on the side of the
oppressed in society, the 'common people' for whose welfare the
politicians show no concern at all. We live in an age wherein the
possibility of material riches is greater than ever before; but it is
doubtful if misery and suffering have ever before reached such
overwhelming proportions. Never before was the difference
between governments' promises and their performance more
glaring, the contrast between their declared aims and their actual
deeds more shameless or hypocritical. All over the continent of
Europe today (to say nothing of India, or China) the populations
are stricken and desperate, while the governments of the great
powers exhibit the inertia of indifference, and complacently allow
individuals and groups, outraged by the sufferings inflicted by war
upon their Allies, to make suggestions for relief (which they
ignore); or impotent attempts at private relief (which they more or
less openly obstruct). The plight of the people in France provides
an illustration of this callous inaction.

Ever since D-day reports on the condition of the French people
have been published in this country. During the German
Occupation, of course, a servile press was only too anxious to
publish the truth about food shortage. But after 'liberation', too
much sympathy with the French was evidently deemed unsuitable
by our rulers, for numerous reports of the well-filled storehouses,
healthy faces, etc., appeared in the press. Perhaps it is not a
coincidence that these reports were issued at a time when the
people of France, having driven out the occupation forces, were
showing the greatest initiative, and therefore making difficult the
reinstatement of a French government under de Gaulle. For
government always requires an inert population whose only
function is to obey the functionaries of the State. Be that as it may,
the attempt to play down the food shortage in France has
continued more or less till the present.

However, it is becoming clearer as more and more reports are
brought back by observers from France, that there is a very serious
shortage of food and also of fuel. A leading medical journal, the
Lancet, for example, has recently published two articles on the
subject. The writer points out that there are gross inequalities in
the distribution of the available food and this is admitted in official
publications. The prevalence of black market methods make it

inevitable that those who have money are able to supplement their official rations. The increase in tuberculosis is spectacularly higher among children of workers than among professional men, civil servants, cultivators, etc. The *Lancet* writer declares that "the ordinary manual worker is in every respect worst off". He tells how because of the lack of fuel, the hospitals are overfilled with "old people suffering from cold, fatigue and respiratory infections".

Undoubtedly an important cause of the food shortage in France was the German Occupation. Enormous amounts of food were demanded both for the maintenance of the occupying army and for export to Germany. But with the driving out of the Nazi administration, these large amounts should have become available for the French people. No doubt the sabotage and destruction of lines of transport, etc., did something at first to diminish this benefit. No doubt liberating armies, no less than occupying ones, require to be fed. Nevertheless one would have expected that by now there would have been an amelioration in the plight of the French. Nothing of the kind has happened, however. "Since liberation", writes the *Lancet*'s correspondent, "despite an improvement in the official ration, there has been a sudden deterioration in the condition of children of the poorer classes in Paris, of whom many have been found underweight. There has also been an increase of vitamin deficiencies in Marseilles."

This result comes as no surprise to those who have followed the fate of other liberated territories. Italy and Sicily are probably considerably worse off than France.

France is ordinarily a food-producing country, with ability to feed the total population with ease. There can be no doubt at all that if the peasants had access to the land, they could increase production so as to overcome the present difficulties. But the de Gaulle government is pledged to maintain private property. Moreover, the peasant cannot get those products from the towns which he needs to carry on production without paying very high prices for them. This is the reason why they continue to sell their products on the black market just as they did during the German occupation, when such black market channels proved very useful to the Resistance Movement. Moreover, inflation makes them distrustful of paper money.

But even if the money system did not dry up the free flow of goods, the lack of transport provides another source of food shortage in towns. This lack provides yet another brake on peasant production. What is the use of producing food if it is going to rot in the countryside for lack of transport? Meanwhile the State departments add typical bureaucratic incompetence and indifference. *Reynold's News'* foreign editor, David Raymond, just returned from France, reports (11th March 1945): "I know of a case where lorry drivers who were going to the country and would be returning with empties, rang up the Paris Food administration offering to load up with butter on the return journey. They were told that Paris had no need of butter. This at a time when the capital had been without fats for six weeks!" (*The Lancet* correspondent writes also "that up to the day I left Paris, 29th January, no fat of any kind had been issued in the ration of the Parisian since December".) David Raymond also speaks of truck loads of salt being washed away because "some bureaucrat ordered elsewhere the locomotive that was drawing the open trucks in which the salt was being consigned. That was when thousands of Parisians were having to eat unsalted food!"

Meanwhile, people in this country have realised the appalling plight of the French, and their immediate reaction is to want to help. There is enough food in this country to avoid actual starvation in France by sharing. *Picture Post* recently published an article on the conditions in France and were immediately inundated with letters from people anxious to send a part of their rations to France. Enquiring into the possibility of getting something done, however, they came up against an official blank wall. "The attitude of the Ministry of Food", wrote their enquirer, "is that this is a matter for UNRRA. An official added that 'we have no evidence that the people of Britain would be willing to give up any of their rations. I don't think they would.' I asked whether, if it were proved that they were willing, the Ministry of Food would release quantities of food in bulk. He said the question was hypothetical, and most of the food that will go to Europe will in any case come from the Americas. Certainly the Ministry of Food will not allow the sending of food, and seem to be afraid that, if sending is permitted: 1. there will be a feeling abroad that our rations in this country must be lavish if anything whatever can be spared, and 2. there might be a counter-campaign to raise rations here." There one encounters the typical bureaucratic preoccupation with trivialities and indifference to fundamental issues. The writer makes it clear that UNRRA cannot do anything, and concludes that "clearly, almost nothing is being done".

24th March 1945   JOHN HEWETSON

Stabilising Poverty

The National Insurance Bill

"Social Security", declared *Reynolds' News* on 27th January, "is to be the birthright of every Briton". It is perhaps natural that the 'socialist' press should hail the National Insurance Bill, because of their allegiance to the Labour Government. But there is no doubt that *Reynolds'* leader writer was expressing the view of reformists in general when he wrote: "We may criticise the National Insurance Bill in detail. But no criticism can obscure the fact that Jim Griffiths's Bill marks the end of a bad era in which the lash of the Poor Law was never far from the backs of Britain's working people".

Such is the reformist point of view; and it seems to us to be exactly the other way about. The National Insurance Bill can be praised in detail; but considered from a general, a historical, a philosophical point of view, it will not stand criticism at all, and must be condemned for the same reason as the Poor Law which *Reynolds'* claims it supersedes.

The Benefits

From an immediate point of view the bill undoubtedly confers benefits. The Unemployment Benefit of 26/- a week is an increase even when the rise in the cost of living since 1932, (142, compared with 1914 as 100) or even since 1939 (155 compared with 1914) to its present level of 203, is taken into account. But it is worth pointing out that it was recognised 10 and 15 years ago, that the UAB was insufficient to provide for adequate nutrition, and that the health of the unemployed was seriously impaired thereby (The Health Section of the League of Nations drew the attention of the member States to this fact long ago). The present increase by no means brings the benefits up to a level which will provide enough food for full health.

Similarly, the increase in the Old Age Pensions (now euphemistically styled 'Retirement Pensions'!) from 10/- to 26/- a week is an obvious gain; and the same may be said of the Maternity Grants and the general provision for lessening the economic burden of a birth. Indeed the very fact that the cost of the scheme in 1948 is estimated at £509,000,000, as against £351,000,000 under the old scheme, shows that there is an improvement in the extent of benefits despite the increased contributions which workers have to pay. But of course that is not the whole story.

Labour Pays for the Whole Cost

At present, where a worker pays 4/7 a week, his employer 'pays' 3/10. But what has to be remembered is that all wealth is produced by the workers, by the application of labour power to natural resources. Workers supply the labour; they make the machines; and they work the machines. When the employer 'pays' 3/10, he is only paying money which the workers have made for him. It is only 'his' money because he owns the means of wealth production, a state of affairs which socialists and anarchists have denounced as immoral and unjust for more than a century. In effect, the workers pay the whole cost of the scheme.

The Philosophy of Insurance

And this brings up the question of the whole idea behind insurance. Originally it arose from the desire for mutual aid. When a misfortune befell a member of society, men felt it was only just that the whole of society should shoulder the burden of the misfortune, so that no individual should be crushed by it. Thus when a man falls out of work, society should see that he — seeing that unemployment is no fault of his — should not suffer by it. To succour him and his family at such a time is only in line with natural conceptions of justice and mutual aid.

But does the new Insurance Bill do anything like that? Would society, if it were free, so far insult misfortune as to offer redress to the tune of a mere 26/- a week? One has only to think what it is like to try and scrape along on such a sum, to see that the idea of a just redress for misfortune, the idea of the community at large lifting the burden from the shoulders of the unlucky individual, has become completely submerged in the cold calculation of the State Actuary, untouched by any impulse of mutual aid whatever.

Ulterior Motives

If a fellow feeling for misfortune is not the guiding principle of the Bill, what is? And here it is necessary to leave the immediate standpoint and widen our horizon to some extent. The Reform Act of 1832 was looked upon at the time also as a 'revolutionary' re-orientation of attitude towards social questions. But even conservative historians now point out that, had some concessions not been made at that time, England would hardly have 'escaped' from revolutionary changes in actuality. Looked at historically, reforms are always mere relaxations of intolerable conditions, only to peg them at a slightly lower level. They are always, from the point of view of the ruling class, designed "to concede the part, in order to maintain the whole".

And in recent years, we have seen 'reforms' used to achieve the immediate ends of the employing class also. "One fundamental feature of the scheme", says the *News Chronicle* (25th January 1946), is that in order to get the benefits you have to make steady contributions. *For most benefits there will be a requirement that, before you can draw from the fund, you must be able to show a yearly average of 50 weekly contributions*, credit being given for contributions when you are sick or unemployed".

This means that the man who does wage work simply to free himself to engage in other activity, who works some weeks, and then stops in order to do the thing he really wants to do, and only returns to wage work when his funds run out — such a man is heavily hit by such a clause. In fact, it is clear that the promoters of the Bill regard the fundamental business of a man between the ages of 19 and 65, as working for an employer or contractor. "There will be no means test. *The tribunal will make its decision on the availability of work and the willingness of the man or woman to take it*". Clearly, if the man or woman is unwilling, if he or she says "That's not the sort of work I want to do", then the tribunal's decision will be unfavourable, and the economic screw will be turned on. The idea of fulfilment in work, of doing something because one likes that kind of work, thinks it valuable, and therefore does it well — this idea simply has no place in the National Insurance Bill.

Organisation of Poverty

Thus we return to our original contention. From a revolutionary point of view, even from a simple progressive outlook which thinks freedom a necessary condition of men's life and activity, the Bill must be condemned. In return for economic benefits — which however will undoubtedly lag behind an increasing cost of living, and require another 'revolutionary' bill in 10 or 15 years time — in return for these merely temporary and evanescent benefits, a worker is tied to the bench for 50 weeks of the year, and must accept whatever employment the Labour Exchange, with its bureaucratic unconcern for any question of personal preference on the part of the individual, chooses to offer.

Rivetting The Chains of The State
It is the old story. Capitalism menaces workers increasingly with insecurity. So the State, acting on behalf of the ruling class, uses that fear of insecurity as a bargaining counter. In return for some relief in crises of unemployment or birth, or in the failing working powers of old age, it fastens the shackles of the State ever more firmly on the working class. It denies once more the right of individual workers to freedom of choice, even in the limited sense of *laissez faire* capitalism; and it affirms the conception of State Capitalism, which is also the conception of the frankly totalitarian governments; *that a man is simply a working unit. He must do what work the State tells him, where the State tells him.* In return, the State values him, if he is out of work or too old to work, at 26/- a week.
9th February 1946

No Health Plan in the Midst of Poverty

When a problem exists, the rational way to solve it is to seek the causes and then repair the trouble in a radical manner. This is the way to solve the problem of present-day ill-health. It is now generally admitted by the medical profession, the sociologists, and even the State departments that the principal cause of the mass of ill-health to-day is *poverty*. But there is no sign that the reform of the Health Services incorporates any serious attack upon poverty.

If one is not going to try and remove the root of the trouble, any changes one proposes in the existing Health machinery are bound to have advantages and disadvantages — as all palliative measures have. In *War Commentary* and *Freedom* we have always stressed the need for a *radical* approach to this question, and therefore any comments we make about the present struggle between the BMA and the Government can only be incidental. The struggle is not between a radical proposal and a palliative proposal; both are superficial, and cannot be regarded as remedies. Nevertheless, some of the issues involved are not without interest.

Trend towards State Control

The Government's proposals for an all-embracing public Health Service is in line with the tendency which has gathered increasing momentum during our lifetimes for the State to gather more and more of the organisations which are necessary for society into its own hands. Hospitals grew up as voluntary institutions relying on contributions for their funds, or as services provided by local authorities. As such they had certain virtues and certain disadvantages. Alongside these public hospital services there existed the general practitioner, and he still remains the foundation of the medical services. Formerly the general practitioner was a 'family doctor' — he lived in one district all his life, and often observed his patients from their birth to the grave. The relationship between him and his patients was often a very good one indeed; he felt that his responsibility was to his patient, and he acted in his best interests alone. Indeed, medical ethics from the time of Hippocrates has been based on this relationship.

Disappearance of the Family Doctor

But in the past forty years, chiefly due to State intervention in the domain of health, this conception of a 'family doctor' has been gradually undermined. Certainly the panel doctor does not fulfil the same role, and in the nature of things it is impossible for hospitals or other institutions to do so. The factors that have brought this about are not simple. The family doctor was paid by his patients. This meant that the poorest could not afford the same degree of medical care as the better off. State intervention in the shape of the National Health Insurance — the panel system — was intended to remedy this position by evening up the effects of wide disparities in income. (There is good reason to think that it has not achieved very much in this direction.)

When the BMA therefore claim that payment by the patient to the doctor preserves the ethical relationship between the two, there is something to be said for their claim. But it ignores the fact that the non-paying panel patient has for years more or less gone without these advantages. The Government, in claiming that a *free* service is necessary for all, are also on the right line as far as it goes. But there is also some truth in the fact that the doctor in such a system — as it would exist to-day — does not solely consider the good of his patient, but also has to consider other interests as well. Thus under the panel system, a doctor can prescribe the medicine he considers best for his patient; but if that treatment is thought to be too expensive, he may be asked to consider cheapness as well as what he thinks is best.

Similarly, there has already developed a tendency for doctors to consider other interests besides those of their patients. Many doctors almost automatically consider the employers' interests when deciding whether or not to issue certificates of fitness or unfitness to work. And during the war lay persons, such as the National Service Officer could query such certificates and order independent medical examinations. Similarly, medical examinations for the army, or undertaken for an insurance firm, are not primarily in the interests of the man or woman examined. The suspicion with which workers often regard factory medical officers is grounded in the feeling — too often correct — that he is there to look after the interests of the boss. Under the older conception of medical ethics he should concern himself solely with the interests of his patients.

Dependence on State as Employer

If doctors are to be employed by the State their livelihood will depend on it, and therefore many will unconsciously modify their behaviour to suit the interests of the State. In Russia, a medical student has a record folder in which is recorded his progress as a student, and which continues with him throughout his employment under the State. It is needless to stress the fact that such a system makes for caution, orthodoxy and mediocrity, because the fear of damaging one's chances of favourable employment if one acts in a way which does not suit the State. In Germany, certain doctors fell so far from considering the welfare of their patients, that they undertook the castrations and forced sterilisations demanded by the Nazi penal codes. Such is an extreme position perhaps. But it illustrates how the function of medicine can be diverted from its true course by giving up the classical Hippocratic relationship with the patient.

High Level of Compensation

It seems likely that the State will win. Bevan proposes to compensate practitioners on a scale higher than that which was expected (£65 millions against a calculated £58 millions), thereby repeating the Labour Government's policy towards nationalisation of industry and the Bank of England. In so far as the BMA is concerned with the financial interests of the doctors, it exerts a reactionary influence. But if it manages to preserve the independence and autonomy of the doctor in his relations with his patients, it will have helped to preserve one of the best traditions of medicine.

Poverty Remains the Real Problem

But in considering the pros and cons of the present proposals it is necessary to keep a sense of proportion. The purpose of a National Health Service is to improve the health of the population. All that the present bill aims at is to modify the existing means of treating ill-health, and therefore it is not likely to be much more successful than the NHI of 1910 was. Tuberculosis is still responsible for more than half of the total deaths occurring in early adult life. Tuberculosis is a disease almost wholly dependent on bad social conditions arising from low wages. and could be virtually wiped out by abolishing conditions of poverty. In old age the deaths from respiratory conditions — pneumonia, bronchitis, etc. — are more than five times as frequent among the poorest sections of the population as among the well-to-do, and the same relationship between poverty and increased death rates exists during the first year of life. Deaths in childbirth, the bulk of heart diseases, and all the major causes of sickness and premature death are similarly affected by economic and social factors. Yet the new Health Bill does not touch these matters.

A radical solution of the problem of ill-health is impossible unless poverty, its principal cause, is removed. But poverty is an essential feature of the present mode of production, and indeed any society in which economic disparities exist. The solution of the problem of ill health demands a radical reorganisation of the very bases of society. In other words, it demands a revolutionary approach.

20th April 1946

POST - WAR

Freedom, June 30 1945.

PART 2

A Phoney Peace
Our struggle against war goes on

The period between September 1939 and May 1940 was popularly known as the phoney war. The period between May 1945 and some unspecified date in the future may well be called the phoney peace. The war has dragged on through many years, under leadership which has told us repeatedly it is inspired and brilliant but has failed to do anything to speed up the six years of drawn-out war, and that war is still unfinished. For even while the black market is raking off quick profits in selling at advanced prices Union Jacks which they bought up cheap after Dunkirk, the war in the East goes on. There is method in this madness. The idea is to get us accustomed to 'war in peace': to be used to what were thought wartime sacrifices and restrictions being carried out in peacetime, and even if Japan surrenders, this 'phoney peace' is scheduled to go on in the name of keeping order, occupation, preparation, and so on.

Our struggle against the war is therefore not ended, nor can it ever be ended except by dissolution of the system which breeds wars. Our first duty as revolutionists in the new period is to get our fellow workers to realise that the immediate necessity is for an end to all fascist tendencies brought in under wartime excuses.

Against the Defence Regulations
Mr Morrison has revoked some of the Defence Regulations — 84 in all revoked and 25 partly revoked — but left the vast majority. This is intentional bamboozling of the public into thinking that the Defence Regulations are finished, and using the phoney peace to get them accustomed to the others staying on. He announced to the House of Commons that the release of persons detained under

153

the regulations had been authorised. This again was a deliberate attempt at misleading the public, since he means in fact that *only* those who are detained under Regulation 18b are released. There are anarchists in jail under Regulation 39a, but that is not revoked, nor are those persons released. Over a year ago — long before the recent trial directed against the anarchist movement — we declared in *War Commentary* that there was a calculated plan of releasing the fascists and arresting the anti-fascists, the revolutionaries, anarchists in particular. That is now proved true. The reason is because the Government no longer fears the fascists: they were 'dangerous' in the event of a foreign invasion (by the Nazis) just as the Communists were 'dangerous' when Hitler was allied to Stalin. Now that there is no possibility of a '1940' the fascists come out. There is, however, the possibility of a '1918' — a revolutionary situation arising out of such problems as demobilisation and the lack of homes for heroes to live in — that is why the Government turns its attention to the anarchists. It will step by step attempt to infringe the rights of freedom of speech, print and assembly as they affect the working class. It is no use imagining that this will be relaxed because the war is over. Restrictions against those who might be in sympathy with the enemy are relaxed. Restrictions against those who are likely to be in sympathy with the international working class in the forthcoming revolutionary situation are only just beginning. Our elementary first demand in the post-war period is a fight against fascism.

Against conscription

Mr Churchill has announced that conscription is to go on — for years. He gives as his excuse the fact of the war against Japan — the phoney peace excuse again — but avoided saying that conscription would finish even then. In fact he gave as his "personal and political conviction" that the "defence of the country should be shared equally by everyone". (This does not include MPs, of course.)

His intention is plainly enough to keep conscription on. First of all to give it a popular coating by saying it is "to relieve" men in the forces from going to the Far east. Then to keep it on for good. Here it is significant to note what has happened in Canada. Canada has abolished conscription. Only volunteers are to go to the Far East. Peacetime conscription will not be operative in Canada. Why? Did anyone vote against it? Certainly not, they never had the opportunity — but thousands voted against it with

their feet, and refused to go abroad; the population gave
enthusiastic support to those who went on strike against overseas
conscription; they fought the civilian and military police to protect
'deserters' and 'draft-dodgers'; soldiers and civilians acted in solidarity against overseas conscription.

We too demand the end of conscription. Already the high-
ranking dodgers here are wrangling quick demobilisation and
a post-war career by flocking to become candidates for
Parliament. The rank and file must voice its demand for like
privileges in no uncertain fashion. It also has to take part in the
social affairs of the post-war world: only this will not be done by
elevation to Westminster one at a time, but by a movement of
industrial resistance that will transform society from a grabbing
capitalist machine to a free world.

The object of the phoney peace period is to say there cannot be
any demobilisation in the nature of 'all out altogether' as Japan
remains to be dealt with. Nevertheless, in the last war such excuses
were put forward and mass solidarity forced on the Government
the necessity for 'all out altogether'. When Mr Churchill saw the
soldiers marching on Whitehall after the last war, he did not make
the sort of heroic speech he makes when the soldiers are in front of
him facing the other side. He hid himself, and they demobbed
themselves.

The masses are tired of excuses that we cannot have the end of
conscription because of the war against Japan — then there will
come the excuse that it cannot be ended because of occupation;
then there will come the excuse that it cannot be ended because of
the need for preparation for the next war with which ever ally we
fall out with first.

Industrial conscription
Industrial conscription must be swept aside. No wartime excuses
for maintaining production could now be operative — but as the
peace is only a phoney one, we are told to remember Japan and
stay under the heel of the Ministry of Labour. The fact that the
worker cannot choose his job leads directly to the laws against
absenteeism, bad workmanship, etc., since by this means one
could get out of a job one did not like. One restriction on labour
means conscription all round. The present laws are industrial
serfdom. We look forward with confidence to the manner in which
these measures will be swept aside, as will the identity card system,
by spontaneous action such as led to the discarding of gas masks,

opened the London tubes in 1940, and made short shrift of such efforts as the 'Silent Column'.

Amnesty!

All these demands are elementary demands of the struggle against home-grown fascism. We must engage in a demand for the release of *all* political prisoners, conscientious objectors and *all* such wartime offenders. There are thousands in prison for such offences. The Fuehrer Churchill has decreed that these shall stay in jail.

The numbers involved, particularly as 'deserters', are so vast that only a general amnesty will prevent a serious crisis, since the numbers already incarcerated are but a fraction of the general total who will be involved. The Government's idea is to hound and starve them out until they surrender or turn to crime. We must give a Canadian answer to the militarists who propose to set up concentration camps which naturally are not to be open for inspection by visiting cameramen. It is indisputable that the projected plans for making Dartmoor a centre for military 'offenders' is now devised by those who want a British Buchenwald as an outlet for their sadistic impulses not for some time to be gratified by total war.

Such fascists must be exposed; such fascist measures must be resisted. We enter on a period in which only the utmost vigilance will prevent our going the way the German workers went; and we shall go not only with our eyes open but with their experience before us. We must never get to the state of affairs where the only means of deliverance lies in the regime toppling over by natural catastrophe or imperialist war. The edifice of tyranny must be cracked with our own hands. The alternative is too costly. Revolution will prevent such a sacrifice. No amount of 'never again' vows and pledges by the thousands who will now — as after the last war — turn to pacifist solutions until the next war, nor of preparation by those now wedded to militarism, will prevent either another world war, or the conditions when serious workers can even consider a world war as the lesser of two evils.

'Total war — partial peace'

As anarchists we opposed the world war, recognising it from the first as imperialist, and not deviating from that stand. We knew that those who pretended that Nazism (or Germany) alone caused the war would have in fact supported the war in any case, whatever the cause and against whomever it was waged. The evil things in Germany were merely useful from a war propaganda point of view: they certainly were true, but did not occasion the war. The war was caused by rivalry between imperialisms. It has incidentally destroyed Nazism; as the last war brought in its train the overthrow of Czarism and Kaiserism; and the next war may bring the overthrow of another imperialist colossus.

But total war is too costly for such incidentals, and we must temper our natural relief at the ceasefire that heralds the end of one stage of the long, drawn-out waste of lives and years that nothing can replace, by the thought that not only does the war go on in peacetime, but that we are back in the 1920 situation, with a quarter of a century experience of political disillusionment to our credit. That last is just as well. The revolutionary movement was in the inter-war period relegated to the museums, anarchism had almost become a piece of folklore. That period of recession in the international revolutionary movement is now ended. The experience in disillusion in political saviours calls forward the best traditions of the past wedded to modern needs: a movement of industrial resistance for the occupation and expropriation of the places of work, an anarchist movement standing for the overthrow of all governments, and all systems of exploitation of man by man. That alone will end the third world war before it begins. And simultaneously with that duty, let us make certain that our movement, struggling for the ultimate social transformation of society, plays the most prominent part in resistance against all those tyrannical measures the State is imposing on us in the guise of total war and partial peace. If there is not a free society on the ruins of capitalism, there will be a third world war. If we have not even managed to preserve the most elementary of personal liberties, not only will we find ourselves in a third world war, but in that third world war Britain's next rival imperialism will be using our plight as an excuse to 'liberate' us.

19th May 1945

Inside Germany

British Soldiers' Impressions

(This article is compiled as a result of an interview with three soldiers on leave from the BLA, taken in shorthand during a conversation, and which they checked and agreed was correct. Two of them were in the same unit, the other travelled in a different part of Germany. Their experiences generally speaking tally. While any impressions gained in the manner described may generally give only a part of the picture, we feel it to be at any rate as accurate as those given by war correspondents whose perspective is much more limited.)

Not much remains of the Nazi structure in Germany. It probably collapsed long ago, control being exercised by the Army, and of course the civilian burgomasters, etc., who were members of the Party, but not necessarily leaders. The SS are generally hated, even by the patriots who regard them as war-dodgers. The Party is seldom referred to openly, except as 'they'. We heard a POW say, "We've had ten years of war, not four like the Yanks. They couldn't let us alone till the world crashed down on top of us. They don't care, they're all right." It is a common belief the Nazi leaders are in safety. No-one we spoke to believes in Hitler's death; some think he is in hiding, we even met some who think he is in safety in England. However, all the reports indicate Hitler is dead. It is doubtful if he could survive one minute anywhere in Germany, let alone outside. The Press reports that "Germans feel little sense of guilt" is perfectly true, as except for a few, none identify themselves with the Party.

Atrocities

It is fairly definite that the German soldiers behaved 'correctly' in occupied countries. That is not to say that the atrocity stories are untrue. With exceptions mentioned below, all atrocities that were committed were done in accordance with the Geneva Convention. That may sound cynical but is quite verifiable. The victims of the Gestapo were members of the underground movement who as *franc-tireurs* and *saboteurs* were unprotected by international law, and we believe even the shooting of hostages is permissible under the 'rules of war'. All this was done under command; there is no doubt at all that the soldiers obeyed the orders, just as they obey orders to go to battle. (This is not to whitewash them for obeying orders but they are not the only ones). In the main the atrocities committed in occupied countries, against the resisters, were done by Quislings, directed by the Gestapo, and the Army was seldom involved. The Resistance movements so far from following the nationalistic line laid down by the emigré governments, often took part in movements to spread sedition among the German soldiers.

The notable exception to this 'correct' procedure was of course as regards the Jews. In Belgium and Holland few Jews are alive except those who were hidden by the local populace, and it is encouraging to know there was a lot of this solidarity. In Germany practically none at all remain, except those who had escaped from concentration camps, etc. We questioned several Germans on their attitude to the Jews. Most soldiers disclaimed any responsibility for the fate of the Jews in the occupied countries. The statement was always made, "Their own people deported them". On reference to Dutch friends we elicited that what was meant was that when the round-up of the Jews was made, it was not done by the Army or even directly by the SS but by the regular police of the occupied countries. Even the rationalistic French Resistance papers bitterly complained of the attitude of the French police at lending themselves to such work. Their victims often committed suicide before being arrested, particularly those refugees who had already experienced concentration camps. The victims were sent by sealed train through Germany to Poland. They were not seen by the majority of the people, and it may be doubted whether the majority of Germans believed Hitler meant business when he said he would exterminate the Jews and Poles any more than our people realise our gauleiters mean business when they talk of extermination.

Of course this does not exculpate the German people, who knew that the Jews were persecuted even if they did not realise they were being exterminated. Unfortunately we cannot find any signs of the concentration camps revelations being untrue. They were designed mainly for Jewish people, but also had a number of German political prisoners and prisoners from other nationalities being 'broken in'. The camps at Buchenwald, Belsen, etc. are the culmination of the campaign which began in 1933 and ended with the mass extermination camps in Poland. In 1933 the Nazis did not dare to introduce mass extermination. There were individual beatings-up, degradation and the boycott. The concentration camps were filled largely with 'politicals'. (Few 'politicals' remain in the camps since most were taken out and sent to the front line; those now in being mostly well-known leaders of the pre-Hitler era and not the rank-and-file of the underground movement.) Until the introduction of the racial laws in 1938 Jews could still live in Germany, however much discrimination was practised against them. The campaign against them was to blacken them as much as possible and degrade them so as to work up such a hysteria against them as would make it possible for the wholesale concentration to take place. Most Germans believe that the Jews are guilty of thousands of offences, and the Nazi poison will take long to eradicate in this respect, but they have been subjected to so much propaganda that they take little impression from it. For instance one soldier said, "Of course, the Jews made plenty of money out of us when they were in power, but seeing the state the Aryans brought us to when they barged into the country I think I'd prefer the Jews", an interesting mixture of having swallowed Nazi poison and anti-serum too! A civilian to whom we spoke thought the Nazi Party was controlled by the Jews! However, few people we spoke to had any real bias against the Jews when it came down to it, and none at all believed the wilder allegations of Streicher, etc. Their attitude may be summed up by one who said, "Supposing Churchill or Stalin ordered pogroms, what would you do?"

We repudiate the idea, as suggested by Montgomery, that any of them put on an act for our benefit, since most of them think British soldiers idolise Churchill and the King, but these we spoke to were quite prepared to run them down.

Political Trends

We met no Communists, and think stories that there is a Communist movement can be discounted. It is generally accepted that 'Communist' means pro-Russian and no-one we met believes in the Communist Party as a revolutionary force, as some in 'liberated countries' still do. The Nazi propagandists built up a picture of Bolshevism as imperialistic, which, being true as well as propagandist, is generally believed. We never went near the Russian Front, but it is generally believed in the West that gigantic atrocities took place on both sides there.

As regards Germany itself, it is finished. The cities we did not see, because all we passed was rubble, where cities once stood. It is impossible to imagine what it looks like from air raid experience in England. One has to picture the devastated square mile of the City of London as representing a whole town and one is near the mark. The people in the country districts often look well fed, both farmers and labourers; in the town districts all look starved. In some of the little towns one sees the real small-bourgeois type, the equivalent of the Cheltenham and Torquay retired business-man, who has not done so badly.

The slave-labourers in the towns were treated abominably, and looked ill and worn. Not all of those in the country do. To our amazement a German farmer told us to leave his Russian labourers alone, as they were better off where they were, and they agreed. This is an exceptional case, and could not have happened except in an isolated district out of reach of the Nazi octopus, but that there can exist people working for nothing who do not want to go home indicates something pretty terrible where they come from.

There was a general opinion that the Allies would come as liberators, excluding the Russians who it is thought want to annex the country (no-one in Germany we spoke to talks as do some of our people in terms of "making it a Communist state"). The air-raids altered this opinion to an extent, but the effect of the BBC propaganda has been to give rise to an impression that the Allies would be less harsh than the Nazis. It is hard to have to say this, because it looks as if one wants to whitewash the evil thing of Nazism, but this is frankly not the general case. The Allies have stopped for instance the concentration camps, etc., and the extermination campaign which Hitler introduced under cover of the war. That is a good thing, but hopes of outside salvation have been dashed to the ground by the inhuman administration of the country.

Devastation
The picture of woe and devastation that is Germany cannot be believed. It is undoubtedly the case that those who pretend that there is a 'campaign for a soft peace' either have never seen the condition of the country or want to hush it up by saying we are being too tolerant. The cities are smashed beyond hope. Sanitation does not exist. Famine is very near, possibly a couple of months ahead. Not a family is left intact - all have suffered some bereavement, none remain together. Many are anti-war — desertion has always been very high, in proportion to the small rate of conscientious objection, largely restricted to the Jehovah's Witnesses. (At a hospital a soldier told us, "If the Fuehrer weren't a homosexual himself he would realise that the reason so many men get VD is in order to dodge the Eastern Front". Incidentally,

stories about the corruption of Nazi leaders are rife, but unfortunately evade the issue of Nazism itself, as against the particular leaders.)

The picture of devastation has been completed by the policy of loot and destruction by the occupying troops, as well as ex-labourers. This falls particularly harshly on the working-classes. While shops, etc. are ransacked, most of these are usually bomb-damaged already. On the larger houses, mansions, etc., Allied guards are often placed, ostensibly to prevent the Nazis from escaping! The working-class places are robbed wholesale while the women stand by weeping, and in one case Russian ex-labourers even took the clothes off the children of one working-class woman. In this instance they were made to give them back by British soldiers, but the soldiers' action was a definite breach of the non-fraternisation orders, and it is usually the reverse, when looters even search the gardens with mine-detectors to see if anything is buried away. Clothes, dresses, watches, etc., all are taken from the people while they stand by; usually what is not taken is smashed in the process. It is doubtful if any prisoner-of-war ever gets to the base with any personal object remaining — watch, cigarette-case, etc. — and what is infuriating is that contrariwise the admirals, generals, etc. are treated with 'traditional courtesy', no doubt a form of mutual insurance. When a few big bug's houses are looted, the Command may take action, and enforce the laws against looting by harsh sentences on soldiers, but that is how they will dodge the issue, for in fact the looting is a direct result of orders, the non-fraternisation order in particular. When the Allied soldiers went into Germany they were prepared to be 'correct', but they got orders to the contrary. The officers would not let us ask for a cup of tea or some boiling water to make some. "What do we do, then?" "If you want anything, take it." That is how it started. It is fantastic to pretend, as the Press at home pretends, that soldiers have not the intelligence or the honour to refrain from mixing with war-criminals. They had sufficient discernment to know who was who, and those who shake hands with Goering are not the people to refuse to trust them. The position now is that one cannot speak to any German, not even answer a greeting and the looting campaign is only a facet of this artificially organised campaign of hatred. Few men will do as we did, mix and talk in defiance of the order, and perhaps one cannot expect them to take the risk when demobilisation is (we all hope) so near.

Non-fraternisation

Take one aspect, the requisitioning of houses by the military. The non-fraternisation order refuses to allow the Germans to be under the same roof as the Allied soldiers. A woman, her mother, and her child, were turned out of their house and asked where they could sleep. "In the pig-sty", they were told by our officer. That is a typical instance. When we admitted once a woman soaked to the skin through sleeping in the rain, to dry herself at her own fireplace, we were told "not to be soft" and severely cautioned. We could not help realising that the officers running this campaign belong to the same stock as those who evicted our forebears from the crofts and commons. It is farcical to reflect that after all this had happened they gave out the order to blanco up, and keep all brasses bright, as "the Germans respect a smart soldier". They can only visualise respect in terms of bullsh!

We would give one further instance, when some of our men gave food to an old woman. On an officer threatening us with a court-martial for fraternisation with Germans we told him she claimed to be a Jewess; the officer then made an anti-semitic remark to the effect that the Jews were as bad as the Germans, this despite the presence in hearing distance of at least two British soldiers of Jewish descent. It is difficult to find any difference between such persons sheltering under Grigg and Churchill, and their Nazi counterparts.

At the moment there appears to be no likelihood of any renaissance in Germany: the important lesson is to know that our gauleiters can behave in the same way when required, just as they evicted our ancestors, burnt their cottages and deported them to penal settlements; as they did in Ireland up to a generation ago, do in India today; and are now behaving in Germany. It may be argued by those who have been assimilating war propaganda that the German leaders ordered such things in Russia and elsewhere first; that is true, but it is no use pretending the people on top are motivated by revenge; it is just the way they have behaved elsewhere, and will always behave when given unbridled power. We shall only stop them doing it at home by a determined movement of resistance such as the French — and Irish — had, otherwise we shall finish up being the home coolies, just as the German workers did when their rulers lost their empire. Meantime we must show the German workers whether or not it is possible to stop actions of the bosses which conflict with our conceptions of humanity.

2nd June 1945

The Cost of War

25,000,000 Dead

The following article is reproduced in a condensed form from the French newspaper Liberation *which published it on VE-Day. We have hesitated before publishing it as the figures seemed to us so high that we thought they were probably due to an over-estimation.* After some of the figures had been confirmed by other sources we decided to publish the article nevertheless reminding our readers that these statistics do not pretend to be accurate but to give an idea of the tremendous losses suffered by all nations in the war in Europe. These do not represent the sum total of war dead; the war in the Far East will undoubtedly prove more costly still than the war in Europe.*

When we establish a record of the losses suffered during these five years of war, we shall see that they are all out of proportion to the wars of the past. Today this record is still incomplete because the counting of the dead, as always, takes place after fighting.

Up to now, we have only fragmentary figures. Put together they express this first fact, unfortunately incomplete, that the war in Europe has taken more than 25 million DEAD.* To put it in a more human way than figures, it means that a population like that of Spain has been crossed off the map and history.

Military Losses
FRANCE: 110,762 killed, 19,315 missing.
USSR: the figures vary according to the sources.
Soviet Sources: 5,300,000 dead.
American Sources: 21,000,000 killed, wounded, missing, prisoners (no distinction is made between civilian and military).
German Sources: 13,400,000 dead.
GERMANY: according to Russian information, 8,500,000 dead up to the 1st October, 1944.
UNITED STATES: 200,000 dead, 97,000 missing, 490,000 wounded.

[* In fact the official figures are nearer 50 million: that is the population of the UK. — Editor]

BRITISH EMPIRE: 310,000 dead, 70,000 missing, 425,000 wounded.
POLAND: 1939 campaign, 900,000 dead, missing and prisoners.
JUGOSLAVIA: 300,000 dead in Tito's troops.
GREECE: 13,000 killed, 70,000 wounded to which one must add 50,000 dead in the partisans' struggle.
Other countries at war: losses unknown up to date.

Civilian Losses
FRANCE: 100,000 dead in prisons and concentration camps in France. 150,000 shot (70,000 in Paris). More than 150,000 dead through bombing.
POLAND: 5 million slaughtered or 14·7% of the Polish population.
JUGOSLAVIA: 1,300,000 killed, most of them through reprisals.
USSR: the Russians talk of millions dead without giving precise figures.
GREECE: 150,000 victims murdered by the Bulgarians, Germans and Italians. 450,000 dead through starvation.
HOLLAND: 125,000 Jews and members of the Resistance Movement killed.
BRITAIN: through bombing 60,000 civilians killed or missing. 100,000 wounded.
GERMANY: the total number of people killed through bombing is still unknown. At Hamburg 100,000 dead; Karlsruhe 46,000 dead. 250 towns have known a similar fate.
JEWS: more than 4,000,000 (including 2,600,000 Poles) have been exterminated in Europe.

This is a first record of the European phase of the second world war. According to the most pessimistic estimates Napoleon's wars, which lasted 15 years, killed two million people. Between 1914 and 1918 the world lost eight and a half million people. Between 1939 and 1945, in Europe, there has been more than 25 million dead.

It is a tragic progression, full of anxiety for those who realise that a new conflict may destroy 20 centuries of civilisation.
16th June 1945   YVES HUGONNET

The Triumph of Brutality

A few weeks ago we were in the middle of the great atrocity sensation. The newspapers published photographs of dead and dying prisoners in the concentration camps. The news reels filmed the horrors and showed them at every cinema in the country. People read the newspapers, went to the pictures, and were suitably shocked or sceptical, according to their state of political disillusionment.

This in itself was of no great significance, for the exposure at this particular time of something which they had condoned for ten years before was obviously a tactical move on the part of the government. What seems to me of much greater social significance is that to-day, a month after the atrocity scandal, people are still attending the exhibition of horror photographs in Regent Street in such numbers that queues of hundreds stand outside the doors all day and every day — including Sunday. They go, not because they are shocked at the deeds of the SS men, but to satisfy a morbid curiosity in looking at these macabre records of human degradation and misery.

The Destruction of Values

It seems to me that these people who stand and wait outside the horror exhibitions are themselves the victims of a subtle psychological process not unlike that which is inflicted physically on the inmate of a concentration camp. They are the victims of a gradual breaking down of ethical standards, analogous to the breaking down of individual human pride and the actual killing of the incurable recalcitrant, which was the object of Nazi practice. They, like many millions of others in Europe, while thinking they were fighting the Nazis, have suffered that brutalisation of feelings and atrophy of values in conduct, which were once considered the characteristics of the Nazi alone.

I need only quote a few instances to show how people who described themselves as anti-Nazis have acted with a needless brutality as great as that of the Nazis. There was the great sadistic exhibition of the public trial of German officers and soldiers in Kharkov, and, following their inevitable condemnation, the public execution and the films showing the details of slow strangling. There was the treatment by members of the French Resistance of women who had consorted with German soldiers. These women had their heads shaved and were paraded through the streets in the same way as Nazis paraded women who had relations with Jews. There has been the continual clamour for victims and more victims on the part of the Communists and other sections of the resistance movements in various continental countries. There was the exhibition of Mussolini and his colleagues following their death, when their bodies were left in the public square for days while people spat on them and fired revolver shots into them. There have been the incidents of elderly Germans, with no Nazi connections, being forced to bury the decayed bodies from the concentration camps, under the muzzles of American guns, in just the same way as the Jews were made to perform revolting tasks at the bidding of the Nazis.

Some of these acts have been performed by individuals, others by the authorities with the tacit approval of large numbers of individuals. Individual Germans have been blamed for not protesting against the atrocities in the concentration camps. But there has been an alarming number of people in England today who have seen nothing very wrong in atrocities committed against the Germans. It would seem that many who thought they were attacking Nazism had developed an attitude not unlike that inculcated by the Nazis. I think it is probable that a great many Germans were not very much moved by what they knew about concentration camps. But I also know that many Englishmen are callous to what they have heard of the Indian famines, that many otherwise decent Americans are supporters of discrimination against Negroes, and that millions of Russians choose to forget the people who disappear into the forced labour camps of the Arctic circle.

The Root of Brutalisation

The root of this brutalisation, which at best is a callousness towards human suffering and at worst an active interest in such suffering, lies in the lack of any real feeling of the integrity of the individual human being. If we regard men as individuals each with the same feelings as ourselves, but each with his own individual nature and needs, then we shall accept and respect their personal rights. We shall treat them with consideration and shall not harm them in any avoidable manner.

If, on the other hand, we regard men as names, as clothed bodies without personal needs and virtues, then we shall lose sight of their rights to freedom, to justice, and, finally, even to pity. We shall treat them merely as objects, whose destruction is nothing in comparison with the supposed good of the collective, the herd.

The difference between these two attitudes is similar to the difference between libertarian and authoritarian philosophies and social systems. If we are given freedom to develop our own personalities, then we shall respect those of other people. If we are compelled to regard ourselves as ciphers to be used for any foul purpose of the collective, to be turned into serfs or cannon fodder at the will of the ruling class, then we shall tend to regard other people also as nameless units without rights or importance.

We cannot blame the people who have become brutalised by the effects of living in an authoritarian world. They also are the victims of an atrocity, for their human feelings have broken in the great Belsen of a war society as ruthlessly as the bodies of Jews were broken in the Nazi hells. For years, even before the war, they were being made callous by the poison of brutalised novels and brutalised films. Then, since the war, they have been conditioned by processes of which the training of professional killers (described by Dwight Macdonald in an article in *Now* No. 4) is only an extreme example. The ideal of the governments has been a series of nations of depersonalised, obedient thugs. Thugs who reacted in the wrong manner, like Hulten, were eliminated, but those who have destroyed German cities and boasted of it have been given medals and praise.

It is inevitable that, after so many years of war and regimentation, people should have become inhuman in their actions. But, where inhumanity is the result of external circumstances and influences warping the mind, we should be careful to condemn the act but to understand the actor. Above all, we should condemn the social environments and the individuals and classes who have caused ordinary men and women to act against the generous and gentle impulses which are the natural expressions of social feeling.

The Myth of Original Sin

The story of original sin has been invented by theologians to explain the cruelties that exist among men. Yet these evils are not born, but are acquired in a society that denies the dignity of the individual and degrades human values below the false values of political abstractions. When men have learnt that the state and the nation are only the phantoms that mask the intention of privileged classes, when they realise fully that mutual respect between individuals is the only basis on which a peaceful society can be built, they will gain a sufficient sense of the value of human happiness to abandon the brutality that is bred in a regimented world.

Before we can live in a society where brutality will be eliminated, it is necessary that we should destroy utterly those institutions of authority that have been its principal cause. But we should be careful in the process not ourselves to become brutal. We should destroy where it is necessary, but only because it is necessary, and we should do it without any feelings of revenge towards what we destroy. The revolution that develops ruthless and brutal methods is already on the way to becoming another tyranny, for it is through this diminution of our feeling for others that lack of respect for individual liberty comes in, and thence the acceptance of authority. We must learn from the ironic triumph which the Nazis have achieved in their hour of destruction, the triumph of seeing their enemies adopting the brutal Nazi rule of conduct.

16th June 1945   GEORGE WOODCOCK

Open the Prisons!

It is significant that the most outstanding institution of modern states is the political police. Italy was the country of the Ovra, Germany of the Gestapo, Russia of the GPU, all dreaded bodies whose names filled people with visions of deportation, prisons, concentration camps, cross-examinations accompanied by beatings, summary executions, refined tortures.

Never, as in the modern state, whether fascist or democratic, have the police been so numerous, the prisons absorbed such a considerable portion of the population, the spying system been so widespread. The concentration camp designed to accommodate prisoners numbering hundreds of thousands has superseded the prison which proved insufficient for Governments who had to put millions of people in prison to maintain their rule.

The horror of concentration camps, this creation of the last few decades, of a civilisation where individual freedom has lost every meaning, has made people indifferent to the horror of the prisons. Yet prisons are increasing in number and absorbing, as statistics have proved, an ever increasing number of prisoners and though the sufferings they inflict may not compare with those of certain concentration camps, they are steadily undermining the health and mind of the men and women condemned to live in them.

It is time we became aware of this cancer at the heart of our society; it is time we realised that prisons are not only tragically harmful to those imprisoned in them but to every one of us, because the fear they inspire forces us to compromises, to cowardices, to betrayals which are unworthy of free men.

The prisons and concentration camps of Germany are being emptied of the political prisoners who have filled them during long years of oppression. Buchenwald and Dachau will soon be empty monuments to the cruelty of a ruthless government. The Allies are proud of the way the evacuation of these camps is carried out. But in Britain, in America and in Russia political prisoners are not 'liberated'. Socialists, pacifists, anarchists who have been sent to prison for holding the same views as their comrades of Buchenwald have to remain in prison.

They don't receive any publicity. When a fascist like Joyce goes to jail, newspapers are filled with stories about him and photographs of him, of his wife, of his cell windows, etc., etc. But the thousands of people who have gone to jail for being opposed to the war, whether for political or moral reasons like CO's or for a dislike of the army, of discipline and the war, like deserters, are forgotten.

When the resistance movements in France finally succeeded in liberating themselves from Nazi occupation, in several towns, the population stormed the prisons and threw the doors wide open. In England, in the day of victory, not a single voice was raised in favour of liberating all those who had been imprisoned during the war. No political party, no parliamentary candidate, no newspaper has taken upon itself to ask for an amnesty. Not only are prisoners left to their fate but every day men are condemned to years of imprisonment for desertion and similar offences arising out of war regulations.

There has been only one protest against the excessive number of prisoners and it has, ironically enough, come from an association of prison warders who find themselves so overworked that they beg the courts not to send so many people to jail.

We cannot dismiss the thought of people in prison by merely declaring that there is nothing we can do about it. Past experience has proved that amnesties can be imposed on the government by popular movements. When amnesties have not been granted, prisons have been forced open as in Spain where in 1936, in particular, prisoners were liberated all over the country by the spontaneous action of the people. On a smaller scale, we have seen recently in the case of John Connor that it was possible to obtain the release of a man providing public opinion is sufficiently vigilant.

Prisons must be fought. They must be fought by a constant agitation for the release of prisoners. They must be fought by direct action, as when the building workers of Barcelona went on strike rather than work on the construction of a new prison. They must not merely be emptied but utterly destroyed, their stones scattered away. Not only are prisons symbols of oppression which must disappear in a free society but one must also remember that, though the revolution will render them useless the counter revolution may soon fill them again.

The French people will soon commemorate the taking of the Bastille, the first act of liberation of the Great French revolution, in other countries too that date will be remembered and lip service paid to justice and freedom. But the only way of serving the cause of freedom would be to repeat the action of the revolutionaries of 1789 and open the prisons all over the world.

The immediate task now is for the workers to impose a complete amnesty by protest meetings, by demonstations, by direct action in the factories. If this were achieved it would be a great victory for the working class, a victory over the bosses' mightiest weapon, the prison and its servants. It would be the first step towards that society where men would be truly free because their freedom would be shared by all.

30th June 1945

'Kill Them Like Flies'

'Kill them like flies — treat them like insects — kill — will — kill them.' 'Them' are the Japanese, the Japs, the last enemies of civilisation. And they *are* just flies: General Slim himself, commander of the British troops in Burma, said so.

The allies bombed Germany into dust, they surrounded armies, killed men and took prisoners. But they are forced to *learn* how to fight the Japanese — with flame-throwers and incendiaries, hand grenades and daggers. In the Marshalls, in the mid-Pacific, tens of thousands of Japanese soldiers have been isolated for almost two years on small atolls just above the level of the ocean. They die from starvation and epidemics like flies. Meanwhile Super-Fortresses bomb Japan, burning down whole cities. The RAF dropped on Berlin 1,500 tons of explosives at a time: the US bombers hurl 4,500 tons of incendiaries on Tokyo at each visit . . . Civilisation is on the march.

The Japanese war-lords are no angels, of course. They are cruel and bestial, and there may be some truth in the accounts of atrocities committed against allied soldiers and of the killing of prisoners. For many years the Japanese have raped, sacked, burned China; they have tortured in Burma and the Philippines; they will continue to do so. It is true that they have no respect for their own lives, nor for the lives of their enemies, but then they do not say: "We fight for civilisation". The Japanese never signed the Geneva Convention, they do not want to be prisoners of war. In Japan a prisoner is a dead man — his family mourns him, he is dishonoured. So it is logical that in New Guinea Japanese soldiers should be hiding out, whilst in Burma they retreat dying.

Death is everywhere in Asia. The war there has no other meaning than extermination — extermination in the most cruel, inhuman way possible. We make no choice: twenty years ago Chiang Kai Shek burned his political opponents in railway engines, today his is the stronghold of culture and humanity. The Japanese will continue to kill and to die, for no one can exterminate a people of one hundred millions, no one can kill a hundred million flies.

Yes, civilisation is on the march. They will send thousands of Super-Fortresses to level the cities of Japan. Hundreds of thousands, millions of soldiers and civilians will die. The horrors of the war in Europe will appear as a pretty fairy-tale if the real show is put on in the Pacific. Here is a good slogan for the manufacturers of insecticides: "Kill Japs and die for it". After all, it is all in the name of civilisation.

30th June 1945

Stalin's 'Left' Turn

Another Political Trick

It seems clear to-day, with the defeat of the German army and the unconditional surrender of the Reich, that none of the major problems of European politics have been solved by the victorious powers. The inevitable contradictions which have been foreseen during the war by a revolutionary minority cannot remain hidden any longer from the public by official and unanimous declarations or promises of a wonderful peaceful world.

Only a few days after the final act of the European war, when the VE-Day celebrations were still going on, when the flags of the United Nations were still displayed in all the public places of Great Britain, France and the USA, the reactionary press of America started to call a war with Soviet Russia inevitable, pointing out that Europe cannot be reconstructed so long as it is dominated by the evil power of Russian Imperialism. At the same time the Soviet papers started a campaign, which still continues, to prove that the Western Allies are collaborating with the big shots of the Nazi régime and to point out that the liquidation of the German Army must be parallel with the extermination of the last survivors of the Nazi régime.

Behind these accusations by the Soviet press and radio lies something quite different. Stalin has once more surprised the world with one of those somersaults of policy which are possible only if you have absolutely no public opinion to reckon with, if all liberty of thought and of expression have been carefully suppressed beforehand.

The trend of the Soviet foreign policy appears now to be concentrating on one major objective: the neutralisation of Continental Europe. It has always been clear to the Russians that to dominate Europe they must dominate Germany, exactly as it is necessary for Germany to dominate Russia in order to keep its position in Europe and the world.

In other words, Stalin would like a friendly Germany, while the western powers are not interested for the time being in the friendship of the German people, and seem to have in mind to exploit themselves the industrial power of the Reich rather than to build up a new German economy.

The British, Americans and French have decided to bring

'order' into defeated Germany, even by means of 'collaboration' with the most reactionary German elements. The Russians are able to establish order by themselves, for the GPU can take care of any internal opposition. There need not be collaboration. Indeed, the fear of Russia still prevailing among many Germans, particularly the bourgeoisie, makes collaboration with reactionary elements difficult for the present. Stalin knows this, and that is why he decided to enter Germany as a 'liberator', while Churchill and Roosevelt spoke of 'conquering'. It is true that the Russian policy during the war was ostensibly one of conquest and of domination. But, now the war is over, Stalin starts to try to win over the German people, to convince them of the necessity of co-operation with 'mighty Russia'. This is the scheme.

First, conditions of life must be improved. The food rations in Russian-occupied Germany are increased (at least temporarily). The reconstruction work is done with the greatest possible speed. The Berlin underground is running. The shops are opening. Cinemas are featuring Russian pictures. The orchestras are playing once more — Tchaikovsky has replaced Wagner. At the same time the radio stations are again on the air. The propaganda from the Berlin stations starts to 'prove' that the Russians have only the best intentions towards the German people, and announcers with German accents ask the listeners to thank the Red Army for liberation from the Nazi yoke. Here is a typical item:

"One Miss Ursel Friedman says: 'Now we know what lies the Goebbels propaganda told about the Red Army. Not only shall we not starve, but the working man gets more than under the Nazis. All this is a revelation to us. We are simply amazed. We shall want to work in any case. It is now up to us to organise the distribution of work swiftly and efficiently. We all see rolling past us the Red Army lorries carrying food to the German population. Altogether a new life is beginning. We have started on the way towards a better world. Even theatres have reopened. Things are looking brighter and they will look brighter still'."

(Berlin Radio, 18th May 1945)

At the same time the new German municipal administration of Berlin takes over. General Barjanin, Soviet Commander of Berlin, pointed out during the opening session of the council that "Marshal Stalin has long ago ordered the preparation of food for German civilians". It seems that Stalin took this measure at the same time as his spokesman Ehrenburg spoke of the awful 'Fritz', the Hun who will have to pay for the Nazi crimes.

So far everything seems clear. The Russian government wants a 'friendly' Germany. So it shows the 'humanitarian' and 'liberal' aspect of the Soviet régime. M. Mikoyan, Deputy-Chairman of the Council of People's Commissars of the USSR, i.e. Deputy to Stalin himself, recently made a tour to study the food situation in occupied Germany, especially in Berlin and Dresden. On his return to Moscow he gave an interview to *Pravda*. Here is what the 'communist' had to say:

"The seriousness of the German food situation is mainly die to the German Government's mistaken policy in agricultural production and distribution. According to the German law the peasants had to deliver all their produce to the State except for a certain quantity they could keep for their own use. They could not sell any grain, fats, meat or potatoes on the free market or through trade organisations. This naturally weakened the stimulus towards increasing production. To enable Germany to feed her own towns, the peasants must be allowed to sell in the free market after fulfilling the compulsory deliveries to administrative organs. Trade in any articles of mass consumption was previously forbidden in Germany and the population had to be content with the very few wares they were given on ration cards. To improve the population's supplies the Soviet Command has allowed free trade in Berlin. This will be another way to raise the standard of living of the urban population."

It will also be another way to return to the most classic system of capitalism. A few years ago M Mikoyan would have been shot as a traitor to the 'progressive' Soviet régime of trade control and of suppression of the 'Kulak' or enriched peasant.

The Russian policy in Germany, the policy of 'friendship' with the German people is only one of the features of the scheme set up by Stalin to form the European bloc to protect the Soviet Union. What Stalin is doing now is a 'cordon sanitaire in reverse'. This cordon sanitaire must of course include countries such as Poland, Czechoslovakia, Austria, Yugoslavia, not to mention Hungary, Bulgaria and Rumania. It is in connection with the formation of this bloc of Central and East European countries, that there appears the 'new' formula of Soviet policy. In fact it is not new at all, as we shall see in a moment.

In his order of the day, announcing the capitulation of the German armies, Stalin spoke of the "historic struggle of the Slav peoples". A few days later, 19th May 1945, one of the Stalinist agents, M. Zdenek Nejedly, Education Minister of Czechoslovakia, emphasised the meaning of this historic sentence. He said in his first speech upon his return to Prague: "I return from Moscow as Minister of Education, firmly convinced that the destiny of the nation, liberty and civilisation have been defended by the Red Army . . . The most important fact for us is that, in the future Europe, the leading role will belong to the Slav nations. The Slav idea, vague in times of Kolkar, has to-day become a reality. The Slav nations, centred around the great Russian nation, represent a force which no European coalition can oppose."

As I said, the idea is not new. Replace, for instance, the word 'Slav' by the word 'Germanic' and see if it does not remind you of something . . .

So to-day, in the month of the 'most crushing victory in human history', power blocs are already forming. I have attempted to analyse the trend of the Soviet foreign policy as it appears now.

Of course, the British and the Americans are preparing to counter these moves. They have their own interests and their own plans. It is perhaps too early to speak of the results which the logical development of the situation may bring. There is not always much logic in traditional politics. But the movements which can overthrow régimes, can also upset foreign policies.
2nd June 1945

DIMITRI TVERDOV

ADMIRALS & CANNIBALS

From an obituary of Admiral McLain, who died of a heart attack, published in the New York *Herald Tribune*, 7th September 1945, under the title 'War Strain Kills', we detach the following passage: "He fought the Japanese as a man who hated them. Once he recommended 'killing them all — painfully', and at the peace he expressed his fears over a situation in which, he said, 'the Jap war lords are not half licked yet. They're going to take a lot more killing in the future. I don't like the look in their eyes'.

He never lacked for colourful, picturesque language with which to describe his enemy. Asked, once, on a radio programme what he thought should be done about a Japanese by-passed island, he replied, 'Oh, let the little (mumble) stay there. They're the type that will eat themselves'.

This should be read in connection with the horrifying stories of cannibalism amongst Japanese which we quoted in the last issue of *Freedom*. American admirals delighted in driving Japanese to cannibalism and then Allied journalists denounced them as yellow beasts!

THE ELECTIONS OF 1945

Vote — What For?

At last, after a decade during which a parliament elected to maintain peace has fought the bloodiest war in history against the principal imperialist rival of the British ruling class, and a hardly less ruthless war against the liberties of the British workers, we are told that the revered constitution of Britain will once more be taken out of the cupboard; the people will again have the pleasure of electing whichever gang of politicians is to filch away their freedom and prepare by power politics for the next world conflict in which they or their sons will die.

Before we go on to discuss the particular issues of this forthcoming election, it is perhaps desirable to enquire *why* it is being held at this time. The ostensible reason for the election is the decision of the Labour Party conference to end the coalition immediately and to withdraw the Labour Ministers from the National Government. This decision was made because Churchill had sent an 'ultimatum' to the Labour Party putting forward the alternatives of either continuing the Coalition to the end of the Japanese war or ending it immediately. It is interesting to note that neither side is willing to accept the responsibility for the decision. The Conservative leaders and their press blame the Labour Party for not accepting the offer to continue the Coalition to the end of the Japanese war. The Labour leaders and their press blame the Conservatives for putting the Labour Party on the spot by making the alternative between an immediate election and an indefinitely long Coalition which the Labour rank-and-file would not be willing to support. These earnest attempts to pass the buck imply a recognition of the distrust which the politicians expect will be awakened in the average elector as a result of this sudden precipitation of the country into an election at a time when the maximum disorganisation still exists and when a very high proportion of the electorate will not be able to vote.

The Trojan Horse

In fact, there is reason to believe that the leaders of both parties
were equally to blame for the springing of the election at this time,
and that the apparent causes were largely manufactured. It is
reasonable to suppose that Churchill's Labour colleagues were
fully aware that Churchill was about to produce his so-called
'ultimatum', and that they had given at least tacit agreement.
Certainly, given the mood of discontent among the rank-and-file
of the Labour Party, the decision to break up the Coalition
immediately instead of carrying it on indefinitely was a foregone
conclusion, and it seems probable that the Labour Party
Conference was quite deliberately chosen as the Trojan horse by
which the idea of an election could be brought to the people.
Obviously, the workers are less likely to be suspicious of an
election if it is demanded by a body claiming to represent the
working class in general, than if it is dictated by the first of a
largely discredited government.

Given the probability that the election decision was 'managed'
by an agreement between the leaders of all parties, we have still to
discover their reason for such a precipitate election. The principal
function of the election seems to be that of diverting the attention
of the workers from the immediate problems and issues of their
daily life, about which they are already showing a great deal of
discontent, and to provide a safety valve which will prevent them
from resorting to really effective methods for changing their
conditions and bringing about their liberation from the state of
military and industrial slavery in which they live. In the
background move the sinister developments of European power
politics, from which the politicians are no doubt very anxious to
divert the immediate attentions of the people under their control.

It is obvious that, after the neurotic outbursts of relief on VE
Day, the people of Britain are rapidly coming to realise just how
phoney the peace is. Already, on the morrow of so-called victory,
food rations have been cut once again, and we are informed that
fewer clothes will be available, while cigarettes have gone into
short supply. 'Peace', for the time being at any rate, seems to be a
leaner condition than war, and in the meantime, the process of
release from military and industrial conscription appears to be
scheduled to last for a good many years before it is finally ended.
Meanwhile, the housing shortage becomes steadily more acute,
and the tensions within industry, which were largely suppressed by

such collaborationist institutions as the joint production committees, are steadily coming to a head.

After six years of war the workers expect something concrete.
They are not likely to be put off for very long with such sops as the
ending of the blackout, the abolition of the regulation against
leaving oars in boats, or the granting of small quantities of petrol
to middle-class car-owners. Already the incidence of strikes in
industry has risen, and sympathy for the strikes seems much
greater than it was during the war itself. A wide movement of
direct action, which might well assume other forms than strikes, is
what the leaders of all parties fear most of all, because it is the only
kind of movement which can directly menace their own power and
interests. Therefore they are prepared at all costs to divert the
people from such actions, and an election, which gives the illusion
of making a change in the existing set-up, and gives the ordinary
man the feeling that he is actually doing something positive
towards improving his conditions, is an obvious manoeuvre of this
kind. It is a fair certainty that the pretence of party struggle which
an election arouses will provide a compensation for direct action
which will stave off trouble for at least some months after the
election.

Fear of Responsibility
The fact that many of the people nominally entitled to vote will in
fact not be able to do so is probably an added reason for holding
the election at the present juncture. The majority of the people
who will be disabled from voting will be working class people who
would be more likely to vote Labour than Conservative. This fact
will give the Tories a fair chance of winning and a certainty, at the
worst, of being in a large minority. It will also satisfy the
disinclination of the Labour leaders to take power on their own
responsibility. If Labour win the election, it is probable that their
majority will be so slight that they can only hold power with the
help of some centre group, and already the idea of a Lib-Lab
coalition is being canvassed. This would be a very pleasant
solution for the Labour leaders, because they would be able to
enjoy the fruits of power, while they could always blame
circumstances or the Liberals for their failure to bring about any
positive improvements in the conditions of the working class.
Indeed, such a solution would probably help the Tories as well, for
they in turn could make a powerless Socialist government the
scapegoat for any oppressive measure the ruling class found

necessary in a situation of post-war turmoil, just as the German Social-Democrats were made to take the responsibility for the crushing of the genuine working-class movements of post-1918 Germany.

What, in fact, is the choice offered in the election to the workers of this country? The Tories speak with a number of voices, to suit every taste. Beaverbrook and his followers talk loudly of the elimination of all controls, by which, of course, they mean the elimination of the controls which wartime managerialism has imposed on individual capitalism. They do not, however, advocate the elimination of that most evil control of individual liberty, military conscription. The 'Left' Conservatives, led by such figures as Quintin Hogg, talk of limited controls, which really means that they favour the monopoly capitalist against the individual capitalist. Meanwhile, Churchill's 'caretaker' cabinet, with its array of big industrial nabobs and young scions of the peerage, is a foretaste of the kind of class cabal which a Tory victory at the polls would foist upon the people.

Labour Imperialists

The programme of the Labour Party, except for the talk of nationalising public utilities and the Bank of England, reads very like a pre-war Conservative election platform, with its demands for continued conscription and for a system of tariffs with imperial preference. Even the nationalisations advocated by the Labour Party are nothing like so drastic as those put into practice by the Nazis in Germany, and it looks as though the Labour Party are really anxious to save private capitalism from the results of its own weaknesses. We have always contended that the Labour Party is as imperialist in its fundamental interests as the Tories. We did not, however, foresee that they would admit it quite so naively.

There is nothing much to read between the lines of the political speeches and programmes. The intentions of the leaders of both parties are obvious. They intend to maintain a war-time economy and a war-time society, in peace time as well as in war, and for this purpose to suppress individual freedom as far as possible. You will find that both sides demand conscription and tariffs, which mean militarism and imperialism, which in their turn mean another war in a measurable space of time.

There is really no choice so far as the worker is concerned between good and bad in this election. The fundamental identity of the interests of politicians was never so clearly shown as at the present time. And, whichever party comes into power, the pursuit of these interests will ensure that neither peace nor freedom will be the result of their rule.

Already, in Europe, the activities of politicians are sowing the seeds of imperialist conflicts. Trieste, Piedmont, the Dodecanese, Syria, Austria, are added to the existing centres of conflict in Greece, in Poland and in Germany. The pre-war disputes over colonies are returning in the feverish atmosphere of San Francisco. And within every country, including England, the war against the common people goes on relentlessly.

Boycott the Election
The function of the election is not to give the common man the chance of deciding how this chaos shall be solved or even of how he himself shall be governed. That will be decided for him by whomever is elected, regardless of election promises or programmes. The true function of the election is to deceive him, and, by giving him a false impression of his power to change things by making a cross on a piece of paper, to divert his attention from those events in the world which would mould his life and may bring his death.

The workers should ignore the elections and keep away from the voting booths. Their liberation from want, war and oppression will not come through the phantom battles of the ballot, but through their own direct action, their own refusal to co-operate any longer in a system that sacrifices their lives to the double evils of authority and property. They can begin by boycotting the means by which their enemies try to trick them into accepting their chains; they should end only when they have destroyed the institutions in whose interests such deceptions are employed.
2nd June 1945

Anarchists and Elections

We have seen many changes in the last few weeks. The peaceful political atmosphere of the years of war has been suddenly troubled by speeches, articles, posters full of recriminations, accusations, insinuations. But the storm is only on the surface; it does not affect profoundly the majority of the population, who are too wearied by five years of war, too sceptical of political parties, too anxious about the future to care much about the election radio squabbles between Churchill and Attlee.

It is difficult to imagine that the average man can be greatly impressed or inspired by election propaganda. But it is not so difficult to guess that he feels slightly disgusted at the sudden turning of coats, at the startling revelations of the misdeeds of friends of yesterday, at the pride taken in disunity where unity had been continually maintained.

What could reinforce his scepticism more than to see Herbert Morrison suddenly charging his late cabinet colleagues with having surrendered to vested interests? And declaring in all seriousness that he had the gravest doubts about the Government using war-time emergency powers for peace purposes — a thing he would not have hesitated to do himself were he still Home Secretary!

Bevin, who on his own admission, has been repeatedly told by the gentlemen of the city what a wonderful man he was, suddenly accuses the steel ring of strangling the steel industry. The man who denounced dockers' strikes is going back to 'his docker's days, on a box at the street corner'.

A few weeks of plain speaking against opponents, of lip-service to the peoples' cause, of talk of justice and freedom, all to be forgotten once the new Parliament is elected — this is what elections mean!

Whether Labour or the Conservatives win the results will differ little, as both parties are based on a policy of exploitation of the workers by the capitalist class or the State; a policy of oppression of the Colonial people; on a Vansittartist policy as far as Germany is concerned.

It is difficult to understand how anyone can still believe that Socialism can be achieved by a socialist majority in Parliament. There have been the examples of Germany, of France, of Spain which have shown that even when a Left wing majority was achieved in Parliament the reactionaries still preserved their power. In Spain they did not hesitate to resort to armed revolt to re-establish their domination. The ruling class plays the parliamentary game as long as it does not imperil its supremacy. When it does, 'extra-parliamentary' methods are used, such as political intrigues, economic crisis, wars and armed revolts.

By playing the game of the ruling class and maintaining people's faith in Parliament the so-called socialist parties prevent people from turning to the real solution of their problems, the overthrow of the State machine and the establishment of workers' control over land and industry.

The role of the Anarchists during the elections may, at first sight, appear merely a negative one. We do not produce any candidates possessing the magic power of solving all the world's problems. We decline to acclaim and serve this wonderful man, the MP who, once in Parliament, is as Kropotkin has described him, "A veritable Proteus, omniscient and omnipotent, today a soldier and tomorrow a pigman, successively a banker, an academician, a street sweeper, doctor, astronomer, drug manufacturer, tanner or contractor according to the orders of the day in Parliament. Accustomed in his capacity as lawyer, journalist or public speaker to talk of things he knows nothing about he will vote on all these questions but, while in the newspapers he merely amused with his gossip and in the courts his voice only awoke the sleeping judges, in Parliament he will make laws for thirty or forty million inhabitants."

The Anarchists do not believe that because an airman has bombed Berlin he will be able to defend the workers' interests at Westminster; they do not believe that a successful lecturer, writer, lawyer, public speaker will solve their problems for them. They refuse to put their faith in incompetent mediocrities who, as experience has shown, once elected to Parliament will be concerned with feathering their own nests or rising to government posts.

We refuse to proclaim ourselves the saviours of the people and we also refuse to take sides in the electoral struggle. All governments, conservative or socialist, exist to defend the interests of a minority. Socialist governments like others have been the tools of the capitalist class and have often voted more reactionary measures than the Tory governments themselves. Higher wages and better conditions are not obtained by MP's as 'concessions' from the capitalist class, they are *forced* upon it by workers' agitation.

If the workers rely on their own strength and are prepared to fight with their own weapons they will soon bring the ruling class to their knees.

16th June 1945

The Election Racket

Democracy is often thought of as synonymous with freedom, but in fact democracy has more in common with dictatorship than it has with freedom, and those who talk of 'vital democracy', 'real democracy', 'social democracy' and the like, merely confuse the issue. The word means 'rule by the people' and suggests what is in actual fact the case, that in a democratic society the people have the right to choose their rulers, whereas in a dictatorial society they get the chance (if at all) only once. By choosing the people who will rule the people themselves do not exercise power, their power being solely a question of choosing which person will form the personnel of the State. Hence political parties, which only aspire to rule, find this arrangement satisfactory to get their personnel into power. It still does not make freedom. The people are still ruled whether in a dictatorial or a democratic way: the difference being usually only one of degree. Some rulers take away civil liberties (which have nothing to do with elections and are such things as freedom of the press, freedom of assembly, freedom to strike, freedom of opinion, religion and non-religion, freedom of the individual from compulsion of various kinds including conscription, slave-labour and the rest). A dictatorial state would not necessarily need to employ the violence used in Germany and Russia — this can and has existed in States with a democratic form, and contrariwise some States in a dictatorial form have not found it necessary to use so much violence as others. The violence is only necessary when there is resistance, or when the rulers are plain sadists.

It can be the case that dictatorial measures are passed and the form of choosing between rulers still remains. Elections have nothing whatever to do with freedom. One can appoint one's rulers but cannot force their actions. Resistance can stop them from doing as they wish, but so it can in any State. Our sole safeguard against loss of civil liberties is the fight we put up against infractions of civil liberty, however large or small, whatever the State is. Politicians can pass laws against the masses, and still retain the right to sit in Westminster.

The Career of Politics

All that Elections mean is there is the picking and choosing of candidates to enter the Parliamentary field. The men themselves look on it as a career, which it is, and we quite understand their choosing the most profitable career open to them consistent with their abilities. The people we fail to understand are the dumb-bells who help them on their career with such great enthusiasm. Here again we can understand the financier on the one hand and the trade union bureaucrat on the other. They want to get someone to represent their interests against encroachments of other vested interests. Their interest in Elections is plain to see. The dumb-bells are those honest, enthusiastic and willing volunteers, who take all the knocks of electioneering and see others walk off with the plums. Afterwards they get disillusioned and blame it all on to the masses being apathetic. Why the devil shouldn't they be apathetic?

We are asked to believe that the Honourable Mr So-and-So is out to do us good. We are flattered. He even shakes our hand (fancy, an Honourable and a Major too, he fought the Battle of Britain single-handed with only one typewriter). "He has served his country well in war", pleads his agent. "All he asks from you is the chance to serve his country in peace." (I wrote this thinking it sounded absurd, and then Brendan Bracken said it about the Hon Max Aitken, son of the wealthy monopolist Lord Beaverbrook). It reminds us of the famous slogan that "The rich will do anything for the poor except get off their backs". If they were honest they would say they wanted power and a career. Everybody knows it anyway, and allows for the fact even if they're electioneers. Instead, however, they are very humble and self-sacrificing, and when they advance their personal career they are 'serving'. This is simply humbug, as is shown by the scramble for seats. Every so often a constituency association says it doesn't want an MP and he stands independently of his association. Although soldiers are harassed for reading anarchist literature, there is a rush from high-rankers for seats in Parliament — we have read so often that "a high officer on Montgomery's staff" is sitting in such-and-such a constituency for any one of the three parties, that we imagine Monty's staff conferences at the Base must be more hectic than the scenes at the Front where the fighting is actually done.

Officer Politicians
The scramble by officers for seats is rather a distasteful one, more so considering it comes at a time when the ordinary soldier is forbidden to take part in politics and every endeavour is made to prevent him from having the slightest interest in the world outside his unit. Most of these officers who are newcomers to the scene

can be easily classified. There are those who are already MPs. Some of them have worked their ticket by being MPs and resigned the peace-time commission when trouble starts (like the hero in 'The Four Feathers' only they don't get any white feathers) yet retain the handle of Major, Captain, etc., which sounds good and means nothing. Some have concentrated on soldiers and done nothing as MPs simply working on staff and base jobs in the forces, and so getting 'battle honours'.

A few have actually taken an active part in the war to justify the propagandist use they make of their titles.

Next come those not yet in Parliament. There is the usual Tory complement of sons of good families who spend a time in the Army after they finish their education, and then pass on to politics, all mapped out for them by the family fortunes. Next come the largest group of all: those who have never before taken an active part in politics, but quite intelligently realise it's a good post-war business — a quick way on to the Board of Directors of any company. These small-time City businessmen have usually made a flop of their own affairs but have had a taste of power by commanding men as officers in the Army, and want to continue what they feel they have a vocation for. There are the go-ahead lawyers who feel they can use the same wangles in making laws as they can in helping to administer them. Most of these don't, however, find their way into the Army. They belong to the pool from which the candidates from Civvy Street come.

Labour Brass-Hats

The Labour Party is going in for officer-selection. They have a better chance than the Tories in selecting men with 'good war records' since the Tories choose men for coming from the wealthy strata (who may incidentally have 'good war records') whereas Labour candidates usually don't have to fish up 'expenses'. However, the Labour Party has only occasionally taken advantage of this (Common Wealth has cashed in on it more) as in the case of an Air Vice Marshal selected as Labour candidate for Newark only a few days after the *Daily Herald* had publicised a very sneering letter about the Liberals choosing an Air Vice Marshal, and so trying to cash in on his rank. The Labour candidates come mostly from the Trade Union bureaucracy — older men, who have been through the experiences of government-within-government, plus the usual lawyers, solicitors and the like. The Liberal Party specialise in the business-man with a flair for politics, plus the inevitable lawyers; the Conservatives in the scion of aristocracy, 'born to rule', and the get-rich-quicker who bought his seat after share-pushing or marrying a duke's daughter, with a sprinkling of lawyers.

All are united in one thing, namely, they all have 'chosen a career'. That career is power. So long as government exists, people will make a career of ruling the lives of other people. That is Democracy. It is a variant of Dictatorship. It is not FREEDOM. If freedom means anything at all, it means the possibility of living one's life without power at all — doing as one wishes providing one does not infringe other people's liberty. Laws and lawyers are unnecessary: politicians not wanted, whether they make a career of ruling or do it for nothing. Freedom is therefore a society in which one is without rule — that is to say, ANARCHY.
16th June 1945

Vote With Your Feet!

There is a story being related nowadays that a psycho-analyst died and by some clerical error of the celestial immigration authorities was permitted to ascend to heaven, where he was met at the gates by St Peter, apparently forewarned of his approach. Peter, puffing and blowing, and much perturbed by something, begged the psycho-analyst's assistance in treating a serious case of paranoia which had just arisen. To the analyst's query as to who was thus affected, Peter replied "It's God, I'm afraid". "Oh," said the analyst, surprised, "and of what particular delusion is His Almightiness the victim?" "It's terrible, terrible!" sighed Peter, "he's strutting around heaven, imagining he's Churchill."

This apocryphal anecdote may perhaps serve to remind us of the extraordinarily *Church-like* atmosphere surrounding our political system today, and the *God-like* attributes assumed on an increasing scale by political leaders of all factions in this country (not to mention the elaborate mythology built around the world's various Fuehrers, Duces, Caudillos, Mikados and Commissars). The most effective weapon in the armoury of organised religion in past ages (apart from the more radical expedients of torture-chamber and the stake and faggots) in its divine mission of persuading the people to recognise its hegemony over their physical and spiritual lives and destinies, was the convenient fact, much emphasised by theological pundits throughout the centuries, that acceptance of the Christian faith and belief in the reality of its various hierarchies of gods, saints, archangels, angels, cherubims, devils, demons, ghosts, hob-goblins and other taradiddles and fol-de-rols in no way depended upon a rational understanding of the dogmas of christianity. No indeed! The divine mysteries of the christian faith were to be shrouded in a permanent and impenetrable fog for the ordinary mortal: in fact, the mere application of his faculties of reasoning and analysis to the claims and taboos of christianity would in itself render him gravely liable to a charge of heresy with its attendant punishments.

The truth of religion was declared in advance to be unassailable by its professional exponents, and to enforce the peoples' acceptance of the Church every means was used to coerce them into support, or at least passive toleration, of its dictates. Just as physical obedience was enforced by the threat of rack or flames, so mental obedience was ensured by the fact that reason was only tolerated in so far as it applied itself to the task of justifying and elaborating the Church's dogmas.

Then, in the eighteenth century came the downfall of God. In the prolonged battles of that era between the established Church and the new 'enlightened' State, the Church received a decisive and permanent defeat; from that time on, power over the lives and destinies of mankind was vested in the hands of the State and its own particular hierarchies of presidents, premiers, dictators, statesmen, politicians, diplomats, police officials, magistrates and military officers. The *idols and images* of religion were relegated to the hearth and the chapel — a subsidiary and comparatively unimportant cog in the repressive mechanisms of the State machine.

The Deification of the State

Slowly but surely, the State and its appendages began itself to assume a pseudo-divine status, for the overthrow of God did not in itself do away with the spiritual subjection of mankind: were people to develop a sense of independence and self-reliance, a desire for absolute freedom, the results would have been as fatal to the new secular State as they previously been to the old Church

State. So the same formula was adopted by capitalist democracy —
reason was only tolerated in so far as it accepted the basic
proposition of the infallibility of the governmental system, the
sanctity of parliamentary institutions and the eternal necessity of
political leadership. Reason might do almost anything — *except*
protest against the whole monstrous edifice of this new Secular
Church; and out of the capitalist system emerged the new heretic,
as well-hated by authority and as ostracised by bourgeois morality
as was the atheist in earlier ages — the revolutionary anarchist.
For he had committed the unpardonable sin in the eyes of society,
he had asserted his will to freedom and his negation of all
authority; consequently the most strenuous efforts of the State
were reserved to oppose and suppress the dangerous heresy of
anarchism.

With the gradual degeneration of the capitalist system, authority
found it necessary to combat more fiercely still this idea of
absolute freedom (in reality the *only* freedom) which had budded
and flowered in the anarchist movement and presented an
increasingly menacing alternative to the weed-bed of authoritarian
society. As the effeteness and retrogressive nature of capitalist
economy became more and more transparent, despite all efforts at
camouflage by the ruling classes, it was clearly perceived by
statesmen and politicians that something more was needed to
bolster up people's slowly waning confidence in the inevitability of
the governmental system.

Divine Leaders

"In human form do men create their gods and with human
qualities do they endow them, that so no sphere of man's activity
may be outlawed from divine sanction." With exactly similar aims
to those of the creators of religions, the leaders of the State
concerned themselves increasingly to surround the figures and
institutions of government with an air of divinity and a halo of
religious zeal and pure disinterestedness: "in divine form do men
create their political leaders" so that ultimately no thought or
action may be free from the dictates of the State. In fact,
politicians have attempted desperately to create a myth of duty
and responsibility towards the people in order to conceal the
patently callous opportunism of their lust for power; in the words
of André Breton, the surrealist writer: "They claim to be on the
side of good sense, wisdom and order, the better to satisfy their
ignoble appetites, exploit men, prevent them from liberating

themselves — that they may the better degrade and destroy men by means of ignorance, poverty and war".

Never has this parade of wolves in priests' clothing assumed larger or more absurdly hysterical proportions than now. Never has so motley a harlequinade postured before the people as at the present day, when, with eyes cast to heaven and their respective 'bibles' clasped reverently in their hands, the political parties prance demurely before us, eager to solicit our benediction and alms so that they may recline comfortably for a few years in the benign climate of parliament house, council chamber and committee room, all emphatic in their protestations of concern for the happiness and welfare of mankind, all proffering unique panaceas whose efficacy they will guarantee if only you will put them in power first!

The gods, popes and bishops of other ages must look down with approbation at the sight of these new disciples, united above their bickerings in one determination: to prevent the people from achieving that freedom which is the natural goal of mankind. In this respect the Tory Church, Liberal Church, Labour Church, Socialist Church and Communist Church are as united fundamentally as were the Catholics, Protestants, Lutherans, Calvinists, Mormons, Catharists, Puritans or Four Square Gospellers. No division between religious sects was ever greater than their unity against freedom of thought; nor is any division between political parties greater than their unity against the concept of individual freedom and all that it implies.

Reject all Gods
We shall in a few weeks be given the Hobson's choice of submission to authority, the choice between one professional parasite and another — the choice of a condemned man between rope, axe and bullet. Is it too much to hope that people will at last *reject* the choice between different evils, and will finally consign all gods and their bastard offspring, politicians, to the dust-bin in the same terms as did André Breton when he remarked: "*I have always wagered against God*, and I regard the little that *I have won* in this world as simply the outcome of this bet. The stake (my life) has been so ridiculous that I am conscious of having won to the full. Everything that is doddering, squint-eyed, infamous, sullying and grotesque is contained for me in this single word: God."

Can we not make that same wager against *human authority* in equally unequivocal terms, conscious of the fact that if we win, the

prize is nothing less than liberty? No ballot box will give us that liberty, though all political parties would endow it with the same apparently miraculous functions as the top-hat from which the conjuror draws rabbits and watches. Only by delivering a well-directed, determined and powerful kick in the backside of all gods, governments and dictators can liberty be realised. And now seems a particularly appropriate time. *Let us vote with our feet!*
16th June 1945   SIMON WATSON TAYLOR

Yer Pays Yer Penny . . .

Speaking at Paddington in support of his protégée Brendan Bracken (15th June 1945), Lord Beaverbrook, the Number One decoy duck of the Tories who is drawing all the Left fire from Churchill on to himself, said: "If ever a man has been maligned, misinterpreted, misreported and attacked, I am that man." This was rather a bold statement for Maxie, as his newspaper combine has been doing that sort of thing for donkey's years. His reporters are constitutionally incapable of putting down one statement correctly when spoken by his political sparring-partners. If Mr Bevin only said "I am a member of the Labour party" the *Daily Express* would not get it correct but be obliged to alter the word 'Labour' to 'Socialist' in Bevin's mouth.

Labour Party
However, in spite of distaste for this crookedness, one must admit that the Labour Party would do better to call itself socialist. This annoys the left sectarians who are insistent that it is only a Labour Party, but the fact must be faced that Labour has left that stage behind. Its origins were clearly as a *labour* party — it was the political wing of the trade union movement. Gradually, with the rise of the ILP and other Socialist elements, it took on a definite social-democratic character. The popularity of the Labour Party in working-class districts has often rested on its representatives — men like the late George Lansbury, Will Thorne, now retiring at 87, the late Fred Jowett of the ILP, were representative workers

who rose up, and however one may disagree with the reformist leadership of the old Labour Party, there is no doubt at all of its specific representative working-class nature. This is not altogether gone; from the trade union movement many figures have risen up (Bevin being the obvious one at the moment), but that period of the Labour Party's history is vanishing. The new generation that has come forward in the Labour Party is of another nature altogether. Hannen Swaffer has been making the point for a long time that the Tories had no right to call themselves 'national' — and now the *Daily Herald* re-echoes with the cry that only Labour is the national party, the Tories representing only one class. The contention is that if you want to vote 'national', you have to vote Labour, and its service candidates up to the ranks of Air Vice Marshall and Lieutenant-General and Commander nearly burst their blood-vessels at Churchill's suggestion that they weren't 'national'.

In a press statement (14th June 1945) Mr Morgan Phillips, secretary of the Labour Party, made the following points as summed up in the *Daily Herald*:

"More than 130 of the candidates have served in the forces in this war. Others served in the last.

They include nearly all ranks from private to lieutenant-general, stoker to commander, and aircraftman to air vice-marshall.

Never has any party been more truly national in its appeal to the country. Of a list of 350 candidates whose careers were published yesterday, more than 120 are university graduates.

No fewer than 105 have held managerial and other high business posts, or public positions other than those in local government.

There are 31 professors, headmasters and lecturers, 43 barristers, solicitors and doctors, and 161 with experience in local government.

Of the 597, only 150 are sponsored by trade unions and co-operative societies.

Of these, more than 100 have had higher or secondary education.

More than 50 have held ministerial posts and would form the nucleus of a Labour Government."

'Left Unity'

Well, that sums up the positions of the Labour Party. It no longer even claims to be a working-class party. That being so, why all the talk about working-class unity? In fact, even that is dropped — the politicians now talk of 'left unity' which is even taken to include the Liberals, who can't even muster a plain 'mister' for their election broadcasts. The Liberal Party in this country was always an

upper-class movement. The original cleavage between Whigs and
Tories was not essentially on class grounds (in fact the Whigs
contained the oldest aristrocratic families) but on the question of
the monarchy. The Whigs defeated the Tories and brought in the
Hanover dynasty. When the Tories finally accepted this
monarchy, they got back into power and kept out the Whigs, who
began to take over the Liberal principles gaining ascendancy
outside Parliament, especially Parliamentary reform, in order to
increase the number of voters, and thus reduce the Tory chances in
Parliament. The struggle of the 19th century to enlarge the
franchise was between Whigs who developed under Gladstone
into the Liberal Party, and the Tories, who were developed under
Disraeli into the Conservative Party. Even the electoral reforms
were not exclusively Whig. Disraeli 'dished the Whigs' by
extending the franchise himself, when the Tories were in a
minority. The theory they both worked on was that whoever
enlarged the franchise got the votes of the new voters, and both
competed to gain popular support by reforms, since in those days
expanding Imperialism had reforms to offer. With the growth of
trade unionism, in those days a force that could gain reforms under
expanding capitalism (which it cannot do any longer), more
reforms were squeezed out of the ruling-class at a time when the
Liberals were in the ascendancy. Contrary to predictions, the
Liberal Party did not become wholly middle-class; nor the
Conservatives wholly upper-class. They both competed for the two
strata of society, and angled for working-class support by promises
only. Lloyd George got popular by introducing the dole — maybe
Woolton will get the same credit for introducing rationing!

The Liberal Party was finally wrecked in the last war.

Since Lloyd George left office it has not resumed power, and
has split in various ways, some climbing on to one bandwagon and
some on to another, some forming the phoney Liberal National
party of Conservatives in disguise, and some deciding they were
Socialists after all. There still remains the independent Liberal
Party. It has more candidates this election than for years, for the
simple reason that there are more candidates this election than for
years — so many businessmen having been out of their
accustomed routine in officer's uniform, and seeking now a quick
way to demobilisation and an ascertained post-war career.

The independent Liberals' reputation for being 'Left' is based
wholly on their foreign policy. The majority were Popular
Frontists in the days when that flourished, the *News Chronicle* in

particular having a reputation for Stalinised Liberalism. At home the 'Liberal' capitalists have taken no steps to earn any such 'progressive' denominations, and the reason they took a 'progressive' line on foreign affairs (in the Left Book Club sense of the word) is quite simply explained by the fact that there they had no power to back their statements by deeds.

The fictitious halo cast by the ever-credulous 'Left' — even parties like the ILP, let alone the Government itself — on the Beveridge Scheme, for better doles, has enabled Sir William Beveridge to revive the Liberal hopes. But with 300 candidates in 640 seats they have no hopes whatever of being the alternative Government. The next premier will be Churchill or a Labour man. All the Liberals hope to do is to increase their parliamentary representation, and we fail to see how this is expected to solve any problems. The old ironic phrase about 'His Majesty's Opposition' became reality when the leader of the opposition was given a governmental salary in 1938, and the Liberals are going to the country with that as their *aim*.

We cannot refrain from pointing out that all the minor parties, like the ILP (confined to a few old strongholds), Common Wealth (typically confined to middle-class districts only) even the Communist Party, who attack us for being irresponsible in opposing voting, are merely making a joke of their participation in the elections by aiming at merely strengthening their parliamentary representation, thus putting up a few candidates here and there, with the aim of having a dozen instead of a handful of Parliamentary representatives. They support Labour candidates in every other district, however! The exception proving the rule is that Mr D. N. Pritt is getting Communist backing at Hammersmith against the official Labour candidate, although Mr Pritt is horrified at the suggestion of his being a Communist — he merely supports them on every line, deviation, dot and comma, but apart from that he is a loyal supporter of the Labour Party and can't understand why they expelled him. (Curiously enough, Mr Maurice Edelman and Mr Tom Driberg are official Labour candidates though they can hardly be said to differ much from Mr Pritt on the Russian question.)

The main Communist contribution to the election appears to be organised interruption going right beyond any bounds of decent heckling. In the main they do it to Tories, but also to Labour speakers opposing Communists. Typical Communist Party tactics, of which we ourselves have had experience.

Lord Beaverbrook seems to try to mollify Communist Party hecklers by his notorious pro-Stalinism (but he's off the party line now) and asking voters "to send back Stalin's buddy, Churchill".

Tory lie
The general line of the Conservatives is to adulate Churchill. It is good to know there is one old-age pensioner they care about, anyway. His poster looks down on us everywhere (he has the fortunate habit of losing about ten years on his photographs and at least twenty on his portraits — on some of them the hair on his head even grows again). It is difficult to see why his opponents claim it is unfair for him to use the publicity they shoved on him between 1940 and 1945. They knew his character well enough, his record of pro-fascism from 1923 to 1940 as regards Italy, and 1933 to 1938 as regards Germany, and yet allow him to get away with the pretence that he "foresaw everything". They pushed him into the limelight for the simple reason that they were supporting a war without a principle, and therefore fell back on the old expedient of praising one leader, and blaming another, reducing the world situation to a Churchill, a Hitler, a Roosevelt, a Mussolini, a Stalin, as if such 'great' men were any more than what Tolstoy called them — "tickets of history", just the label on the bottle of poison.

Behind Churchill's banner (trade union as it were) sadly the Big Business representatives, and society idlers, in uniform for the duration. The *Daily Express* angle on the elections is illuminating — it harps on "giving youth a chance" and assistance to servicemen running for Parliament. Now the vast mass of youth and of servicemen have no such opportunities. They ask us to give such opportunities to a very small minority. But why? If they are out to 'do the public good' one might say that people 'with a good war record' are the last people to choose — "they've done their bit in the war, now let someone else do the work" might be the reply. But that is nonsense because the *Daily Express* like the candidates themselves and everyone else bar the enthusiastic volunteers, who do the real work of the election, knows that these people aren't out to 'do the public good' primarily, even though in many cases they believe they will, but are out for a career.

A 'human story' in the *Daily Mirror* sums up the matter perfectly. Mr Robert Boothby, Conservative MP (who was told off once by Mr Churchill for being over-enthusiastic about the defence of Czechoslovakia in 1938 as it became known Mr

Boothby had financial interests in Czechoslovakia — we poor fools couldn't see why the entire bunch weren't similarly reprimanded for being over-enthusiastic about the defence of Britain in 1940); is engaged to a Swedish Hollywood scriptwriter, who is attacked in the US press as a pro-Nazi propagandist. The lady told the reporters that if Bob were elected she would marry him, but if he were not elected she would not, as she would feel then that she had ruined his career and she would always feel a reproach for it, as after all, "a man's career comes first".

It's all very true and all very touching, but why *do* they pretend to be altruists?
30th June 1945   A. M.

The Anarchist Movement in Scotland

"Vote — Not Me": this inscription seen on the walls of a Glasgow factory gives an idea of the attitude of the Glasgow workers towards politicians and governments. They are increasingly aware that their problems will not be solved through party politics but through their own action in the workshops. The propaganda which our comrades have tirelessly carried out during the past few years is, in no small degree, responsible for this healthy attitude of the workers.

Meetings both outdoors and indoors are extremely well attended and the most popular ones are those held at factory gates in the lunch hour. It is always with great reluctance that the meeting breaks up when the time to go back to work arrives. Meetings are held at Steven's Yard on the Monday; Royal Ordnance Factory, Dalmuir, on the Tuesday; at Barclay Curle's and Jarrow's on the Wednesday. Meetings have also been held at John Brown's shipyard where the Communists gave our comrades a rather hostile reception. This did not prevent the crowd from being about 1,000 strong.

On the Sunday no less than six open air meetings are held: at Shettleston at 3.00pm, Maxwell Street at 7.00pm, Brunswick Street the whole afternoon, Jail Square at Paisley from 7.00pm, Hamilton Cross at Burnbank at 7.00pm and on the Mound at Edinburgh from 3.00pm. All meetings are very well attended, particularly in Brunswick and Maxwell Street, where the police had to interfere a few weeks ago as the crowd was preventing the traffic from following its usual course. Our comrades are able to hold all these meetings thanks to a particularly good team of open air speakers who think nothing of spending three hours on the platform speaking and answering questions. Eddie Shaw, Jimmy Raeside, Frank Leech, Jimmy Dick, Eddie Fenwick, Dennis McGlynn and many others take the platform regularly.

The influence of anarchist ideas is worrying the Communist Party, who put the rumour round that the anarchists are being paid by the Tories to prevent the Communist candidate for Glasgow Central Division from sailing into Westminster. Strangely enough, the Tories do not show any gratitude towards the anarchists. In fact, they were very worried about the lack of enthusiasm for the polling booths displayed by Clydeside workers. *The Daily Record*, Scotland's foremost morning paper (Kemsley Press Ltd.) came out with the headlines: "Use your vote, for lose or win, apathy is the blackest sin". The Tory press knows full well of course that the lack of interest in the elections is not a sign of apathy but a manifestation of the people's disgust in the various political parties. The anarchists did not urge the workers to adopt a merely passive attitude towards elections, and posters were put up declaring "Don't Vote. Organise to take over industries", "Government is for slaves. Free men govern themselves". On election day they toured the Glasgow streets with the loudspeaker, exposing politics and politicians, and advising workers to stop using their votes and start using their brains.

The fruitful growth of anarchist activities in Glasgow should be an encouragement to comrades in other parts of the country who at present may appear to be working solitarily and to little obvious purpose. What has been done in Glasgow can be emulated elsewhere — there is nothing in the Clydeside air that makes it the only place where libertarian ideas can flourish. The large and growing anarchist movement in Glasgow was built from the work of a few original comrades for whom at times the struggle seemed thankless and without result. But they persevered, were joined by other enthusiastic workers, and now they are beginning to see the results of their efforts as anarchism becomes a real revolutionary influence on the Clyde. In other areas the same can be done. Much hard spade work may be necessary in the beginning, and then, perhaps, when it is not expected, the results of all this labour may appear and astonish even those who work for it, as it has done on the Clyde.

14th July 1945

Direct Action for Houses

A little while ago *War Commentary* reported the arrest of seven families who had settled in an empty 20-room mansion and a cottage at Blantyre. However the case ended it was, as this paper pointed out, "an indication of the kind of incident which is likely to become frequent during the aggravated housing shortage after the war." And now we read even in the reactionary dailies, reports of the activities in Brighton of the 'Ex-Servicemen's Secret Committee', whose 'vigilantes' so far number over 400 members. Working at night, they break into unoccupied houses and install the homeless families of serving men, with their belongings and household goods. At their open-air meeting on Sunday 9th July, the movement's secretary described how they had received enquiries from London, Portsmouth, Sheffield, Liverpool and other parts of Britain, and added: "I have told them, 'If you see a house, take it and let the law do its damnedest'. We have started a movement which we hope and pray will spread over the length and breadth of the land." Delegates of the Brighton movement have now visited London to attend a secret conference with the object of developing a similar organisation there.

The Brighton ex-servicemen evidently do not intend to be fooled again by the 'Homes for Heroes' patter of the politicians. They know that houses will only be provided as the result of their own militant action, and not through petitions, recommendations or ballot-paper crosses.

Historic housing struggles

We often hear of the housing achievements of the Vienna Municipality of the 1920s, but we are never told the story of the determined action of the workers themselves which forced the authorities to provide houses. After the First World War, Austria was suffering the results of military defeat, blockade, famine and inflation, but her most desperate problem was overcrowding. In March 1921, 200,000 people silently demonstrated outside the Rathaus in Vienna carrying banners with the words 'Give us Land, Wood and Stone, and we will make Bread!' But the Viennese workers knew that a demonstration by itself would accomplish nothing. The returning wounded soldiers didn't wait for houses to be built for them — they demanded that the government should hand over to them part of the ex-emperor's hunting park. The government refused time after time to consider their request, so the ex-soldiers took a cartload of picks and shovels to the Lainzer Tiergarten and 'dug themselves in'. They went on to build foundations till the government was forced to recognise their *fait-accompli* and the 'Kriegsinvaliden' settlement was begun. The workers of the Hirschstetten appropriated bricks from an old fortress, and again in the industrial quarter beyond the Danube the transport workers and others coerced the authorities into action by first taking the initiative themselves. They begun work on the houses, and the government *afterwards* legalised the affair by leasing the land. In the same way the postal workers and many more, by their own action *forced* the government to initiate the Vienna Municipal Housing and Town Planning Scheme.

An English instance of working class expropriation during the same period is given in George Woodcock's *Homes or Hovels* (Freedom Press, 6d):

"One example was that of a camp of huts which had been built in Durham during the 1914-1918 war to accommodate Belgian refugees. There were about 650 concrete huts, with drainage, water, electricity, roads, a school and a hospital. The whole place was surrounded by heavy park railings with locked gates. At the end of the war the refugees returned home, the camp was deserted and locked up. Meanwhile, the housing shortage on Tyneside had become acute, and one night the gates of the camp were broken down and a number of working-class families established themselves in the huts. The number soon increased, and before the authorities awoke sufficiently to take action a large settlement was already in being. The government, realising that some considerable measure of force would be necessary to eject the new dwellers, gave in and accepted the situation."

Another more publicised instance was the 'Blitz Hotel' incident of a few years ago, in Glasgow, where families of 'squatters' in a war-damaged building refused to leave until alternative accommodation had been provided for them.

Housing and Ill-Health

Sir John Orr, in a recent speech showed that many social evils like high infantile mortality rate, high general death rate, crime rate, juvenile delinquency, tuberculosis, etc., can be directly attributed to malnutrition and bad housing. We don't need to be reminded of how food was systematically destroyed, to keep prices up, while millions went hungry, but it is not widely realised that in the same way, the housing shortage is not a question of productivity — the land, materials and workers exist — but an economic question. A society based on profits and dividends will not provide homes at rents which working class folk can afford, *because it wouldn't pay.*

"Though more than one-third of all houses in England and Wales were built since 1918, more than three-quarters of all houses of low value in 1938 had been erected before 1914, and they provided the houses of perhaps eight in every ten working-class families."
The Times, 3rd February 1945.

It should also be pointed out that, of these houses one-third were actually built before 1861, and that these figures do not include Scotland whose housing standards are lower still. This is the lesson of the past, and it will be repeated in the future, unless the workers act. If the lavish promises of the politicians *are* fulfilled, they will only succeed in housing the highest-paid workers, and the lower middle class, while the ordinary working class family can only hope for the older and obsolete houses from which the more fortunate people have moved, when they become new slum areas and rents are lower through deterioration and sub-division. But while the workers should not be deluded by the idea that they can get adequate, healthy, and pleasant homes without the destruction of the capitalist system, they should study the day-to-day possibilities of action for the lowering of rents and the prevention of rent increases.

The Great Rent Strikes
Remember the Glasgow Rent Strikes of the 1st World War period. All over the city, when rent increases were made the house wives banded together street by street, refusing to pay, and forming the Women's Housing Council. They spied on the movements of bailiffs and rent-collectors, barricaded their homes, put the furniture of evicted people back into the houses as soon as it was pitched out, and even had actual fights with the factors. The men came out from the big shipyards and works, and the government, finding that their promises of enquiries and legislation did not satisfy the workers, or prevent more men from stopping work, were forced to pass the First Rent Restrictions Act, while the landlords had to withdraw the increases. As one of the workers' delegates said, "The Country can't do without the 8,000 workers, but the country can do without the factors." The Glasgow Rent Strike was important as a tendency towards the social and political strike, one of the most potent of our eventual weapons against our

rulers. The Glasgow workers knew that they could not rely for support on the official Trade Union and Labour leaders, (I expect they remembered the words of Robert Smillie, MP, years before, when he said to a woman who was trying to prevent the sheriff's officer from turning her out, "I'd advise you to get out of the way and let the man do his work. You can't do any good."). The workers' task, now, just as it was in 1915 is, as John MacLean said then, "to take the initiative into their *own* hands".

The second great Rent Strike Movement grew from London in the years just before the second World War. In 1938, 250 tenants at Quinn Square, Bethnal Green, started a strike to demand not only the repayment of money charged above the limits of the Rent Restrictions Act, but for a general reduction of rents in future. They succeeded and were followed by a strike of 131 tenants of Southern Grove, Mile End, who picketed, barricaded, and demonstrated to get repairs done and rents lowered. They too were successful and shortly afterwards workers living in three London areas, Holborn, Stepney, and Poplar, whose flats all belonged to the same landlord, struck:

"900 tenants secured a victory and signed an agreement which established a flat rate for every type of dwelling and provided for adequate repairs and redecorations to all flats to be started immediately and carried out periodically." (*Reynold's News*, 16th April 1939)

The Stepney tenants conducted the Langsdale Mansions strike and the 'Great Brady Street Battle', as well as many others. The 340 Brady Street tenants barricaded their homes and fought the landlords for 21 weeks, after which they won big reductions; the return of evicted tenants; and an agreement by the landlord to carry out the necessary repairs to the extent of £2,500 for the first year, and £1,500 for each year afterwards. Rent strikes also occurred at Amersham, Balham, Bellingham, Dagenham, Hammersmith, Hampstead, Hendon, Holborn, Maldon, Woolwich, Wood Green, and many other places in and around London.

In the Municipal tenants' strike at Birmingham, 40,000 people fought for 19 weeks to prevent rent increases, and 15,000 of them got reductions amounting to £30,000 a year. The continued success of these Rent Strikes and their rapid spreading, frightened landlords everywhere into doing repairs, and some even *offered* to reduce rents, while the government at the beginning of the War passed the second Rent Restrictions Act, (although this has been widely ignored or evaded by landlords).

There has been much less of a struggle against the burden of rates, although, as Sir E. D. Simon says, quoting the case of a man trying to move out of a slum area into a new housing estate, and finding that besides having to pay say, 5/- more a week in rent, he has also an additional 4/- in rates: "Surely no other tax existing in this country even approaches in harshness and injustice this tax on a poor father of a large family, of 10% of his income for rates alone, levied just because he is making special sacrifices to bring up his children in good conditions". He points out that "a rich man living in a large house will often not pay as much as 1% of his income in rates". Certainly, few taxes are so designed as to make both the poor poorer and the rich, richer. Councillor A. B. Mackay, of Glasgow explains how our rating system benefits the landlords:

"The landlord class had unbridled control of legislation for centuries and they abused their power, legislating in their own class interests, shifting the obligations which lay on their lands on to tax and rate payers, while they continued to take the ever-increasing value resulting from the energy and expenditure of the community. The device by which the landlords effect their depredations is very simple but very effective. Where their lands are unused, or used for a purpose of lower utility than the optimum, they are returned in the rating books at a nominal amount or a low valuation. They, the landlords are all right. The fools — the rate-payers on full land, building and improvement value — will do the paying while the landlord waits till a public body or a private person will pay up the inflated price which scarcity of land provides."

The middle-class ratepayers' associations show on which side of the fence they stand when they continually call for a reduction of rates made possible by cutting down those social services from which the working class benefits. They do not demand a proper rating of their friends the landlords.

A quite unique form of Rate Strike was that made by George Lansbury's Poplar Borough Council in the early 1920s, when they refused to levy the LCC's Poor Rate because it imposed an indefensible burden on the working class boroughs to the exclusion of the wealthy ones. Once Lansbury and his council had been jailed, it was found that because they wouldn't alter their view, they would have to stay in prison indefinitely. The only way in which the authorities could solve the absurd situation was to change the law! There have been sporadic Rates Strikes amongst the workers, but never to the extent of the Rent Strikes.

From the examples mentioned, we can see how effective direct action can be when applied to our housing problems. It works, it gets *results*. Already the Brighton Corporation has promised to requisition houses officially for its homeless people. But it wouldn't have even come 'limping along behind' in this matter, but for the action of the Vigilantes. Our message to them should be:

Act on your own — no reliance on the politicians, especially those who try to cash in on your success.
Stick together, and work on as big a scale as possible!
Don't give up, and don't give a damn for the authorities!

If the Vigilantes have these three pre-requisites for successful action, INDEPENDENCE, SOLIDARITY, and DETERMINA-TION, we can be sure that their movement will 'spread over the length and breadth of the land', and may have consequences and give opportunities which it would be criminal for the workers to ignore.

28th July 1945   COLIN WARD

The War in the Far East

During a recent London strike a Labour stooge asked the workers "What would you say if I told you you were letting down the boys we sent to Burma?" and an anonymous voice replied, "We'd ask you what bloody right you had to send them there." We cannot sum up the position better. During the election campaign many candidates were questioned about the war in the Far East. It was obvious from their surprise that they had never questioned the need for it at all, since all parties had tacitly agreed to place it, alongside the German monarchy and the brothel-keeping bishops, amongst the subjects beyond controversy which no loyal Briton would worry about. They 'explained' the war in terms of backing up the troops in Burma, etc., and rescuing the prisoners-of-war in Japanese hands, all obviously consequent upon the fact of a war, and nothing whatever to do with the need for war. They could not explain the war any other way, and fell back on attacking the Japanese system, but were quite unable to suggest any alternative to it. In the end, most of them fell back on sheer crude racial hatred of the lowest type.

War propaganda for the Japanese War is in fact relying solely on crude 'anti-yellow' stuff, the vilest of all coming from the United States, which since the downfall of Nazi Germany is perhaps the world centre for racial hatred doctrines. It is not hard to discern that the main objection to the Japanese system of government from these sources lies in the fact that its subjects do not belong to the brownish-pink 'white' race. The harsh discrimination against Japanese-Americans is nothing but the logical outcome of the discrimination against Afro-Americans and similar racial minorities in the States. The war with Japan gives them a good excuse to peddle this line, which has spurted forth emulations of Nazi principles ranging from the erasure of the names of Japanese-American veterans of the last war from memorial stones to the wholesale deportation of families out of their homes and farms.

In so far as there has been any propaganda over here in regard to the Japanese war, it has timidly followed on the American race-hatred line; our Government has not given us such a full dose of colour-prejudice and 'Japanese-are-animals' bilge, for the simple reason that it knows people not brought up to colour-hatred will not swallow it, and its sole effect will be to further widen the gulf between its European and its Asiatic subjects.

Putting aside the crude propaganda which taken to its logical conclusion means that we have to fight everyone whose features are different from our own, we find that no ideological excuse whatever is put forward to justify the war against Japan. It is true the system of government is attacked, but only on occasion. Most war propagandists, even those careful to differentiate between 'Nazis' and 'Germans', 'Fascists' and 'Italians', merely refer to the 'Japs'. Some consider the Emperor to be a peace-loving man who wants to rule constitutionally but is in the hands of his military caste. Others (anxious to have a figurehead to pin all the evil on to) have fastened on the Emperor as the source of all evil, Hirohito being conveniently rigged out beside Hitler and Mussolini. Yet others picked on Tojo during his tenure of office. Some attack 'Jap militarism' but what is the difference between 'Jap militarism' and the 'Prussian militarism' we crushed for ever in the last war, and any other militarism? Why do none of them attack the system in Japan, as they did that in Germany and Italy? For a very simple reason. The system has no fancy name such as 'Fascism', it is plainly Capitalism, and if our ruling class were hesitant about calling themselves anti-fascists, they are even more hesitant about calling themselves anti-capitalist.

'Re-education'

It is significant that whereas they spoke of 're-educating' the Germans, nobody talks of 're-educating the Japanese'. It would be a joke for Britain and the USA to speak of re-educating a people they themselves had educated. The evil the Japanese ruling-class were taught they executed, even if they have succeeded in bettering the instructions. When the great Western powers found the old feudal land of Japan unlocked, they had before them an open field. Closed for centuries to the foreigner, Japan was suddenly opened to the capitalist world. They took her in hand, an infant sprung upon the world, and moulded her in the most profitable course to themselves. The country was rapidly industrialised. The old feudal barons, the ancient aristocracy, survived by adapting themselves to the new regime, and becoming big industrialists. The working-class and the peasants remained in abject misery, only increased by the 'benefits' of the West.

This hardly bothered the 'educators'; they were pleased to see a docile proletariat. When the proletariat became less docile, and

the military caste was obliged to carry out a few massacres to keep
them down, the effect on the international conscience was to cause
a jump in Japanese bonds.

In those years Japan was boosted to British children as 'the
Britain of the East'; it was glorified in song and story as the 'land
of the Cherry Blossom'; and Edwardian music-hall audiences were
encouraged to sing of the Japanese soldier 'off to fight for the
freedom and right of dear old Japan'. The song is not so popular
today.

Japanese civilisation is older than ours; the Japanese are not a
backward people in the technical sense; as a result, the Japanese
capitalists learnt more quickly than was expected. They developed
into a menace to their capitalist neighbours, economically and, as
a consequence, militarily. First of all, Russia. Then, Germany.
Then, China. Then, Britain and America and their satellites. At
last Japan ceased to be 'a land of happy smiling people'. We
suddenly began to realise that atrocities were committed there.

For what purpose is the war in the Far East dragging on? Some
talk of annexation and colonising the country, thus clearly
demonstrating the real imperial nature of the war. It cannot be to
're-educate' them. We have already done that. They say they are
going to crush Japanese militarism but to destroy militarism means
to destroy government, and what are they going to put in its place?
They cannot destroy capitalism there without putting in a workers'
regime; and no-one in their senses imagines the capitalist class
here is going to do that. The fact is that they can only retain the
same system in Japan as operates at present, after perhaps some
controversy as to whether to treat Hirohito personally like
Goering or like Badoglio. Their choice is capitalism or revolution;
and they will inevitably choose capitalism.

The government has made no ideological smoke-screen for the
war against Japan as it did in the war against Germany, because it
cannot. The invasion scare can hardly be used now even by senile
tribunal chairmen; and no thoughtful person can accept a
'Vansittartist' case against the Japanese when, more than in
any country in the world, there is the widest gulf possible between
the upper classes and the lower. The only evidence offered against
this is the way in which the lower classes allow themselves to be
killed in a war (a fact for which allied soldiers are praised!); which
is, on reflection, scarcely surprising when one considers their low
expectation of survival and poor prospects in life.

We are entitled to say, therefore, that the war has taken an even more sharply and obviously imperialist character; that the main issues are obviously the re-conquest of colonial possessions, for the profit of Stock Exchange operators and City and Wall Street bondholders, anxious for their tin and oil and rubber, and oblivious to the blood and tears and sweat.

Against this cynical exploitation of human life for a few people's selfish gain plus the swaggering political desire to assert 'national honour', what can be done to prevent this holocaust in the Far East, which may well, failing a surrender by the Japanese generals, drag on for years, wiping out the best of the coming generation?

It has been seen very plainly that political power is worse than useless. Few soldiers want to go to the East, far fewer want to stay there. They actually had the 'opportunity', technically, of 'ruling themselves' in the democratic fashion; that is to say, an election was held. It is reported from all sides that a majority of troops concerned who could vote, voted Labour, and obviously this was primarily because Churchill was on the other side. They voted against Churchill as a symbol of reactionary imperialism and because they wanted to go home, but obviously the Labour Party will not fulfil their wishes. It consistently announced its full support for the Japanese war, win or lose the election, and in fact it was just Hobson's Choice. Their votes did not enable them to decide what they themselves wanted to do. Democracy means choosing people to rule you. Doing as you want to do yourself (without interfering with anyone else!) is not democracy, but anarchy.

The only way in which imperialist adventures of this nature will be ended is by fraternisation between peoples when this is possible; by refusing to obey the dictates of discipline and instead following natural inclinations. The Canadian soldiers won a major victory in preventing their Government from sending conscripts to the East. It may well be that in future generations when Vimy Ridge is a forgotten memory of a barbaric past, Canadian soldiers of our generation will be remembered for the solidarity aroused by the 'zombies' in their struggle for elemental human rights, and, whether they were conscious of it or not, laying the foundations of internationalism.

If their lead were followed universally, the Japanese capitalists, still cut off from their foreign backers but without a war to bolster up their regime, would speedily fall a victim to the workers and peasants of Japan and its Empire, who have in past struggles shown their will to resist under the harshest tyranny.

28th July 1945   JOHN BAYA

The Only Answer to the
Atomic Bomb: ABOLISH WAR!

The recent complacent announcement by the Allied leaders of the atomic bomb, explodes once and for all the myth of the moral superiority of the American and British ruling classes over the Nazis or the 'dirty Japs'. Undoubtedly, had the Germans used this monstrous device before the Allies had a chance to put it into operation, they would have been regarded as having reached the depths of moral depravity. When they produced the flying bomb and the V2 rocket, the leaders of British and American opinion were full of the most self-righteous indignation, which is made to appear all the more hypocritical now that it is revealed that all the time experiments were going on in Britain and America to perfect this weapon which makes the most violent weapon of the Nazis seem a silly toy.

The atomic bomb, we are told, can cause the same amount of destruction as 20,000 tons of TNT. This, it should be remembered, is equivalent to rather more than the weight of explosives contained in all the flying bombs which were discharged by the Germans against Britain. It is equivalent to 2,000 of the largest blockbusters which the RAF dropped on Berlin, and a single plane, we are told, could do as much destruction as 5,000 British planes bombing Berlin. After hearing this news put forward by the Allied leaders with glib complacency, as if they were announcing some quite ordinary and pleasant event, we find it impossible fully to express our horror that men who pretend to be working for the benefit of the human race should display such hypocrisy and such a complete lack of any sense of moral values.

While the Allied leaders were begrudging small quantities of money to be spent on vital social services, while they delayed housing and pretended they could not spend money on hospitals or education, they spent the colossal sum of five hundred million pounds on perfecting this machine of destruction.

Atomic energy can be used as easily for constructive as for destructive purposes. For years scientists have been endeavouring to gain the means of research in order to use this energy for beneficial purposes, such as power in industry and transport, etc. But throughout this time they have been labouring under the opposition of vested interests whose profits would be affected by such a discovery, and it is only when atomic energy seems a likely way of winning a war and causing mass destruction and death on an unprecedented scale that they are given the opportunity to put their discoveries into effect. It is a scandalous reflection on our contemporary society that so many of the important and potentially beneficial inventions should have been brought forward only because they also proved effective destructive agents in modern warfare. Nor can the scientists themselves be allowed to go without condemnation. Admittedly, in a sense they were the victims of the system, in that they could only develop their discoveries by agreeing to adapt them for destructive purposes. But in thus yielding, they have become the greatest enemies of mankind, and it is impossible to excuse them for the part they have willingly played in furthering the destructive desires of political and military leaders.

The atomic bomb is a weapon in the hands of the ruling class which cannot be underestimated by the workers. It has been said that, like gas and bacteriological warfare, it is so frightful a weapon that no government would use it for fear of reprisals, and from this idea it has been suggested that its advent may mean the end of major wars because they will be too frightful in prospect for governments to embark on them. This, however, is not borne out by historical examples. Although none of the warring powers used gas on enemies who were as well equipped for retaliation as themselves, they have had no compunction in doing so where the enemies were weak, as the Italians did in Abyssinia. And the present use of the atomic bomb against the Japanese shows that governments will not scruple to use it where they can do so with impunity.

So far as the relationships between governments and their peoples are concerned, we cannot escape from the fact that the power of the ruling class is made all the greater by the discovery of a weapon which does not need large masses of people for its manufacture or operation, and can therefore be entrusted to small and select groups of reactionaries who will not be subject to the same influences as conscript armies or large masses of factory workers.

While we are fully aware of the terrible possibilities implicit in this new invention, and of the way in which it may be used against the struggling workers, we cannot fail to point out that, in a free and co-operative society, the discovery of how to use atomic energy could be turned to the lasting benefit of the human race. All that the so-called Utopians like Kropotkin and Godwin envisaged in the past from the discovery of new forms of energy could now be realised in a few years by the use of this vast new source of power. Disagreeable occupations like coal mining could be eliminated, and a new era of leisure and abundance could be initiated by the responsible use of this discovery. It is the crime of society dominated by authority and property that it should in fact seem to offer us little more than a new era of fear and destruction. *11th August 1945*

Russia's Little Brothers

The influence of Russia continues to grow in Eastern Europe, and, however it may be affected in the future as a result of the advent of the atomic bomb, there is at present no sign of any force that is likely in the near future to prevent Russia from consolidating its mastery over all the minor countries of Central and South-Eastern Europe.

This ascendency is expressed ideologically not in revolutionary or even in pseudo-revolutionary ideas, but in a revival of the Pan-Slavist nationalism which was one of the great bulwarks of Tsarist Russia, and which made so many Russian liberals of the nineteenth century unwittingly play a reactionary role that assisted the purposes of the Romanoffs.

Cleverly, the Russians have left it for their satellites to be the most enthusiastic propagandists for the new pan-Slavism. Characteristic of their statements was the speech of Lausman, the new Czech Minister of the Interior, at Bratislava.

"For the first time in our history we are the neighbours of our socialist brother, the Soviet Union, with whom we intend to ally ourselves to defend security in a spirit of brotherhood and Slavonic reciprocity. We know that such a grouping will result in a barrier of Slavonic countries around us, against which any Fascist tendencies will break."

This pan-Slavism is further illustrated by a growing hostility against the Western Allies, which appears to be strongest in Yugoslavia where, in Trieste and Carinthia, the Russian zone of influence impinges on the Anglo-American zone in Italy. The Belgrade paper *Politika*, for instance, on the 18th July, said in its editorial:

". . . the action of the Great Western Allies in liberated Europe are diametrically opposed to what they solemnly pledged, as for instance, freedom, democracy, the right of national self-determination, the punishment of war criminals and the destruction of the remnants of Fascism."

These statements are true enough in themselves, but they are obviously used for purposes of falsification when they are combined with an attempt to prove that the Russians have acted with complete unselfishness and consideration for the rights of others.

"One cannot speak of a sphere of interest in connection with the Soviet Union, because it is not an imperialist state. It is a peace-loving country, which actively opposes every imperialist war."

One wonders just what the Finns or the Lithuanians would say about this in private, or how it would fit in with Russia's last minute dash into Manchuria to be sure of getting a share of the spoils before the attack on Japan was finally ended.

Anti-Greek propaganda
The combination of Slavonic racialism and the Russian policy against British influence in the Balkans appears in the ferocious anti-Greek propaganda which is being carried on in Yugoslavia, Rumania and Bulgaria alike. This is built up in the form of a paranoic myth of Greek imperialism which reaches the most fantastic heights of invention.

In Rumania one of the semi-official papers, *Romania Libera*, declared, "To Southern Europe, Greece constitutes a near and immediate danger . . . a new hotbed of war is being formed in the guise of a greater Greece." Similar accusations are being made in Yugoslavia, and the Communist paper *Baba* 'exposed' the existence of a "Greek Turkish Aegean bloc which is evidently aimed at the democratic Balkan nations." But the campaign reached its height in Bulgaria, where the Sofia daily *Narod* went so far as to assert that "Greece still entertains megalomaniac ideas of capturing not only Belgrade and Sofia, but even Moscow."

Slavonic racialism is demonstrated in practice by the expulsion of Germans from Poland and East Prussia, and of Germans and Hungarians from Czechoslovakia. These expulsions are carried out with considerable ruthlessness. The Hungarian press is full of complaints of the treatment of Hungarian peasants by the Czech bureaucrats who are conducting their expulsion, and the treatment of the Germans who are being expelled from Czechoslovakia is even worse. Most of these Germans and Hungarians belong to families who have been settled on Czech territory for many generations, and who have had no contact with fascism or who have even been hostile to it. Nor is their expulsion likely to aid the economic balance of Czechoslovakia, for the majority of its skilled artisans and industrial workers were Germans, while its best farming was carried on by the Hungarian peasants. This internal disturbance is likely to cause the Czechs to become even more dependent on Russia and to turn their country into an economic colony of Russian industry.

Expulsion of Germans

In Poland the Germans are rapidly being driven over the Oder. An example of the conditions of their expulsion is given by a recent order of the Mayor of Kattowicze, which instructed all persons of German nationality to report for evacuation at an assembly point "with hand luggage not exceeding 20 kilograms (about 45 pounds). No indication is given of what will happen to the rest of their belongings.

Meanwhile, even the bonds of Slavonic racialism do not make the little countries of Eastern Europe show any great altruism towards any of their Slavonic brothers — always excepting their big strong brother, Russia. Mutual expressions of esteem among these countries are accompanied by declarations of an intention to hold on to whatever they already possess in the way of land or resources. A Czech leader, Lausman, declared:

"We want to maintain for ever the best possible friendly and good-neighbourly relations with Poland. Although Poland made the greatest sacrifices in this war, she must understand that the Teschan area has been and will remain ours."

And president Benes declared, "Every country cares primarily for its own kith and kin, and wishes its compatriots to live within its borders."

Here, then, we have the indications of Soviet policy in Eastern Europe; to establish a sphere of influence based on the old Tsarist idea of Pan-Slavism, to unite its subject peoples against the outside world by this myth of a common blood, and yet, at the same time, to keep alive the old points of difference between the various national units in order to prevent all the little brothers from discovering that they may have a common grievance against the big brother.

'Democracy' in Eastern Europe

Meanwhile, at the same time as the local bosses of all these little countries strut about and pretend they are the equal partners in a great league of Slavonic peoples, the Russian government quietly maintains its control over all their vital affairs. It is the Soviet Military Command which imposes or lifts curfews and tells who shall leave or enter each country. A group of pro-Russian Poles who came to England recently admitted:

"Poland must give up any idea of having a foreign policy of her own, or an independent army to support it. We will be allowed wide cultural autonomy, and if we will be satisfied with that, we can share in Russia's brilliant future."

The same applies to all the Central European and Balkan countries. However much they may be allowed to talk of independence and democracy, to shout at each other or at the outside world, for the forthcoming period of history they will work in the shadow of the Red Army and the OGPU. Their foreign policies, their military affairs, their police, their immigration bureaux and their concentration camps, the nuclei of political power, will be under the control and supervision of the Moscow central command. This is the meaning of the word 'democracy' in the context of Eastern Europe, where it is constantly on the lips of puppet politicians and military adventurers.

25th August 1945

France Today
by a French correspondent

It is a truism to say that the French situation is dominated by extremely difficult economic conditions. The newspaper *Resistance* has published figures showing the depreciation of the buying power of the franc. In 1939 it was possible to buy for a thousand francs a man's suit or seven pairs of shoes. In 1945, the waistcoat alone cost a thousand francs. One can also buy for the same sum one shoe, left or right, as one wishes. The situation is no better regarding food. For a thousand francs one could obtain in 1939 a banquet for a whole family. Today, a meal on the black market for one person will cost a thousand francs.

It is obvious that in these conditions one should have witnessed an enormous increase of all wages. This is not the case. Employees are still being paid salaries of three thousand francs a month while the increase in the wages of industrial workers has no bearing with the increase in the cost of living. To live at all decently one needs in France today five to six thousand francs a month; only a small minority possesses this minimum income.

The food distribution is so bad that all the newspapers, including the Gaullist newspapers, are obliged to organise periodic campaigns to demand the resignation of the food minister Ramadier and to denounce the black market. In fact, the black market can only exist with the complicity of the government.

A few months ago, the newspaper *Paris Presse*, a staunch supporter of the government, strongly denounced the corruption of the ministries and pointed out that the big racketeers of the black market were able to work in all safety because they bought from the government departments the necessary papers to legalise their traffic. On the other hand the repression against people who go to the countryside in order to provide themselves with food is extremely well organised.

The Parties and Trade Unions
The attitude of the so-called working class parties and organisations is simply scandalous. For example, at the last meeting of the national council of the CGT (corresponding to the TUC in this country), these gentlemen found the workers' demands for an increase in wages completely out of place. But

they stressed the necessity to work for the war and, by implication, to make sacrifices for it.

The Trade Union bosses have the support of the Communist Party. Here is a fact which I can guarantee as completely authentic: In an aircraft factory in the Paris district, an old syndicalist militant had organised a campaign to demand an increase in wages. He was immediately accused of being a *provocateur* and Tillion, the communist Minister of Air, menaced the factory to deprive it of orders if that worker were not sacked immediately. This fact is, I repeat, absolutely authentic. And it is not an isolated case. The communists have set up a system of denunciation of all those who protest against their conditions. All those who present demands are accused of being anarcho-Trotskyists. During these last few months the campaign against all the movement to the left of the Communist Party has been resumed with a violence unknown since 1936-37. In this campaign the communists are not alone. In March, Teitgen, Minister of Information, broadcast a speech dealing with the 'uneasiness' existing in France. According to Teitgen, it is the militants of "a so-called 4th International" who systematically spread disorder.

'Anarcho-Trotskyists'

During the last few weeks the campaign against revolutionary elements has been intensified. A weekly newspaper called *Nuit et Jour*, has published an article dealing with what it called "the latest shape of Nazi propaganda". Extracts from this article have been reproduced in another weekly possessing a big circulation, called *J*, which is obviously under communist control. The article says: "We learn that a satanic agreement has been reached between Trotskyism, this kind of anarchy of the 4th Fascist International, and nazism pure and simple which still hopes to survive by underground work in various countries. The Germans are proposing to assimilate themselves all over the world with the Trotskyists, that is to say the anarchists, enemies of communism in every country and who are certainly responsible for the death of the Russian ambassador to Mexico, Oumanski."

Why this violent denunciation of the Trotskyists and the anarchists as Nazi agents? The newspaper *J* gives one of the reasons when it declares: "We are witnessing in France today, particularly among some young people, a renewed activity of those suspicious elements, who must be denounced wherever they encrust themselves, as the agents of fascism and reaction."

It was inevitable that, in view of the attitude of the Communist Party concerning the most elementary demands of the workers, in view also of the incredible corruption existing in the Socialist Party (SFIO), the people should try to find some new organisation in which they can have some faith.

It is this faith which, as *J* says, must be destroyed. The method is exactly the same as that employed some time ago in Moscow, but the reasons behind it are rather different and we shall only be able to appreciate them fully in the near future.

Change of line

The Communist International is preparing a new turn, but this time a turn towards the left. The preparatory signs for this new *volte-face* are sufficiently clear to all those who are somewhat familiar with the methods used by the communists. First of all, on the international plane, there is the complete renunciation of Ilya Ehrenburg's Vansittartist policy. After Alexandroff had attacked Ehrenburg in *Pravda* for saying that "the whole of Germany was responsible for the crimes of Hitler", Ehrenburg has been obliged to disavow his jingoist propaganda of the last few years.

Alexandroff's article has had other repercussions. It is significant that in the 'Victory issue' of *L'Humanité* (the organ of the French Communist Party), one does not find any longer the Germans referred to as *boches*, as was common practice up to a few days ago. It also refers to the crushing of 'German fascism' and 'Hitler's Germany' and not merely of Germany as it did before.

From the dispatches received from the part of Germany occupied by the Russians it seems that they are trying to put up a 'liberal' attitude towards the German population. On 10th May, Robert Reuben, wrote that, in the eyes of the Soviet military government, the German people have been the victims, not only of Nazi propaganda but also of Nazi oppression. When one remembers what communist propaganda used to turn out only a few weeks ago about the wicked *boche*, one can only reach the conclusion that the Party line has changed once more.

Eliminating witnesses

It is in this new twist in their policy that we find the reason for the Communist Party campaign against revolutionary elements. During the whole war the communists have denounced the Trotskyists and the anarchists as German agents because they maintained that the German people were not responsible for the

Nazi's crimes. In order to prevent possible sympathisers joining the ranks of movements to whose ideas the Communist Party is now paying lip service, it is necessary to discredit them and assimilate them to the fascists. This will also make it easier to eliminate them physically if necessary. This method has been used before during the Moscow trials.

That the Communist Party everywhere is the direct agent of Moscow's foreign policy is a banality. But it is in France that this attitude of the Communist Party is more blatant, and one wonders if they will be able to execute this new somersault without losing the support of the bourgeois elements which they have secured thanks to their ultra-patriotic policy.

The complete absence of ideology has permitted the Communist Party to gain a fairly astonishing electoral victory, but it has its drawback in the lack of stability of its membership. The small bourgeoisie which has supported the Communist Party during the municipal elections will not follow it so easily if it takes a somewhat revolutionary turn.

The Elections
The success of the Communist Party at the elections is astonishing not because of the trend it indicates, as in the present economic conditions the masses could only turn to the left, but because of the methods used by the Communist Party to succeed in dominating most of the great industrial centres and particularly Paris.

The communists have, for the purpose of the elections, allied themselves with practically everyone. In some districts they have allied themselves with reactionaries in order to beat the Socialists, in others with the Socialists in order to beat the moderates and reactionaries.

We do not possess yet a complete picture of the election results. But whatever they are, the victory of the Communist Party seems certain. This victory, however, can only have a meaning if it corresponds to a clear line of the national as well as the international plan. In fact, on the internal plan the directives of the Communist Party are perfectly vague and on the international plan one can see the beginning of an important change.

The political struggle in France has become, during these last few months, extremely violent. On the Atlantic front, for example, during the offensive on Royan, where there was still a pocket of German troops, a bloody struggle took place between the FFI and the soldiers of the Leclerq division. The soldiers of Leclerq are, on the whole, reactionaries as they have been recruited in North Africa with officers belonging to the colonial troops; the FFI are mostly controlled by the Communists. The fact that this incident took place in spite of the orders of the Communist Party which forbids any political struggle as detrimental to the war, shows that the control of the Communist Party over its members is not as well established as it wishes to be.

There would still be many things to say on the general situation in France today, but information is difficult to obtain as one cannot rely on the press, which is submitted to severe censorship. I hope, however, to be able in future articles to give a more detailed account of the political situation in France as it develops itself.
19th May 1945

Pétain's Trial a Legal Farce

After long days of trial, endless statements by the witnesses for the prosecution and for the defence, the sentence against Pétain has at last been given. Practically everyone in France expected the solution which has in fact been adopted. By finding Pétain guilty and condemning him to death the Court gave moral satisfaction to the Resistance; by not putting the sentence into effect the opinion of the pro-Vichy elements is respected.

The whole trial was absurd from beginning to end. It was pretended that the trial was conducted according to legal procedure whereas in fact Pétain having received his power from the National Assembly he should have been judged by that same Assembly. One also witnessed the grotesque situation of Pétain being prosecuted and judged by men who had taken their oath of loyalty to him as head of State. Mornet, the public prosecutor had furthermore been appointed by Pétain as President of a Commission whose job was to denaturalise French Jews.

The prosecution charged Pétain with having asked Hitler for an armistice in June 1940. But the witnesses called by the prosecution had all shared in the responsibility of ending the war. Paul

Reynaud, who was Prime Minister at the time, called Pétain to the government knowing full well that the Marshal preferred an armistice to military capitulation on the field. Daladier came into the witness box to try to prove that the French army could have carried on the struggle at the time when the armistice was signed. But Daladier was the man who signed, together with Chamberlain, the Munich agreement in 1938. Albert Lebrun, who was President of the Republic in 1940, came to declare how desperate he was at the signing of the armistice. But evidence proved that this 'witness' had sent letters of congratulation to Pétain after he had gained power. And a French paper reminded the public that Lebrun was present at a Council of Ministers when General de Gaulle was sentenced to death as a traitor.

In short, the whole trial proved that practically all the members of the Government of the Third Republic had accepted the armistice of 1940 as a necessity. The whole atmosphere of the trial could only have a demoralising effect on the French people. It was a disgusting exhibition of dirty linen being washed in public. The trial is reported to have cost £1,000 a day, yet at one time the newspapers reported that the accused was asleep (he seems to have slept most of the time), as well as several of the jurors, while the others were engaged in doing crossword puzzles.

The only possible conclusion from all this is that only revolutionary justice could have demanded an account from the men who are responsible for the sufferings of the French people. During the trial of Pétain a guilty man was judged by his accomplices and was merely condemned to satisfy public opinion: that is to say, in order to preserve the interests of the bourgeois state.

25th August 1945

Atrocities of the Mind

The August number of the New York monthly *Politics* devotes its editorial to what are justly called the 'atrocities of the mind' perpetrated by the notorious General Patton. Its front page carries a picture of Patton addressing Sunday school children. He said to them:

"You are the soldiers and the nurses of the next war. There will be another war. There always has been. Sunday school will make you good soldiers."

This speech gave a fair indication of the typically fascist attitude towards war of this amiable soldier (how many similar quotations we could pick from the works of that other friend of children, Adolf Hitler!), but it is milk and water in comparison with his speech to his soldiers before D-Day. This speech was recorded by OWI, the American army information service, but has never been officially released. By comparing a text published unofficially by a *New York Daily News* columnist and some notes taken by a man who was present when the OWI recording was played, the editor of *Politics* arrived at the following version of Patton's speech, "shortened for space reasons and also edited with regard for the sensibilities of the postal authorities . . ."

"Men! This stuff we hear about Americans wanting to stay out of this war — not wanting to fight — is a lot of bull__t. Americans love to fight, traditionally. All real Americans love the sting of the clash of battle. America loves a winner. America will not tolerate a loser. Americans despise a coward. Americans play to win. That's why America has never lost and never will lose a war, for the very thought of losing is hateful to an American.

You are not all going to die. Only 2% of you right here today would be killed in a major battle. Death must not be feared. Every man is frightened at first in battle. If any man says he isn't, he's a goddamned liar. But a real man will never let the fear of death overpower his honour, his sense of duty to his country and to his manhood.

All through your army career, you've bitched about what you call 'this chicken__t drilling'. That drilling was for a purpose — instant obedience to orders and to increase alertness. If not, some sonofabitch of a German will sneak up behind him and beat him to death with a sock full of s__t.

An army is a team. It lives, sleeps, eats and fights as a team. This individual hero stuff is a lot of crap. The bilious bastards who wrote that kind of stuff for the *Saturday Evening Post* don't know any more about real fighting under fire than they know about f__ing.

Even if you are hit, you can still fight. That's not bull__t either . . .
every damn man has a job to do. Each man must think not only of himself
but of his buddy fighting beside him. We don't want yellow cowards in this
army. They should be killed off like flies. If not, they will go home and
breed more cowards. We've got to save the f__ing for the fighting man.
The brave men will breed more brave men.

Remember men! You don't know I'm here . . . let the first bastards to
find out be the goddam Germans. I want them German bastards to rise up
on their hind legs and howl: 'JESUS CHRIST! IT'S THAT
GODDAMNED THIRD ARMY AND THAT SONOFABITCH
PATTON AGAIN!'

We want to get the hell over there and clean the goddamned thing up.
And then we'll have to take a little jaunt against the purple-p__ing Japs
and clean them out before the Marines get all the credit.

There's one great thing you men will be able to say when you got home.
You may all thank God that thirty years from now, when you are sitting at
the fire with your grandson on your knee and he asks you what you did in
the Great World War Two, you won't have to say: 'I shovelled s__t in
Louisiana'."

The editor of *Politics* rightly describes these utterances of Patton
as "atrocities of the mind: atrocious in being communicated not to
a psycho-analyst but to great numbers of soldiers, civilians and
school children", but they are something more. They are among
the danger signals that show more clearly every day that, although
Nazism has been defeated in Germany, its spirit is still alive as ever
in the world, and that whether Hitler is dead or alive, the brutality
and the homicidal neuroses which underlie the actions and ideas of
the Nazis have come to life again in the minds of many people in
the countries which were supposed to be fighting for the kind of
world in which the Pattons and Hitlers would be obsolete.
Unfortunately, it is a type which is likely to afflict us for a good
time longer — for as long, in fact, as ordinary men and women,
ordinary workers and soldiers, will allow themselves to be the
tools of such hysterical megalomaniacs.

6th October 1945

The End of Lease Lend

The National Debt grew out of the effort to subsidise mercenary
troops and mercenary governments all over Europe a hundred
years ago, in an effort to crush France, first of all in her
revolutionary period, afterwards in her imperialist period when
the former was crushed. In the last world war the National Debt
reached its zenith, because then the strain of total war left the
entire capitalist fabric weakened. The contradictions within
capitalism made it quite absurd to rely on private capitalists and
bankers whose wealth represented only the labour and materials
on which the Government could draw anyway, and like other
European powers, the Government was obliged to borrow from
America, the newest and strongest capitalist power.

As they borrowed on so vast a scale, and all they borrowed was
blown sky-high, the debts contracted to the USA could never be
repaid. Apart from Finland — which alone kept up the interest on
her debts as a propaganda gesture which failed to work in the end
— the Governments just defaulted on the payment of interest on
the accumulated debts. In the Second World War, President
Roosevelt realised the futility of going through the same comedy,
and evolved the Lease Lend Plan. Mr Churchill now refers to it as
a "most unsordid gesture" but at the time it was correctly
represented as a plain business deal.

Obviously America could never collect on the debts being run
up by the nations she was subsidising in order to keep down
German imperialism. The idea was that they should borrow what
they needed from a mutual pool and what was still standing would
be collected afterwards.

We got tanks, planes, ammunition, battleships, Spam, oil and
dried eggs; the Americans got bases in the Bahamas, upkeep of
troops abroad, Ministry of Information lecturers and the defence
of her interests via a few million corpses. The arrangement thus
worked perfectly well on both sides. The authors of the Lease
Lend Plan realised the contradictions of capitalism in that you
cannot work everything out in money values — and decide how
much Britain owed for crashed aeroplanes, or alternatively how
much the USA owed for Britain's supplying the pilot's corpses;
what indemnity Britain ought to have for a village wrecked by US
troops, or France for whole towns eliminated; what debt Britain

and France ought to contract for the bombs to destroy a German town, and so on.

US businessmen naturally took advantage of Lease Lend to push their goods to the four corners of the earth and create a demand for them at the expense of rival export markets. The sudden ending of Lease Lend does not mean that they are going to walk out on this profitable field. What it does mean is that they know that Europe and Asia cannot do without them now, and they want to dictate terms while the scarcity of war is on, knowing that in a few years economic nationalism will try to drive them out.

The King's Debt

The net result will be to increase the intensity of the trade war, and since we shall not be asked to share in the profits whoever wins we may refrain from taking sides. The aspect which chiefly concerns us, however, is that one result of the end of Lease Lend in what is in fact the concluding stage of the war and not the beginning of peace, will be the further increase of the National Debt, in order to subsidise a war that has already been won. As the capitalists have not the patriotic illusions of the workers, it is not just Wall Street, but an international capitalist clique which has decided we have not paid sufficient. Untold numbers have given their lives, or their features, all have given the best portion of their years, some their homes, their interests, anything or everything they had.

In spite of all this, our real rulers do not think it indecent to send in the bill. The capitalist class, of America in name but internationally in fact, send in the bill for their war. We have been fools in defending them from rival hoodlums but at least we can decline to pay the bill for doing so.

William Cobbett remarked a hundred years ago that while the name of the King is affixed on all our institutions — the King's Army, the King's Navy, the King's Prisons, the King's Courts, etc. — the debt which springs from these institutions is never called the King's debt, and it is in fact the only case in which the nation is honoured so much as to have anything called after it. So far as we are concerned, if King George VI, as the symbol of the real rulers, cannot meet his obligations, that is his worry, and we ought not to pay.

This is a practical issue and not a plaintive abjuration to Mr Attlee, for the bill is not paid by the Chancellor of the Exchequer but by you and me. In particular by means of income tax, the legalised robbery by which money we earn is stolen from us by the

Treasury, thus ensuring we work harder and get less. Pay-As-You-Earn (PAYE) is the legal pickpocketing by which we are paying for the privilege of having suffered. Shall we go on paying it?

Post-war processes are speeded up or slowed down not because some Ministers are efficient and some inefficient, but by reason of the temper of the people. Once the homeless seize empty houses, the Ministry of Health tries to get it organised properly, just as the LPTB made arrangements *after* the shelterers seized the tubes in 1940. The Ministry of Labour give out perpetually contradictory reports as to demobilisation only according to the demonstrations of unrest which they find manifested. The one thing that they fear is direct action. The Chancellor of the Exchequer will find PAYE a very satisfactory arrangement so long as we put up with it. He will see approval in our docility. One or two mass demonstrations of refusal to pay the rake-off would stir him up. Strikes in key industries to demand payment of income tax by the employer would likewise convince Mr Dalton that he never intended to keep the scheme anyway. While we go on paying and grumbling and filling up forms for the Inland Revenue we will foot the bill for the war.

The old highway robber was a gentleman. He demanded your money *or* your life. The modern capitalists want both. The answer is to defend our interests as vigorously as we can until such time as we bring his robbers' castle crashing down over his ears.

8th September 1945   A. M.

FAMINE IN NORTH AFRICA

One day in June of this year, 64 natives were found dead from starvation in the area of Casablanca and Settat alone. All the wheat supplies in Morocco have been exhausted, bread is being made from barley. It is doubtful if the present harvest will provide even enough seed for the next year's sowing of wheat and barley. There will be nothing available for consumption. For lack of food-stuff, cattle are being slaughtered right and left, and soon none will remain. North Africa will soon have a famine that will even be worse than the Indian famine of two years ago. UNRRA hasn't moved into North Africa at all — only Arabs are there. (*The Call*, 10th September 1945)

Political Police Exposed

Since the beginning of tyranny, a system of political spying has been a necessary part of the edifice of government. Informers have carried tales of disaffection to the wielders of power and have received due reward for their filthy work, while those who have worked for liberty have been persecuted as a result of the activities of such degraded men.

With the rise of the modern state, the system of spies has become organised into a secret or semi-secret police which has had for its peculiar province the safeguarding of the ruling class by observing and persecuting its opponents. Some of these political police organisations have gained worldwide notoriety. Before 1917, the famous Czarist Okhrana, or Third Division, aroused horror among all Western liberals, but since that day there have been far more formidable organisations for suppressing political oppositions, particularly the late Gestapo of Nazi Germany and Ovra of Fascist Italy, and the still flourishing Ogpu of Stalinist Russia (it goes by another title today, but 'a rose by any other name would smell as sweet!').

All these really famous bodies of political police have flourished where the system of government was or is openly despotic or dictatorial. Democratic politicians have made great use of them in their own propaganda, and have claimed that in their own countries such institutions could not exist. But those who know the ways of politicians will also know that it is a favourite device of theirs to accuse an opponent loudly of a fault which they themselves are guilty of committing in order to divert attention from their own failings. And in this case there is no exception. So-called democratic countries have also their political bodies, and the existence of such organisations has been a living disproof of the freedom which they pretend to confer on their subjects. While a single political policeman exists, no country can make the pretence of freedom.

'This could happen here'

We are often told that in England there is no political police — that such an institution would be incompatible with the spirit of British democracy. Churchill in his election campaign tried to discredit his opponents by declaring that if the Labour Party were returned to power they would institute a political police to crush

opposition to their rule. The obvious inference was that no
political police was in existence under Churchill and, while people
laughed at Churchill's accusations against the Labour Party, they
did not go so far as to question the deliberately false basis on which
he made his statement. Of course, Churchill's accusation was true
in a degree, because the Labour Government have continued to
operate the political police which Churchill used against the
people who opposed the war, but which he chose to ignore in his
statement.

For England has its own political police force — the Special
Branch of Scotland Yard — of whose very existence many people
seem to be unaware, although it has gained a certain unsavoury
fame in the past year or so owing to publicity given to its actions
against minority groups, particularly the Trotskyists and, later, the
Anarchists.

The Special Branch was actually founded in the early years of
the present century. A certain facade of spy-hunting and so forth
has been used to give it justification, in spite of the fact that all the
real work in this connection is done by MI5 — the sinister military
intelligence organisation which also plays a part, difficult to assess,
in the political life of the country. But despite all the various jobs
of such a kind that happen to come within the province of the
Special Branch, its main function in the eyes of the ruling class — a
function whose importance has grown steadily since its formation
— is that of spying on opposition political groups and
revolutionary movements, and endeavouring to suppress them
whenever their activity frightens the government. The fact that no
separate body of political police exists in this country has been
used as a reason to contend that we have no political police at all.
But this is a self-evident fiction, when one considers the activities
of the Special Branch, which, although it may be nominally only
one department of the Metropolitan Police, is in reality a
miniature Gestapo in all its fundamental characteristics of political
discrimination and underhanded spying.

Pedigree of the Special Branch
Even before the advent of the Special Branch, political police
activities were not unknown in England. Our present spy
inspectors and sneak sergeants are all in the fine old English
tradition of the informers Oliver and Castle, who gained such evil
notoriety for their activities against the workers' unions in the

early days of the nineteenth century. Later, in the 1850s, Herzen, the friend of Bakunin, records the use of detectives to report the activities of political refugees in England. In particular, he describes the case of Rex v Bernard, where Judge Campbell allowed the defending counsel, in spite of protests, to describe a political detective as a 'spy'. So that even the English judicature recognises the contemptibility of the miserable individuals who search out its victims, and by permission of a deceased old gentleman in a horsehair wig we have the right to call our friends of the Special Branch by at least part of their real title.

At the beginning of the present war the Special Branch was reported to have a staff of 180. Since then, it has increased considerably, and a good deal more of the workers' money has been spent on keeping these renegades who are willing to serve the ruling class in any way for the suppression of their fellow workers. The Special Branch is not a body of political experts. Most of its members are ignorant of elementary social facts and have no understanding of the ideas of the people they try to suppress. This ignorance, of course, is in the interests of their bosses, as they are less likely to become sympathetic with revolutionaries than intelligent men would be. It is a revealing fact that some of the leading men of the Special Branch reached their positions by way of the vice squads. They have two functions, and no more — spying and bullying.

Police methods have never been over clean. The object of the average policeman is not to see that justice is done, but to obtain convictions, irrespective of the merits of the case. At one time, in certain police forces, promotion was based more or less on the number of convictions an officer obtained, and always the police are forced on by pressure from above to obtain a continual stream of 'criminals' to show their superiors how efficient they are. Moreover, although all policemen were not necessarily psychopaths, the police force undoubtedly attracts sadists and power maniacs of various kinds, and also brings out the latent neuroses in many men who would be harmless in normal life. The ruling class desire a body of men who will be actively interested in preserving both property and the state, and they are ready to accept the aberrations of those whom they find to be good and enthusiastic servants. Indeed, the extra-legal cruelties and oppressions of the police are all part of the terror by which people are held in awe by government-made laws.

Paid informers

The Special Branch is no better than any other police force in its methods, except that it has not been able to act on so grand a scale as, say, the Ogpu. Its officers have spied and threatened in order to gain information regarding minority opposition groups. They have made use of informers and tried to corrupt honest men to this loathsome trade. Only recently two men who appeared in a London court on a black market offence admitted that they were paid by the police to act as 'narks'. The police made no denial. We have also seen the signed confession of a man who acted as an informer to the Special Branch against a small opposition political group.

But there are even more contemptible forms of spying into the private affairs of revolutionaries and oppositionists. When the letters of a number of anarchists *all* arrive later than they should and mostly bear signs of having been opened in transit, when telephones are persistently eccentric in their action, all we can say is that we do not believe in fairies, especially when police officers mention in conversation facts which can only have been heard over the telephone.

A statement signed by many leading writers and published widely at the time of the anarchist trial early this year drew attention to the extra-legal methods used by the Special Branch in conducting their searches. In the case of the searches of the Freedom Press premises and of the houses of anarchists, no attempt was made to decide what material was relevant to the charge. Files, card indexes, typewriters, letters, etc., were all bundled into sacks, taken away and kept for months. In the case of Freedom Press, the result was a complete disruption of the normal business of the office, an effect which had no doubt been intended. In the case of private individuals, not only political documents but also valuable literary and professional manuscripts were taken away to be subjected to the prying noses of Scotland Yard. The whole affair was reminiscent of the attacks by fascist bands on the offices of revolutionary newspapers during Mussolini's rise to power in Italy.

Irregular searches

The abuses of law in connection with searches could be discussed at much greater length. In one case, when a comrade was away, the police broke into his studio, ransacked it, and departed without leaving any notification. In the case of the Trotskyists, men and women were subjected to gross personal indignities in the police search for mythical documents. In the recent prosecution of Albert Meltzer, the police, after his arrest, went and searched his room, without either he or his landlady being present, and many papers were taken away — this although Regulation 88a, which authorised the search of premises for political documents, has been recinded. A further instance of the abuse of law was the searching of Tom Earley and Cecil Stone when they were arrested for selling *Freedom*. It is not the usual practice to search minor offenders of this kind, and it is obvious that these, like the other political searches, were aimed more at humiliating and terrorising opponents of the government than anything else.

A further completely extra-legal practice on the part of the Special Branch is to visit the employers and landlords of members of political minorities and inform them of the opinions of their employees or tenants, with a few added words of advice. As a result of such despicable acts, a number of anarchists have recently been sacked following police visits to their places of work. It was a curious coincidence, moreover, that Freedom Press received notice to quit its premises in Belsize Road just before the December raid, and that the deal for the first new premises to be found was almost closed when the owners suddenly called off negotiations without giving any reason.

The police, as all people who have had any contact with them soon discover, are incapable of telling the truth consistently, and in more than one recent case where anarchists have been concerned, police officers have deliberately given false information in the witness box in order to prove their cases.

Another interesting point of the Special Branch activities is that, although it is a department concerned with political offenders, its officers are always ready to use non-political excuses in order to frame their victims. Philip Sansom was sentenced on a ridiculous charge of possessing an army overcoat. Albert Meltzer was sentenced for failing to notify a change of address, but the charge was brought by a Special Branch officer. Moreover, it has been through the activities of the Special Branch that a number of aliens have recently been interned again because they associated with unorthodox political groups. One of these was Josef Moravak, a proved anti-fascist who is now held in the concentration camp at Stanmore because he associated with anarchists and came under the notice of the Special Branch.

The Black Records

Perhaps the most sinister part of the political police in this country
is the complicated system of records which are kept of left-wing
people. This library of dossiers dates from the beginning of the
present century, and includes the records of hundreds of
thousands of people who have shown any kind of activity in
left-wing opposition or anti-war groups. The authorities set so
much store by it that they evacuated it to the country during the
war, so that the bomb we all hoped would fall on Scotland Yard
would have been of no use after all. It is obvious what use would
be made of such a system of records if a really reactionary
government came to power in this country, and this institution, if
nothing else, shows how the Special Branch has been built up as a
skeleton Gestapo for use in some future eventuality.

In spite of the fact that a Labour Government is in power, the
Special Branch continues to function, to spy, and to persecute.
The library of dossiers is still retained, containing no doubt the
records of many members of the present House of Commons. This
surely is a testing point of the sincerity of the Labour Cabinet. Will
they continue to use such reactionary institutions? It is possible,
though highly improbable, that they are only dimly aware of what
goes on in the dark places of Scotland Yard. If this is so, it is time
they made an enquiry into such reactionary bodies. A Labour
Government that keeps a political police and political dossiers for
the use of future reactionaries, stands self-condemned as
reactionary itself.

6th October 1945   JUNIUS II

HER MASTER'S VOICE

"Soviet Union is giving Warsaw a gift of a new radio station which
will be audible throughout the entire world, Moscow radio announ-
ced yesterday.   (*News Chronicle*, 12th July 1945)

Warsaw will be able to talk to the world, but the words will be
put into her mouth by Moscow.

'WAR CRIMINALS'

The Nuremberg Red Herring

The long series of trials of war criminals and collaborators continue to drag their sorry length across the contemporary international scene, and their effect so far has been not to breed just indignation against the psychopaths who stand in the dock, victims of their own perfidy and scapegoats of a corrupt society, so much as to reveal that their corruption permeates the whole of the world they represent, and lays its evil shadow on the judge as well as on the victim. If the war had ended the other way round, one reflects, the British and Russian governments would have provided the victims for very similar trials, and it cannot easily be said that British armament manufacturers were any less guilty of the war than Krupp, or that Stalin was any less bloodthirsty to his enemies than Goering. No doubt the trials would have been arranged in a different way, but their conclusions would have been similar, and designed for similar propaganda ends.

But, in fact, the propaganda that it was hoped to gain has gone rather flat in the process. Laval, for instance, cut a better figure than his judges, and the only effect of his death has been to give him a martyr's crown, while, if he had been allowed to live, nobody would ever have regarded him as other than an unsuccessful rogue.

The Belsen trial revealed the 'horrible monsters' in the dock to be psychological cases who were as much victims of their environments as the people they killed and tortured. To execute them is an evasion of the real issue, that while society is based on force, in certain acute situations it will breed sadism of this type among servants. But to admit that it would have meant a denial of the very basis of government, and no set of judges can afford to do that. So Kramer and his associates in their turn became the victims of the code of violence that made them the torturers they were.

Now we are witnessing the trial of the really *big* war criminals by the pure Allies who never started a war in all the centuries of their existence. But when we look at the figures in the dock, we begin to remember by association other figures — British politicians who

welcomed the coming of Nazism to Germany, British manufacturers and financiers who helped to put the Nazis in a position to
make war, Russian politicians who made a pact with the Nazis,
and all the rest of the sinister figures who helped in the conspiracy
to crush the working class which culminated in the great climax of
the war. Why are they not also in the dock? Ribbentrop, let down
by his former friends, begins to wonder why at least they are not in
the witness box. But, we are told, it is unlikely that British
politicians would be allowed to give evidence, for fear of revealing
secrets of national importance. For fear, in other words, of
betraying the plot against freedom in which they were accomplices
of the men in the dock.

If a soldier or worker had shot Goering or any of his associates
in the heat of anger, we should not have blamed him. But when we
see these men standing before their fellows in tyranny, we protest
against the whole ridiculous pageant of 'justice', which we realise
as well as the ruling class is merely propaganda to deceive the
workers.

But it is unsuccessful propaganda. People are losing interest in
it, and in Goering and Co. Now they have ceased to be real enemies
of freedom. As George Orwell said a few weeks ago in *The
Tribune*:

"Actually there is little acute hatred of Germany left in this country, and
even less, I should expect to find, in the army of occupation. Only the
minority of sadists, who must have their 'atrocities' from one source or
another, take a keen interest in the hunting-down of war criminals and
quislings. If you ask the average man what crime Goering, Ribbentrop
and the rest are to be charged with at their trial, he cannot tell you.
Somehow the punishment of these monsters ceases to seem attractive
when it becomes possible: indeed, once under lock and key, they almost
cease to be monsters."

It is time the workers looked to the enemies who still have the
power to hurt them instead of troubling with those who have lost
that power. Goering and his friends, whatever their past crimes,
are broken, discredited men, who are being sacrificed because
they are no longer of any use to their class. But the sensible man
will remember that revenge is a poor substitute for freedom, and
that such circuses are designed not for our benefit so much as to
hide from us the fact that the function of the Nazi leaders, the
suppression of the individual in the interests of the state, is still
being carried on by others who now pretend to be their enemies.
1st December 1945

Sham Justice

In most countries the trials of 'war criminals' have been held during the past months and the Nuremburg trials, which are to continue for a number of weeks more, are the show-piece both insofar as the criminals concerned in it and in the sense of the theatrical in the spectacular arrangements made for the staging of it. In this country it was necessary to have a trial or two to satisfy the public's lust for the macabre, and during the last few weeks a number of minor 'war criminals' have taken their stand in the dock at the Old Bailey. In most cases the people affected have been former members of the defunct British Union of Fascists, and they have all more or less been charged with the same crimes, of assisting the enemy by broadcasting and writing for him. For this they have been branded as traitors by the national press.

I looked up the definition of traitor in the *Oxford Concise Dictionary* and this is what I found: "Traitor — one who violates his allegiance or acts disloyally (to country, king, cause, religion, principles, himself, etc.)". This definition, if accepted, must render the law on the question somewhat vague. A man who is loyal to himself, to his principles or to his cause may at the same time find himself in conflict with his king and country. Ethically, surely a man should be loyal to himself and his principles because this is something over which he has control. In the case of king and country it is an accident of birth whether he is born in Franco's Spain, democratic Sweden or Hitler's Germany. But then justice today is not concerned with ethical questions. This is clearly shown by a case in the writer's own experience. When I was in Wormwood Scrubbs prison recently, there were two men working alongside one another in one of the workshops. One was a German and the other an Englishman. The German had been sentenced by an English court to two years imprisonment for having taken part with others in beating up a German who had betrayed military secrets to the British which had allowed them to locate and bomb a secret factory in Germany. The Germans considered this man a traitor to the fatherland, while the British had made him out to be a anti-Nazi patriot! The Englishman sitting alongside the German had been sentenced at the Old Bailey to ten years penal servitude for the same crime as the anti-Nazi German, but the other way round! Thus we see 'justice' at work:

in one case the traitor was sentenced, in the other the man who beat up a traitor is sentenced and the traitor glorified.

The case of Joyce — and to a lesser degree Amery — points to the hypocrisy of law and justice as understood in present society. The anarchists have no reason to speak on behalf of fascists. In all countries where fascism has achieved power anarchists have been among their first victims. But this fact must not prevent us from exposing the sham justice that has been shown in the Joyce trial. Sir Hartley Shawcross, Socialist Attorney General, based his case on the grounds that Joyce owed allegiance to the Crown. We will just mention in passing that from the legal point of view the allegiance was based on the fact that he held a British passport to which, as an American citizen, he had no right! A few weeks later at Nuremburg, Sir Hartley had obviously forgotten what he had told Joyce about allegiance and declared for the whole world to hear the following noble words: "*There comes a point when a man must refuse to answer his leader if he is also to answer to his conscience*". These are words which should not easily be forgotten; they are words which should be handed down from father to son. But before doing so, and possibly finding ourselves up at the Old Bailey, perhaps someone would enquire of our rulers whether these fine sentiments are for export, or whether they only apply to the German people *vis a vis* their leaders who are now in the dock!

If the British Government want to make the fact of being a militant fascist punishable by death then let them have the courage to say so. The trials at the Old Bailey are just a farce and Joyce and Amery just scapegoats, for if it were justice that was being meted out to them by the courts then, as the *Manchester Guardian* pointed out, their fate would be shared "by many who walk untouched among us".

29th December 1945   V. R.

British Lidices

When the Nazis destroyed a Czech village called Lidice a wave of indignation swept all 'democratic' countries. But during the last month villages have been burnt or bombed to the ground by British troops and air force among almost complete indifference.

Yet the facts are revolting enough to move people's conscience. On the 13th December newspapers announced that, following the murder of the British major and the Red Cross girl working near Padang in Sumatra, further reprisals had been taken in addition to the arrest of several Indonesians and the shooting of others who attempted to escape. Tabag village where the bodies were found had been burnt down.

The following day it was announced that from Batavia a battalion of Indian infantry with strong tank and artillery support set forth for a punitive expedition to Bekasi, the small town where the crew and passengers of a crashed Dakota were murdered three weeks before. Petrol was poured over the buildings and the town was razed to the ground. Efforts were made to spare the houses of the Chinese but in the general conflagration they too caught fire.

In Indo-China British troops used methods singularly similar to those used by Mussolini in Abyssinia. While Tabag was being destroyed, Spitfires 'shot up the emplacement' of a native position in Indo-China. The report admits that the British Commander declared that he "undertook the mission reluctantly". An official declared: "It was not considered cricket to use the RAF for offensive action against people who are unable to retaliate in kind".

When Germans burnt villages to the ground they committed atrocities, when the British do it it's 'not playing cricket', but the effect on the population is the same. It is to foster hatred amongst nations and races and make impossible a peaceful and happy world.

29th December 1945

'Go to Hell' Cry to Britain
Stop British intervention

Our Labour War Minister J. J. Lawson, chose the moment when British marines, soldiers and airmen were shooting down the people of Southern Asia to pay this tribute to the British soldier:

"It has been said that the British soldier is the best ambassador we have. I think he is better than most ambassadors. By the peculiar nature of his tasks the British soldier is in some directions a genius. He has certain gifts of his own. He always seemed to make people laugh. I have never known an ambassador who could make people laugh."

The soldiers of the Labour Government of Britain are not ambassadors of laughter. Java is bombed by rocket-firing Mosquitoes and troops are concentrated at key points 'ready for anything'. Indo-China is submitted to military rule, Indian demonstrators are fired upon.

The man directing Britain's foreign policy, Ernest Bevin, who declared at the Conference of the Labour Party in 1939: "I am anxious to prevent the Labour Movement fighting for the preservation of the Paris Bourse, the London Stock Exchange and Wall Street", is not only asking British soldiers to die to defend the interests of those big three, but also to defend Dutch interests in Indonesia.

What is the Atlantic Charter?
Let us remember once again the big lie, the principle of the Atlantic Charter, which says: "Britain and America respect the right of all people to choose the form of government under which they will live, and they wish to see sovereign rights and self-government restored to those who have been forcibly deprived of them". Millions of people have died thinking they were defending that principle. Now men and women who dare to inscribe that principle on their banners are shot down by the 'defenders of democracy'.

The other war to end wars and to make the world safe for democracy ended in the Amritsar massacre. There are massacres every day now in Indo-China, India and Java. The men who sit in judgement on the murderers of Lidiee are ordering Javanese villages to be burnt to the ground as reprisals.

What is the crime of these 'extremists', of these 'rebels', of these 'undesirable elements' and 'rioters'? Pandit Nehru declared a few days ago in Lahore: "Four hundred million Indians can no longer tolerate British domination. We are now very impatient to throw away the yoke of slavery. We are now terribly sick of the British Government; we say, 'go to hell'."

'Go to hell' echo the Indian masses, 'you have robbed us of our riches, you have forced our women and children down the mines'. 'Go to hell' echo the Indo-Chinese people, 'you are protecting French business people and officials who have starved us for generations, who have poisoned us with opium and alcohol in order to increase their profits'. 'Go to hell' cry the Indonesians, 'we have worked on tea and rubber plantations at starvation wages, we have been sent to terror-ridden concentration camps in the jungles of New Guinea as soon as we have dared to protest'. In 1938 the profits of the Dutch firms derived from their richest enterprises were over £25 million. The wages in Dutch concerns ranged from 2s 6d to 7s 6d a week at ten hours a day. The average income of the inhabitants of the colony was 1½d a day. This is not propaganda put over by 'extremists', they are figures published by the International Labour Office. No amount of bombing of Indonesian radio stations can destroy these fearful facts.

Dutch hypocrisy

What answer does the Dutch government give to these accusations of exploitation and oppression? There is Queen Wilhelmina's sickening hypocritical speech from the throne at the opening of the Netherlands Provisional Parliament:

"I deeply regret the suffering which inevitably overtakes the population of Java until order has been restored. We are continuing to try and salvage the future of this ravaged land for the Dutch and for the Indonesians — the future of a commonwealth built on the voluntarily accepted solidarity of the parts of the empire."

The "voluntarily accepted solidarity" has already manifested itself in thousands of casualties among British and Indian troops and Dutch and Indonesian civilian population.

The excuse for British intervention, that India, Indo-China and the Dutch Indies are not fit for democracy, is farcical. Is Portugal with its fake elections a democracy? Is Spain with its prisons full of political prisoners a democracy? Is Poland, ruled by the GPU? Is Hungary, under the heel of Butcher Horthy? Yet all those countries are recognised by Britain as independent and we are proud to call Portugal our oldest ally!

The Chairman of the Labour Party, Harold Laski, has condemned the policy of the Governments in Indonesia and Indo-China. He said: "It makes the British claims to have been engaged in a war for democracy and freedom a hollow mockery all over South East Asia". If this represents the view of the Labour Party why is a Labour Government ordering British and Indian troops to shoot down and bomb Indonesians and Indo-Chinese? Why is it putting the French and Dutch back in the position where they can ruthlessly exploit millions of people who have clearly shown their hatred of foreign rule?

End Intervention in Asia!
The shedding of blood in South East Asia must be stopped. No faith can be put in the Labour Government. They have shown themselves cold-blooded imperialists like any Tory government. America is standing aloof supplying lend-lease weapons to crush the Indonesians, but letting Britain do the dirty work. Russia, so articulate on the question of the atomic bomb, has refrained from coming out on the side of colonial people.

The only effective help has come and must continue to come from the workers. The Australian workers who have refused to handle supplies for the Dutch, the British seamen who refused to carry Dutch troops, have shown the way.

When Britain tried to crush the Russian revolution, dockers refused to load the 'Jolly George' with munitions. Bevin was with the dockers then. Our answer to him now must be in the spirit which animated the dockers of the 'Jolly George'.

NOT A SOLDIER — NOT A ROUND OF AMMUNITION — NOT A MACHINE GUN — NOT A PLANE FOR BRITISH INTERVENTION IN ASIA.
1st December 1945

The Big Three Meeting

The Big Three have met once again. This time Russia's suggestion has been followed and they have met in Moscow. Didn't Mr Molotov say at the conference last September that everything was going wrong due, partly at least, to the London atmosphere which was not suited to really serious conferences. And then, the presence of the not-so-big-Big-Two annoyed considerably the Commissar for Foreign Affairs.

But, what has not changed is the conspiratorial atmosphere which surrounds all international meetings, particularly since we have entered the era of atomic democracy. All that the Press has been allowed to publish on the Moscow gathering strangely resembled health bulletins. One day it was revealed that "The talks are proceeding positively rather than negatively" and the next day it was triumphantly announced that "they are going on well". Recent history shows how much one should rely on health bulletins. The day before Patton died it was announced that the general's condition was 'excellent'.

The only possible explanation for the silence which surrounded the meeting is that Messrs Byrnes and Molotov thought that it would be embarrassing if the public came to know the background of the revolts in Iran, how the Chinese question was settled, the bargainings over Germany and their real feelings about the Circus of the United Nations which began its work in London on the 10th January.

The problem of Iran is becoming increasingly more complex. Only fellow-travellers or morons can have believed that the autonomist movement in Azerbaidjan was a popular revolt against a government with fascist leanings. The gentlemen of Teheran are no democrats of course, no more than King Ibn-Saud of Arabia or the Egyptian government. But that's not the point. The Iranian government is threatened with extinction because it has refused petrol concessions to Russia. Geologists estimate that the petrol reserves of Azerbaidjan are amongst the most important in the world. This alone would justify a 'popular' revolt. But Azerbaidjan is also a strategic point of first importance. It is on the Northern land route to India. If the Red Army settles down in that province it will constitute a real and immediate threat to the lifeline of the British Empire. While Soviet diplomacy exerts a pressure on England and America at Teheran it launches an attack against Turkey, who is an ally of the same powers, and who defends the Northern approach to the sea route towards India.

Middle East problems which have, during the last few months occupied such a prominent place, are so intimately inter-linked that it is difficult to separate them. While Russia is trying to acquire new sources of petrol England and America struggle to preserve theirs. It is possible to say to-day with a degree of certainty that nothing will be done to allow European Jews to settle in Palestine. Let us leave on one side the question of principle. On both sides of the Atlantic many tears have been shed over the "unfortunate survivors of Hitler's massacres". These are merely crocodile tears. The US Congress has passed resolutions asking Truman to obtain from Attlee a promise that Jews should be allowed to enter the Holy Land. Truman will do nothing of the kind. He knows that the Standard Oil of California and the Standard Oil of Texas have received important concessions from Ibn-Saud. Truman 'knows' that thanks to these concessions this blood-thirsty, medieval, autocratic king of Arabia has become "a good democrat and a good ally". He knows too that if he upsets him America may lose fuel bases in a part of the world which is strategically of primary importance particularly in view of the desire for expansion of our Soviet Ally. Truman therefore prefers to allow several thousand Jews to enter America and pacify in that manner liberal electors and the Jewish minority which represents several million votes in the United States.

While at the Moscow Conference the American Government have not modified their position regarding the atomic bomb they have, nevertheless, made a few concessions to Stalin. Thus Tito has been recognised in London and Washington. But it looks as if the latest Kremlin demands will meet with fierce opposition. These demands which we have mentioned before, menace not only Turkey but the whole structure carefully worked out by Britain in the Near and Middle East.

The method used by Stalin is remarkable in itself. His declarations of the 'historical right' of Russia over some Turkish province reminds one without great effort of German 'rights' on the Sudetens. The method used is the same. The aim is the same. In 1938 we knew that Hitler was massing important military forces on the border of Czechoslovakia. To-day Stalin is massing important military forces on the border of Turkey as well as in the Caucasus, Bulgaria and Rumania. The fact is that, though the Press hardly mentions it, the Bulgarian Army has never been demobilised. The only Russian soldiers to leave Bulgaria were old or one-legged men. We know too that the Russian fleet on the Black Sea is more powerful than ever. This explains why the Turkish government answers the menacing demands of Russia by coolly declaring that they are ready to make war. Needless to say that the Turks have consulted the other Big Two beforehand.

On some questions however, complete agreement has been reached in Moscow as, for example, regarding the Chinese Civil War. The Yenan Communists have been abandoned by Stalin even before the Americans attacked them. Already last August there had been the Moscow-Chunking pact by which Stalin recognised the authority of Chang Kai Shek as the central government of China. Later an agreement took place between Chunking and the Soviet authorities according to which Russian troops would occupy Manchuria till the arrival of Chang Kai Shek's troops, to protect it, in fact, *against* the Communists. Fellow-travellers should be careful not to condemn too violently the attitude of the Americans in China. There was a time when Stalin was playing Yenan against Chunking but he does no seem to need to do this any longer. Apparently Stalin has found ground for agreement with Chang Kai Shek the specialist in bloody exterminations of revolutions.

After the serious 'discussions' they had at Moscow, American, British and Russian statesmen will not be able to take a nice rest at this puppet-show which is called the General Assembly of the United Nations. It is not difficult to foresee that nothing will be done in London. The debates will be open to the Press, of course, but only because they will be without any interest or importance.

12th January 1946   KATHERINE WARREN

Patton Explains

General Patton who achieved fame during the war more by his brutality and showmanship than his military achievements, met with a timely death, in a motor accident, shortly after the end of the war. His memoirs have now been published in America and they will not disappoint those who saw in him the incarnation of militarism with all its violence and stupidity.

Of the famous incident when Patton struck a bed-ridden soldier across the face, during one of his visits to the Italian front, he writes:

"I am convinced that my action in this case was entirely correct, and that had other officers had the courage to do likewise, the shameful use of 'battle fatigue' as an excuse for cowardice would have been infinitely reduced."

In another part of his book, he writes:

"One of the great defects in our military establishment is the giving of weak sentences for military offences . . . I am convinced that, in justice to other men, soldiers who go to sleep on post, who go absent for an unreasonable time during combat, who shirk in battle, should be executed.

It is utterly stupid to say that general officers . . . are not capable of knowing how to remove the life of one miserable poltroon."

Patton was not only convinced that he had supreme power over men, God was also to be bullied to do what he wanted. Shortly before Christmas 1944, Patton recalls:

"The weather was so bad that I directed all army chaplains to pray for dry weather."

He called Chaplain O'Neill of the Third Army into his office and the conversation went along these lines:

General Patton: Chaplain, I want you to publish a prayer for good weather. I'm tired of these soldiers having to fight mud and floods as well as Germans. See if you can't get God to work on our side.

Chaplain O'Neill: Sir, it's going to take a pretty thick prayer rug for that kind of praying.

Patton: I don't care if it takes the flying carpet. I want the praying done.

O'Neill: Yes, sir. May I say, general, that it usually isn't a customary thing among men of my profession to pray for clear weather to kill fellow men.

Patton: Chaplain, are you teaching me theology or are you the chaplain of the Third Army? I want a prayer.

O'Neill: Yes, sir.

The prayer was issued to the troops, and the next day the weather cleared.

7th February 1948

An Old French Tradition

The *New Statesman & Nation* recently (9th July 1949) published an article with the somewhat strange title 'A Meditation on Being Beaten Up' by a Mr Robert Payne. The writer happened to be passing through St. Germain des Près in Paris on 1st July at 5 pm when about 400 students who had just finished their *bachot* examinations were showing their feelings by singing and shouting and dancing in the middle of the streets, and not unnaturally holding up the traffic in the process. Then the police vans arrived and in Mr Payne's words:

"Their tyres screamed, and their sirens screamed louder. There was panic among the students, for the police cars drove straight at them — I still cannot understand why none of the students were run down . . . The police cars came to a stop. The police jumped out with truncheons, revolvers at their sides, their faces set for murder — the ugliest brood of Frenchmen I have ever seen. They simply threw themselves at isolated and defenceless groups of students, hurled them on to the pavement, cursed them in the foulest language, and then frogmarched those who were in their power to the police vans. After about four quite obviously innocent students had been clubbed and thrown into the car, I took out a piece of paper and began to take down the numbers on the collars of the more brutal policemen."

The next three minutes were eventful for Mr Payne and he has a vivid recollection of them.

"Three policemen charged me, swore at me, threatened to 'kick my arse right the way through', and then in unison decided to give me a lesson. Evidently, even in France, one should not take down numbers on collars. I remember five terrific blows on the side of my head, and then the whole of the Boulevard St. Germain began wheeling like a futurist painting. I was frog-marched to the van. I remember thinking: In the van it will be all right, it will be quite calm and probably very hot, for it was a hot day. But this is not at all the technique. The moment you are thrown into the van the beating begins again, and there are very well-fed policemen waiting to club you at the moment you are thrown in."

Eventually when the van was stuffed full with victims they were driven to the police station.

"The guardroom was filled with brutal, coarse-faced clowns who played dominoes, swore, waited for orders, and refused to answer any questions of the prisoners except with threats . . . There was no longer any physical brutality; but the psychological brutality remained — threats, silence, the long wait before the names and the charges are written in the dossier. When it came to my turn to be examined, I was asked who I was. I said I was a professor, their faces fell, almost on their knees they asked me to leave."

Mr Payne was lucky, since he escaped the traditional *passage à tabac* (beatings with truncheons) with which the French police defend the law. And Mr Payne is obviously naive when he attributes this police violence to the bad example given by the Nazi occupation forces. And in a subsequent issue, a correspondent rightly points out that this kind of treatment existed long before the war and quotes from personal experience in 1938 when he was detained 17 hours because he had left his passport behind at his hotel only five minutes walk from the police station.

But these are minor incidents in a long history of police brutality, and readers of this column may recall that *Freedom* revealed a number of cases including one in which the victim died as a result of the beating-up he received at police headquarters.

In France everybody knows what it means to fall into the hands of the police. In hospitals doctors and nurses often have their victims as patients. Besides our contemporary *Le Libertaire* (which recently published a courageous editorial denouncing police violence), few voices are raised in protest. When one discusses these matters with Frenchmen they shrug their shoulders adding, "Nothing can be done. Everyone knows about it, but we can do nothing to stop it".

In Paris the visitor immediately feels the power of the police. They are everywhere; van-loads of them seem to be on the move wherever one turns; police posts are to be found in the most unexpected places, and when one sees them close-up with their revolvers at their sides and white truncheons (and at demonstrations some carry Tommy guns) one feels that the police rule Paris. And are there really no men of goodwill to support the Anarchists in demanding that police brutality shall cease in France?

6th August 1949   LIBERTARIAN

The Case of Dr May

The case of Dr Alan Nunn May the young scientist who was sentenced at the Old Bailey to 10 years imprisonment has aroused considerable indignation among many people in this country. The charge to which he pleaded not guilty in the Magistrate's Court but to which he pleaded guilty when he appeared at the Old Bailey, was that "he gave to an unknown person for a purpose prejudicial to the safety and interest of the State, information about atomic research calculated to be useful to an enemy".

The prosecution's case rested on a statement made by Dr May when he was seen by Lt Col Burt head of the Special Branch of the CID of the military Intelligence authorities.

"About a year ago, while in Canada, I was contacted by an individual whose identity I decline to divulge. He called on me at my private apartment in Montreal and apparently knew I was employed by the Montreal laboratory, and sought information from me concerning atomic research . . . After this preliminary meeting I met the individual on several subsequent occasions while in Canada . . . I gave the man a routine report on atomic research as known to me. This information was mostly of a character which has since been published or is about to be published."

Mr Gerald Gardiner defending remarked that Dr May told him that the person to whom he gave the information was Russian. From Dr May's statement he declared that he only embarked on this affair because he thought he was making a contribution for the safety of mankind. "I certainly did not do it for gain." It was clear from the whole case that Dr May was a person who had taken Mr Churchill's perorations about our great ally, Russia, seriously and was a victim of his political beliefs, deserving a staunch defence, at least by the Communist Party. But remembering the Communist Party's attitude to their National Organiser when he was sentenced to seven years imprisonment for passing on information to Russia we were prepared for dead silence on the subject. This was in fact the attitude of the *Daily Worker*. A routine report on the trial — no comments. But the *Daily Worker* has now seen which way the wind is blowing. Letters have been published in the National Press and the *News Chronicle* devoted its editorial column to the case. So now the *Daily Worker* has 'courageously' joined the fray — indignant letters to the Editor which had probably been in the Editor's basket a week, followed by an Editorial Comment in the

Daily Worker of May 14th entitled 'Case for Mercy'. We quote a passage from the Editor's comment:

"What Dr May was in a position to disclose was fundamental scientific data relating to atomic energy — in other words, data of a kind which was always made public in the period before the war. Indeed, without the international exchange of scientific information present day developments in the utilisation of atomic energy would never have taken place.

Many scientists are of the opinion that such fundamental scientific data should be shared and that scientific discoveries should not be converted into secret diplomatic weapons. Dr May's action was a consequence of his passionate adherence to this view."

And to think that the *Daily Worker* might easily have withheld this brilliant defence of Dr May if the Capitalist Press had not published letters defending him and if the Association of Scientific Workers had not made a plea on Dr May's behalf! For surely such a comment could have been written the day after Dr May was sentenced and not a fortnight after. It would have been much more effective, and would have prevented those who follow Communist Party diplomacy from inferring that Dr May had been dropped by the Communist Party in the same way as Springhall was.

So far as we are concerned we protest energetically against the conviction. We feel however that Dr May's case would have been much stronger if instead of disclosing the information on Atomic energy only when approached by a Russian agent, he had called a public meeting and at that meeting either disclosed the information or at least made a very strong plea that data on atomic energy should be internationally shared. He would have had strong support from scientific and technical workers throughout the country.

The case of Dr May also raises some very important questions on the Freedom of the Individual in Society and we propose to deal with this question in a future issue of *Freedom*. Meanwhile we have drawn the attention of the Freedom Defence Committee to our views on this case in the hope that they will be able to give it the utmost publicity.

18th May 1946

The Eisler Case

The action of the British Government in arresting Eisler has given rise to justifiable misgivings in liberal circles, for it clearly shows how political expediency overrides principles of civil liberty, and hence how insecurely those civil liberties are maintained.

That Eisler is a Communist is neither here nor there. Nor does it matter that the Communists, and even their stooges in the National Council for Civil Liberties, show no concern for the principles of civil liberty when it is a question of victimising their political opponents, e.g. Fascists and Trotskyists. Because Eisler and his associates are indifferent to such conceptions is no reason at all for denying them the advantages of an immunity from unwarranted police action. We are here concerned with the principles of liberty, and questions of expediency have nothing to do with such principles. Eisler was escaping from the USA on a Polish ship, when British police boarded the ship at Southampton and, disregarding the protests of the captain, removed their man by force. It was quite clear that the British Government has acted at the request of the US Government, but whether they have any right to take a man off a ship belonging to another country is not at all clear. The whole episode is reminiscent of those cases where Nazi or Russian police have kidnapped a political refugee and brought him into their own territory for the purpose of exacting the revenge of a totalitarian government on its opponents. When Eisler appeared at Bow Street, Communists demonstrated outside with posters saying, 'No American methods here — release Eisler'. It would have been just as true to say, 'No Soviet methods here' or 'No Fascist methods here', but that does not in the least alter the case.

It seems that it is up to the Home Secretary to decide whether Eisler's alleged offence in America is 'criminal' or 'political', for if the latter an extradition order should not be granted. We pass over the impertinence of such an enquiry, and will content ourselves with remarking that such a distinction is not supposed to be valid in this country, for 'no one is penalised for his political opinions'. This is definitely not true in America where anti-syndicalist laws are in force in several states, and anti-anarchist laws also.

In the past, the right of political asylum in this country has been extended to all political refugees, even those charged with

assassinations if it is clear that such assassinations were of a
political nature. This conception of political asylum was very
strong in the nineteenth century, but has steadily weakened since,
considerations of expediency gradually gaining more and more
ground.

There remains one more aspect of the Eisler case. If he is
committed, the circumstances of his arrest could well be held to be
illegal, in which case a judge should dismiss the whole charge. On
one occasion when the Home Secretary disregarded a writ issued
by a judge, the judge committed him for contempt of court! So it is
still open to the judiciary to make a stand for the principles of civil
liberty.

28th May 1949

WAR & CRIME

Who are the Criminals?

So much publicity has been given to the 'crime wave' that one would imagine, from merely reading the newspapers, that the country was full of raging bandits who were staging hold-ups at every street corner. Yet such an idea is obviously exaggerated, and it is therefore desirable to give some attention to this 'phenomenon' in order to see just what it is and just what lies behind the great propaganda bogey into which it has been built up.

It must be admitted, of course, that there is an appreciable increase in a certain type of crime, the hold-up, with or without violence. It was hardly to be expected by any sensible man that the state of affairs would be otherwise. For six years men have been taught to use lethal weapons, to value human life very cheaply, and to commit acts of violence without any undue perturbation. Certain sections of the forces, such as the Commandos, have been given the training of professional thugs, being taught not merely to shoot, but also such 'useful' arts as the way to murder or capture and tie up a man without making any disturbance. It is hardly a surprising thing that in some at least of these millions of men the habits and ideas of violence should have become so deeply ingrained that they are unwilling to relinquish them, but instead decide to turn them to use in earning their living by crime.

The other end of this process can be seen at work among children. It is admitted that there has been a rapid increase in child delinquency during the war. Yet what else was to be expected, when in their schools these children had heard war praised daily, had seen on the films hundreds of exploits in which violence and murder were shown as virtuous acts, and had taken in there poisonous teachings from almost every children's paper that had passed into their hands?

Our Bandit Society

Our present system is based on banditry, on the robbing of the poor by the rich, on the violence of authority, and if necessary, the violence of war as a means to ensure the continued suppression of the poor. But, as repression always leads to resistance in some form or another, so authoritarian societies always produce an unofficial violence that runs counter to the official violence. The acts of bandits and child criminals are acts of rebellion against a tyrannous society. They do not arise out of any inherent evil, but out of instinctual processes of struggle against imposed authority. Yet this fact should not lead us to imagine that such acts are necessarily good. On the contrary, they represent forces which can very well be canalised by a clever authoritarian movement to serve its own ends. All the fascist and proto-fascist movements from Napoleon III onwards have found their early nuclei in the organisation of such irrational rebellions against a corrupt society.

A merely destructive feeling of rebellion, if it remains on the emotional or instinctual plane, can be used by anybody who is sufficiently clever. The only kind of rebellion which is of real eventual value is that which is based on a clear and reasoned awareness of the social issues and is devoted towards a constructive end of building up a real and stable freedom in place of the capricious violence of authority.

But there is another reason for many of the crimes which are taking place today, and that is the presence of large numbers of deserters in the large cities (there are estimated to be 10,000 in London alone). These men have found the army unbearable, for one reason or another, and, tired of waiting for a release, have taken the quickest way out. Once away from the army, they have found themselves unable to earn a living by ordinary methods because of the fact that they cannot get regular work without employment cards, which involve some kind of direct contact with authority. Accordingly, they have been forced to earn a living as best they can by some kind of irregular employment, by racketeering or by robbery. They have had no alternative, unless they choose to give themselves up for two yars at Stakehill or some other concentration camp. They have no prospect of release from their present life, unless the government issues an amnesty.

The Government's Responsibility

For this situation the government is almost wholly responsible. It is the inevitable product of the system of military conscription, and while the authorities try to keep men in the army against their will, there will always be deserters who will have to live by some extra-legal means. The majority of deserters engage in innocuous minor rackets and keep themselves as far out of the public eye as possible. But there are always a few who in sheer desperation or bravado indulge in sensational or violent crime. For this problem there is only one solution — the immediate ending of conscription, rapid demobilisation, and the granting of an amnesty to all deserters to enable them to become once again useful members of society.

This is as much as seems necessary to say about the 'crimes' themselves. But, as I indicated at the beginning of this article, there is more to the 'crime wave' sensation than immediately meets the eye, and the sudden declaration of an impending drive against the bandits cannot be dissociated from the government's proposals for a strong, centralised police force, or from the ambitions within the police force itself to become an autonomous body, playing its own reactionary part in influencing policy within the country.

Almost immediately after the 'crime wave' had been built up into a large-scale newspaper and radio campaign, the police chiefs began to talk of enlarging the force, and a figure of 16,000 extra policemen was named. Then, on the 11th December, the police issued an appeal for people to volunteer as part-time special constables (*Evening Standard* 11th December 1945):

"Object of the call to civilians is to enable regular policemen to be taken off routine duties and transferred to crime detection . . . Volunteers will be given training and uniforms. On duty the 'special' will have all the responsibilities, powers and privileges of the regular police."

The Police Hoax
This appeared to be a temporary affair to tide over the time until the 'crime wave' had ebbed. But the next day, when many of the suckers went along to offer their services, they found that they were expected to guarantee their co-operation for a period of years (*Evening Standard* 12th December 1945):

"All applicants were told that they could join the Special Police only on a three-year agreement. It would not, the police say, be practical to train and equip men merely to cover an emergency in crime such as the present one."

The reasons behind the actions of the police became clear. If they were really desperate for assistance, they would take volunteers on any terms. But in fact they can afford to do without men, *unless they are willing to sign on for three years*. In other words, it is not unreasonable to contend that the police do not really want helpers at present, but want to set up a large auxiliary force which will have another function than that of assisting with the present 'emergency'. They are anxious to increase their own power.

Meanwhile, those who are not willing to act as specials are being asked to become informers. Scotland Yard appeals to all people to ring up 999 if they see anything unusual were featured in newspapers and on the radio, and no doubt by now a number of perfectly innocent people who have behaved unconventionally or who aroused suspicions of the inquisitive, have been subjected to the unpleasant attentions of the police.

A Show of Power
A further step in the assertion of police power was the comb-out of the West End on the night of 14th-15th December. More than 15,000 people were stopped by the police for questioning, and nearly a thousand were taken in to police stations for further grilling, although the police had in the end to release most of them.

This demonstration of police power — for it can be regarded as little else — represents a sinister incident in peace-time. During the war some kind of plausible case might be made by war supporters for police check-ups, but in peace-time such an infringement of individual freedom as this plague of 3,000 human locusts invading the centre of London and interfering with the freedom of movement of thousands of men and women is a clear demonstration of arbitrary force. It means that the police are telling us our wartime slavery is here to stay.

Let us not be gulled by the bogey of an exaggerated 'wave of crime' into accepting the steady increase of police power at the expense of our freedom. When we are asked to help the police in this consolidation of their power, let us remember that the words *informer* and *nark* have a very unsavoury history in the language of the working man.

Police power will always be more than anything else the buttress of authority. It will never end crime, for that is a phenomenon which cannot be dissociated from the system of privilege and property. One kind of criminal gains his property by legal thefts. The police are his friends. The other gains it by illegal theft. The police are his enemies. But when there is no property and no

privilege, then there will be no theft. And assuredly there will be
no police. The society where men enjoy freedom will have shaken
itself free of such parasites.

29th December 1945   GEORGE WOODCOCK

Demand Amnesty for Deserters!

At the end of the war, *Freedom* was the first paper to advocate an
immediate amnesty for all deserters, not only on the grounds of
the elementary justice of such a procedure, but also because a
failure to take this step would involve consequences which would
be harmful, not only to the deserters themselves, but also to a
society that forced these men into keeping themselves alive by
furtive and anti-social means.

Our contentions have since been abundantly vindicated. Forced
to live in hiding, without rations, without legal jobs, a great
proportion of the deserters had only the alternatives of indulging
in some kind of criminal activity or of giving themselves up to
endure perhaps years of imprisonment or brutal detention for an
action which they obviously did not regard as wrong. Naturally
enough, most of the deserters elected to remain at large, and there
is no doubt that their needs was one of the most important
contributory factors to the recent crime wave.

We take no moralistic attitude towards 'crime', nor do we in any
way defend the property society which the criminal attacks. But
there is no doubt that a perpetually criminal life is harmful to men,
and wastes in a rather futile struggle abilities which could be used
to more constructive social ends. For the criminal's position
society is ultimately to blame, and in no instance so much as in that
of the deserters, who are forced into their life by the existence of
conscription and the refusal of the government to allow them to
return to society as responsible and useful individuals.

The Government offer
At last, after eighteen months of hesitations and of refusals to

grant an amnesty, the Minister of Defence has brought forward a scheme which even right-wing papers like the *Evening Standard* describes as "a half-measure which is unlikely to yield effective results". All in fact that the government really says in this greatly publicised offer is that deserters who give themselves up by 31st March will have this fact taken into consideration when their cases are considered, and that they will have their previous service restored for the purposes of the release scheme if they serve satisfactorily for a further 12 months.

The whole announcement has a vagueness about it that is certainly menacing and seems deliberate. There is no actual guarantee of clemency, and no sentence is named as being the maximum a deserter can expect if he gives himself up. Furthermore, most deserters have been forced to commit technical crimes of one sort or another, in direct consequence of their illegal positions, and they will obviously fear that such acts will be brought against them in addition to the actual offence of desertion.

Indeed, it would be difficult to imagine an offer less likely to induce men to leave their present life and go back to imprisonment and at least a year of army service before they can hope for a release.

Amnesty the only solution

The only solution to the present situation is in fact that of a complete amnesty for all deserters. The Government's answer to this is that it would give the men preferential treatment over those complying with their military obligations. To this we would answer that if the Minister for Defence had been for years on the run, without ration books or identity card, in perpetual fear of arrest, and forced to live by all kinds of furtive expedients, he would begin to think that these hunted men had already suffered enough, merely for having refused to continue their subjection to military conscription.

The government, as all governments do, is looking at the situation from the wrong end of the telescope. They see the fault in the individual, the wicked deserter who will not submit himself to military discipline and decided to try and live his own life. But the fault in fact lies in the state and the army which conscript and regiment men until they are unable to stand it any more and have to revolt against it. This is shown by the fact that in recent months the number of deserters in this country has actually increased by 5,000. This large number of men who were actually waiting for their discharge and knew that desertion would involve later demobilisation, actually felt the life of the army so impossible to bear that they had to embark on desertion, with all its very unpleasant consequences.

But the sinister aspect of the Government's announcement is not only in its maintenance of a vindictive attitude towards the deserters themselves. It appears also in Alexander's final remark:

> "The Government requests the co-operation of everyone, particularly friends, relatives and employers of these men in securing their surrender."

In other words, everyone who knows of a deserter is expected to lower himself into that most despicable function of informer, with the threat that if he does not he will fined heavily or sent to prison. This kind of appeal is on no higher level than the appeal which the Nazis made to children to spy on their parents. It is a cynical attack on those individual loyalties and solidarities which decent men and women show to each other in adversity, and which represent one of the most powerful forces for mutual aid within society. It is in making such demands on its subjects that government shows itself to be so fundamentally immoral and inhuman.

The only real solution to the problem of desertion is to remove it completely by ending militarism and the army. But since these things are not likely to cease within the next year or two, it seems to us more than ever necessary that we should press for an amnesty, which is an immediately practicable objective. When we first advocated this measure, in association with the Freedom Defence Committee, we were almost alone. Now many other people have come to admit the justice of our attitude, and when a paper like the *Evening Standard* finds itself forced to write an editorial demanding an amnesty, it is evident that there is already a very large public opinion which desires an end to the continued vindictiveness of the Government towards deserters.

In every way you can, demand an amnesty for the deserters and for all other people who are now in prison or on the run as a result of the war. The most elementary justice demands this, but it is also the only practical way of solving a pressing social problem and restoring these men to useful and constructive lives.

1st February 1947

Oppose Conscription!

The Individual's Right to Resist

That the Labour Government is having some difficulty from an opposition within the party to introducing conscription is an encouraging sign, though too much should not be built on it. The number of Labour MPs who voted against the second reading of the Bill (72) was higher than any other 'rebel' vote, and it appeared to secure some effect, for the Cabinet announced its intention of reducing the period of service from 18 months to 12 months.

Such a reduction, of course, makes nonsense of the Government's claim that they had examined the question very carefully and had come to the conclusion that every able bodied man must serve a year and a half. To make such a substantial reduction shows that there never was such a necessity, and no doubt much ridicule could be heaped upon the Government's head on that account. Unfortunately, there are indications that to adopt the course of mere ridicule would be to miss recognising that the Government has been pretty astute in this matter of reducing the training period. For it seems likely that they not only foresaw the opposition from their own back-benchers, but also gauged its quality correctly.

Socialist Tradition Quickly Shed

Opposition to conscription has been traditional in this country right up to the recent war. Chamberlain, as late as April 1939, declared that he would never bring in conscription in peace time. When he did bring it in — one month later — the Labour Party were loud in their denunciations. It is really disturbing to see the readiness with which the traditional attitude is shed. Rhys Davies, opposing the Bill, said that he was surprised to see George Isaacs, the Minister of Labour, supporting it, "for he has denounced it much more bitterly in the past than I have." Nor do the socialists appear to have forgotten their anti-conscription past, they merely seem to think that 'times are changed'! The *New Statesman* in its leading article (12th April 1947) which contains no criticism of the measure, blandly remarks that "Considering Labour's tradition of opposition to conscription it was surprising that only 72 out of a party of close on 400 opposed the Bill."

The *Tribune* (4th April 1947) feels the need of justifying this revisionism, with somewhat lame excuses: "On the conscription issue, the pacifist and liberal opponents had really no case other than their conscience (*sic*). Every socialist country today practises conscription, and refusal by Britain would again have been regarded as a contracting out of international obligations."

Thus, those who make the decisions as to whether the workers shall or shall not be conscripted are quite unruffled by any adhesion to principle — whether socialist or simply liberal opposition to compulsion. There can be little doubt that the *New Statesman* is correct when it says, "Long before the debate on conscription the Prime Minister knew that those who objected on principle to National Service were a relatively small minority."

Knowing this, what is more simple than to pitch their demand high — at 18 months — and then make a 'concession' by knocking off six months, and so satisfying these socialists who are so lightly encumbered by principles?

No doubt there are a few MPs who really are concerned with the principle of the thing: but such idealists do not flourish in the House of Commons.

What is the use of conscription?

An interesting reflection is that there has been no one to question whether conscription is a necessary measure. The official enquiry into the National Service Acts after the 1914 war (of which Sir Ian Hamilton was the chairman) expressed the view that conscription had been a failure, and that the maintenance of voluntary recruiting would have satisfied the needs of the services more quickly and more satisfactorily. Hence conscription must serve some other need than its apparent one, and it is doubtless the assistance it gives a government in controlling its subjects that makes it such a desired measure.

It is also worth reflecting on the view expressed in *Freedom* some months back — that if the government tries 'the voluntary method' first and does not receive much response, it has in effect received a positive mandate from the country against the measure proposed. The need to impose conscription itself indicates that the population (who are supposed to be 'represented' by their government in a democracy) don't want it. But these are academic considerations, and a socialist government dismisses them with contempt.

Individual resistance

If the Bill becomes law, as seems likely, the opposition in Parliament will have done what it could and failed. But the matter does not rest there. For it is still open to the intended conscripts to refuse to be conscripted, to express individual resistance. (We are always hearing that this is what the Germans should have done against Hitler.) It has been held that no law is binding which violates the conscience of the individual, and to refuse military service at the close of a bloody war which seems only to have made a bloodier world is not only in line with conscience, it is also good common sense.

19th April 1947

Army Trained Gunmen!

No Solution Without Amnesty for Deserters

It is not difficult, if one goes about it rationally (rather than with the shallow enthusiasm of so-called 'dispassionate' judges) to put two and two together on this gunman business. The war trained thousands of men to accept acts of violence without stirrings of conscience — indeed as laudable behaviour. At the same time the silly inelasticity of red tape drove twenty thousand odd soldiers to desert — with the inevitable consequence which we have pointed out so often in *Freedom* that, debarred from legal means of earning a living, they have been driven into a life of crime.

Deliberate psychological conditioning in brutality plus deliberate exclusion from legal existence, practically speaking, equals gunmen. It could hardly be otherwise. What is surprising, perhaps, is that there are not more of them and more desperate crimes of violence. It seems that despite psychological conditioning, and the practice of 'praiseworthy' violence, the human material is still sufficiently recalcitrant to retain a natural distaste for such acts. That the gunman is the exception rather than the rule in a post-war world is something of a tribute to the sociable habits of men.

Official Hysteria

When the sequence of cause and effect is as clear as in this case of the contemporary crime wave, remedies are proportionally easier. It is not possible to undo the fact of the war and its methods; but it is at least open to everyone to recognise the immediate evils which result from it, and which may therefore be reckoned up as part of the inevitable cost of any future venture of the same kind.

Moreover, the gunman is still the exception which proves the rule of human sociability: it requires the exceptional circumstances created by the outlawing of deserters to bring out these exceptions. Hence the outlawing of deserters must be ended. The government have already admitted that they know this root cause of the crime wave, and they have tried to remedy it by their appeal for deserters to give themselves up. This remedy has proved a complete failure — only about three thousand out of the twenty responded (and the 'lenient' treatment they received was quite severe enough to scare off any others from giving themselves up!). The obvious indication, therefore, is to declare an amnesty for *all* deserters, and thereby cut the base from under the crime wave.

It might be added that the need for all this is all the more urgent since the psychological effects of living outside legal society are such as make it increasingly difficult for a man to return to normal social life. Criminals are made by the circumstances of their position. Hence the longer an amnesty is deferred, the more difficulty in rehabilitation will be experienced.

But does the official mind show any sign of grasping these obvious and common sense facts? Not in the least. Instead, we see the police using the public alarm as a cover for inconvenient cordoning-off and round-ups and check-ups which cause immediate dislocation, create a condition of police-mindedness which is extremely undesirable (to put it no more strongly) — and to have as their result the arrest of a mere handful of deserters.

Meanwhile, members of the government have used the occasion to demand 'more powers' to put down the gunmen — that is, a permanent increase in the powers of the executive in order to deal with an essentially transitory problem. Judges have been ordering flogging, and the yellower newspapers printing articles supporting corporal punishment. Instead of an elementary use of reason, the official reaction is one of hysteria — but with a shrewd eye to the main chance of getting some increase in official powers out of the situation. One suspects that the hysteria is a simulated one just in order to make something out of it.

Nothing can Justify Flogging

The position regarding flogging is perfectly clear. A Royal Commission has investigated it to see if it is effective either as a deterrent or as a reformatory measure. They enquired whether the fact that a man could be flogged for certain crimes had any effect in preventing such crimes from being committed. As a result of their investigations they came to the perfectly unequivocal conclusion that it did not have the slightest effect on the commission of such crimes.

They also enquired whether flogging discouraged men from committing the same crimes again. Result: it has no such effect.

They also found that flogging had an actively deleterious effect on the criminal who experienced it — it made him worse.

These results are perfectly clear and no one has been able to overturn them. Yet judges go on ordering flogging, and presumably will continue until they are themselves restrained by law from doing so.

So far we have only looked at the practical aspect of flogging. But there is also the other side, the moral aspect. The government and the law may accept a morality which seeks to justify the infliction of violence on an individual as a remedy for the infliction of violence *by* that individual; but such an Old Testament procedure hardly commends itself to normally intelligent men and women today. And since it is becoming increasingly evident that anti-social behaviour towards one's fellows is a sign of psychic sickness, retributive measures become even more out of date. There are undoubted difficulties in the way of persuading such individuals to seek the appropriate treatment for their psychic ill health; but that should not prevent a recognition of the general causes — war training and refusal of legal status to deserters — and steps suitable for their removal. At the present moment there is no sign whatever of any such recognition in official circles. On the contrary, war training and conscription are to be made even more general, while the law continues its idiotic circle of punishment and the manufacture of criminals.

17th May 1947

Gang Children and Education

During the war years there has been a steady increase in child delinquency. This increase has taken place in working class cities and districts, particularly Glasgow, Birmingham and London, and it has a clear relationship with the economic condition of the children's homes and the type of education which is meted out to them. Children whose homes provide no comfort and no kind of diversion must be expected to roam out to get their entertainment in the streets. And children who are taught daily in their schools and at the cinema to admire the gigantic gang violence of war are very naturally inclined to practise their own forms of gang violence. Hence we get the social problem of the youth gangs who annoy the police and the respectable during the blackout hours of our industrial cities.

In Birmingham recently an attempt was made at the Sherborne Street Centre to provide a means to deal with these children which would not involve the violence of the law. The centre provided recreation and means of doing constructive work, and threw itself open to as many children, regardless of their standard of respectability, as were willing to attend it.

A report of the activities of the centre was issued recently, from which it seemed that the non-coercive methods used had been successful to a very great extent in detaching children from a life of gang hooliganism. This was because the centre provided something real and constructive to direct their energies, and bears out the anarchist contention that men will usually choose some kind of integrated work in preference to the pointless existence lived by the majority of slum dwellers. The whole nature of the development of the centre also shows that an efficient form of educative activity will always do more than coercion to solve the problem of the anti-social being.

But the report shows another side of the picture when it reveals the circumstances under which the children live.

"Some boys and girls come to the Centre utterly tired out, too tired even to read or talk for some time. Consider 'A', aged 18, who is at work at 4.30am, reaches home at 4.30pm, has tea and then delivers newspapers and helps in his father's shop until about 7.00pm . . . Also the case of 'H', aged 16½, who on one day had been moving, unaided, 1 cwt. barrels of provisions from 8.30am to 6.00pm . . . Often enough the home is the most unrestful place for the young folk. A small kitchen-living room with a table which is never cleared, often a tired and irritable mother with young children — the only possible rest place is bed. And these young folk need something more than just work and bed — they do not want to go to bed immediately after leaving work."

A further quotation shows the low standards of sanitation and health that prevail in the environment in which the children live:

"The verminous cases mentioned above, the number of girls suffering from fainting, headaches, etc., girls suffering from malnutrition due to the hand-bag dinner (and the absence of a substantial evening meal now that 'it is not worth while cooking because father and older brothers get their main meal at the works canteen'), septic sores, eye and teeth troubles gave cause for worry . . .

"Washing provides a difficulty. Few of the members have baths in their homes and they complain that, when they attend the Public Washing Baths, they have to wait for very long periods — and they refuse to wait. The boys can take hot showers at the Gymnasium on the Section evening. But the girls are less fortunate. The home custom is for the girls to have a full wash in the kitchen on Friday evening if and when fathers and brothers go out. The girls state that overtime and late return cause the adult male movements to be erratic as to time and, if the coast is not clear — no bath!"

Finally, an extract which shows the miserable results in intellectual development achieved by the normal state education:

"The general reading level is very low; few read at all, some read only the penny 'comic', only three had current City library tickets, and eight were members of the Twopenny Libraries."

These revelations of the conditions under which the delinquent children were brought up are in a way the most significant part of the report for they show a state of affairs which obtains in most industrial districts. They also show that, however well-intentioned the efforts of such centres and however successful they may be in providing a more pleasant alternative for the children than hooliganism, they touch only the surface of the problem, aim only at curing the symptom and not the disease. For the seeds of the disease lie not in the streets where the children prowl at night, but in the poverty-stricken, overworked life of their homes and places of work. Until poverty is abolished, such measures go only a negligible fraction of the way towards curing the plight of the poor.

The efforts of such reformers may be honest in their intent. But there is a blatant cynicism in such official pronouncements as the recent one of the Minister of Education that after the war every child will receive a secondary education. It is obvious that, in the majority of cases, a good education can only be fully effective when it is linked with economic security and comfort. The child living in a slum home, unless he is exceptionally acute, can find no place in his environment for the qualities of good education. To attempt to impose on children a liberal education when their home environment is kept by property interests at a level of squalid poverty is a heartless mockery. It is useless to impose culture on a boy or a girl if there is a virtual certainty that their adult life will be confined in the alternating cycle of a regimented factory life and a tired home life which will kill the desire for any but the most mechanical of enjoyments.

It must be borne in mind, however, that not a cultured but an obedient mind is the main object of State education. Children are taught not for their own benefit, but in order to mould them into the pattern required by the State. Any lengthening of the period of education will be used by the State to increase its hold on the children, and when secondary education is applied to all we can expect it to take on an even less liberal and more openly propaganda nature than it has to-day. Furthermore, the government no doubt see in the extension of the school age by a couple of years a means of easing the chronic unemployment problem that will arise when war production ends and demobilisation commences. What they choose to disregard is the unpleasant fact that in our present society the keeping of the child from remunerative work for a year or two will mean an extension of malnutrition among the poorer families.

Education can only be used to its full effect in a free society, where the needs of the State do not warp its nature, where the scholar is not subjected to the deadening influence of a poverty-stricken environment, and where work has become a vocation, as opposed to the mechanical toil of the modern factory. Education will then aim, not at the creation of the robot desired by all rulers, but at the integration of natural human desires and aspirations, and the creation of a free and well-balanced mind, capable of appreciating and using in full measure the physical and intellectual gifts of a society based directly on life instead of on the abstractions of religions and politics which govern our modern systems of official education.

Mid-May 1943   GEORGE WOODCOCK

The Problem of Juvenile Delinquency

Juvenile Delinquency in an English Middletown, by Hermann
Mannheim (Routledge, 12/6).

A considerable literature has grown up in recent years on the
subject of juvenile delinquency — chiefly as a result of the great
increase in juvenile crime during the war and post-war years. It is a
subject which has considerable interest for people of progressive
outlook, but the very investigation of the subject is really a
fundamental criticism of the ideas of punishment inherent in the
system of law. For as soon as one begins to probe into the factors
which cause juvenile crime one has already begun to abandon the
idea of individual responsibility in these matters which provides
the sole philosophical and logical justification for punishment.

For it is clear that if the environment in which these young
delinquents have been reared is partly or even mainly responsible
for the crimes they commit, then it is the environment, not the
individual delinquent which must be 'punished'. It is necessary to
say at the outset that none of the investigators of delinquency
proceed to this logical position. They seek means of mitigating the
circumstances which enquiry after enquiry has shown to be the
causal factors, but they always seem to see these circumstances as
special and peculiar ones, instead of regarding them as the
extreme manifestations of faults which run through the whole
social structure.

The present study was an intensive examination of a number of
delinquents in Cambridge before and during the war, whose object
was the elucidation of certain environmental factors, such as the
effect of size of town, of the nature of the housing, etc. But its
chief interest for readers of *Freedom* lies in the general questions
raised.

First of all the nature of the crimes: the huge majority — 94 per
cent before the war and 93 per cent during the war — were
offences against property. In the pre-war group 74 per cent of the
objects stolen were valued at less than 20/-; the figure falling to
42·9 per cent during the war (one wonders if this fall is merely a
reflection of the rise in prices occasioned by the war?)

Then there is the nature of the delinquents. This enquiry, like so
many previous ones, shows that the majority of juvenile
delinquents come from broken or unsatisfactory homes, many of

them being illegitimate. The problem has indeed been spoken of as the problem of the 'affectionless' character. The case history of many individual instances shows the same pathetic facts; a child whose emotional stability has been sapped by a lack of love in his upbringing; who feels himself to be outside society, and has no feeling of membership of or solidarity with the community; whose 'crimes' (it seems absurd sometimes to describe their petty offences in such a strong term) are sometimes consciously recognised by the child to be an expression of hostility towards society, and then the pitifully inadequate means of redemption for these lost children.

There can be no doubt of the good intentions of the probation officers and welfare workers and even of the juvenile magistrate's courts — for who could deal with children's offences with the unsympathetic attitude of the religious approach which regards each offender as strictly responsible for his offence? But the sorry decline from the probation officer, the welfare homes and Child Guidance Clinics whose aim is clearly to help the child, to the Remand Homes, the Borstals and finally the prisons, whose aim is equally clearly to protect society, shows only too clearly how inadequate are the means of reclamation available.

And in all these studies, the child delinquents may be the 'offenders' but it is society which comes up for indictment. Once again the preponderance of property offences show how powerfully rooted is contemporary crime in the property structure of society. One cannot but recognise that the majority of these offences would automatically disappear in a society which did not express its value through individual property.

Much more important, however, is the inability of society to provide the atmosphere of love which could counteract the absence of love in the upbringing of these delinquents. And what a reflection on society is it that to the misfortune of a loveless childhood the courts can usually only add some form of additional legal punishment. The alleged need to protect society only too clearly aggravates the lovelessness at the bottom of the delinquent's situation, and confirms his progress from juvenile to adult crime and the ghastly waste of lives in prison sentences and careers of crime.

Again and again, the investigator uncovers unsatisfactory home conditions, only to find that progress is blocked by the refusal of the parents to co-operate. And since their own unsatisfactoriness is presumably the product of their own emotional and social difficulties, this refusal is more likely to be an inability to co-operate. If the home is hopeless the next resort is to the Home. And even the most exceptional of these cannot adequately — in existing circumstances — replace the lacking parental love, while the majority must offer the cold and disapproving touch of institutionalism.

In conclusion, one feels all the time the unreality of our society, its complete absence of community feeling. No doubt each of these children has been observed by a sympathetic neighbour; but our economic and social structure makes it impossible for these to take over the responsibilities of the inadequate parents. Indeed, if they tried to do so, the law, in its determination to protect society (which in this case means protecting the state from having to shoulder economic responsibilities for children which in law rests on the shoulders of the parents, however inadequate) would obstruct such a social and human endeavour. In practice the care of the delinquent child lies between its unsatisfactory home, and the equally unsatisfactory Home.

But in a free society, not split by class differences, and in which the individual is not overburdened by the need to look after himself and his dependents in competition with his fellows, communal feelings would have free play, and a child which lacked love at home, would almost certainly receive some measure of compensation from those individuals whose sympathy and love for children is seemingly boundless even in our society. Indeed, such an integral society would do much not merely to repair and reclaim the delinquent child; it would also strike at the root of delinquency itself by removing many of those problems which make for unsatisfactory homes.

That these studies of the sociologists disclose the inadequacies of society in relation to juvenile offenders is clear. It is for anarchists to point the way to a social structure which meets these criticisms.

10th July 1948   J. H.

POST-WAR STALINISM

The Russian Elections

For the first time in eight years the Russian people have gone to the polls to elect a new Supreme Soviet of the Union of Socialist Soviet Republics. The Supreme Soviet consists of two Parliaments: the Soviet of the Union and the Soviet of Nationalities and is elected every four years.

The Soviet of the Union has 656 seats and is elected on the basis of one deputy for every 300,000 of the population. The Soviet of Nationalities has 631 seats on the basis of twenty-five deputies from each constituent republic, irrespective of its size, eleven deputies from each autonomous republic, five deputies from each autonomous province and one deputy from each national region. Voting is by universal suffrage for all who have reached 18, 'irrespective of sex, nationality, race, faith, social origin, property status or past activities'. Candidates must be over 23.

The Supreme Soviet of the USSR elects a Presidium of the Supreme Soviet of the USSR composed of 37 members and endowed with great power. Theoretically the legislative power belongs to the Supreme Soviet but the Presidium has the right to issue decrees which have the power of law. The members of the Presidium cannot be removed by the Supreme Soviet in case of an insoluble difference arising between the Soviet of the Union and the Soviet of Nationalities.

The Supreme Soviet of the USSR also appoints the highest executive and administrative organ of State Power: the Council of People's Commissars of the USSR who deal with the international organisation of the country.

The term Supreme Soviet is highly misleading. It has nothing in common with the Soviets which were formed during the Russian revolution and were councils of workers' delegates (or peasants and soldiers) elected by a relatively small number of people and directly responsible to them. The deputies in the Soviet of the Union each represent something like three hundred thousand men and women and remain in office for four years. Not a very direct kind of representation!

What is the difference between the Russian parliamentary system and that of democratic countries? The main difference is that under the Soviet régime there are no opposition parties. The right to nominate candidates is reserved to official bodies that is to say, Communist Party organisations, trade unions, co-operatives, organisations of youth, cultural societies. The candidates who are not Communist Party members are described as non-party but they are in fact supporters of the Party. Stalin stressed the point, in his election broadcast on the 9th February, that non-party people were now united with the Communists in one common team of Soviet citizens which forged the victory over their country's enemies.

"The only difference between them," said Stalin, "is that some belong to the party while others do not. *But this is a formal difference*" (italics ours).

Under the Soviet system there is no chance to choose between candidates representing two or more policies as there is only one Party in the State, the Communist Party.

The choice of the candidates is not left to the electors at the time of the election. Several candidates are nominated for each constituency and except in constituencies which have such illustrious candidates as Stalin, Molotov, Kalinin, Voroshilov, Zhukov, etc., a certain amount of discussion takes place before the solitary candidate is decided upon. Once he is chosen voting becomes a pure formality, the only way to express opposition to the candidate is to abstain from voting but as in the plebiscites organised in fascist countries great care is taken to get a maximum of voters to the polls (age is no excuse, in Georgia an old man of 118 went to the polls!)

In a police state such as Russia it is probable that more than mere persuasion is used to ensure that the great majority of people fill in their ballot papers though, of course, propaganda is used on a big scale. It is aimed at giving the electors the illusion that they have power to pass judgement on the Communist Party. Stalin declared at the beginning of his speech: "The Communist Party of our country would be of little worth were it ready to accept the electors' verdict". Having no rival parties to oppose it, being supported by a Party controlled Press and radio, having at its command the army, the police and millions of bureaucrats it would be very difficult indeed to understand why the Communist Party should be afraid of the electors' verdict.

No wonder Stalin's speech was 'confident' (*Daily Worker*). He was spared the exhausting propaganda tours that politicians such as Churchill or Roosevelt had to undertake in order to secure re-election. Not for him the speeches on top of cars or standing in the rain, not for him the last minute Press campaigns skilfully calculated to destroy weeks of propaganda work. Stalin's re-election was preceded by a unanimous concert of praises. *Pravda*, for example, paid this inspired tribute:

"It is indeed happiness, real happiness, to meet Comrade Stalin. If one translated the endless acclamations into the language of simple words they would read: 'We are proud that the greatest man of our day, the brilliant creator of victory, the saviour of civilisation, the leader of the peoples, belongs to us, to our country, to our people. We know and are deeply convinced that the greatest man of our time could not appear in any other country but ours'."0111

And from Radio Khaborovsk (6th January 1946):
"Yesterday's pre-election meeting in the Stalin precinct of Moscow left one with an unforgettable and inspiring mission. It reflected with great power and sincerity the boundless love the people bear for their great leader, wisc teacher and father, Comrade Stalin!

'Dear Comrades', declared the woman worker A. A. Slobnow, 'it is the great fortune of our people that during the difficult years of the war it was Comrade Stalin, deputy of the entire people, who stood at the head of the state . . . Glory! Glory to our own J. V. Stalin'. These words are an expression of the innermost thoughts, feelings and hopes of the Soviet people."

When the votes were counted in Stalin's constituency in Moscow, it was found that 100 per cent of the voters had cast their votes for Stalin.

Probably nobody dared to give Stalin the advice Kingsley Martin gave to Tito a few days before Yugoslavia's elections: "I hope you will get 75 per cent", said K. Martin, "If you get 90 per cent, it might be a good idea to destroy 25 per cent of your vote".

Stalin is different, of course, but 100 per cent does not sound very convincing, somehow.

23rd February 1946   M. L. B

Russian Imperialism
How Menacing is it?

Faced with the accomplished fact of Communist success in China it may be that the government has had no other choice than to accept the situation. Yet the equanimity of the Western powers in the face of this new situation has indeed been remarkable. In appearance the extension of Russian influence into Eastern Europe and China gives a new access of power to the leaders of the Soviet Union; but it is as well to give consideration to certain other aspects of the development of Russian imperialism which are less regarded.

The extension of British influence overseas during the seventeenth, eighteenth, and nineteenth centuries provided an enormous access of power to the British ruling class. Not merely was great wealth extracted from overseas empire, but the export of industrial goods and industrial capital provided an immense stimulus to the development of home industry, against which the difficulties of imposing colonial rule on newly-subject peoples provided only small off-setting disadvantages. The situation is quite different for Russia, still a comparatively unindustrialised state unable to fill the demands of its home economy adequately, much less supply the industrial needs of an increasing number of satellite countries in the colonial manner.

Moreover, whereas it was once easy for Britain to maintain an economic stranglehold on subject countries without the need for a large administration for direct political subjugation, Russian imperialism has to rely on armies of occupation, utterly subservient quisling governments, or a highly organised and loyal political police (or all three). In such circumstances considerable dilution of Russian power occurs with each acquisition of territory. It may be that considerations such as these lie behind the apparent unconcern with which American ruling circles regard the acquisition by Soviet Union of such a vast territory as North — and perhaps also South China.

Problems of Transport
Nor does the reverse side of the picture end there. One of the great difficulties which Kaiser Wilhelm II had to face in the pursuit of German imperialist ambitions was that of transport. For that

reason the Berlin-Baghdad railway became a political objective of the first importance. But while he was struggling with the almost insuperable difficulties of overland transport to the Middle East, the British were in a position to send an almost unlimited quantity of shipping through the Mediterranean. Sea power is still of overwhelming importance in the successful development of overseas empire.

Now, in the case of China, the problem of transport is simply vast in its extent and complexity. Overland solutions to the problem can scarcely be achieved within fifty years — a long time at the modern political pace. So even if China is overrun by the Communist Party, and even supposing that Russian industry was able to supply the needs and reap the profits, it still remains true that the supplying of China with industrial goods and capital is still easier for a maritime power like the United States — or even Great Britain. Meanwhile the weakness of the Chinese economy makes it easy for any power trading with it to interfere in internal affairs simply by manipulating its needs for overseas supplies.

Security for the Older Imperialisms
In the light of such considerations as these, the Western powers may well be reflecting that the failure of Napoleonic France, and both Imperial and Nazi Germany to shake the position of the older and firmly established imperial powers, is likely to be repeated by the renascent Russian imperialism of Stalin. Indeed, political leaders in the West no doubt feel confident that, as in the past, a new attempt to shake Anglo-American world hegemony may only succeed in establishing it all the more firmly.

Such prospects are doubtless cheering enough for experienced imperialists; for workers all over the world they only darken the outlook still further. To be involved in struggles which only end in establishing the yoke of imperialism still more firmly than ever is dreary indeed. As such prospects become clearer the revolutionary solutions advanced by Utopian Anarchists and 'dreamers' may gradually be seen to be practical, though they will never be easy.

China: Despair, Reform or Revolution?

From time to time events in the Chinese civil war bring China into the newspapers of the West. But in betweenwhiles no one thinks of the largest country of the world, with its population numbering a fifth of the world population, which has been sunk in a seemingly endless war since 1927. It is well to reflect on this interminable struggle while evaluating the present 'crisis in China', for it is doubtful if the Chinese peasant any longer thinks in terms of 'decisive phases of the struggle', 'critical moments in the campaign' and all the other catchwords of Western observers for whom the agrarian millions in China hardly exist.

Nevertheless, it is inevitable that the virtual loss of North China to the Communists should seem an event of importance to those observers outside China who regard the struggle — correctly enough — as lying between the Soviet Union and the United States. For the situation of the Nationalist forces now seems fairly desperate, and American newspapers are already talking about 'the loss of China' and discussing desperate measures for the recovery of the Nanking government, or alternatively seeking to diminish the importance of the blow.

The balance of power

The attitude of the British Government is difficult to assess, but it may be inferred from certain important articles in *The Times*, whose general trend is to try and maintain that Chinese Communism is somehow different from the genuine Moscow article, and is not seriously to be feared. There is indeed an attempt to whitewash the Communists at the expense of the Nationalists, attention being drawn to their provision of 'efficient government', their agrarian reform, and so on, by contrast to the inefficiency, corruption and general contemptible nature of 'the carpet baggers of Nanking'.

This point of view is castigated by the more realistic *Economist*, indeed the ease with which it is demolished makes it perfectly clear that *The Times'* line on China represents less the government's beliefs than its probable policy. One is perhaps justified in concluding that the British are seeking once again to play their old rôle of rejoicing third holding the balance of power. Having no direct concern in the struggle in China itself, they no doubt hope

that the two other great powers in the world will exhaust and
weaken themselves on the battlefields of China, and hence
relatively increase the power of Britain.

Chiang Kai-shek's star wanes
In America there are two schools of thought; those who think the
checking of Russian expansion in China is more important than
checking Russian expansion in Europe, and those who think the
reverse. It looks as if the latter are in the ascendant at the moment,
probably as a result of Marshall's damning of the Nanking regime
eighteen months ago. In any case, the incompetence of the
Nationalist regime is such that the American aid intended to equip
the armies more efficiently gets side-tracked into the deep pockets
of the functionaries. Those who are most concerned about
American interest in China recognise that the first condition of the
increase in American aid is a radical reform of the administration
and in the agrarian field. The *Economist* even goes so far as to
hope that "upheavals in the Nanking government may well come,
of themselves, as a result of the military defeats of recent months."
But one may infer that such a process would not be willingly
permitted to go too far, and although Chiang Kai-shek's star has
undoubtedly declined, he is still praised in American editorials, his
counter-revolutionary prowess in the past being no doubt still
remembered.

Unpopular opinions
The position of anarchists towards the protagonists in China was
stated seven or eight years ago, at a time when Chiang Kai-shek
was being lauded to the skies and participated in the councils of
Roosevelt and Churchill. Nothing can obliterate the bloody record
of the Generalissimo in the years after the revolution of 1927
which makes him rank as a butcher of revolutionists and
working-class militants second only to Stalin. Nor have anarchists
ever been taken in by the 'reforms' of the Communists which left
the system of landlordism substantially untouched and dismantled
the peasant councils set up at the revolution.

Parallels with Spain
The present position on China has many parallels with that of
Spain after the counter-revolution had destroyed the revolutionary
resistance to Franco. The workers on both sides are in the grip of
rulers whose aims are dictatorial and reactionary, and for them

there is little to choose between the protagonists. They must be deadly weary of a war which has gone on for almost a lifetime with the Japanese invasion as a few years incident. Deadly weary of chronic famine conditions which make army rations a sufficient incentive to recruit fighters on both sides. Twenty hopeless years behind them and a hopeless prospect in front.

The new social revolution

Such a situation augurs poorly for the only immediate prospect which offers hope for the future, a new social revolution. Yet, if the incompetence and internal divisions of the Nationalist regime of Chiang were to lead to the seizing of initiative by the workers and peasants, the whole struggle in China would take on a new complexion. Throwing off the fetters of landlordism and debt and the depredations of the armies, the social revolution would offer a far more serious threat to the Communist regime in North China than even the Nationalists have done. And not by force of arms but by example and the well-known tendency of revolutions to spread and overwhelm the Communist dictatorship from below.

It may be utopian to hope for such a response from exhausted men and women, but all the world's revolutions have seemed visionary and improbable a few weeks before their outbreaks, and at all events such a prospect would have far more to offer than the indefinite battleground of the great powers, with its famines and slaughters and endless columns of refugees, which is the pattern of life for the Chinese people yesterday and today.

27th November 1948 ANARCHIST

The Lysenko Controversy

Attention has already been drawn in the columns of *Freedom* to the controversy in Russia between Lysenko and geneticists alleged to be 'subservient to Western pseudo-science'. We ventured to suggest that the suppression of certain scientists and the science of geneticists might well create more of a storm in this country than many a more extensive or far-reaching repression in the Soviet Union. It now looks as if this prophecy will be justified, for the Lysenko controversy has been discussed on the wireless in several programmes and also in the daily and weekly press, while the Royal Society has also had occasion to comment on the matter.

Protests by British Scientists
It appears that the Royal Society has addressed several enquiries to the Russian Academy of Sciences regarding the date and place of death of its former President, Vavilov. None of these enquiries has received an answer, though Vavilov was an honorary member of the Royal Society and a geneticist of such international repute that he was elected President of the International Congress of Genetics held in Edinburgh in 1939. Vavilov was attacked by Lysenko and discredited. He disappeared and is thought to have died in a forced labour camp, but so far no account of his death has been disclosed by the Russian government or the Academy of Sciences.

When at a recent Congress, Lysenko attacked the remaining few of Vavilov's colleagues among orthodox geneticists, and succeeded in getting their institutes closed down and themselves dismissed, he did so with the official approval of the government. And in addition he laid it down that science should be political, or, in *Pravda*'s words, "the most important principle in science is the .ty principle". This was too much for the Royal Society, and Sir Henry Dale, its president, resigned from the Russian Academy of Sciences, of which he was an honorary member. He addressed a dignified letter of protest regarding Vavilov's death and the political element introduced with official approval by Lysenko, and his very restraint provided the most scathing comment upon the subordination of scientists in Russia. Since then, several other foreign members of the Russian Academy have also resigned.

Internationalism of Serbia

It could be said that these eminent scientists could have made their protest earlier, and that by making it now they expose themselves to the suspicion of having succumbed to the current anti-Russianism of politicians who were lauding 'our gallant ally' only a few years since. But in their defence it must be said that scientists have sought to make science an international brotherhood, and with considerable success. And that the intrusion of political partisanship into their relationships would be exactly the fault of which they now accuse the Russian government. That they have raised this protest, and on such ground, is greatly to their credit.

Lysenko an Ignoramus

Several points of interest have emerged in the course of the recent broadcasts. Dr Darlington and others have witheringly attacked Lysenko's experimental premises — his refusal to submit his results to statistical analysis — which he denouces as bourgeois — and the inability of other experimenters to repeat his results. But it is especially interesting to hear Dr S. C. Harland state that to discuss genetics with Lysenko was like trying to explain the differential calculus to a man who did not know his twelve times table. After several hours conversation with him fifteen years ago Dr Harland regarded him as a man devoid of any grasp of genetical principles or plant physiology

Stalinist Defence

Professor Haldane showed himself to be a typical Stalinist in his extraordinarily feeble defence of Lysenko and the recent decrees against the very genetics of which he, Haldane, is an exponent. He claimed that he could not decide the issue without reading the 500 page report of the proceedings of the Congress. But it does not seem necessary to have read the whole report to form some kind of opinion about the subordination of science to party needs, the dismissal of geneticists of international repute and the closing of their institutes, or the denunciation of the work of Mendel and Morgan, which as Haldane very well knows is fundamental to modern genetics, as 'fascistic' and 'bourgeois'. He prudently did not speak of these things, and merely sought to draw red herrings across the trail — being witheringly rebuked for his many attempts to mislead the uninformed general public in a letter from a leading New Zealand geneticist in the same issue of the *Listener* which published his contribution to the discussion.

Not the least amusing — and instructive — aspects of Haldane's squirming defence of the indefensible, was his citing of the colchicine treatment of seeds in an implied defence of Lysenko's claims; amusing because Lysenko has himself denounced this treatment as 'bourgeois'!

Inheritance of Acquired Characters

In another broadcast, Professor C. H. Waddington (who in his Pelican *The Scientific Attitude* had shown himself rather uncritically laudatory of the position of science in the Soviet Union) discussed certain political aspects of the Lysenko ideology. Most interesting was his suggestion that the revival of Lamarck's long discredited idea that acquired characteristics could be handed on to offspring was due to the need to bolster up confidence in the Soviet Government's ability to 'control nature'. For, clearly, if by altering the environment of a plant one can affect its offspring which will then continue to breed true, one can overcome agricultural difficulties which have proved very considerable in the past, and which have only been begun to be solved by the most advanced geneticists of the school officially discredited in Russia.

The revival of the idea of the inheritance of acquired characters is most interesting in this connection. It has no real scientific basis, but yet its substance is embedded in the ideas of the ignorant, and it is often appealed to in support of anti-revolutionary arguments. Thus, when reformists say that anarchism could not possibly come in a short time *because of centuries of capitalist conditioning*, they are really implying that we *inherit* ideas which were conditioned in our forbears by the conditions of capitalism. And it is obvious that if the effects of the environment are inherited by offspring then the 'living down' of reactionary conceptions and habits of economic competition will be a much more formidable business than revolutionists expect.

Actually, the fact (established by orthodox biology) that the germ cells which bear the structure of inheritance are virtually uninfluenced by the environment of the individual parent, means that the future generations will be genetically, at least, untramelled by the unsatisfactory environment of the past and present. Here, at all events orthodox science is on the side of revolutionary conceptions as Kropotkin insisted, and Lysenko and the reformists are ideologically in much the same boat.

24th December 1948 JOHN HEWETSON

Seen in a Crooked Mirror

Nineteen-Eighty-Four by George Orwell (Secker & Warburg, 10/-)

If it is true that satire admits an element of hope, then this novel is not satirical: it is a grim and convincing attack on the centralised State and on modern warfare, and its power is due to the complete pessimism with which every page is stamped. It is certainly Orwell's most considerable book to date, and is the most powerful novel of its kind to appear since *Brave New World*.

The story is set in a future when the world is divided between three totalitarian powers which are perpetually at war with one another. It would not be possible for any of the three to win the war, and in fact the authorities have no intention of ever bringing it to an end; its real purpose is to hold in being the existing hierarchy in each State. Since few men can remember what peace was like, the idea of peace has disappeared: *war is peace*, as the Party slogan proclaims. In London, a city of Airstrip One, part of Oceania, the Party rules through four ministries. The central character, Winston Smith, works in the Ministry of Truth. Here, among other things, novels and songs are composed by machinery for the *proles* (a large submerged class of illiterates, quite powerless), and Winston in the Records Department is occupied in the continual falsification of history. "Who controls the past controls the future: who controls the present controls the past", says the Party, and its rule is based mainly on its complete destruction of all historical records. Every day yesterday's truth is altered so that it will conform with today's events. It is true in a way that the past still exists in memory, but this way is distorted by the technique of *doublethink*, which is a kind of schizophrenia by means of which one can remember a thing and simultaneously forget it, believe a statement and at the same time disbelieve. Thus there is no past and no future, but only a continuous present in which the Party is all-powerful; there is no more history. The Party is timeless, its leader, Big Brother, is eternal. Within this eternity Winston Smith is the only living man who believes that there is an objective standard of truth and that political freedom and equality are desirable. The story is about his meeting with a girl called Julia, their love affair, and their attempt to join a revolutionary organisation. It would be a pity to give away Orwell's plot, which is worked out with terrifying completeness. Sufficient to say that he discovers that the ultimate aim of the Party is simply to increase its power over men: that is, to increase human suffering: that is, to produce an eternity of pain. "If you want a picture of the future, imagine a boot stamping on a human face — for ever."

The novel has the complete credibility of a nightmare; it is this quality of dream which lifts it above the level of the political horror story. As a piece of craftsmanship it is subtle and almost perfect. Orwell does not begin by presenting a future world of whose plausibility the reader has first to be convinced; he begins with the world as it was until recently: a drab, exhausted, broken London, dusty under desultory rocket-bombs. Because one knows that this world really existed, one accepts the truth and Orwell then proceeds to introduce a gradual heightening of the truth. One grants the premises; the poetic logic is perfect; and so one accepts the conclusions. (Possibly this foundation in present truth will eventually weaken the novel; in the future the reader may not be able to assent to the premises; otherwise the book bears all the marks of permanence.) If one takes the story to pieces, few of the parts seem original. Much has been learned from *Darkness at Noon*; there are many reminders of Dickens; there are even touches of horror from the Gothic novel and the Yank terror magazine — no doubt derived from Orwell's researches into boys' fiction. Orwell's astonishing success lies in his imaginative grasp of all these elements, and his moulding of them so that each seems perfectly placed and genuinely recreated. Perhaps the best example is his handling of the love affair. From the first this is slightly repellent, and there is a moment when Julia actually seems — hearty, swearing, bashing you in the back with her hockey bag — to become a kind of Girl Guide leader on Victoria Station. Yet in a world of fear and ugliness in which a strict military chastity is enforced by the Party, love would degenerate into this kind of physical scramble, and even the lovers would be unaware that any degeneration had taken place. This is probably Orwell's deepest insight; his treatment of the sexual problem is always acute.

Only an honest man could have written this book, and it is desolating that in our world such honesty should lead to such despair. Out of his despair, Orwell has made a protest more complete and more sustained than any other writer of his generation, and for this he deserves our praise and gratitude. I don't think any sensitive reader could ever completely forget *Nineteen-Eighty-Four* — a crooked mirror held up before us with terrible determination — unless the book fails in its purpose and

we ourselves enter the mirror world of doublethink and
forgetfulness. It is our task to ensure that that does not occur, to
oppose the world presented by Orwell's novel, to alleviate human
despair and restore the honesty and faith of free men.
11th June 1949   L. A.

Challenge from a Fellow Traveller

Will you allow me to comment on the article entitled 'The Stalinist
Fifth Column' in your issue of 14th May 1949, which, as it is
unsigned, I take as being editorially approved, and in which you
discuss the Congrès Mondial des Partisans de la Paix held in Paris
from 20th to 25th April. As a delegate to that Congress from a
group of Scottish Nationalists (United Scotland Secretariat) I fall
to be classed by you amongst "fellow-travellers and other weak
heads", though my individual insignificance is a guarantee that I
was not among those you refer to as "carefully hand-picked". I
would like to ask two questions, and to make two brief comments
on the Congress.

First, I would ask, do Anarchists object to 'fellow-travellers' as
such, or only to travelling along with Communists? I ask because I
seem to be a 'fellow-traveller' with both Anarchists and
Communists. As a Scottish Nationalist I advocate to the best of my
ability the kind of social and political organisation and
co-ordination which is generally spoken of by some such epithet as
'syndico-anarchist'; but outside the political sphere I repudiate
many ideas which certainly obtain considerable authority among
Anarchists, if they are not an absolutely essential part and *sine quâ
non* of Anarchist doctrine — for example, many of the ideas on
sexual behaviour, especially in regard to juveniles, which I find
advocated in *Freedom*. On the other hand, I am not afraid of
finding myself in the same train as Communists on certain matters;
and when they take their stand against the Atlantic Pact, which as
a Nationalist and a Pacifist, I repudiate with every ounce of energy
I can muster, I am delighted to co-operate with my Scottish
Communist comrades. The Paris Congress met, specifically

pledged to oppose the Pact, and to rally world opinion against it, while claiming also the wider object of advocacy and defence of world peace and co-operation of all peace loving peoples, and the co-ordinating of public opinion generally for the preservation of peace and the support of the United Nations Charter. With all of these purposes, provided in the last instance my own country, Scotland, is recognised as entitled to a vote in the councils of UNO, I am in sympathy, whether or not Communists also support them. So my second question is: provided you admit me as a 'fellow-traveller' with yourselves (which perhaps, of course, you don't) do you consider I should refuse to travel along with Communists in their march against the Atlantic Pact, at the risk of having to keep silent, or at least of finding no effective way of voicing and working for my own policy of opposition to the Pact?

To come, however, to more important matters, may I point out just two aspects of the Congress which are left unmentioned in your article? Firstly, when a man of the intellectual standing of Frédéric Joliot-Curie declared that science must refuse to submit to any policy of secrecy, and must be free to share its discoveries internationally among all scientists, irrespective of political frontiers; when he repudiated the suggestion that atomic scientists, himself included and indeed one might say at their head, should use their knowledge for purposes of war; when he showed us the possibilities for human welfare and advancement which lie in the right application of atomic energy to the purposes of peace and construction in place of destruction, I refuse to believe he merely spoke with his tongue in his cheek, or with a mental reservation in favour of Communist 'interests' or the USSR. For apart from the question of a personal integrity never yet called in doubt, the whole tradition of French thought gives the lie to such a suggestion.

The second point which you omit to mention is, I feel, indeed fraught with promise for the world today, in the tragic moral conditions which confront us. This was the immense part played by men and women of colour in the Congress, the almost preponderant rôle of Africans (including American negroes and West Indians of African descent) and of Asiatic peoples, a preponderance willingly accepted by the fraternal sympathy of their white comrades from Europe and the Americas.

These are the two points I wish to raise; there are many more one could stress, but my letter is already too long. If no room can be found for it in the pages of *Freedom*, where as I know your space is limited, I would like to think it will at least be read by the comrade who, presumably, recorded his own experience of the Congress in your article.

11th June 1949   M. P. RAMSAY

Editor's reply: The warning was needed!

The Warning was Needed!

From the foregoing letter it seems that our epithet of 'weak heads' was not too strong. And does one detect a streak of malice in her last sentence — for it goes without saying that anarchists were not represented at the Congress, as the whole content of our article made clear. But to deal with her points, we will discuss them in reverse order. It is indeed tragic that the Stalinists can draw so freely on men and women of colour. Nothing is more desirable than that white and coloured workers should join hands in the fight against oppression; but that means Africans and American negroes joining with the workers of the Soviet Union as well as the workers of the West to throw off *all* oppression, Soviet imperialism as well as Western. It does not mean joining with your own oppressors' rivals for world power.

We shall be more convinced about Professor Joliot-Curie when he demands freedom for science in the Soviet Union and urges the Soviet Union to publish its atomic secrets. So far he shows only the familiar transferred patriotism of all the other Stalinist intellectuals.

Now on the question of fellow travelling our correspondent does not quite seem to understand the accepted meaning of the term. Applied to Communist fellow travellers it implies conscious or unconscious acceptance of being used by the Party for its own ends without actual membership. Lenin enunciated the doctrine behind this practice quite clearly: Communists must enter other organisations in order to dominate them or to break them up. It is difficult not to feel repelled at the moral obliquity of this doctrine, which has done more than anything else to break up what mutual solidarity used to exist on the left. But it is quite clear how the tactic can be resisted — by refusal to co-operate with any Leninist outfit, whether Stalinist or Trotskyist, which employs it. We do not think it too strong to call the unconscious tools weak heads, while the conscious fellow travellers cannot escape the stigma that attaches to decoys, narks and other such fry.

Does our correspondent not realise that the Communists have been systematically exterminating not only our anarchist comrades (in Russia, Spain, Poland and all the countries of eastern Europe) but all revolutionary socialists as well? How can one retain any moral integrity at all while collaborating with such people? In our article we did not use the term "Red Fascism" lightly.

Our correspondent's letter clearly shows that the warning we issued to uncritical pacifists was only too sorely needed. It lends added point to the final paragraphs of our article.

11th June 1949   EDITORS

Russia's Grip Tightens

The Communist Party purge in Hungary has attracted considerable interest in the capitalist press without much in the way of explanation or understanding. The news interest in this, and other intra-party struggles arises for the sensational press in the fact that the latest purges involve the highest leaders, like the Röhm-Heines purge which Hitler carried through in June 1934. But this very fact deprives these affairs of immediate interest for revolutionary workers, for our sympathies are not engaged by the victims; all of them prominent as were Röhm and Heines — in securing the counter-revolutionary coup of a party dictatorship. We cannot shed tears over these butchers when they feel the same whip that they have themselves forged and ruthlessly applied to workers and revolutionists as well as other oppositional forces.

There is, however, another aspect of the arrest of the Hungarian leaders, Rajk and Szonyi; it follows a whole series of similar purges in which not merely erring rank-and-filers are weeded out, but which involve the top line Communist leaders who have often been most active in bringing their party to power. Hungary is not alone in conforming to a pattern.

The leading Polish Communist, Gomulka, was purged some months ago. He confessed in the best Bolshevik recantation manner, and does not seem to have been extinguished. Kostov, in Bulgaria, has been deprived of all official positions. Less lucky than these, General Koci, of the Albanian Communist Party, has been shot. And then there is Tito. Communist leaders in Rumania and Czechoslovakia are restive and anxious. That some changes are brewing up in Czechoslovakia is shown by the desertion of several members of Czech diplomatic corps abroad.

The capitalist press interprets these desertions as indicating recognition of the 'superiority' of the Western way of life, but it is quite clear that it is personal fear which inspires them; the deserters have been quite happy when the heat has been turned on someone not themselves. Revolutionary circles are apt to fall into another error — that of regarding these party purges as indicating opposition to the party, and therefore as evidence of weaknesses or at least of weakening. Such explanations take too much at their face value the charges of Trotskyism, treachery, etc., which are levelled at the fallen, and which are, in reality, no more than Leninist-Marxist terms of abuse, mere name calling.

Not Weaknesses, but Strengthening of Reaction

One sees going on the liquidation of high-up party leaders all over the Iron Curtain countries, over which the Communist parties have imposed most brutal dictatorships, more efficient and more thorough than that of the Nazis. One's knowledge of the situation of the workers and of the opposition elements under the Cominform regime (and under Tito) makes it tempting to treat all this purging as signs of cracking up, of weakening, of the existence of opposition with which the authorities have to make a serious reckoning.

It is necessary to take into account other less obvious features, however. First, all these countries behind the Iron Curtain are better regarded as what they really are — satellite states of Russia. Second, the simultaneous character of the purges suggests that they are made necessary not by the existence of opposition but by directives from the centre — from Russia. All these party leaders who are now victims of the purging process are activists who have taken a very prominent part in the successful bringing to power of their parties. Mostly they are not Moscow trained, but owe their positions of prominence to their own participation in the underground struggles of the war years. They do not conform to the type at which Tito directed his sneer that they arrived from Russia in passenger planes, smoking pipes. All of them are charged with nationalist deviationism. In short, it is apparent that by their personal achievements and their national successes they were unsuitable tools for the imposition of control from Moscow. Their crime, like Tito's, consists of unwillingness to make their countries completely subservient to Russia. That they are all being eliminated can only point to one explanation; that the imperialist hold of Russia on the satellite states is being ruthlessly tightened.

This is the fact to keep firmly in mind. Sympathy with the

purged leaders is quite out of place. The capitalist press, anxious to discredit Russian Communism from a merely capitalist angle, takes these opportunities to represent the purged in as sympathetic a light as possible. But it is important to distinguish clearly between them and the revolutionists who were the first victims of the new Communist states. All these ex-party leaders have the blood of the workers on their hands; all of them have been not merely consenting parties to the methods of the Communist dictatorship, but its chief architects.

What we are witnessing in these intra-party struggles is not internal weakness and potential opposition, but the tightening of central authority not simply of the Communist government in the countries themselves, but the central control by the Russian government.

Imperialist Consolidation

This process is not one which can be disregarded. In the past, the spectacle of revolts of colonial peoples against British imperialism being crushed by the British army units has brought home to revolutionists the power of imperialism. What we see today in eastern Europe is the consolidation of Russian imperialist power, and in effect the incorporation of the Cominform countries within the structure of the Soviet Union.

The importance of such a process lies in its effects on the potential internal opposition to the regime; it inevitably weakens it. What we are seeing is the strengthening of dictatorship, the grim tightening up of the most oppressive regime whose success means despair for the workers.

Duty to the Revolution in the West

It is useless and presumptious to call on the workers under the Communist heel to revolt — and to wait for them to do so. It is true that their emancipation can only come from themselves, but it is unreal and unfair to expect them to initiate the process. The way to undermine the totalitarianism of eastern Europe is to make the social revolution in the West. progressive reformism, even if successful, has here little effect against the totalitarian regime; but the tendency of the revolution to spread which has been noted in all past revolutions and against which reactionary regimes take elaborate precautions testifying to their fear of it — this tendency holds out hope to the oppressed millions of Russian imperialism as well as to the millions under British rule.

25th June 1949

The Stalinist Fifth Column

As the cold war between East and West hardens, the Stalinists have gone into action with their customary energy to build up fifth columns in the democratic countries. How feeble by comparison the similar efforts of the fascists and nazis before the last war seem in retrospect! The technique is to organise congresses mainly for intellectuals round some seemingly unexceptional slogans such as 'the desire of the common peoples of the world for peace'. Fellow travellers and other weak heads are carefully handpicked, speeches are made denouncing warmongers — Anglo-American ones only, of course — solidarity is expressed on an international scale from delegates 'representing', as the saying goes, 'millions of the oppressed and peace-loving peoples', etc., etc. The aim is not to ensure peace, but to build up fifth columns in the midst of the rivals for world power of the Soviet Union. The chief weapon is publicity.

On a tiny scale we saw the technique used during the second winter of the war in this country as 'The People's Convention', when obedient intellectuals, not distinguished for genuine anti-militarist activity, luke-warmly urged peace. (Need one add that all that was before the break-up of the Soviet Nazi pact with the German invasion of Russia on 22nd June 1941?) Since the war, the same methods have been used on an international scale, first in Poland at the Wroclaw Congress of Intellectuals last year, then at the 'Cultural and Scientific Conference for World Peace' in New York at the end of March, and more recently still in the rally of the 'Partisans of Peace' at the end of last month in Paris.

Some Dissentient Voices

One may derive some slight satisfaction from the fact that despite careful hand-picking and grooming, the British delegates have shown an obstinate tendency to say what they think instead of what they are told. Thus, even the very reliable crypto, Konni Zilliacus, was rather coolly received when he said that reform was better than revolution, and said kind things about the Labour Party. No doubt, however, he was thinking of his rather shaky position in the ranks of Labour, and had Transport House in mind rather than his immediate audience.

Mr Harvey Moore KC, however, was definitely forgetting the Stalinberry rules when he said that the advocacy of peace meant opposition to war, and especially civil war, e.g. in China. For this piece of heresy he was roundly hissed by an audience which had just gone into a delirium of joy over the news of the capture of Nanking by the Chinese Communists — or ought one to call them 'partisans of peace'?

These dissentient voices scarcely disturbed the Nuremberg-like unanimity of the congress in Paris, and may even be useful as indicating the 'independence' and 'free nature' of the discussion: the significance and danger of these performances lies elsewhere, and the threat is less to the rival imperialists than to those who seek social justice and the ending of imperialism and war — to the advocates of revolutionary anti-militarism in fact.

Dangers to Internationalist Anti-militarism
The insincerity of the fellow travellers, their slavish dependence on Moscow, their manifest concern for their personal appearance in the limelight — all these factors make these antics repellent to ordinary people. But by their enormous publicity, their claims to 'represent' *all* lovers of peace, they succeed in identifying all anti-war activity, and all anti-militarist activity with their own tawdry pageantry. Nor do the pacifists help matters by willingly supporting these crypto Stalinist performances. Paul Robeson and Charlie Chaplin and Picasso also play right into the hands — not of peace, but of Red Fascism and Soviet Imperialism. Peace is not to be secured by transferring one's disillusioned patriotism to the other side, nor is the cause of true internationalism served by lip-service to Russian nationalism and expansionism.

It is an urgent necessity for revolutionary anti-militarists to dissociate themselves and their aims as sharply as possible from disguised Soviet militarism. If they do not succeed in doing so, not merely will they find their arguments discredited in advance when the next war comes by their association with the enemy-to-be, but they will find that the home government will suppress them with ease as being thoroughly identified with the Russian Fifth Column. And when that happens they will deserve scant sympathy.

The danger can be combated by unequivocal adherence to internationalism, to revolutionary anti-militarism, to the ideal of social justice instead of jingo nationalism *of whatever brand*. And also by determined, persistent, and radical exposure of the true nature of this fifth column activity, as the greatest danger to the cause of peace and justice. This can be done in everyday propaganda which forms the major propaganda activity of a

movement. It can also be done by courageous and determined action among the intellectuals themselves by raising opposition within these parades. How this was done at the New York Conference will be described in the next issue of *Freedom*.
14th May 1949

Marxism and the Tito-Cominform Struggle

It has been the proud boast of Communists that Marx and Engels had discovered certain contradictions in the capitalist society which made its collapse inevitable. 'Overproduction', unemployment, falling wages, the struggle of the great powers for markets overseas and the resulting wars were, according to them, bound to lead to the breakdown of the old system and its replacement by Socialist States whose new ruling class, the proletariat, would guarantee peace and plenty, prevent the reappearance of national antagonisms and herald a new era of international solidarity. On the strength of these discoveries, Marx and Engels claimed to be the exponents of 'scientific' Socialism and spoke with condescension of those 'Utopian' thinkers like Proudhon who advocated a free society because he thought it ethically desirable rather than because he considered it economically unavoidable.

A hundred years after Marx's materialist conception of history, that is to say his doctrine that economic forces are predominant in the direction of human affairs, had been expounded in the *Communist Manifesto*, it received a great shock through a conflict in which the protagonists are those very States which have advanced the furthest on the road to authoritarian Socialism. It is not surprising therefore that the Tito-Cominform dispute has among many questions also raised the following: "What is the Marxist interpretation of the dispute and how valid is it?"

Among the various charges against Tito there is one which always occurs. Instead of building Socialism the present rulers of Yugoslavia have detached themselves from the 'peace-loving bloc' by reintroducing private capitalism in the towns, supporting the richer peasants against the poorer in the countryside, and by trading with the West instead of with the East. On closer examination, these charges made both in 1948 and today seem baseless when made against a country in which even lemonade kiosks are State-owned and in which the number of collective farms run by party bureaucrats is higher than in any other Russian satellite State. Unlike Poland, Yugoslavia did not at the time of the Cominform resolution have a trade agreement with either the USA or Britain; moreover most of its raw materials were exported to the Soviet Union at less than world prices in return for armaments for Tito's army.

Since the economic factors, in direct contradiction to the Marxist theory, have played a purely secondary rôle in bringing out the dispute, one must look elsewhere for the forces which caused it. One of the chief characteristics of the Stalinist form of government is that its rulers require absolute obedience from all their subordinates. Party purges, concentration camps, never-ending propaganda and the control of production and distribution become the most powerful weapons to enforce this obedience, consolidate the dictatorship and perpetuate the régime. To this end all means are admissible; a Trotski can be chased round half the world and murdered, a Bukharin becomes 'son of a bitch' at his trial, millions of peasants can be uprooted and moved to another continent in order to introduce 'Socialism' in the countryside and a little-known Tito could be sent by the Comintern in 1937 to purge the Yugoslav CP of 'all alien, vacillating elements'.

When that same man 11 years later, basing his stand on the geographical position of his country and on the wartime record of the Yugoslav CP as compared to that of the other European CP's, tries to prevent the USSR from gaining complete control of a State machinery which he thinks is due to him alone, then the Stalinist world changes its views. The Cominform journal which 18 months ago boasted that Tito's Yugoslavia was making such progress that it was beginning to surpass Britain in certain fields, now blames the Marshal for turning the same country 'into a chamber of horrors'. Although the entire Communist élite in Eastern Europe has taken part in the quarrel the only thing both sides can agree is that their opponents have fatally deviated from Marxism-Leninism and are using 'Nazi' methods. Or to quote some of their more colourful, 'scientific' statements, the Cominform has 'sunk into the deepest mud' while the present rulers of Yugoslavia are 'thievish as cats and timid as hares'.

9th July 1949   I.A.

Stalin's Empire of Yes-Men and Mummies

A four-line item tucked away at the bottom of the page was all the space the national press gave to the news that Kostov, former Communist Vice-Premier of Bulgaria had been hanged as a traitor.

Traicho Kostov is yet one more prominent Communist leader to be liquidated in carrying out Russia's policy of stamping out any non-conformism in the Eastern bloc countries. The trial conformed to the usual pattern, from the violent language of the prosecution, the vocal hostility from the public benches to the now traditional custom of the defence lawyer being so overwhelmed by 'proofs' of guilt put forward by the prosecution that he turns against his client and adds his denunciation to that of the prosecution.

But Kostov was a harder nut to crack, since he pleaded 'not guilty' and refuted the written statement he had made before the trial started. What is more he maintained this attitude to the end of the seven-day trial. The reports state that: "In their final pleas to the Court, Kostov was the only one of the accused to claim innocence. He denied briefly and without emotion, charges of espionage and conspiracy but made no attempt to refute any charges or testimonies by his fellow accused which they repeated against him in their final statements."

The charges of which Kostov was found guilty were: (1) Kostov had been a police agent inside the Communist party since 1942; (2) After 1944 he had worked for the British intelligence; (3) Kostov, acting on instructions of British and United States agents, had got in touch with Marshal Tito and plotted to make Bulgaria a Yugoslav 'colony'; and (4) With Tito, he had planned the assassination of the late Bulgarian Premier, Georgi Dimitrov.

As the *Manchester Guardian* points out in an editorial comment (10/12/49) the Russians could not afford to admit that they wanted to put a stop to a policy of "fairly free discussion" within the parties "provided always that an outward appearance of unanimity is maintained". That is why the Bulgarian Government has had to try to associate Kostov with a murder-and-espionage story for which witnesses can be provided. And this is why Kostov's plea of not guilty considerably upset Russia's plans, and it would seem that the sentences imposed were meant to deter others from following Kostov's example, for the accused who all pleaded 'guilty' escaped the death sentence, whereas Kostov, who pleaded 'not guilty' has paid with his life.

An interesting parallel is to be found in the recent trial in Sarajevo (Yugoslavia) of nine Russians accused of espionage. The sentences ranged from three to twenty years hard labour; the accused who received the highest sentence was the only one to plead 'not guilty' to the main charges!

A second interesting parallel is the background of the accused. Kostov, who was accused of espionage for Tito and the Western powers, had a long record of service in the CP. Only two years ago, the Central Committee of the Bulgarian CP issued a long statement on the occasion of Kostov's fiftieth birthday, some extracts of which we reproduce below:

"Great are your achievements, Comrade Traicho Kostov, as the builder of the party, as teacher and instructor of the party members. Under your leadership and your heroic example, thousands of party members were educated into absolute loyalty to the party.

Your deep Marxist-Leninist theoretical knowledge, your great culture, your famous industry and steadfastness, your modesty, your iron will, your unquestionable loyalty towards the party and the working class are those Bolshevik characteristics which beautify your whole fighting life, forever united with the struggle of the party.

A loyal colleague of George Dimitrov, and his first assistant, you are to-day one of the most loved and respected leaders of our party, a great statesman and builder of new Bulgaria."

And now we are asked to believe that the man who, among other things, sent Petkov to his death was, all the time, plotting to assassinate Dimitrov and was spying for the Americans!

In the Yugoslav trial of nine Russians spying for the Soviet Union, the ringleaders were 'an orthodox priest', a 'Tzarist law student' and a woman who 'admitted co-operating with the Gestapo'. A curious and unlikely collection of Russian spies, almost as curious and unlikely as the 'Titoist-American Spy' Kostov.

Without appearing cynical one cannot but think that it was fortunate for Dmitrov (and Moscow) that he 'died' before the Kostov trial started. The Reichstag fire 'hero' might have quite easily found himself in the dock alongside his 'loyal colleague'. Instead, by dying just at the right moment, he is being built up as a hero and, according to a press report, his body is being preserved by the same secret process used for Lenin's remains.

There is no doubt that in the Stalinist Empire there is room only for 'Yes men' and mummies.

24th December 1949   LIBERTARIAN

Tito versus Stalin

It is so typical of the brazenness of the Communist leadership that a complete *volte face* in policy is explained away with perfect calm and all that was said or written before in support of the opposite point of view is discarded without a word of explanation or even an apology. Or is it that the readers of the *Daily Worker*, for instance, who have been lapping up for years now 'eye witness' accounts of the work of the great Marshal Tito and his followers, just don't care whether what they read in the Communist Press is fact or fiction and therefore are conditioned for changes of front without apologies? Somehow we do not think that all the *Daily Worker*'s readers are as blind and brainless as all that, and yet that paper 'owned by its readers' in its only editorial comment on the Tito crisis makes no mention of how it came to support this 'Trotskyist' in Communist clothing for so long, but instead uses the old nationalistic trick of rallying its supporters by warning them that the 'reactionaries of the Capitalist world' are 'rejoicing' and that they must close their ranks to resist any attempts to drive a wedge in the ranks of the faithful. Anything but the hard facts and significance of the Stalin-Tito feud which however much they may deny it, is, particularly since Tito has refused to capitulate in the best Moscow Trials tradition, threatening the 'unity' of the Communist and Communist dominated countries.

The Cominform Statement

The statement is a long, rambling document in which the Communist phraseology and slogans abound. It consists of eight points, the first of which reveals that it was the 'action of the Central Committee of the All-Union Communist Party (Bolshevik)' which took the initiative in uncovering the incorrect policy of the Central Committee of the Yugoslav CP and above all the incorrect policy of Comrades Tito, Kardelj, Djilas and Rankovich. The second point deals with the 'hateful policy' of the Yugoslav Party 'in relation to the Soviet Union and to the All-Union Communist Party' and specifies in this connection such acts as the 'belittling' of Soviet military specialists, 'discrediting' the Soviet Army and subjecting Soviet civilian subjects in Yugoslavia to a 'special regime' which consisted in their being watched by Yugoslav spies and followed! All this, according to the statement, indicates that the Yugoslavs began to identify the foreign policy of the imperialist powers and to act accordingly. And finally, the Yugoslav Communists spread calumniating propaganda borrowed from the 'arsenal of counter-revolutionary Trotskyism'.

Internal Deviations
The third point deals with the Yugoslav Party's policy inside their country and with 'their retreat from the Marxist-Leninist position'. Fourthly, the leadership is accused of revising the Marxist-Leninist teaching about the Party and is accused of 'letting the Party dissolve itself in the non-party Popular front' which includes various classes and variegated political groups, among them some bourgeois parties. Fifthly, the 'bureaucratic regime within the Party' is ruinous for the Party. 'There is no internal democracy in the Party and the type of organisation encourages within the Party military leadership methods similar to those of Trotsky'.

They refused 'Brotherly Help'
Point 6 condemns the attitude of the Yugoslav Party to the 'brotherly help' offered by the Russian and other CP's and attacks the leaders for being 'afflicted by inordinate ambition, grandeeism and cunning calculation'. The seventh point deals with their refusal to come to heel or in the words of the statement for replying 'negatively to numerous proposals of the brotherly CP's to discuss the situation'. Eighthly, as a result of this attitude the Yugoslavs have moved to 'dissassociate themselves from the United Socialist Front against Imperialism and set out on the road of treason to the international solidarity of the working people and of transition toward the position of nationalism' and consequently they have put themselves outside the family of 'brotherly Communist Parties and outside the United Communist Front and thus also outside the ranks of the Information Bureau'.

This, very briefly, is the charge sheet which sounds too good to be true. It contains everything from the charge of Trotskyism and deviation from Marxist-Leninism to the classic personal attack — 'inordinate ambition, grandeeism and cunning calculation'. The document also reveals that Tito's major crime is that for one reason or another he has refused to be dictated to by Stalin. Perhaps Tito fancies himself as a second Stalin (and the *Daily Worker*, for one, did much to build up that myth around Tito) and is blind to the fate reserved for those who show themselves too independent where Moscow is concerned. Or perhaps Moscow has shot her bolt for such a document as the Cominform statement, in our opinion, presupposed the grovelling acceptance by the guilty party. Instead, all the Communist Parties have paid lipservice to Moscow's pronouncement *except* Yugoslavia!

Now one must await events. Will Moscow accept defeat, or will the Red Army bring a little concrete 'brotherly help' to Tito and his friends? Only when the answer to this question will be given will the politicians be able to draw conclusions for the next move in their game of power politics.

For us the scene is unchanged. Or should we revise our opinion of Tito if he successfully resists Stalin, and say that there are now two Stalins in Europe. Instead of one Stalin and a stooge?
10th July 1948

4,000 Spanish Refugees have disappeared in Russia

Former Communist Party 'General' Challenges Party to Deny Statement

There was a time when the name 'El Campesino' was on every loyal Communist's lips. He was a symbol of that courage and self-sacrifice which, we are told, were an inspiration to a whole people at war with the forces of Fascism; and such qualities are only to be found in Communists. El Campesino was the first Spanish Communist to rise from the ranks to be 'General in the People's Army'. He, Lister and Modesto, were described by a Communist-inspired publication (in 1940) as "three of the greatest and best-known" leaders of the Spanish People's Army, and Moscow recognised in El Campesino the "Tchapaiev of the Spanish War".

Such biographical details are necessary (and could be easily supplemented by reference to Communist publications of the Spanish War period) by way of introducing El Campesino to readers who did not follow events in Spain in 1936, and to recall his deeds to the faithful Party followers whose short memories (when expedient) are only too well known.

For, El Campesino is in the news again. His rôle is a less heroic one than when, as the story goes, he defied Franco's troops, who declared he had been killed by climbing onto the roof of a house encircled by the enemy of the Teruel front to show that he was alive and full of fight. In the five-hour battle that ensued he is said to have lost a thousand men but himself succeeded in escaping.

His new rôle
Today he is a *former* Communist whose experiences in Russia have destroyed his faith in the Stalinist regime. The book on which he is at present engaged, and to be published in Paris soon, promises to reveal some interesting facts about the Communists' rôle in Spain and conditions in Russia itself which, incidentally, will confirm many of the things the Anarchists said at the time and which the Communists denounced as "Trotsky-fascist disruptive propaganda", etc.

A Paris daily paper has published three instalments from El Campesino's forthcoming book. The first deals with the story of what happened to the gold from the Bank of Spain. El Campasino has first-hand knowledge, since he was instructed by José Diaz, then Secretary General of the Spanish Communist Party, to arrange to collect the gold and load it on to lorries. The operation was undertaken by trusted Party members, many in the uniforms of Assault Guards, and in an hour the 7,800 cases of bars and coins were loaded on to 35 lorries, carrying indicators which led unsuspecting onlookers to believe that they were carrying explosives. On 28th October 1936, the cases were transferred to a ship bound for Odessa. Like so many contrite ex-Communists, El Campesino is "full of indignation against myself and all those responsible for the theft. I am convinced that José Diaz himself must have deeply regretted his part before his tragic death in Tiflis." But we are also asked to believe in El Campesino's "involuntary complicity" in the affair. Yet he tells us that a similar operation occurred in Catalonia this time under the direction of a "Communist battalion commander, Manolo. Six lorries loaded with gold were sent to France and, according to El Campesino, handed to Maurice Thorez, who is still leader of the French Communist Party. Other consignments of gold were sent to Thorez in this way and a further 2,500,000,000 francs were received by the French Communist Party from Dr Negrin (then Spanish premier) for the purchase of arms and for propaganda as well as funds for launching the pro-Communist daily *Ce Soir*. And that is only part of the story.

How right were the Anarchists when they pointed out that what arms were received by the Spanish workers from Russia and other sources had been paid for handsomely with hard gold. And how indignant were the 'innocent' Communists and fellow travellers!

Spanish Communists in Russia

The defeat of the Spanish workers by Franco's army and the betrayal of their revolutionary aspirations by such leaders as El Compesino, was accompanied by a mass exodus into France of Anarchists, Socialists, Communists who feared reprisals. El Campesino tells us that in France a committee of Communist leaders was created to 'screen' those Communist Party members who were seeking asylum in Russia. Priority was given to three categories of 'comrades'— members of the NKVD (secret police organisation) who, it is interesting to note, were "mainly women"; well-known militants whose position was compromising; Spanish and foreign militants "who had given signs of lukewarmness during the civil war or who knew too much. Not having been able to liquidate them in Spain, as had been the case of a number of their friends, they were to be sent to Russia and made to disappear." The first contingent, under the direction of Togliatti, Modesto and Lister, left in April 1939.

Altogether 3,961 Spanish refugees arrived in Russia in this way. They had been preceded by 1,700 children accompanied by 102 teachers.

El Campesino claims that of nearly 6,000 Spanish refugees in Russia, only 1,200 are still alive today, and challenges the Communists to disprove this figure.

Those 4,800 Spaniards who have disappeared or have died in Russia include two whom we have mentioned earlier — Diaz, Secretary of the Spanish Communist Party and organiser of the transfer of the Spanish gold to Russia, and Manolo who was responsible for taking the four lorries from Catalonia to France and of handing them over to Thorez. Dead men tell no tales.
11th November 1950

THE POLITICS OF HUNGER

The Real Conditions in Germany

At a time when the newspaper reports about conditions inside Germany are obviously distorted and partial, it is useful to have some other source of information. The following account was sent to Freedom *by a correspondent in Germany.*

The working populations in all countries have been the chief sufferers from the war, and this is as true of Germany as of other countries. The German people are starving. 2,400 calories a day are the minimum necessary for a human being; but if a German gets 1,200 he is lucky. He will probably get even less this winter unless there is some change in the administration of the country.

There is no rationing of clothes — they are unobtainable. The Black Market flourishes. A pound of coffee fetches 350 marks (£8 15s). This causes some slight inconvenience to the soldier of the occupation forces. After he has sold his coffee, he wants to change his marks into English currency. Yet by the Regulations he cannot change more than the fortnightly amount of his pay. He gets over the difficulty however by selling his surplus marks privately at about 80 to the pound, and then sends the notes home. There is a similar regulation in the American zone, but the American soldier does not seem to have so much difficulty either, for the US Military HQ in Berlin recently stated that GIs have sent home 11,000,000 dollars more than their pay allowances during the first four months of the occupation. In October alone half a million dollars in excess of pay were sent home, showing how ineffective are these regulations.

With cigarettes, coffee and chocolate the allied soldier can buy anything he wants. A girl will sell herself for a bar of chocolate or a packet of cigarettes.

Requisitioning

In accordance with clause 19 of the proclamation of the Allied Commanders-in-Chief, houses, cars and furniture can be confiscated at will by the military government. They are simply 'Requisitioned for Military Purposes'. It is said that there have been cases of high ranking officers having cars painted over in RAF colours, complete with RAF number plates, and shipping them to the UK. Even the entire production of factories — making cigarette lighters for example — have been dealt with in a like manner.

When a German is thrown out of his house under a requisitioning order, he applies to the Buergermeister and joins a long waiting list for 'other accommodation'. The best houses have been taken over for officers (sometimes two officers to a house) even in towns where there are good military barracks. The conquerors must have the best.

No Lifts for Germans

The only serviceable trains are used by the occupying forces. Germans travel in open trucks and these are packed. On the autobahns large notices forbid service drivers to give lifts to Germans. People of all ages can be seen sitting dejectedly by the roadside with their bundles of possessions beside them, miles from anywhere. At night the headlights of one's car pick out white appealing faces.

The Quest for Fuel

In the early morning and at dusk the streets are filled with civilians in search of firewood. Members of all classes join in the march, pulling odd assortments of barrows and carts. Success rarely crowns their efforts chiefly because of the non-availability of tools. But the energy which they put into this quest testifies to the lack of gas and electricity.

Misery from Bombing

Despite the bombing raids on Germany, the Allied armies still had to fight their way in, and one has the impression that the suffering and misery caused to the civilian population is out of all proportion to the military advantage achieved. The effect of these raids is illustrated by the case of Hanover. Before the war it was a beautiful city, a centre of art and culture, rich in architecture, music and literature. The second residential city of Germany, it was known as 'Die Stadt in Gruen' — 'The Town in Green'.

It has been officially estimated that 80 per cent of the city has been destroyed. Of approximately 148,000 houses, only 1,000 remain standing. The peacetime population of 470,000 has been reduced to 300,000. To-day, Hanover is a city of wild-eyed, bewildered people, a city of destruction, crumbling buildings, endless queues, want and depression. Every large German town has the same story to tell.

Birds of a Feather
The filling of administrative posts in many cases with Germans who had served under the Nazis has already shown that the alleged anti-fascist attitude of the Allies is only a thin veneer. Military Government is, in fact, not anti-fascist but simply anti-German in outlook, and also displays the usual class prejudice of the officer type. Displaced Persons who are working in the Nazi Labour Corps are being provided for in an institutional sort of way. But 'displaced' landowners who fled to Germany when Russia annexed the Baltic States, and who are in fact pro-Nazi, are welcomed by the officers, and dinners are given in their honour. These people invariably say in conversation with the British, "You'll have to fight the Russians, you know". They receive more sympathy for having had estates taken away from them, than the ordinary displaced person who has lost everything, and has no prospects at all.

German Soldiers' Homecoming
Men of the Wehrmacht returning mostly from PoW camps in the East, are half starved and dressed in rags. Boots are long since worn out, and their feet are swathed in old clothing. None are really physically fit. Allied Administrative officers say that in normal times 85 per cent of them would be hospital cases. But such are the conditions of housing and feeding in the big towns that those who possibly can move on must do so. Wehrmacht women and Red Cross nurses came back with the troops and they too are mostly ill. Some claim to have marched as much as 300 miles, and evidence seems to confirm this. Many of them have children with them, and no one can deny the care which these bedraggled mothers have lavished on them throughout the difficult journey.

Forced Labour

The German population mostly works for the Military Govern-ment, and all Army units have their share of forced labour as a result. All classes are to be found in the labour corps; school-teachers, ex-luftwaffe personnel, office workers, etc. They are paid on an average 3 marks a day (1/6). The male labourers do anything from road-mending to window-cleaning; the women are put to work in the kitchens, and as waitresses in service messes.

Germans' Attitude

In the British zone the German population, and especially the older people, are mostly servile and eager to please. But this is not due, as the Hun-baiters would have us believe, to 'German cunning'. It is partly thankfulness that the wholesale destruction and slaughter is over, and that they find themselves in the British instead of the Russian zone; and also the terrible shortage of all basic commodities makes the population so abjectly dependent, that they become servile in consequence. Allied personel are not allowed to make way for Germans on the pavements, and the population quickly make way for them, with however, a few exceptions.

MG's Fear Disorder

But with the approach of full winter, and increasing shortages of fuel and food, there are signs that the attitude of the Germans will change to opposition, and the Military Government is fully aware of this. Already in the British zone the training of a German police force is well under way. Forty separate police forces have been formed and it is officially estimated that 40,000 policemen distributed among them will be necessary. As an Allied journal puts it, "They are steadily being trained in their local forces, and they may well prove a useful adjunct in the maintenance of law and order in the coming winter". The fear underlying these last few words is evident.

12th January 1946

World Starvation Now Admitted

Not Due to Natural Causes, but to the Price System

It is no pleasure for those who have for months been warning against the danger of famine to say, "I told you so!". Starvation for millions of people is too grim a prospect. Nor is the fact that the United Nations have now recognised the palpable fact of mass hunger any guarantee that anything will be done about it.

Speaking at the UNO General Assembly on 13 February, Ernest Bevin stated that in the first six months of 1946 importing countries will require 17,000,000 tons of wheat and flour, whereas the expected supply is estimated at only 12,000,000 tons. He added that there were good reasons for thinking that "the deficit will be even larger than the 5,000,000 tons already mentioned".

To indicate the extent of the likely famine, Bevin declared: "We are dealing with 1,000,000,000 of the world population who in the next few months may be faced with famine . . . It is estimated that in Europe there are 40,000,000 people consuming an average of 1,500 calories a day. This is an average figure. Many millions are below it, and it is impossible to know the number of those who are hungry, in addition to the Far East. *It must be a terrifically large figure.*"

We have pointed out for weeks now the plight of the people of Germany and Central Europe. Bidault and Wellington Koo pointed out to UNO the serious conditions in France and China respectively. There can now be no excuses; Bevin gives 1,000 millions — half the population of the world — as facing famine. For months Governments have been trying to cover up the starvation conditions which face workers almost everywhere. If they are forced to admit it now, we may be sure that they do not exaggerate the picture.

India and Malaya

In India it is officially estimated that there is a grain deficit of 3,000,000 tons, and there are no reserves. Indians are rationed to 1lb of grain a day, and are subsisting on 1,000 calories daily — just over one third of the 2,800 calories regarded by nutritionists as adequate to maintain health. Indians had the worst diet of any country in the world *before* the war; yet the *News Chronicle* states that their diet to-day provides half the calories they had in pre-war days. A repetition of the 1943 famine is expected.

In Malaya, the food situation is desperate, and the cost of living is anything from 5 to 20 times the pre-war level. The position of children was made worse at the beginning of the reoccupation by the British, because an order from London suddenly cancelled the meals which had been given free in the native schools. Another factor which contributes to the starvation is the price of rubber. The Government, by arrangement with America, has fixed the price at 10d per lb. At this price the growers cannot make a profit, and so "rubber cannot be produced". (*Manchester Guardian*, 10th February 1946). The same source adds that "labour cannot be got at this price level. To give native labour even a bare livelihood it is agreed by all that wages must be three times the pre-war level". These observations give the key to the *economic* causes of the world famine.

Capitalist Economics the Cause

The distinguishing feature of the capitalist system is that goods are produced in order to be sold. Production therefore depends on the existence of a market, and if there is no market, if people can't buy the goods, they won't be produced. Nowhere is this truer than in agriculture. The farmer or peasant has to lay out money and labour for months before he sells his product and recoups himself. Now if the workers in general are paid such poor wages that they cannot afford more than a dead minimum (and sometimes not even that) then the farmer doesn't produce more than a minimum of the food, for he will lose his outlay if the product can't be sold, or is left to be bought up by the government for less than cost.

Furthermore, if there is a bumper crop, the goods flood the market, the price falls, and many farmers are ruined just because the good crop has lowered prices below the level at which he can recover his outlay, and begin to lay out again for the next season. The US crop of last season was a record one. Common sense immediately tells one that this is singularly fortunate seeing that the crops in S Africa and in India have been poor. But common sense and humanity are not the dominant factors in capitalist economy — the market is the only consideration. And a good crop means lowered prices. Consequently the US Secretary of Agriculture has already suggested that crop quotas may have to be reduced next year to *protect farm prices*. In plain terms, this means that American farmers will be encouraged to produce *less food this season*. This advice was given when Europe was already starving, and in total disregard of the chronic famine conditions in India and China.

Why cannot the surplus food be given away free? Because if it were, the price of food offered for sale would fall still further and the profits of the food producing industry would also fall still further. To protect the price of food — and this means to keep the price above that at which millions of people can afford to buy it — only two courses are open: not to produce the food in 'excess' in the first place, or to destroy the surplus by ploughing crops in, burning wheat, or throwing fish back into the sea. Prices are raised, and the producer is able to make a profit (often only enough to allow him to struggle through next season); but inevitably a large section of the population goes hungry.

Government's Futile Appeals
It is not the wickedness of individual capitalist producers which is at fault. Often the farmers and peasants live almost on starvation level. They are at the mercy of the market — of the capitalist mode of production. In India, it is exactly the peasants who provide the bulk of the starving population. Modern famines are not due to any 'wickedness' on the part of the primary producers (though we would not say the same of the middlemen who hoard the much needed food until they can sell it at outrageous scarcity prices), they are inevitable symptoms of the market economy of to-day.

Governments understand the position alright; that's why they offer subsidies, why they enable restrictionism to be practised on the scale which makes famines possible. They are acting as one would expect them to act — in the interests of the big concerns involved. The State is the executive committee of the ruling class, and it is simply unrealistic to expect them to act in the interests of society as a whole. Only the individuals who compose society can do that, by organising themselves in such a way that they control the economy directly.

The State, however, through its spokesmen like Bevin, Byrnes, and all the rest of them has to *appear* to concern itself with society as a whole; otherwise it would never continue to rule. But in face of this world wide food shortage, a problem that requires the energies of society as a whole to solve it, all that governments can do is to issue appeals to farmers to grow more food! Obviously if it were economically feasible for the farmers and peasants of the world to grow more food there would be no famine. If the poverty of the workers the world over permitted of it they would buy more food, and the very fact that they could buy, would provide the demand without which, under capitalism, no supply can be forthcoming.

It is useless for Bevin to imply that the causes of the famine are natural causes — the crop failures in South Africa and India. The United States have had a record crop for two years running now, and have ample reserves. We are always hearing about this 'age of transport', about technical progress having established the effectual unity of the world, and so on. Under a rational system of economy crop failures in one part (even if they were due to natural, instead of largely economic causes) could be compensated by the plenty elsewhere.

World Solution

The capitalist press, both left and right, shows itself utterly incapable (?unwilling) to realise the full extent of the problem. The Tory papers groan about ration cuts and make anti-Labour Party propaganda out of the situation. The working class of this country have been and still are undernourished. But there is no problem at all here comparable with that in Europe, or India, or China. Meanwhile, the Labour press seeks to excuse Bevin's complete failure to mention economic causes in his survey of world food conditions, by declaring that the people of this country are better fed now than they were before the war, and calling for a tightening of the belt. As if the cutting down on dried eggs in this country of 47 millions will make any difference to the lot of the 1,000 million whom Bevin says are facing famine!

To remedy an evil, one must look to its cause. The cause of the present famine, and of the chronic food shortage of decades past, is the capitalist mode of production. Its solution is the abandonment of that economy, which ties the producers to the market which demands scarcity in order to keep prices up. Human beings *need* food. And production must be to supply *needs* — Human needs, not market needs. The peoples of the world will have to break the State power which exists to defend the market economy and the handful of capitalists who profit from it before they can produce enough to satisfy the elementary food needs of men.

23rd February 1946

The Ration Cut in Germany
Big Three Bargain While Germans Starve

At its Glasgow Conference in early December, the Union of Anarchist Groups accepted a resolution on the imminent danger of famine in Europe. Our movement foresaw the situation which now faces so many millions of people in Europe, India and China, and called on the working class in this country and America to assert themselves in practical solidarity with workers the world over in order to save the victims of the coming famine. We do not regard the people of Germany and of Japan as enemies; for us they are our fellow workers, exploited just as we are. Even if we did regard them as enemies, the desperate plight in which they are now placed would be quite enough for us to stretch every nerve in order to help them. We print in this issue of *Freedom* a declaration of our Dutch anarchist comrades towards the Germany of the workers, and we endorse their humane views. Human needs, human pains are everywhere the same; they cry out for redress without distinction of nationality.

The situation of millions of people in the world today is so tragic that one can hardly bear to let one's mind dwell on it. Horrible as war is, the horrors of capitalist peace seem even more ghastly, for they are more widespread and impersonal, while the sufferers are more helpless and uncomprehending.

To add to the misery of lack of fuel, appalling lack of housing, and food shortage, the occupation authorities in Germany now propose to make the situation even worse by making drastic ration cuts. The average ration hitherto has been 1,500 calories daily — just over half the amount usually reckoned as the minimum to keep the sedentary person in health. But it is now announced that this amount is to be cut to nearly 1,000 calories daily, and the press openly discuss the inevitability of increased disease and death rates. The Government, in deciding not to make any ration cuts here in order to make food available for Germany, calmly envisages 'civil disturbances' as a result of the food situation, and talks of the necessity of increasing the policing forces of occupation.

It was suggested that a pooling plan should be established whereby the four occupation zones should have a common distribution of available food stocks. This has broken down, and Lieutenant General Clay, the US Commander in Berlin, stated on

2nd March that "the food situation in Germany has now reached a point where pooling the existing supplies will help no one".

One of the most offensive things about the whole tragic business is the half-ashamed, half-gleeful way in which the capitalist press describes the plight of the German people. "Germans are last in the queue for world's food" is the announcement in the *News Chronicle* for 28th February, and it is typical.

But what is really much more shocking is the glimpse we get of the reasons for the hold up of relief, and of the obstacles in the way of the reconstruction of German economic life — insofar as that is possible under capitalism. "Big three bargain over German food, steel" runs the *News Chronicle*'s headline on 4th March, and Denis Weaver writes:

"Some pretty hard bargaining is understood to be going on within the Allied Control Council of Germany this weekend. It concerns not only food but steel, and on the outcome may depend more than the exact rations of bread or cereals Germans are to have in the British zone . . . Neither has agreement been reached on another vital question — that of how much steel Germany is to be allowed to produce. The Russians want a lower figure: Great Britain a higher one. According to my information a connection between these two unsolved problems has been suggested on the basis of a bargain implying concessions by both sides.

Germany, in fact, is assuming more and more the shape of a vast chess board upon which games are played which have little relation to the German people as such."

These discussions epitomise the way in which world decisions are reached today. Bargains about steel, about rubber, about oil — there are the concerns on which the lives and welfare of millions of workers hang. But they hang on these decisions, not as primary factors which govern the discussions, but as mere incidental results of their outcome. No doubt the stock exchange is doing very well; but meanwhile hundreds of thousands of men, women and children face the pain and misery and anxiety of starvation, lack of shelter and lack of food.

Excuses to Save Capitalism

There is famine in Germany, India, Japan, and certain Allied European countries. Obviously such a widespread food lack requires fairly radical measures for its relief. Yet we find the spokesmen of the governments talking in terms of raising the extraction rate of flour from 80 to 85 per cent, reducing the amount of barley available for beer, or appealing to civilians to eat less. Manifestly, such measures can only have a very slight palliative effect.

These attempts to shave a little off the national larders in order to provide a few scraps for the famine areas appear even more ludicrous and shameless in view of the reports in the financial papers about the destruction of wheat in Argentina.

Furthermore, the present famine condition was expected, for as long ago as last autumn the Allied Commanders in Berlin had ordered the digging of mass graves because they anticipated that the people would be too weak to do so when the time came to fill them. All this attempt to treat the famine as an emergency which has descended out of the blue is simply an attempt on the part of the governments to cover up the chaos which their administrations bring to the populations they claim to look after. The excuse is so transparent that even left wing papers have criticised the government on these grounds.

I do not doubt that individuals in the government want to save the lives of the starving. What they are obviously unwilling to do is alter their system of economy so that these lives *can* be saved. Instead they simply make ineffectual gestures to make people think that something is being done.

The drought in India and South Africa, and the consequent failure of the crops, is given as the cause of the present world food shortage. But it clearly does not greatly affect the position of Europe, and is chiefly used as an excuse. In the present technical state of agriculture it is quite absurd to claim that crop failures in certain parts *cause* generalised famine. The real cause is the failure to have any margins to allow for such natural disasters, and on looking into the matter further, one finds that this failure is due to the operation of capitalist economy.

The statistics of world agriculture recently published as a White Paper by the government make this clear. Australia and Argentina have had to cut down their grain exports during the war years because of the loss of European markets. Hence the acreage under wheat in Argentina fell from 21,302 millions in 1938 to 14,183 millions in 1945, while in Australia it fell from 14,350 millon to 10,950 millions in the same period. Not having the incentive of profit, the farmers have let all these potentially productive acres go out of cultivation, with the result that there is no margin to meet the sudden occurence of crop failures elsewhere. The farmers cannot be blamed, for the loss of markets ruins them and they cannot just grow a surplus if there is no prospect of selling it.

The same difficulty faces the American farmer under the capitalist system, and prevents them from responding to the 'appeal' of the British and American governments that they should grow more food. "American farmers", says the *News Chronicle* for 13th March, "are reluctant to grow as much wheat as is needed, because they feel they may be left 'holding the bag' in later years when harvests in Europe and India are normal again."

It is useless to deplore this 'selfish' attitude on the farmers' part. Thousands of them were ruined during the early thirties by the collapse of world agricultural prices. If they behaved as their hearts would urge them and grew food for other men's needs instead of according to the dictates of the market, they would be driven out of business in a season — before their philanthropy had got very far. The root of the trouble lies in the capitalist system, and this cannot be disguised by excuses. It happened in exactly the same way after the last war, though in a less catastrophic form, and workers will continue to starve so long as the market system of economy endures.

The other disgraceful excuse which the governments fall back on is to represent the position as if there were only an amount of food in the world to feed a proportion of the population, and the rest must *inevitably* starve. This is Malthus up to date with a vengeance. They state the problem as though it was a question of deciding merely *who* are going to be the unlucky ones in the allocation of food. Thus, to refuse food to Germany, and cut their rations down to Belsen levels, is frankly stated to be a death sentence on millions of Germans, chiefly infants and very old people. But, say the government spokesmen, "it is a reprieve for millions of Indians". Sir Ben Smith urges the US government to deny food to the Japanese so that starving Allied countries "can be fed". Time and again the columnists write that the German people must come at the end of the world queue for food. The whole problem is represented as though we had to choose between the Indians or the Germans — and all the time wheat is being destroyed in South America and US farmers are holding down their food production for fear prices will collapse.

While governments make these dirty, shameless excuses, millions of men and women face miserable extinction from starvation. The market system must be swept away. Workers must take over the land themselves and work it to serve men and their needs instead of markets and the stock exchanges. Only then will this ghastly tragedy become a forgotten nightmare.

23rd March 1946

World Food Situation
Underlines Degeneration of Socialist Thought

Here are some scattered observations involving the feeding of ordinary people in different parts of the world. The universal food shortage is terrible enough. But in another way the indifference of men — especially those who claim to believe in what used to be called the 'brotherhood of mankind' — is scarcely less terrible or sinister. Let us look at the world.

News Chronicle report of 28th December 1946: "Rome, Friday. Carrying banners saying: 'We don't want to die of hunger' and 'We're hungry, give us food', housewives in the seaport of Bari sacked shops today in a demonstration against the high cost of living. Police in light tanks fired at the rioting crowd, killing one and injuring fourteen. Reinforcements of troops and armoured cars have been sent to the town."
The old, old story. They asked for bread and got — bullets.

Robert Root, *Worldover Press* correspondent in Berlin describes (on 27th December 1946) the hunger of school children in Germany. If a hot daily lunch cannot be provided very soon without cutting rations in return, one American official says, "it is inevitable that there will be a tremendous wave of sickness and epidemics in winter. The children are obviously underweight and undernourished and will not be able to withstand the rigours of the oncoming cold weather. In my work in the schools I have noticed an alarming increase in the number of cases of children who have broken out with an ugly-looking and irritating skin disease due to malnutrition."
Root goes on to remark that one bad effect on morals has been the stimulation of food thefts. "In some areas, half the delinquencies among school children have been such thefts. In the Kreuzberg district, 62 per cent of the delinquencies were of this type in the first six months of the year."
51,580 children, or 40 per cent of the children in the United States' sector of Berlin, are without shoes. Almost as many are completely without winter clothing.

"Two fishermen made a catch of 100 stones of sprats at Folkestone yesterday. But there were no buyers and the whole boatload was dumped back into the sea." (*News Chronicle*, 28th December 1946).

Now it is gratifying to know that the food situation in this country is improving, even if one knows that the prime cause of malnutrition here is the inability to buy what food is available, so that increased supplies from abroad only filter through to those most in need if they cause the price of food to be lowered. But congratulation on the score of this increase is out of place in view of the news from Germany and Italy, not to mention the almost permanent famine conditions among Indians and Chinese, or among the native population of South Africa.

Once again the destruction of fishermen's catches shows that the market economy of capitalism lies at the root of the famines today. But this has been pointed out too often in this paper to require elaboration here. What we are concerned with is an ethical aspect of preventable misery which is too often overlooked.

Socialism, by its very name, affirms the feeling of kinship with one's fellow men, and it is this *feeling*, this direct apprehension, which underlies the socialist internationalism. The anti-militarist tradition, once common to the whole of socialist thought, but now upheld almost solely by anarchists (and not, alas, by all of those who describe themselves thus), was erected on the knowledge that it was wrong for men to engage in the mindless mass destruction of their fellows. There is an element of intellectual casuistry in the conceptions of 'progressive' and 'reactionary' wars, which led Marx and some of his followers to take the German side in the Franco-Prussian war of 1870. Such niceties may apparently suit the immediate programme of politics, but they are alien to the ethical traditions of socialism. The great American socialist, Eugene V. Debs, declared: "While there is a lower class, I am in it; while there is a criminal element, I am of it; while there is a soul in prison, I am not free", and he was affirming the sense of kinship with other men — all other men — which is basic to the original socialist conceptions. Charles James Fox, the Whig leader of Pitt's time, expressed the same feeling when he said on seeing a man driven to Tyburn to be hanged, "There, but for the grace of God, go I". The anarchist insistence on international solidarity represents the strongest statement of this feeling.

Unfortunately, the liberals abandoned universal kinship in

favour of national loyalty long ago, and the socialists have now followed them and suppressed them in rabid nationalism. Almost the only other body which maintains the feeling of practical human solidarity is the Quakers, who explicitly keep free from politics.

Throughout the period of European starvation, socialists have been most careful, on the rare occasions when they have advocated mitigating the lot of the starving 'ex-enemies', to insist that they do not do so for humanitarian reasons. Mass starvation breeds epidemics, they point out; and our troops may be infected. Indeed the sickness may spread over here. Self-interest demands, therefore, they declare, that Germans and others should be maintained just above the danger line. These are their arguments when they are in favour of humane measures. But much more often they ignore the famines, remarking that 'they have no reason to love the Germans'.

The collapse of Socialist Internationalism in 1914, and the increasing development of Socialist Nationalism since, shows the degeneration of socialist thought since Debs' time. Significant of the general trend, the 'Communist International' (which was neither communist nor international) never had even a spark of ethical feeling, and its theoreticians derided any such as 'bourgeois illusions'. The lack of this warmth of feeling, only too starkly shown by the socialists of today, is mainly responsible for the emptiness, the disillusionment, the impotence of political socialism. But for people with revolutionary conceptions, for anarchists, for anyone with any depth of humanity, such warmth is an integral part of their make-up. For such people Debs' words have never has such poignancy and relevance as they have today.

18th January 1947

German Workers Demand Food

100,000 in Dusseldorf Strike

The long-suppressed discontent of the German people with the worsening food situation has at last begun to come to a head. This is taking place most actively in the Ruhr, which has been one of the worst-hit areas and which has the most solidly working-class population in Germany.

The demonstrations began with a three-hour strike of 35,000 workers in public utility concerns, who marched to the Military Government headquarters in Wuppertal in a great demonstration protesting against the catastrophic conditions and demanding some alleviation. For the period of the strike, water, gas and electricity undertakings did not function, and the trams ceased to run.

This was the largest demonstration in Germany since the end of the war, but more was to follow. On the 27th March, 1,500 women in Cologne protested against food shortages and the continued requisitioning of houses for British families. On the same day 4,000 people in Aachen marched to the Military Government headquarters and presented a petition.

On the next day there was a general strike in Dusseldorf. All transport services and factories in the city were closed down, and more than 100,000 people came into the streets to demonstrate against the military authorities. Military cars were overturned and stoned, and windows were broken in office buildings.

Since then, there have been demonstrations in Dortmund and other Ruhr towns where, among others, the miners, who receive specially large rations, have struck in solidarity with the rest of the population.

These demonstrations and strikes have been occasioned by the steady decline in the food situation in the British zone. At the beginning of the autumn, promises were made that the ration would be in the neighbourhood of 1,550 calories. But the authorities have failed miserably even to reach that wholly inadequate level, and during the past few weeks the actual rations received have sunk to about 800 calories. Apparently there is now plenty of grain at Hamburg and Bremen, but the transport system to the Ruhr is quite inefficient, and, in addition, it is estimated that within two months some 30,000 tons of grain have disappeared in transit — no doubt finding its way on to the black market to feed the well-to-do.

The growing discontent of the Germans is likely to break out into even greater demonstrations unless conditions change, and the Control Commission authorities are palpably worried. But, instead of immediate supplies of food, they are already resorting to the showing of force by parading tanks in the streets, and they will doubtless attempt a bloody suppression of any rising that takes place at the present time.

5th April 1947

German Currency 'Revolution'

Reformists are fond of attacking revolutionary methods on the grounds that change must be gradual and that any sudden change can only produce misery and hardship. This attitude, however, does not prevent reformists from going in for the most thoroughgoing social jobs when it suits them. The new currency reform in Western Germany is an example of far-reaching interference with the social and economic structure — carried out from above. It dislocates the pattern of life as completely as any revolutionary manoeuvre and has, indeed, been referred to as a revolution by decree.

Such measures, one might remark, are commonplace enough in self-styled 'revolutionary' regimes such as those of Stalin and Hitler, Tito and Central Europe. That the Western democracies resort to the same kind of method serves to show that the pattern of government is fundamentally the same wherever it manifests itself.

Of course, the social and economic situation of Germany urgently requires some kind of reorganisation. For months, years even, the struggle for the simplest kind of life requirements — food, shelter, clothes — has been the prime preoccupation of the bulk of the people. Rations have been unable to secure food enough for all, and every German has had to deal on the black market which flourishes everywhere at fantastically inflated prices. It has been said that it is more profitable for a man to keep three chickens and sell the eggs than to go to work in industry. The devalued currency makes it not worth while for farmers to sell their produce on the ordinary market, so they hoard it for the black market.

Meanwhile, the dismantling of any industry which can be termed a war plant (i.e., which is a potential competitor with Western heavy industry) has completely disorganised the structure of industry itself. Since the ending of the war, Germany has presented the picture of millions of people starving, with no productive work to do, unable to create a reasonable standard of living for themselves by the obvious method of applying their labour to natural resources in order to create new wealth.

This is the situation which the new currency reform is designed to meet. On Sunday, June 20th, the old Reichmarks became invalid and were replaced by the new Deutschmarks. Just how drastic the changeover was is explained by the *Observer*:

"Sunday, June 20th, 1948, does in one day what the German inflation of 1923 did in one year: it wipes out all savings and all money fortunes in Western Germany. Moreover — a truly unprecedented measure — it puts, for one week, all Germans, rich and poor, on exactly the same cash level. Every man, woman and child will have exactly 40 new marks, or about £3, to spend for the next week. Only thereafter will wage and salary differences re-assert themselves; partial conversion of former cash holdings, at a 'drastically reduced' level, will again come later.

"The conversion rate has been deliberately left open till all such holdings — at present unknown and variously estimated at 60 to 80 billion old marks — have been surrendered or registered, together with exact information as to their derivation. This is officially explained with administrative reasons, but it also serves the purpose of discouraging war profiteers, tax dodgers, and black marketeers from declaring all their holdings. Undeclared holdings will become entirely and finally worthless."

The occupying authorities in the British, French and American zones hope that this measure will destroy the barter economy and force production and trade out of black market channels into the 'normal' channels. They plan at the same time a tax reform for 'equalising burdens' to be brought into operation before the end of the year. To quote the *Observer* once more: "German capital and landed interests are not again, as in 1923, to be allowed to profit at the expense of savers and money owners. Moreover, it is intended to spread the internal cost of the war and defeat more evenly between those who have lost everything and those who have kept all or most of their belongings. 'Equalisation of burdens' is to be sought by way of forced mortgages on landed property and a capital levy on other property."

The *Observer* takes throughout an optimistic view of the currency reform: but it does not disguise the effects. "At the same time, the whole poverty of the German economy, hitherto partly disguised, will be brought into the open. Prices will have to find their new level, inessential trades will collapse, manufacturers will no longer be able to keep redundant employees on their pay-roll, and instead of hidden under-employment inside the factories, widespread open unemployment is expected for a time, which can only be absorbed through the effects of ERP, combined with a careful credit policy. In the meantime, Western Germany will inevitably pass through a period of great social and economic straits."

It is inevitable, also that those who will suffer most material hardship (though perhaps not most material loss) will be the poorest.

It is hoped that the currency reform will put Germany back on to a stable monetary basis and enable Western German production to come into line with Western economy as a whole. Objections have been raised on a number of features: the separation of Western and Eastern Germany by a currency barrier as well as by a political barrier, only makes more definite an already accomplished fact. Russia has absorbed the Eastern Zone into the Russian economy; the Western powers are now doing the same with Western Germany. A much more cogent objection is to the pettiness of the aim in itself. The economic pattern of capitalism is disclosed all over the world: to try and solve the tremendous economic and social problems of Germany by seeking to rebuild German economy within this unhealthy framework is to take drastic measures for an altogether too petty end.

Revolutions may be drastic in their methods (quite often in history, they have been peaceful and constructive), but at least they have the justification of a high aim — the establishment of equality and social justice and the elimination of those forces which make for social injustice and misery. To use such drastic measures for such a threadbare aim as the re-establishment of the German capitalist pattern of society, is altogether ridiculous, and the suffering incurred will be just so much waste.

26th June 1948

Berlin: Price in Human Misery

With a few commendable exceptions, the press has treated the blockade of Berlin almost wholly in its political aspect — the struggle between Russia and the West. There can be no doubt at all that in doing so they are reporting what, for the governments involved, is the most important aspect, and the one which determines the kind of action taken. The unpalatable side of the business — the distress of the Berlin population caught between the grindstones of East and West — has been barely considered.

Months ago, when the struggle began openly with the currency reforms in the Western zones and the counter move of blockade by Russia, we drew attention to the fundamental immorality of manoeuvres in a political game whose ill-effects are visited not upon the immediate opponent but upon the masses of the population instead. Political moves are justified by reactionaries and reformists alike by an appeal to the logic of expediency: a certain action is justified because it 'prevents worse befalling'. In a world of practical necessities it is not possible to disregard such considerations; but it is incumbent upon those who take it upon themselves to justify power politics to see to it that what does follow from actions promoted by expediency is not in fact disastrous to the populations involved. For after all, the justification of government itself is that it protects the interests of the people, the nation at large, the community. The situation of Berlin provides one more example of the fundamental falsity of this justification.

For responsible people, it is axiomatic that one faces up to the consequences of one's actions: only so can one assess their value in the light of events. The basic irresponsibility of so-called democracy — as understood either by the Russian or the Western governments — is indicated by the fact that the press reports the arguments of expediency but wholly fails to make known the results of those arguments on the condition of the people of Berlin. The only papers to make such disclosures have been those with an insignificant circulation — the *Manchester Guardian* and the *Times*.

What Has Happened?
The currency reforms of several months ago in the Western occupation zones had certain effects which we shall touch on later.

The most important immediate effect was the counter move of the Russian occupation authorities in closing the road and rail connections of Berlin with the West, thereby depriving the population of the Western zones of the city of their food supply. We shall not discuss here the question of whether the Western powers should or should not have accepted this challenge; that is for the believers in political expediency to explore. The fact is that they did take up the challenge, and therefore took upon themselves the task of supplying Berlin by air transport. The Air Lift has been an extraordinary operation, a triumph of organisation and resource. But it remains a move in the struggle between the Powers, and the relative success or failure which attend it is worked out in hardship not for the Kremlin or the Russian Occupation Authorities, but for the German inhabitants of Berlin.

How successful has it been? The blockade has extended for more than a hundred days. The *Manchester Guardian* estimates an average of 3,500 tons a day, and states that the Allied view of the city's requirements is 4,000 tons a day, while the Berlin city government estimates needs at 6,000 tons a day (though this includes other items besides food).

So far disaster has been staved off, and rations are said to have been largely met. But in the past rations were supplemented by the black market which was necessary to all classes, and the *Manchester Guardian* writes: "All that has been stopped and about the only additional source of supply is black market potatoes after the best Eastern German harvest in twenty years. The old, the poor, and the unemployed are striving to do something almost unheard of — live on their rations. *Moreover lack of money often makes it impossible to buy all of them.*"

Warmth for the Winter
So far, no fuel has been flown to Berlin for the civil population, who now face the formidable cold of a Berlin winter. How serious this prospect is is shown by the fact that calculations have been made as to how far the need could be met by felling the trees of Berlin itself, and by making inroads into the woods near Berlin. The trees in the city's streets could provide 70,000 tons, or 1½ cwt. for each household. This figure illustrates more vividly than more important ones the desperate shifts to which political struggles can reduce a population, for it indicates what formidable sacrifices (consider what London would be like — for decades to come — if

every tree were felled) have to be considered, and for what miserable returns. There is not space to discuss the light-famine but it seems that there will be no artificial light after 5 pm this winter.

The Russian authorities just look on. Not indifferently however; what concerns them is how much credit they lose, and how much the British and American administrations gain or lose by the air lift. Both sides view the reactions of the population merely from the point of view of how it affects their credit. One does not say they are wholly unconcerned about the humanities involved, but we do assert that such questions are relegated to subsidiary positions, and denied the primacy that is their due.

We have seen that the currency reforms initiated the particular round of stroke and counter-stroke for which Berlin is the battle-ground. It has had disastrous results on its own, for it has created a drastic shortage of money in the Western zones. Charitable endeavours have come to an end, welfare projects which sought to alleviate the grosser hardships have dried up. "The uncontrolled economic policy which is at present being carried through", writes the *Times*, "has, among its various consequences, also hastened the 'return to normal' *and further weakened the power of the workers*. (The trade unions lost nearly all their funds in the currency reforms and the individual worker is engaged in a desperate struggle to keep up with ever-rising prices.)" We have seen that the currency reform has deprived the poorest section of the Berlin population of the means to buy the whole of their rations.

The Counter Blockade

In providing the air lift the Western powers could claim that they were only doing what they could to counter the wholly unjustifiable Russian blockade. The sorrows of the workers could be turned almost wholly to their political advantage. Now, however, in the manner of politicians, they have joined the Russians by blockading the Russian zone. Two blacks make a white. Needless to say the Germans who happen to live in the area of Germany occupied by Russia have to feel the weight of this counter move. Their sufferings become the stakes in the struggle and are added to those of the Berliners.

According to the *Manchester Guardian* "There is every indication that the Russians are fighting a losing battle in their zone and are attempting to counter it by pumping in food from

Poland, Czechoslovakia, and the Union itself and by organising a police force of great size wielding despotic powers. The food ration in the Soviet zone still lags far behind that of Western Germany and, paradoxically, that of Western Berlin. The latest reports show that meat and fat deliveries are again three weeks in arrears and that recourse is being had to substitutes of skimmed milk cheese and stale fish. Industries are running short of raw materials and textile exports are falling away as the quality of goods can no longer be maintained. General Clay has made it clear that the battle of the blockade is by no means as one-sided as first appeared."

It may not be one-sided for the power contestants, but it is one-sided enough as far as suffering goes. The powers *may* reap some benefit: the German workers — and more particularly the old, the infirm, the unemployed — pay the price.

Benefits of Rule

So much for the material miseries of the German people in this struggle. Within the framework of the political conception there is little enough that can be done about it. But the whole page of this history demonstrates the mechanisms whereby government is the enemy of the people. By an economic fiat expressed as currency reform the workers have been robbed and reduced to still greater economic servitude. By a political counterstroke normal modes of transport have been interrupted, creating a situation of near disaster. Such strokes are only possible to those who control economy and transport — the governments involved. The people would not feel such strokes on their own backs if they themselves controlled economy and administrative machinery. But they cannot achieve such control *with* a government. The emancipation of a people from such ills requires the dismantling of all power institutions — in a word, the abolition of the state and the institution of government.

16th October 1948

POST-WAR POWER STRUGGLE

The New Red Scare

The ending of the war, and the development of rivalry and tension between Russia on the one hand and Anglo-American imperialism on the other, has resulted in a radical change in the governmental attitude towards the Communist party and its representatives. Two years ago they were still useful to the Governments, playing their part of jackals to the ruling class by persuading the workers to toil harder in the interests of the Allies. Communists everywhere were more royalist than the king, performing without hesitation any betrayal of the workers that might be necessary for the carrying on of the war. Now, however, the position has changed. The Communists have become suspect as the representatives of a potentially hostile imperialist power. They are regarded as representing the fifth column of Russia, and this is, of course, true enough, at least so far as the leading groups of the various parties are concerned. But the fact that the interests of Russia have led the Communist parties in some countries into pursuing a pseudo-revolutionary line has undoubtedly drawn in to them a number of quite sincere workers who really believe they are fighting for their own liberation.

The Pseudo-Revolutionary Line
The changed role of the Communist parties has become more evident in the dominions than it has in England or America. While in England the Communists still carry on an equivocal policy of half-support for the Labour Government, and in America they give their support to the more totalitarian section of the Democratic Party, in the dominions they have found that the only way they can get any mass support is to pursue a pseudo-revolutionary line. In these countries they have found difficulty in gaining the petty-bourgeois core on which they rely in England and America, and are forced to make their base among the more

exploited workers. Consequently, in South Africa they exploit the grievances of the coloured workers and appear as their champions, in India they appeal to the more depressed sections of the population, in Burma they follow the at present popular nationalist line, and in Canada they try to build their support among the unskilled workers of foreign origin.

The result of these activities has been that the various governments in these dominions have begun to take action against the Communists. While they were stooges the CPs were tolerated; now that instructions from above tell them to change the line and pretend to be champions of the workers, they are being regarded as enemies, and the most flagrant means of suppression are being used against them.

Recent weeks have seen a whole series of attacks on the Communist Parties in various parts of the Empire, in which the most elementary rights of civil liberties have been attacked.

Indian Police Terror
In India, on the 14th January, extensive raids were carried out on offices of the Communist party in Bombay, Delhi, Calcutta, Benares and Lahore. The searches, conducted by hundreds of police officers, lasted for hours, documents were carried away, and many people were arrested — 31 in Bombay alone. The raids were not restricted to Communist organisations alone. In Calcutta the offices of the peasant organisation, Kisan Sabha, were raided and its secretary arrested, and in Bombay similar action was taken in the offices of the All-India Students' Federation. There is some doubt as to the responsibility for these arrests; the Central Government attempts to shift the responsibility on to the Provincial Governments, but the fact remains that the raids took part at the same time in different provinces with a simultaneity which could hardly have sprung from individual initiative. What is really significant is that the Congress leaders obviously agreed that the raids were necessary. The ostensible purpose of the raids was to search for clues as to how the Communists obtained the information on which their weekly, *The People's Age*, based an article which revealed the Government's plans for suppressing an Indian rising should the Cabinet mission fail. It is, however, pointed out that the article was printed six months ago, and is obviously being used merely as an excuse to hamper the Communists' use of free speech or a free press.

In South Africa the opening stages have just commenced of the

trial of eight Communists who are charged with sedition. The
immediate charge refers to the recent strike of 50,000 miners in the
Rand, an event which was caused, not by any agitation from
Communists but by the universal discontent of the native workers
with their conditions. In connection with this charge, it was
revealed by the defending counsel that the Crown had actually
refused to give any particulars before the trial, so that the defence
was unable to subpoena the necessary witnesses. The prosecution
then hinted at further charges in connection with military secrets,
but these have not yet been revealed.

The Canadian Spy Scare

The question of military secrets brings to mind the Canadian Red
Scare in connection with the leakage of information regarding the
Atomic bomb. There a Royal Commission issued a report in which
it named some 18 people as having been involved in giving away
information. These people have since been brought for trial, and,
although their cases were not dealt with at all fairly, five out of the
fourteen already tried have so far been found not guilty.
Nevertheless, their names still stand in the public report, and so
far no effort has been made to compensate them. The conduct of
the trials has come in for some very severe criticism, not only from
Stalinist sources, but even from Conservatives and Liberal
supporters of the government. The *Toronto Star*, a newspaper
supporting the Government, stated:

"It is true that nobody was beaten up in the spy investigation, but people
were held *incommunicado*, deprived of legal advice and of communication with their friends, and examined without the benefit of counsel."

The Conservative leader, John Diefenbaker, went so far as to
accuse the Government of sweeping away Magna Carta, Habeas
Corpus and the Bills of Rights.

All these instances show that the Communists are likely to be in
for a thin time with the various Anglo-American governments in
the near future. As the tension with Russia grows, so they will find
themselves among the persecuted minorities.

We hold no brief for the Communists as such. We know that if
they had the power they would be even more ruthless; that no
anarchist, for instance, would be allowed to raise his voice. We
know also that when *real* revolutionary groups have been framed
and persecuted on a number of occasions in recent years, the

Communists have not only given them no support, but have even helped to attack them.

Freedom Must Be Defended
But it is the whole question of freedom of speech and action with which we are concerned. Whatever our disagreements, we must protest against the withdrawal of these rights from any group. For once the right to persecute for political action has been granted, it can be extended into any field. To-day the Communists are being persecuted because they are playing at revolution in the interests of the Russian government. But if their persecution is allowed to continue, it will only give the governments a justification to persecute any genuine working class movement that arises. No doubt the ruling classes will do that in any case. But there is no reason for us to help them by standing by and tacitly conceding the principle of persecution in the case of the Communists.

The worker who has seen the Communist party in action at close quarters is unlikely to fall into the error of thinking them revolutionaries merely because they are persecuted as a result of a gang war between two sections of his enemies. But he will realise that the tolerance of police persecution and judicial terror in any circumstances can lead only to his own eventual harm.

1st February 1947

World Power Politics

Russia and America Stake Their Claims

Having no political ambitions like the political parties of left and right, anarchists are not obliged to employ the prevaricating jargon whereby political moves are dressed up to appear as if they were animated by some kind of morality. Ernest Bevin may describe the Marshall plan as having "behind it a conception of great co-operation between Europe and the wonderful and powerful Western Hemisphere", but it is obvious enough that it is in actuality just another step in the power politics which twists the fate of millions of ordinary men and women and children.

The struggle for spheres of influence has been sufficiently evident since the moment that the war ended, and the various moves and counter-moves have been noted as they occurred in *Freedom*. Moves which demonstrate the expansionist rivalries of Russia and the United States on the one hand, and on the other measures for the protection of the communications of the British Empire taken by Conservative and Labour governments alike. It is sufficient here to recall the Azerbaijan 'revolt' in Persia, the complicated policies in Greece, and the endless discussions on the future of Germany. Both Russian and Anglo-US spokesmen define their respective policies in terms of protecting democratic rights, safeguarding freedom, eliminating fascist elements, and so on. But, as a result of the friction they initiate or maintain, the workers pay the price in economic misery or political oppression or both. The administration favoured by both groups are united in determined repression of any independent moves on the part of the working class and peasants to improve their situation without reference to their too eager 'protectors'.

Truman Doctrine and Marshall Plan
The so-called Truman Doctrine was clearly directed to checking the expansionism of Soviet Imperialism and ensuring the predominance of American Imperialism. The offers to Greece and Turkey and the guaranteeing of territorial integrity of these countries on the Russian fringes was an indication of US power policy.

On the other hand the Russian puppet States from the Baltic to the Danube indicate quite clearly that Russian political control is not going to permit American interference.

The political crisis in Hungary (referred to on another page) is revealing in this connection. The political leaders of the Smallholders Party are evidently the willing agents of American economic policy — doubtless because they have good reason to fear Russian control. Their 'democratic' victory in the last elections (59% of the votes, as against the Communist 17%) has not the slightest significance in the light of the power struggle, for the rulers of Russia have not scrupled — as *Freedom* pointed out in the last issue — to abduct politicians for extracting confessions, while the rulers of America reply with economic pressures by cancelling half of a 30 million dollar loan. Neither power has any concern for the well-being or the wishes of the mass of Hungarian workers and peasants.

Regarding the international situation from the broader European point of view, the Hungarian situation fits into a general pattern — the pattern of the Truman Doctrine, the Marshall Plan, or whatever other fancy name power politics masquerades under.

While the Hungarian Communists kick out the politicians who look to the West, the Christian Democrats in Italy kick the Communists out of the Italian government (using rather less brutal methods). And at the same time, and also in the West, the French Premier Ramadier also sacks Communist ministers while the American government not only applauds but offers subsidies for the purpose of combating French Stalinism.

What is happening, in fact, is a recognition of spheres of influence. The Russians can have the eastern states of Europe, except Turkey and Greece (and the oil countries of the Middle East) while the Americans will look after France and Italy (? and Spain). The frontiers of these spheres of influence are drawn by weight of power.

Britain as the Rejoicing Third
Such a situation restores the British government to its traditional position of holding the balance of power. British Imperialism hopes to be the gainer from the weakening struggle of the other two major powers, and it is a mistake to underestimate its capacities in this respect.

It has been noticeable that during the Hungarian crisis, the British Government and the British press have made what capital they can out of it, but they have made no move which might

seriously embarrass the Russian *fait accompli*. It is legitimate to
conclude that Russian influence in Hungary is conceded. In short,
we are seeing once again the whole dirty business that became a
commonplace between 1933 and 1939; where sanctimonious
principles were loudly paraded, but workers were massacred by
police states without the 'freedom-loving' nations moving a finger.
Let property be threatened and they will intervene to the utmost;
but for mere workers' lives and liberties — well, that is a different
thing altogether.

Don't Take Sides: Support the Workers!

But it is useless to take sides, and reproduce the war 'to end
fascism' all over again. If men languish in political gaols under the
Russians, they rot in economic misery under American-sponsored
capitalism. The two 'alternatives' may differ, no doubt; but only in
degree, not in kind. It is not so much one ruler or the other; it is
for the ruled against *all* the rulers that one must struggle.

German Workers on Strike

The chaotic situation in Germany illustrates the same power
conflicts on a smaller scale, with the various German politicians
throwing in their lots either with the West or with the Russians.
But lying dormant beneath them all are the millions of German
workers. In this issue we publish a manifesto on the strikes and
demonstration in the Ruhr in the spring. As we go to press 30,000
workers in Cologne have come out on strike as a demonstration
against the cut in the bread ration from 1,500 to 1,000 grammes a
week, and the measures taken by Military Government to prevent
any supplementing of rations. The Cologne workers have sent
emissaries to the workers of Dusseldorf to describe their
conditions to them. Now the workers in the Ford, the
Klöckner-Homboldt-Deitz engineering works, the Westwagon
railway wagon repairing plant, the Felten and Guillfaune factory,
the Karlswerk cable factory, the Kalk chemical (fertilizer) factory,
and other plants have stopped work. In addition there are said to
be widespread go-slow movements, and sabotage of the
dismantling of factories for reparations which would create still
more unemployment and misery.

   Our position is clear: we are for the German workers in their
struggle against oppression and starvation. But it is our position
also the world over. Hating Bolshevik Imperialism, we do not
embrace American Imperialism. Rejecting private capitalism, we

do not rush into the arms of Russian State 'collectivised' capitalism. We refuse to take up the struggle on behalf of one or other of the ruling — that is to say, exploiting — groups. Our position is alongside, the ruled, the oppressed; in short, we are for the workers, whether they are groaning under military occupation, or the Russian police state dependencies, or the British Empire and its subsidiaries, or whether they are suffering under a capitalist economy propped up by American loans paid for by the exploitation of the American workers.

Support for one or the other imperialisms means support for power politics, *means support for the coming war*. Support for the workers whatever their 'nationality' (a meaningless term when applied to men and women who sell their labour to live) means support for the revolution, means joining in the fight to destroy war, injustice and oppression. It is the workers whom anarchists support.

28th June 1947

The War Scare

The arrival of sixty American super-fortress bombers at English airfields during recent days, can be regarded as an apt symbol of the war-scare which is being consciously worked up by the governments of the various nations at present concerned with the future of Europe.

We do not for a moment say that the talk of war is all bluff; indeed, war enters thoroughly into the calculations of politicians — otherwise they would not be devoting their energies so assiduously to the making of bigger and better munitions and armaments. War is always the final card in the hand against imperialist rivals, the trump to play when the workers become restive and the established order needs the wastage of war to get rid of its economic surplus and the slavery of war to dragoon its subjects into obedience.

Yet war exists in politics, not merely as a fact, but also as a threat. The menace of war can be used to induce in the peoples an attitude of fatalism which makes them abdicate their own responsibility and fall blindly into the attitude of accepting whatever happens, as if they had no control over it. That is what is happening to-day. Millions of peoples in all countries, faced by belligerent moves of one kind or another on the part of their governments, are talking of the coming war as an accomplished fact, as if, firstly, the governments had actually decided on it, and, secondly, the war could not be stopped even if it were decided on.

On the first point, we would hazard the opinion that, although there is always the possibility that governments may over-reach themselves in belligerence and topple almost unwillingly into war, at present no government has any immediate desire to embark on a war.

A war in the future might be of two kinds — ideological or imperialist. But it cannot be ideological, since there is nothing fundamental over which the two groups of powers, with their similar imperialist and totalitarian outlooks, would care to quarrel. Both sides base their rule on the predominance of a privileged ruling class over a depressed class of workers; the Anglo-American bloc is no more genuinely democratic than the Russian state is genuinely revolutionary, and from an ideological point of view they can be friends as easily as Hitler and Chamberlain were in 1936, as Hitler and Stalin were in 1939, and as Stalin and Churchill were in 1942.

If, therefore, war breaks out it will be an imperialist struggle, like the last war, over markets. And this again seems unlikely, for the immediate future at least. Russia at present is still in such a condition of chronic under-production that the question of economic domination over foreign markets hardly enters into the calculations of her rulers, who are concerned more to get as much as they can of the manufactured products of the technically more advanced countries of Eastern Europe, and whose failure to satisfy the potential market in Jugoslavia was a leading cause of the split with Tito.

America's Markets
The potential market for American capital in Western Europe and Asia is very wide, but its actual value at present is slight precisely because of the destruction of the recent war, and it is for this reason as much as any political action against the Communists that Marshall Aid is being sent to Europe and China — to build these countries up to the level when they will once again become good customers of American capitalism. In these conditions it is

unlikely that the American Government will willingly destroy the results of this preparatory work by embarking immediately on a destructive war.

Russia, on the other hand, is still economically to a great extent in the position of a colonial country, in spite of her strategic domination over so much of Eastern Europe. There has been much evidence in recent years that Russian industry is well behind American, and the veiled eagerness of the Russian government to conclude treaties that will give them machinery and manufactured goods shows that their own industrial system is still not in a position to embark on an unaided war. It should not be forgotten how much of the Russian armament in the last war was actually manufactured in England and America.

It should also be remembered that war on an atomic scale is so much greater a danger to vested property interests that any previous type of warfare that the ruling classes may well be very cautious about using it except in an extremity.

That extremity may come. The very building up of armaments itself creates a danger of war, and at some future date the saturation of world markets and the growing discontent of the workers may force the capitalists once again into war as a desperate way out of their difficulties. But in our opinion that danger is not so imminent as the war scare leads many people to suppose.

But to-day, the talk of war remains a potent weapon to bludgeon the people into submission and apathy. It is a common subject of Stock Exchange chatter that 'the country is going to the dogs' and will only revive when slave labour is reintroduced, as it was during the last war, and a similar point of view seems to be held widely among American financiers and capitalists. So, in the hope of bluffing the people into submission, the Berlin situation and the arrival of American bombers are built up for all they are worth, while the Russians, on their side, play at being tough in order to recover their loss of prestige owing to failures in France and Italy and the defection of Tito.

Fatalism is no way out
At present, so far as England is concerned, they seem to be succeeding pretty well. Everywhere one hears fatalists talk about the coming war, ending in the weak lament, "There's nothing we can do about it". In so far as war is ever inevitable, it is this feeble lack of resistance and responsibility on the part of the individual that makes it so.

For capitalists, bureaucrats and generals cannot themselves make wars. Wars are made in reality by the masses of soldiers and factory workers who allow themselves to be gulled or dragooned into fighting or toiling, into losing life, or freedom, or both, in serving the interests of their masters. It is these individual men and women who can decide once and for all that war will not happen, if only each one of them assumes his individual social responsibility to resist in every way he can, to withdraw his active and ideological support from the state and, in collaboration with his fellow workers of all kinds, to refuse any participation in war. Much less than a general strike stopped war in 1921 when the British and other imperialists were bent on an imperialist conflict. All power is ultimately economic and rests with the workers; it is for them to realise their responsibility and frustrate the policies that may lead, by folly or design, to a new and more destructive war.

24th July 1948

Beware of War Talk

The talk of war gathers in intensity and every day brings news calculated to instil into us a sense of imminent national peril and of resignation to military preparations and civilian sacrifices. Reports of the economic crisis, the production drive and export programme have given place to those of the international crisis, fostered for their different purposes by the rival powers.

To the rulers of the Soviet Union the conflict over Berlin, magnified into the threat of war, is a means of bringing together under her wing her brood of satellites, and of repairing the damage to prestige caused by the ugly duckling Tito. The crisis has its uses for the Western powers also. It will put M. Marie's precarious government more firmly in the saddle in France, it will focus national support for the policy of the American administration while the 'firm hand' policy may strengthen Mr. Truman's chance of re-election and will give new impetus to the latest 'red scare' witch-hunt.

In this country the war rumours are taking second place to the Olympic games. The Prime Minister [Mr Attlee], sweating at

Wembley while the athletes marched past, pulled out his watch. At that moment Mr. Bevin was putting over his latest 'try-on' in the House of Commons, telling them that a decision would have to be taken within a few days on whether the release of men from the Army, now running at the rate of 20,000 a month, would have to be slowed down. With threats and warnings of this sort the idea of the inevitability of war is to be drummed into us until we accept it as easily as do the fair-weather pacifists on the Government benches. Consternation, resignation, preparation — these are the ingredients of a war scare, and passing hopelessly from crisis to crisis, we are to be persuaded to accept all sorts of continual inconveniences, restrictions, sacrifices with that awful temporising that poisons the enjoyment of life. From war to economic crisis, from economic crisis to war scare, from war scare to war economy — this is the melancholy switchback upon which we are travelling.

The editorial of the last issue of *Freedom* showed why we may suppose the present scare to be largely an exploitation of the threat of war rather than of its immediate likelihood. On the other hand, the war preparations are real enough. The United Nations have shelved their plan for general disarmament after two years of futile debate; the price of crude rubber has risen steeply as America and Russia compete for the world's supplies; the sixty super-fortress bombers sent to this country by the USA have been followed by military staff officers. Some demobbed RAF officers have been recalled for active service and it is announced that twenty-thousand more workers may be recruited in the Government's Royal Ordnance factories under a plan to increase production of munitions and stores for the services.

A headline in the *News Chronicles* for 27th July 1948 reads: "Slump in US would mean War, says President". This remark, confirming as it does, our last editorial, is most interesting. Mr Truman did not say "Soviet control of Germany would mean war", nor did he say "Bolshevik Barbarism" or "Stalinist Imperialism" will mean war. He made it clear that a slump, the result of capitalist overproduction would be the cause of war. It is against this background that the present row amongst the 'Big Three' should be measured. The 'crisis' is regarded by all its protagonists as a softening-up operation for their various populations to prepare them for, to gain their sanction for, the Third World War, which the rulers of Britain, Russia and American will believe to be inevitable, as indeed it is unless the peoples decide otherwise.

7th August 1948   COLIN WARD

Marshall's Miracle

The State Department's report which gives estimates of the food, raw materials and machinery that will be shipped by the United States under the Marshall Plan, if Congress gives its approval, has sharpened the controversy as to the merits, or otherwise, of this scheme.

Mr Truman and his associates have candidly presented the scheme as an essential instrument of American foreign policy and seem certain that it can 'achieve miraculous results'. The British Labour Party has now unreservedly rallied to these views and has called a European Congress of the Socialist parties in countries adhering to the Marshall Plan to be held in March. But the Beaverbrook Press and the Communist Party oppose the Plan as undermining Britain's independence, while claiming that they are not opposed to American aid.

On one point, however, there is general agreement, from Mr Truman to Mr Pollitt — that the Marshall Plan is being used as a political weapon. The issues become less clear when the economic aspects of the Plan are being discussed.

The United States would like the world to think of the Plan as a crusade against police States, totalitarian rule, political and moral chaos. They have abandoned the rôle of the philanthropist assumed at the beginning and taken up that of the crusader. There is a third rôle which they could play with little effort, but which is deprived of glamour, that of the business man. A 20th century business man, of course, who has mastered the art of buying the right kind of government as if it were a new piece of machinery and who is more fond of waving the torch of liberty than his cheque book. A 20th century business man who becomes a Tom Paine when the business rival is Stalin and who remains a plain business man when the customer is Peron.

The Marshall Plan is not, as it has often been described, an 'example of a responsible and unselfish action'. The Marshall Plan is business and as such it is outside ethical considerations. It can only be good or bad business, and the report recently published, seems to indicate that it is not bad business.

It would be ridiculous, of course, to believe that America is merely trying to get rid of her surplus production. The plan will mean 'sacrifices' which have been accepted all the more readily because it is understood that they will fall on the shoulders of the American worker rather than on those of the capitalists.

One can also see at first glance that the plan for future European recovery is going to mean the immediate recovery of certain American industries. Originally, the Marshall Plan was to provide (on a credit arrangement) bread for the workers and raw materials and plant equipment for industry. Now, very substantial trimmings have been added. The biggest item of the exports to Britain is tobacco and France and Switzerland are also to receive considerable quantities although they have not asked for it. It will neither feed nor give labour to European workers but it will help the badly hit American tobacco industry.

It is also difficult to understand how an 'unselfish' administration could propose to increase by 34 million dollars American shipping construction during the next fiscal year, while it suggested that shipbuilding in Europe should be curtailed during the next four years.

It is a truism to say that the Marshall Plan will render Western Europe politically and economically subservient to the United States. The only two alternatives which have been put forward are that of the Beaverbrook Press, which demands greater efforts and sacrifices on the part of the workers (while advocating at the same time the re-introduction of the basic petrol ration to show clearly that the workers alone should make sacrifices) and that of the Communist Party, which would like to replace the Marshall Plan by a Molotov Plan.

These two plans being obviously incompatible, Europe is being divided into two sections which should, rationally, complement each other. Before the war more than 60% of the total imports of countries now behind the iron curtain came from Western Europe while only about 15% came from Russia. These countries, on the other hand, were exporting many of the agricultural products and raw materials which the countries in the Marshall area must now import from America. As if frontiers were not bad enough, we now have iron curtains, dollar areas, sterling areas, etc. It is impossible for Europe to achieve a healthy economy until these artificial barriers disappear.

We cannot accept the Marshall Plan any more than we can accept capitalism and imperialism. We cannot support a Molotov plan any more than we can support totalitarianism. We refuse to take sides. One does not choose between plague and cholera, particularly when one does not believe in miracles.

24th January 1948

Churchill Foretells Future

Churchill was in his element once again at the Conservative Party conference, when he rivalled his 'blood, sweat, toil and tears' speeches of the last war with some gloomy prognostications of future events, giving his opinion that the atom bomb in the hands of America was a "sombre guarantee of peace and freedom", and making the blood of his audience curdle with hints of what would happen if and when the Russians begin to make atom bombs in quantity.

We have had such 'sombre guarantees' of peace before in the shape of bigger and better armaments among the various world powers competing for domination; always in the past the race for armament has ended sooner or later in war, and there is no reason to suppose that it will be any different this time, that Churchill's 'sombre guarantee of peace' will not in fact hasten the advent of war.

But perhaps the most interesting point of Churchill's speech was his attack on his old friends in the Kremlin. We are told that:

"The fourteen men in the Kremlin, who rule nearly 300,000,000 human beings with an arbitrary authority never possessed by any Czar since Ivan the Terrible, who are now holding down nearly half Europe by Communist methods, dread the friendship of the free civilised world almost as much as they would its hostility."

It is, to say the least, strange to reflect that these are the very same group of men (with one or two minor changes) with whom Churchill wined and dined so well in the banqueting halls of the Kremlin a very few years ago, and whom he then welcomed as brothers into the alliance of 'freedom-loving peoples'. Can the same men have been good democrats in 1945 and the reverse in 1948? Rulers do not change as quickly as all that; the alteration of attitude is to be found in the kaleidoscopic pattern of political alliances, and this is merely another illustration of the old political axiom that a change of circumstances, a veering of interests, will make the ally of yesteryear into the enemy of today. The Communists are not the only expert acrobats in the political arena.

16th October 1948

Can We Secure Peace?

During the recent war, *Freedom's* predecessor, *War Commentary*, pointed out that capitalist economy has reached the point where it can only maintain itself at all on a war footing. War has become less a struggle between nations than a mode of economy, an end in itself. As early as 1942, *War Commentary* had pointed out that the capitalist class would seek to prolong the war for as long as possible, and that the signal to end it would be the actuality or the threat of revolutionary action on the part of the workers. The course of the war in Italy after 1943 tended to bear out the analysis of *War Commentary*, and the war was in fact spun out for half as long again as its predecessor of 1914.

War has become a necessity for capitalism because the contraction of the world markets have closed all other means for the maintenance of industry. And since profits cannot be secured unless production is proceeding, the whole drive of capitalism itself is now directed towards preparation for war or its actual conduct.

The cycle re-starts

It is impossible not to recognise that the cycle is starting all over again. In 1911 the then rulers of this country began an armaments programme with the building of dreadnoughts. In 1935 the Baldwin administration initiated a new re-armament programme on the grounds that the only way to prevent war was to be fully prepared — *Si vas pacem, para bellum* (If you desire peace, prepare for war). Inevitably the process of history unfolded itself for the nth time and war preparations became the phoney war, which in turn gave place to the genuine article itself. In 1911, in 1935, in 1948, the preparation for war does not serve the political end of prevention: it is the outcome of the economic necessities of the market economy of capitalism. And it leads inevitably to war itself.

Once this is grasped — and the reiterated cycles of history render it impossible for any but the completely blind or the hopelessly wishful to disregard the underlying process — it becomes apparent that the peoples and their rulers are not faced by a matter of *choice* at all. We do not choose or reject war, it is not a matter of good or ill will, of pacific humanitarians or war-mongers; *war today is a necessity to the economic system under which most of us groan.*

And beyond the economic drive, there is another rather dreadful aspect of the matter. Economic questions provide the need for war, but it is obvious that wars are only made possible by the willingness of workers to fight them, and it is at least theoretically true that wars will cease when men refuse to fight. Unfortunately, it is only too plain that for the majority of people war provides an interest in life, a tangible object to work for, which is lacking in peace time. It is by no means uncommon to find people who are distressed to find themselves compelled to admit that they are happier during wartime than they are between wars. It is the pointless deadlines and impotence of peacetime capitalism that makes war, for all its horrors, a relief. It is this that makes the acceptance of yet another war once again likely.

Opposition to war alone insufficient

These two factors, the incorporation of war into the full-time structure of capitalism, and the paradoxical fact that it is more psychologically acceptable than capitalist peace, leads us to the same practical conclusions.

Before 1939, there was mobilised a formidable expression of opinion in opposition to war. For example, the peace ballot with more than a million signatories; while the climate of opinion in 1935 made it expedient for the Baldwin administration to fight the general election on a disarmament ticket although it fully intended to initiate the opposite. Then there was the growth of pacifist bodies, with their impassioned opposition to war and their total ignorance of politics and economics — in a word, of the world in which we live. Finally, there was the formidable demonstration of relief (at the expense of Czechoslovakia) at Munich in 1938, a relief expressed not merely by the populations of Britain and France, but also of Germany.

It is evident enough that war is not deferred because 'nobody wants war'.

It follows therefore that the attempt to mobilise 'anti-war' opinion, with all political shades under the umbrella of pacifism will fail once again. But meanwhile, the unfounded and unhistoric optimism of such blanket movements has the effect of deflecting attention from the underlying trend of economics (of war economies we should now say) which remains remorseless so long as it goes unrecognised. Pacifist movements of this kind provide blinkers which effectively prevent a rational attack on the causes of war.

For it is now bitterly plain that war is inseparable from the market economy of capitalism, and that the march towards war can only be halted by the ending of the capitalist mode of economy, by revolutionary action on the part of the peoples of the world.

Ugly bedfellows

If pacifism provides blinkers to conceal the true trend of events, still more havoc is caused in the ranks of would-be resisters by the propaganda of the communists. When one says that war and capitalism are inseparable, one by no means excludes the 'Socialist Sixth' from the process. For the Russian government is a monopoly capitalist of gigantic proportions, and the Russian economy is as dependent on the market considerations which are the core of capitalism as any of the 'reactionary imperialists of the West'. War is as necessary for the Russian ruling class as for any other.

Meanwhile, however, the present direction of war preparation towards an expected conflict with Russia has turned the Communists of the West (not, needless to say, of the East) into vociferous pacifists. And this carries with it the serious disadvantage that a man is to some extent judged by the company he keeps, so that the government can regard all anti-war activity as 'objectively' pro-Russian. And, just as in the years before 1939, many pacifists' horror of war made them almost apologists of Nazism, so the same emotional need turns many today into fellow travellers. Nothing could be more disastrous or disillusioning for the anti-war movement than to get itself tied up with the policies of the Kremlin-King Street.

The endless vista

It is necessary furthermore to take an even longer view than that of the increasingly close-up one of World War Three. For the processes of capitalism are subserved by war, and so far have survived it, have even been rejuvenated by it to some extent. As far as Germany is concerned the Allies seem to have won set and match for good. And Russia may be knocked out of the contracting group of great powers (France being a seceder willy nilly). But there is still the rivalry between the British and the American empires. The allies of yesteryear have already fallen out. The same thing will happen to the allies of today, for after World War Three capitalism will still need its increasingly permanent war economy.

Thus the immediate needs of our troubled time demands that we reject the preventative methods which have never worked in the past; the ending of war requires the ending of capitalism. And if sceptics say that that will not end war because human nature requires it, we can only retort that in the past human nature only required it every fifty or so years, and didn't demand it as a permanent feature of life.

The immediate needs require us to destroy war by folding up capitalism. And so also does the endless vista of war with America, and perhaps afterwards war with a new great power (for was not Russia 'knocked out' at the Crimea?) of the East, all for the sake of a mode of economy which creates misery and poverty as well as war.

Let us be practical

With this deadly future in front of us it behoves us to be practical. And that means ignoring the repeated advice of the practical men who urged us on against the Kaiser, the Fuhrer, and soon the Politburo. Ignoring all those who tell us about seeking peace by preparing for war, all those who tell us that revolutionary ideas are visionary and pernicious utopian wool gathering. Our backs are to the wall, and we can no longer close our eyes and apply interim remedies which are no remedies at all. It is absolutely necessary to grasp that the struggle against war is the struggle against capitalism itself; that system by which goods are only produced if there is a market for them, or if there is no market, then rearmament and war itself must supply the impetus to production.

That is the sober truth. The revolutionary struggle against war may be difficult, may be a long term struggle; but it is the only one that offers any prospect of success, any widening outlook for mankind.

13th November 1948

Brothers No Longer

The American Loan has been received with a great chorus of bitter condemnation by the British ruling class. Our businessmen are busy declaiming from the house tops how *they* bore the brunt of the war and how *they* lost all their markets while they were working for the government on cost-plus contracts. Our politicians are taking on the tragic attitudes of women of easy virtue who wish to make out that an unfair advantage has been taken of them, and from all sides we are treated to a continual repetition of the ingratitude of the American government and its capitalist accomplices.

Far be it from us to defend the American government. On the contrary, we regard with disgust the consummate hypocrisy with which, after the protestations of brotherhood that have been made during the war years, after the moral humbug to which American politicians have treated us for so long, they can turn to make a commercial advantage of the present need of the British people for raw materials and foodstuffs imported from abroad. But we do not think the British governing class are any less culpable than the Americans in this matter, for the whole situation arises out of the very nature of the system which they maintain and represent.

Indeed, looking at the matter objectively, it has done what any sharp capitalist would not have done in the normal course of business. They have granted a loan at a fairly low rate of interest, on the understanding that the money would be spent on American goods. And, seeing that the firm with whom they were dealing with was desperate for credit, they have taken the opportunity, as any astute capitalist would, to drive a bargain of their own by hustling the British representatives into accepting the terms of the American proposals on the Bretton Woods scheme, which would mean the end of any form of discriminatory trading agreements between countries to the exclusion of others.

The British ruling class brings up the question of how much they have lost through the war. But this is an argument which does not hold much water between capitalists, for the Americans can point out that the British capitalists went into war of their own free will, to serve their own interests, and that in any case there has actually been a substantial increase in industrial profits in this country during the war. As for the grievances of the British about not being able to carry on reciprocal agreements within the Empire, the American capitalists would undoubtedly say that he is not very much interested in maintaining the British Empire.

We have put the matter in this way merely to show that, according to ordinary capitalist ethics, there is nothing particularly shocking in the American loan agreement. It only becomes shocking when it is seen in its proper setting, as a sign of the corrupt social order of financial and economic exploitation from which it springs. Any isolated act of capitalist trickery is evil not so much in its own right as from the nature of the system of property and government that produces it.

It has been said often enough by some of the Labour Ministers who are now busily engaged in the racket themselves, that capitalism of any kind is bound by its very nature to expand and seek new markets. And as the process of industrialisation spreads over the world and reaches the former consumer countries, turning them into producer countries in their turn, the markets steadily become more and more reduced.

In every major war since the middle of the eighteenth century, markets have been a dominant factor, and the last war was no exception. It was fought because the German capitalists wished to make Europe and the Levant their economic province and the Japanese to turn the East into a great market for their own manufactures, to the exclusion of British and American capitalists.

Britain and America fought this war to save their markets from imperialist rivals. Now these rivals have been eliminated. But the economic struggle for markets goes on. Not only are Britain and America lined up for a great conflict over the markets of Europe and Asia, but the war has turned other countries, formerly of colonial status such as Canada, Australia, Brazil and even India, into potential competitors in this war of trade. The former allies, having defended the rivals who threatened their trading supremacy, now draw apart and embark on an economic war of the kind which is the inevitable accompaniment of a market economy. The conditions of the American loan mean merely that the American capitalists have seen a strategic opening and have made use of it. One thing that becomes abundantly clear now that the war is over is that America holds the position of the greatest imperialism the world has ever known, and that its politicians intend to take every advantage of their positions. Would the British ruling class have done any different if the roles had been reversed?

For the workers everywhere this return to the struggle for

markets means only a new misery. Already, unemployment is becoming more than a threat to the American workers, and it will not be long coming to British workers. The new circumstances like the old, will produce crises, economic and otherwise, which the ruling class will turn to their advantage against the workers. Instead of being the means of leisure and abundance, the new potentialities of industrial production will merely contribute to poverty and degradation in all lands.

The only remedy to this situation is the abandonment of capitalism, with its market economy and its attitude of production for profit instead of use. In place of this should be built not a socialist structure of state capitalism, which will merely repeat the same faults in a different way, but a society whose production and distribution will be divorced from the idea of profit and hence from the ideas of exchange and markets. Goods should be produced for use, and should be given to people, not because they can pay or because they have anything to give in exchange, but solely because they need them. This use of the economy will only be achieved when the means of production and distributon are owned by the community and are operated by the workers for the benefit of the whole community.

29th December 1945

THE WELFARE STATE

State Medicine

The subject of the National Health Scheme has scarcely been discussed on its own merits, for it has become a struggle between the Minister of Health and the Negotiating Committee of the British Medical Association. And since both sides appear to have acted in domineering and sectional ways this struggle has itself been complicated by questions of prestige and petty triumphs.

At the present time, the Panel system makes those engaged in the lower income groups eligible for free medical treatment. And as far as it goes, that is all to the good. But it only goes as far as to cover those 'gainfully employed', to use the Ministry of Labour's elegant phrase. Wives and children are not covered and have to buy their medical treatment, so that the poor inevitably get less attention than the rich. Meanwhile, the standard of panel medicine is not very high — which is why so many people view with misgivings its universal application. It is not well paid, so that doctors inevitably pay more attention to the private, fee-paying side of their work. Patients who are well off therefore view the panel with distaste, those who are poor regard their doctors with disillusionment and bitterness. Yet in the existing social environment things could hardly be different.

Commonsense and justice demand that the needs of the sick should receive adequate attention regardless of their capacity to pay. This principle is recognised and is the basis of the proposed Act, and as such it marks an advance.

The difficulties arise when such social advances are taken up and applied by the State. Inevitably, the first question is that of how a comprehensive scheme is to be paid for, and the concern for questions of expense which already affect the existing Panel system, will certainly be carried over into the new Act. And the same goes for the red tape, the form filling, and all the rest of bureaucratic absurdities inseparable from centralisation. Nevertheless, the fact remains that the extension of the scheme to wives and children will benefit the lowest income groups. And the increased separation of medical attention from direct remuneration is at least potentially a tremendous advance.

All the same, the scheme ignores the fundamental factor in present-day ill health. Public attention is focussed on such questions as the sale of practices and the extension of specialist services, while causes of ill health are simply neglected. For the new comprehensive scheme will still have to try and repair the effects of diseases principally caused or aggravated by poverty; and patients will still be hampered in their ability to benefit from medical attention by their overriding need to go out and earn wages. The chief killing diseases will still be many times more common among the lower income groups than among the higher, and the anxiety which characterises the lives of the great majority of people will still inflict chronic ill-health on thousands.

The new scheme has been criticised because there are not enough doctors to operate it; it will undoubtedly intensify the hastiness by which panel practice is marred. Yet the elimination of poverty would so reduce the illhealth that the remaining sickness could receive proper attention and time. At no point does the new scheme even recognise that the elimination of poverty is the first problem in the struggle against disease. It can hardly be expected to do so since the very existence of the State which is to take over medicine depends on the economic servitude of the mass of people. Authority demands obedience, but can only exact it where poverty is widespread, and economic uncertainty the rule. The State cannot radically attack ill-health, for by eliminating poverty it would undermine its own authority.

24th January 1948

The New Health Service Examined

On July 5th the new National Health Service will come into force, and on the same day the National Insurance Scheme. It is possible to make some estimate of how it will work, and since it is a positive manifestation of reforming activity it serves to illustrate both the merits and defects of reformism. In this article I am mainly concerned with the National Health Service but it is important to realise that the new Service is intimately bound up with, is in fact dependant on, the Insurance Scheme which comes into operation on the same day.

The Idea of Insurance

The aim of an insurance scheme is a good and sound one; it is to try and spread the burden of individual disasters over the community as a whole and so mitigate their effect for the individual. Illness is such a disaster, old age and the concomitant inability to work (i.e., earn a living) another. If every member of a community makes a contribution a common fund can be created from which those incapacitated by illness or old age can draw in time of need. The conception is basically one of mutual aid and many of the old sick clubs had no other aim. This aim has been fairly thoroughly adulterated by the modern insurance companies which operate in the capitalist way with interest, and have become immense financial powers. Every insured worker knows furthermore how quickly a few non-payments of stamps is followed by 'falling out of benefit', but, by contrast, how unwillingly some times the insurance society is to cough up the money in time of absence from work through sickness. These delays are no doubt due to the business of checking up on the validity of claims; but they effectually efface the mutual aid aspect and substitute cold actuarial calculation, with all its indifference to the sharp prick of need. It does not seem likely that the centralisation of insurance under the government will humanise the process in any way. No doubt it will merely introduce the inefficiency of red tape.

The Scheme Itself

The pamphlet issued by the Ministry of National Insurance explains the scheme thus: "In return for regular weekly contributions, it will provide the cash benefits during sickness, injury, unemployment and widowhood, payments at childbirth and at death, and pensions for industrial disablement and on retirement from regular work. It is compulsory, and takes the place of the present Unemployment Insurance, National Health and Contributory Pensions Schemes, and the Workmen's Compensation Acts. The money to pay for these benefits comes partly from weekly contributions by insured people and employers and partly from payments out of taxes."

The amounts paid are considerable, being 9/1d a week for an adult working man, of which he pays 4/11d and his employer 4/2d. 'Self-employed' adult males pay 6/2d and 'Non-employed' 4/8d. A man's contributions may be increased to cover his wife if she is not working in outside employment, and so not paying contributions on her own account.

No doubt the partial financing of the scheme out of taxation is intended to lower the burden of payment for low incomes, and in effect increase it for high incomes. But that does not mean that the aim of the scheme is to operate the idea of 'to each according to his needs' — irrespective of capacity to contribute. The Ministry's pamphlet makes that clear: "If you are self-employed or non-employed and your total income is less than £104 a year, you may be able to claim 'exemption' from the Scheme. If 'exemption' is granted you will not pay contributions, *but you may lose benefits*". (My italics.)

Gains Under the Health Scheme
The chief advantages come from what is in essence the extension of Lloyd George's National Health Insurance to cover not merely employed persons, but also their families. Medical treatment is therefore free to all in the sense that individual acts of medical service do not have to be paid for in the shape of fees. This means that as much medical service as the occasion demands can (in theory) be supplied without worries about doctor's bills. How satisfactory that service will be will depend on the individual doctor and the conditions under which such insurance practice is carried out.

There is no doubt that this provides considerable benefit, especially in regard to the treatment of children, many of whose minor ailments are to-day neglected because of the burden of fees. Such neglect may lead to serious disability later on; 'running ears', for example, if untreated may lead to partial or total deafness with all its curtailment of earning power, not to speak of its crippling of individual development.

The fact that the rich are also provided with free treatment is a somewhat acadaemic advantage of the scheme. Poverty compels panel patients to put up with the inevitable hours in surgery waiting rooms; but the better off will prefer to avoid long waits and the company of the 'lower orders' by paying fees to doctors practising outside the scheme. The envious type of socialist would doubtless like to see this loophole stopped for the well-to-do; to do so would not improve the lot of the insured patient, however, and the aim should be to raise the standard of comfort in treatment for them rather than to engage in more levelling.

Some snags

An obvious snag is the high contributions. This increase when added to the income tax, trade union contributions, and any other incidental deduction from the wage packet, will lighten it considerably on Friday nights. The struggle put up by the doctors against the Act has also been motivated in part (some will say a very small part, but they will be mostly reformist social types) by a realisation that the conditions under which medical services will be given will be very far from ideal. If looked at in detail, however, the scheme will probably seem to have more advantages than snags.

It is quite otherwise if one looks at it in broad outline, and also in its political implications. A German woman, long resident in this country, remarked to me, "So they are copying Hitler already!" and the remark is not wholly fantastic.

The idea of mutual aid inherent in insurance scheme aims at insuring against natural catastrophes — or should do. it is obviously idiotic to incure against the effects of, say, bad drains, for the rational thing to do is to improve them. The Labour Party's Scheme derives from the Beveridge Plan, and its whole conception is a liberal one. When the Beveridge Scheme first was published we denounced it in *War Commentary*, *Freedom*'s predecessor. We pointed out that it made no attempt to eliminate poverty, only to insure against its worst effects. As such its effect was actually to stabilise poverty; by seeking to make it just tolerable. The same criticism must be brought against the scheme of July 5th.

There are in addition other hidden trends of a pernicious character. The operation of the scheme provides a complete register of every man, woman and child in the country and a means of checking up on them. This is illustrated by the new medical cards. Instead of the complicated system of Approved Society's name or symbol, and the individual's number with the Society, the new card has quite a simple system of letters and a short number. They use, in fact the National Registration numbers. This means that the struggle to abolish identity cards has been partially hamstrung by their virtual incorporation into a social service.

And yet another step has been taken along the road that ties the population to the State by making it dependant on a State operated scheme for an essential social service. Such measures were a substantial factor in securing the stability of the Fascist regimes, and of the new one-party democracies and their prototype the Soviet Union. Such schemes owe their pernicious effects to the fact that they encourage the irresponsible dependance of individuals on the State. The fact that the alternative, under capitalism, is destitution and the sharper anomalies of poverty, does not make the Liberal-Socialistic alternative a sound proposition.

Towards the Slave State
The only rational insurance against the evils of poverty and industrialism and old age under the wages system is the abolition of poverty and the wages system, and the transformation of industrialism to serve human ends instead of grinding up human beings. Once again the evils of the old system and the evils of the reformist adjustments of it is seen to lie in an anarchist solution.
12th June 1948   J. H.

20th April 1946   *Drawing by Philip*

Increases for the Over-paid
No more for the Workers

When, in the early months of 1948, the Government introduced its White Paper on incomes, advocating the freezing of all wages except those of the most obviously under-paid workers, it was plain to most of us that nothing but hardship would follow for the working class. True, it was promised at the same time that a check would be kept on profits, but since the Government's export policy demands the highest possible production with the lowest possible costs ('to effectively compete in foreign markets') it was equally plain that the manufacturers' incentive would not be seriously tampered with.

The employers, after all, are in business for the one and only purpose of making money; if that purpose is not fulfilled the whole basis of capitalism becomes uncertain and the solution (in our market economy) is to nationalise the industry and make the taxpayer shoulder the losses until production costs and selling prices can be rationalised — as is possible in any monopolised basic industry.

The workers, however, have nothing to invest, and nothing to sell but their labour power. They, therefore, are not in industry to make a profit; they are in it to make a living. They work or starve, and while the employer receives back more than the value of the goods produced in his factory, the worker receives back less than the value of the goods he produces at his bench. This is because not only do all the overheads of the plant have to be met by the productivity of the worker, but also the employers and shareholders have to get their profits — out of that same productivity.

Only wages frozen

It has been no surprise to us, therefore, to see that the only freezing that has resulted from the White Paper has been that of wages, while profits — and prices — have in the main continued to rise. A sop was given the trades unions — who would have been just as servile without it anyway — in the form of capital levy on the rich, and we heard harrowing stories of Lady Mountbatten and others having to sell some of their investments to meet the levy — the £60,000 she had to fork out, for instance, was equal to her income for a whole year. Obviously, it was a matter of great hardship for her — she would have to scrape along on a mere £30,000 pa for the next two years.

But as far as the workers are concerned, the White Paper has proved a godsend for the employers — whether they are private or the State. In fact, particularly if they are the State, for nationalised boards are in the very strong position of being the sole employers in an industry and so can force their workers to accept their terms. And since these State Boards are manned by ex-bosses of private enterprise, they know all the tricks of 'handling the men'. Also, of course, the same State runs the army which provides blacklegs when necessary, and runs the arbitration tribunals (theoretically neutral!) to which disputes are referred, and runs the police courts in which strikers are prosecuted for damages. It will be noticed that in outlining this position the existence of the trades unions, as defenders of the workers' rights and conditions, has been ignored. This is intentional since, as such defenders, the trades unions no longer exist and we are not interested in maintaining the myth so beloved of Socialists, Communists and Conservatives alike, that the trades unions are essential for the welfare of the workers. They are essential for the welfare of the State, for which they are disciplinary organisations, but it is time the workers realised their essentially reactionary function and turned towards the creation of militant rank-and-file organisations.

The growing gap
Since the recent budget, the trades unions have betrayed a certain uneasiness — and well they might. In the nationalised industries particularly, more and more concern is being shown by the workers at the growing gap between incomes and the cost of living, and the blatant manner in which Cripps added to living costs while at the same time reaffirming the wage-freeze, has not been lost on the rank-and-file.

On the railways, workers are gaining strength for their suggestion for a nationwide strike in support of their claim for 12/6 a week wage increase, rejected by the National Board. At present, the net basic wage for a family man can work out at little more than £4 per week — pitifully inadequate for these days. In the Post Office discontent is growing after the Postmaster-General's refusal to grant a 12½% increase in wages, and in the mines, as discussed elsewhere in this issue, a large scale strike is the miners' answer to the Coal Board's refusal to grant the right to concessionary coal.

Everywhere we see the productive workers penalised to pay for the capitalist programme of the Labour Government, but how does that Government treat the unproductive 'workers' upon which the continuation of capitalism depends? In a far more generous spirit. Let us not forget that one of the first acts of the Labour Government in 1945 was to increase MP's salaries from £600 to £1,000 a year. Let us remember how only last year (after the appearance of the White Paper) the Treasury raised the salaries of its own officials (while offering the cleaners ¼d!) and let us note the news that High Court judges are to receive increases of salaries, finding their £5,000 a year (let's be fair — less tax) "inadequate", to quote the Labour Attorney General Sir Hartley Shawcross. And — most iniquitous of all — the Oaksey Committee is recommending raising the pay of police officers by no less than a basic guinea a week for constables — more for higher ranks.

More for the parasites
The income of police constables, one of the lowest forms of animal life, is today valued, taking wages and allowances into consideration, at no less than £415 to £522 per year according to service. A copper therefore receives approximately twice the railwayman's pay, and is going to have it increased, while the railmen are refused an increase. The Government, it is true, may not grant the full increases suggested in the Oaksey Report, but in view of the importance for the Government — for *any* Government — of maintaining this standing army of unproductive parasites at full strength, there is not much doubt that increases will be granted — to attract more men into the force, and away from useful work.

This is how government's operate. Their hired thugs, the operators of their repressive law and prison systems, are well looked after, while the workers who produce the wealth and upon whom society depends for its well-being are exploited mercilessly. We do not advocate the unending continuation of this futile struggle for more wages. However much the workers earned, by the very nature of capitalism, it would be insufficient for a full life, for always would there be parasites battering upon them.

The answer to low standards of living is not to be found in money. The answer is the complete abolition of money, of inequality and of social injustice. It is the establishment of a free society where the needs of the people are the reasons for production and needs are met fully, freely and fairly.
14th May 1949

The State or Liberty?
Is Socialism compatible with individual freedom?

The central tenet of anarchism has always been opposition to the whole idea of government, of the political control of the people as a whole by a few of their fellows. It follows logically from this that anarchists are far less concerned than those who believe in the necessity for government with the question of who compose this ruling minority. Socialists are apt to find our attitude incomprehensible and to describe it as 'irresponsible', for to them it is axiomatic that the Labour Party is better than the Conservatives. If one's vision is limited to matters of mere reforms, it is not difficult to point to some advances for the workers after almost any political party has been in power for an effective number of years. Even fascists can point to reduction in unemployment or to this or that public works. And these questions of relative merit form the endless stock-in-trade of election battles.

In times of a boom in trade a government can often claim the credit for an apparent advance in the economic status of some of the workers; if such a claim cannot be expected to take in the electorate a slump in trade or the 'sabotage' of the political opposition is brought up to explain or excuse the situation. The plain fact, however, is that the general condition of the workers has for centuries been such as utterly to preclude the possibility of full human stature or the realisation of the immense and untapped potentialities of the peoples as a whole. If this fact is faced, doubts arise as to the validity of the reformists' arguments, and the suspicion grows that the anarchist contention may have more in it than a superficial glance suggests. When that suspicion has taken seed, the horizon opens up, and the possibility of a society freed from the petti-fogging vision of all the political sections, together with the inequality, the regimentation, and the squalor that go with their administrations, is seen to be more than an impracticable dream.

Bevan dots the I's
In his speech before the opening of the Labour Party conference, Aneurin Bevan lent considerable point to anarchist criticisms of governmentalism, albeit in a speech intended to boost Labour socialism. In a democracy it should be apparent that government serves the interests of the people as a whole, even though

minorities are from time to time discontented. Yet all governments are forced to attack large sections of their subjects, seeking to attach to them the blame for their own failures to serve the general interest. The Labour Party is no exception. Speaking of the trade unions, he declared that it was "necessary to tell some of their people in industry that they were beginning to lose faith, and that some of them appeared to have achieved prosperity in excess of their moral stature, and that some of them had got what they had got too easily, and that if they had had to struggle more for it, they would value it more now." It seems he was not speaking of the J. H. Thomas's or the George Gibsons, not even of Labour MPs who voted themselves a £400 a year rise in pay at a stroke — nor again of working class cabinet ministers at — is it £5,000 a year? It seems he was speaking strictly of workers in industry who go on strike, for he went on to say that "they were in danger of throwing away, by a few months of dissipating anarchy, what they had spent a lifetime to build up".

We will pass over the absurdity of the suggestion that industrial workers have secured their far from adequate wages without a struggle; nor will we dwell on Mr Bevan's use of the term anarchy, though as an intelligent socialist he cannot be ignorant of its meaning. What is interesting is the attitude of the ruler hectoring the ruled, the men who take the decisions blaming those who have no share in framing them for their own failures. For this is characteristic of all governments, whether left or right.

Materialism and liberty
But Bevan went on to say things which throw into even sharper relief the differences between the socialist and the anarchist way of looking at things. "The verdict of history", he said, "is against us . . . Not in the history of mankind had any society been able to build up the complicated furniture of civilisation on the basis of individual liberty. It had never happened. All history proved so far that only the disciples of oppression had been effective in building up social wealth. They now had to show that if the disciplines of oppression were no longer in existence, the disciples of dignified self-restraint could take their place."

There is an unpleasantly menacing quality in these words. In them one sees the pre-eminent importance which even non-marxist socialists attach to *material* goods, for it means in plain words that one cannot have the advantages of cheap shoes and all the other shoddy products of civilisation without the policemen and the national insurance snooper. Indeed, the complicated furniture of civilisation, as the workers know it, is a very poor return for the sacrifice of individual liberty. But Bevan does not say that social wealth must be built up *with the aid of workers' freedom*, but only that dignified self-restraint must save the Labour administration the embarrassment of themselves applying oppression. One might remark that the Labour Party have shown no delicate shrinking from the task of disciplining the workers. One might also speculate on what exactly 'dignified self-restraint' means — presumably it means that if the workers don't like particular measures enacted by 'their' government, they mustn't give effective expression to their discontent, but must kiss the rod instead.

What is much more interesting is the implied reversal of socialist teachings here. For in the past, socialists used to say that capitalism had solved the problem of production, socialism would solve the problem of distribution while releasing still further productive energies. There is nothing in the past teachings of socialists to suggest that the oppression of capitalism was a necessary part of the building up of social wealth; only that it was necessary to maintain the unequal distribution of wealth. With socialism this necessity should disappear.

Bevan actually gives away the fact that the Labour Party is operating capitalism while trying to give it a socialist gloss. For while inequality exists, while profit for the few is still the driving force of production, while national economies seek to force their way competitively in the world markets, a 'socialist' government, just like any other government, must continue to use oppression.

Liberty and dignity
In Bevan's speech individual liberty appears as a desirable by-product to material prosperity — perhaps even it is incompatible with it. Anarchists insist that individual liberty is essential to men whether they have material prosperity or not, and the verdict of folklore and tradition and literature is the same, that freedom even in frugal circumstances is better than unfree wealth. This is not to glorify poverty of to overlook its stultifying and destructive influence. But anarchists today declare that individual liberty is the pe-condition for the erection of a society possessing true social wealth. Its suppression is only necessary in a society which maintains all the old divisions with unequal remuneration, extreme division of labour, and the vesting of

responsible decisions in the hands of a few central planners and administrators, and a few managers and directors. Indeed it is difficult to see how dignity, even if self-restrained, can be achieved without full individual liberty.

Where lies the choice?

Bevan's argument was directed to suggesting that if labour unrest brought down the Labour government, the Tories would get in. And the world would then say that in Britain the democratic way had been tried, and since it had failed there only remained the way of oppression. We rather doubt if on the issue of oppression there is anything to choose between Labour and Toryism. But even if there were, the choice is between more radical political differences than between one party and another; it is between government from above and free organisation from below — between governmentalism and anarchy in its true sense of absence of rulers.

We have said that for anarchists the choice of rulers is comparatively unimportant, for we seek to eliminate government altogether. This does not mean, however, that we are indifferent to the question altogether, for that would be entirely unrealistic in these days of unlimited brutality in government. During the past thirty years the political parties have sought the electoral way of defeating totalitarianism, without much success to their credit. Anarchists have been — and still are — in the forefront of the struggle against political oppression; but they do not advocate the milder forms of the whip, but its total abolition. The defeat of oppression in this country will not come by voting Labour instead of Tory at the next election, but by the establishing of the social revolution. The Spanish workers' struggle, still continuing after ten years, remains the most formidable blow struck at the totalitarian trend of our times. And the anarchist workers' collectives in Spain, whether in industry or in agriculture, proved that material improvement can be achieved in the most dramatic way, even in the most adverse circumstances, from the free communalisation of industry and the land, organiscd by the workers themselves.

11th June 1949

Stinking Fish!

Can We Take the Party Programmes Seriously?

Two thousand five hundred years ago Aesop the slave told the story of the two crabs. They both walked sideways, one on its Left side and one on its Right. Consequently each thought that he alone was going forwards while the other was in reverse. One day the Left-handed crab chided the Right-handed one pointing out that it looked very awkward and was quite unlike the way the rest of the world walked. "Indeed", replied the other crab, "I walk as well as I can and I'm sure I'm on the Right road. If you would like me to do it a different way I wish you would set me an example, and show me the proper way because I have always noticed that you walk sideways yourself."

The party leaders have been getting very active lately, sharpening their claws for the electoral battle. The Labour Party has published its policy in the pamphlet *Labour Believes in Britain* which has been followed by the Conservative statement *The Right Road for Britain*. Herbert Morrison got very crabby about this. "The miserable little things", he said, "would not publish their programme until they had seen ours". And since the theme-song of *The Right Road* is "Anything you can, I can do better", his peevishness is understandable. But due to their habit of walking sideways, our political crabs cannot see that the Right road and the Left road are one and the same; they see, in their opposite numbers, the faults which are so glaring in themselves.

Mr. R. A. Butler, one of the builders of the Right road (subject of course to the approval of the Grand Lobster himself) observes that : "Policy making presents the politician with many temptations. It is so easy to give way to the natural desire to be all things to all men, to disregard unwelcome facts and to tell people only what they obviously want to hear." He was thinking of course about the Labour programme, but anyone not walking sideways can see that it applies most forcibly to that of the Conservatives. And when the Chief Crayfish of the Left, bristling with indignation, says that the Tory policy statement is "one of the most dishonest documents that I have ever read. There seem to be increases for everybody, but nothing as to how they are going to find the money or who is going to find it", anyone not walking

around in a shell is bound to draw the same conclusions about
Labour Believes in Britain.

Abraham Lincoln is reputed to have said "You can fool some of
the people *all* the time and you can fool all the people *some* of the
time but you can't fool all the people *all* the time". But since
Lincoln's day the politicians have become more audacious and
ambitious. They are trying to prove him wrong. For the Tories, no
longer content with the support of some of the people — the
privileged ones — now seek to fool the ranks of organised labour:
"The Conservative Party supports the Trade Union movement
. . . we hold the view that the Trade Union movement is
absolutely essential to the proper working of our economy and of
our industrial life". And the Labour Party which has hitherto been
content to fool the industrial workers, and the public-school
socialists, now woos the middle class and praises its "responsibility
and forbearance".

Everyone knows that the Conservative Party is the party of
monopoly and big business, but now we learn from *The Right
Road* that "It would help small traders and manufacturers to carry
on their independent economic existence in fair competition with
one another, with large trading and manufacturing concerns and
with the Co-operative Movement". Indeed the Tory solicitude for
the Co-ops is so great that it warns them that "their interests are as
much threatened as those of other traders by specious plans for
further nationalisation". In the same way, private enterprise and
"the small man" are given re-assurance and congratulations in
Labour Believes in Britain. "We believe in the right to strike" said
Churchill at Wolverhampton. "We cannot have strikes", said
Attlee at Durham.

What conclusion is any thinking person to draw from all this
contemptible deceit and duplicity? As the Irish say, "The only
difference between them is that they're the same". Can we take
seriously the pretensions and high-minded platitudes of these
confidence tricksters? If they tried their three-card trick at a race
meeting we would think it an insult to our intelligence. Are we to
tolerate their ridiculous audacity in spheres where our lives and
happiness are in their hands?
6th August 1949

Devaluation:

The Real Gap Widens

Much has been made recently of the Dollar Gap and the proposed solution which has come in the form of devaluation. By the manipulation of commodity prices, currency control clauses in the Marshall Plan and a higher price for gold, the five hundred million citizens of the sterling area are to have 'another chance'. Now we know, of course, that the primary occupation of that ill-assorted combination, politician, economist and civil servant, is to balance figures, make profits, strengthen their hands. They have created the problem. Now they attempt a solution. They may succeed temporarily, juggling their exports to balance dollar imports, even if capitalist methods have to be used by socialists, fascist methods by trade union leaders . . . no matter, as long as the books are balanced and the trade graph is rising. They will then be satisfied that the Gap has been closed.

Already, however, the closing of one gap is leading to the widening of another. The effect of devaluation will be that the rich will become richer and the poor poorer. But few politicians, and certainly no economists, will apply themselves to the closing of this gap.

Devaluation is meant to help the country by assisting manufacturers of finished goods to sell them at competitive prices in the dollar market. By doing this successfully their profits will increase, shareholders' dividends will improve and more will be paid to the government in taxes. The obverse aspect of this cheerful picture, however, is that it can only be attained by the workers suspending their claims for higher wages and better living conditions, for such a rise would mean higher costs for manufacturers and more money in the hands of the working masses when it is necessary that their spending power be reduced to a minimum. So the British worker, influenced on all sides by appeals to his patriotism, is to take the coming rise in the cost of living without a murmur. For the business man and the Companies, the necessary incentive is provided by the probability of higher profits. But for the worker the incentive comes in the form of the old plea — "It's the only way out".

The disparity between exploiter and exploited is, however, nowhere more obvious than in the colonies and South Africa. The raw materials which, overnight, have become twenty or thirty per cent more valuable in terms of sterling, are the very commodities which rely on the slave labour of uneducated or near primitive peoples. The labourers who produce, in remote parts of the world, the rubber, tin, gold, copper and oil, are the people on whom the devaluers rely for their solution. Already, in fact, there have been big increases in the wealth of certain groups. Shareholders in London and Johannesburg have made profits of fifty per cent by simply lifting the telephone receiver. Companies have found their capital increased by a similar amount. Tens of millions of pounds were added to the sterling value of shares on the first day of devaluation.

But the cheap labour of the Rand, Malaya, Rhodesia, West Africa, and the East Indies, by which the Labour Government is trying to save itself, will receive not the smallest fraction of benefit. Once more, as with its predecessors, this trade union government is going to balance its books by further and more severe exploitation of the indigenous colonial peoples over whom it claims benevolent trusteeship.

By the 'luck of the draw' the immediate financial problems of South Africa are postponed. Malan and that most valuable of institutions, the gold mine, are given a new and profitable lease of life.

But for the natives in their compounds outside Johannesburg, for the youths fresh from their tribal lives who come to the city, conscripted by want, what benefit? After a few years, as before, they will return to their tribes, permanently stricken with phthisis, without pension of any kind. The gold mining companies face a future of prosperity. But there will be no relief for the hundreds of thousands of discarded human wrecks.

The Mining Editor of the *Financial Times* writes: "Since the end of last year, the steady increase in the supply of native labour engaged on the Rand has been one of the most welcome features of the industry's experience".

Yet he is not alone in his refusal to consider the human aspect of the matter. People belonging to every group of the community have been misled into believing that the economic sphere holds a permanent solution, that dollar parity is paramount, that this is no time to consider individual grievances or specific cases of hardship. Well, we have seen nations induced into that way of thinking before. In some ways the closing of the Dollar Gap is to serve the same function as war. The aspirations of the worker and the individual are to be ignored or sacrificed to overcoming this latest crisis. His lot will be, as in war, to work harder and for less, for the paradise that is just around the corner.

But experience is teaching us that, no matter how hard we work, governments will find new ways to dissipate the wealth that accrues from this. In our own case Palestine is no longer an expense. Now it is Hong Kong. The price of our Far East commitments is £80,000,000 annually. Now it is the atom bomb, the Brao, the armies of occupation dismantling factories which could be producing the things we need. Lord Citrine at £8,500 a year. And the Duke of Windsor has dollars to buy a new house in Florida.

So from crisis to crisis, and one waits a little impatiently for signs of a wider recognition of the root causes of it all. Yet if devaluation, by making it apparent that, Labour or Conservative, trade union leaders or political leaders, the lives of workers and individuals can never be more than expendable and malleable entities, an important lesson will have been learnt. The disillusion is already beginning. An awareness of the extent to which they have been betrayed is increasingly apparent among all sections of the working class. Their trade union leaders have betrayed them. The political party in which they placed their faith has betrayed them.

Soon they will have tried all the conventional expedients. Soon there will be no-one whom they can trust but themselves.

Then it will happen.

1st October 1949   CHARLES HUMANA

Build Your Own House!

There must be many of us with the ambition, more or less secret, to build our own home — not to be able to get a builder to do it for us, but actually to do it ourselves. Those of us who make our own furniture find it far more satisfying than simply buying the cheap and often shoddy stuff most workers have to be content with. To be able to create the entire dwelling place, however, is something few of us will be able to do this side of the revolution.

And yet, is it impossible? In Birmingham, 50 workers in the Post Office factory are getting together to do just that — build their own houses. First to get the idea was the secretary of the factory's British Legion branch, the ex-service members of which were 'browned-off' with living in rooms or with in-laws. So they got together, fixed up for someone to teach them how to lay bricks, got an architect to design a bungalow, which was promptly corrected by the men's wives, found a site, fixed mortgages with a building society, put up £1,000 between them for equipment, sorted themselves into gangs, elected their own foremen, and got to work.

They have worked out their own 'points' system to establish the order of possession, and the first two couples will soon be moving into brand-new homes of lounge, kitchen, bathroom and three bedrooms, which will cost them £600 apiece.

The men themselves have drawn up their own rules, including disciplinary ones to prevent slackening-off after a majority get housed, and are working three evenings a week, and all day Saturdays and Sundays.

We have always maintained that the housing shortage is completely artificial and could be cured by the direct action of the community. These 50 telephone mechanics, clerks and storemen are showing what can be done with the necessary determination *now*. When all financial and other restrictions are swept away the problems of creating the things we need will be even more certain of solution.

20th August 1949

WAR CLOUDS IN THE FAR EAST

Malaya

The process of dividing the world between the Great Powers appealed greatly to the public imagination in the nineteenth century, and inspired the Imperialist dream of 'painting the map red' that captured British enthusiasm and reached its climax when Mafeking added a new word to the language. Perhaps part of the impregnability of that illusion was the fact that nobody was compelled to do anything tangible in order to justify their proud imperialist claims, other than the pride-conscripts who officered the army and the hunger-conscripts who served in it. And they were doubtless fortified in their practical contributions to Empire-building by 'the lordliest life on earth' in far off countries where they became a special privileged caste, providing each rank understood its place in the then appointed scheme of things.

The traditional British Army and the British Empire were irrevocably joined together. The British Army was always there to defend the interests of imperialism; it took the flag to follow trade wherever it went. No matter where British traders and settlers had established themselves, by means of commercial penetration which invariably began with self-humiliation before the dignitaries established there and finished with the self-complacent superiority indelibly associated today with 'Poonah', the Army finally stepped in to assert the rights or claims of the commercial penetrators and eventually annex the territory.

The Malaya Story
The news that the Guards are going to Malaya must be a whiff of nostalgia in the nostrils of the retired colonels at Bath and Cheltenham. All the build-up of a nineteenth century campaign is

362   [1948]

there. British planters and settlers have been murdered by Chinese terrorists. The Russians are blamed for causing the trouble (they always were and only the use of the term 'Communist' by the Press seems a trifle anachronistic). We must step in to defend the peaceful Malays and restore outraged British interests. The Cabinet has been urged not to delay, and they are now sending the Guards. The Press rushes in with happy little stories of last-minute military marriages. The Singapore gentlemen for whose benefit the troops are going out, have hastily prepared the ground for the Army by decorating their clubs with banners saying, 'For officers and civilians only'. We await the beleaguered garrison story to make the atmosphere perfect.

Empire No Longer

But, unfortunately, behind all this window-dressing is the glaring truth that the nineteenth-century British Empire does not now exist. The spirit of public enthusiasm died in the First World War, when the clash between imperialisms brought home the fact that a heavy price was to be paid for world sovereignty, and the first public reaction against militarism took place in the revulsion from the senseless waste of lives in trench warfare until to-day the Army is insufficient to police the world. Moreover, a glaring truth has been brought home to the imperialists, which is that the only way to colonise is to exterminate the native population to the point where it becomes negligible, as in America and Australia. Although the comic columnists may extract that sentence from its context to horrify their sentimental readers, it is unfortunately true that colonisation and humanitarianism can never mix, and the only way the coloniser has ever established himself is by quickfire and ruthless wiping out, such as Andrew Jackson undertook. Hitler learned the lesson and used it in Europe. Britain's Empire in Canada and Australia and its lost Empire in the United States, were firmly established on that principle. It was unable to do so in India, where it was faced with an old and complex civilisation, and that explains why it is on its way out in India. The followers of Malan would like to use these methods in South Africa, but are late on the scene, and will eventually find, as outlined in these columns before, that the Africans are awakening to consciousness and will not tolerate such methods used on them and will be provoked to a defence that will shatter white hegemony.

The eventual outcome of imperialism is the awakening of the oppressed peoples to a sense of independence, often expressed in nationalism, and no matter what sacrifices are poured out by the metropolitan power, in the finish all they will have to show for it are the neat white cemeteries in bizarre surroundings in the most distant corners of the world. The experience of the long occupation of India, and the late desperate struggle to hang on in Palestine, would prove this without doubt; and the fact is that the British Empire does not now come under the control of men determined to hang on at all costs until thrown out. This romantic Churchillian policy which not even the Conservatives now uphold, has been superseded by a realisation of the facts of power politics to-day and the struggle between America and Russia; and all the 'Four Feathers' atmosphere that may surround the Malaya adventure is only there to please the gallery.

No More Isolated Struggles

There is a tense situation in Malaya which is accentuated by many factors. Undoubtedly the major factor is the Japanese occupation which exploded the legend of white superiority, and yet was succeeded by the Singapore Old Gang. The internal politics of revolutionary movements have something to do with it — the Communists are strong because, as in Burma, they collaborated with the Japanese and received military training during the years of the Russo-Japanese pact, and only towards the finish, with a change in policy from Moscow, did they switch from being pro-Japanese to anti-Japanese, when their superior military training enabled them to dominate the resistance movements. Coupled with this is the factor that Chinese Communists are the nearest highly-organised movement able to give them support since the Indian Congress trailed off into national diplomacy and away from anti-imperialism. But the Communists are not so powerful as to be able to dominate Malaya in the fashion depicted by the Press, except that the publicity given to them naturally tends in their favour. Surprisingly enough, the Malayans are not receptive to the clarion calls for 'defence of Christian civilisation' or (for the benefit of the overwhelming mass of non-Christians in the world) 'defence of democracy' — far less 'our Western standard of values'. They know exactly what that means, and it means something much more different in the Far East from what it does to the after-dinner speakers in the Guildhall. The mass of them are bound to be apathetic in any struggle involving the sovereignty of the West, and more inclined to side with the East if this is represented by anybody with the faintest regard for their interests. It has been fortunate for the American State Department that the 'East' has so far been represented by totalitarian powers with no regard for anybody but themselves.

To-day, there is no isolated struggle, but every outbreak is caught up in the vortex leading to the Third World War. Nineteenth century Imperialism is dead and damned, and this latest military adventure, coming so soon on the heels of the Palestine episode as to enable the now superfluous Palestine Police to be rushed to Malaya, is a test of strength between America and Russia who will both be interested to see 'their side' win. The aim of the more utilitarian Imperialists is to re-create an Empire in Africa; they have little hope of remaining in Malaya for ever, and well appreciate that when it eventually is necessary they will have to evacuate Malaya just as they did in Palestine, in spite of all the 'reasons' now advanced for going there. But, in the phrase which will be Mankind's Famous Last Words. "We have to honour our commitments."

4th September 1948   INTERNATIONALIST

Is there a Solution in Asia?

Rivalry between great powers has brought present situation in Korea

By the time these lines are in print, the situation of world politics regarding Korea may have completely changed the headlines of the newspapers, for the parallel between Attlee's Flight to Washington and Chamberlain's to Munich twelve years ago is obvious enough. But just as Munich made no change in the fundamental pattern of affairs, so the present international rivalries will remain the same, whatever is the result of the Washington meeting. And since it is this basic pattern which is the most decisive factor in shaping events, it is important to keep it constantly in mind, and not to permit revulsion in the face of the threat of war — natural enough to all men, and all the more so for anarchists with their traditional and well-founded anti-militarism — to deceive our judgement.

The basic pattern is the rivalry between the great powers. And it is this pattern which has brought the present situation into being. The American occupation of Japan after the war was clearly motivated by the military necessity to possess a base over-looking the Far East. Such a base could only be regarded by the rulers of Russia as — what in fact it is — a military threat. And here let us state that it matters not at all that politicians and publicists claim 'unaggressive intentions' for such bases. Even if one allows that they are taken and fortified 'in case' of aggression by another power, then one must also logically admit that another power must take these fortified bases into account and seek to neutralise them militarily 'in case' . . . etc., etc.

Move and Counter Move

When the Soviet-assisted Red Chinese army ousted the American-assisted Koumintang army from China, the pendulum of international rivalry had swung once again. So America neutralised Formosa. It is not difficult to see that the next step was the Chinese neutralisation of Korea. (If we use colourless terms like 'neutralise', it is for convenience and brevity. We do not for one minute forget what we have already written regarding the moral baseness of fighting out international rivalries on the territory of a small nation, and to a considerable extent with the lives of its nationals, in an undeclared war which is also conducted — bloodlessly — in the embassies and at Lake Success.)

The situation which the Americans face in Korea is the bargaining pressure of Chinese Communists in their demands on Formosa, and the factors which operate in these political auctions are just these factors of force and strength, although they are always rigged out in fancy dress for public viewing. A writer in the *Observer* (3rd December 1950), discussing "How it may look to the Chinese", obligingly supplies this diplomatic camouflage in advance, tinged nevertheless with contemporary realism:

"Then came the American neutralisation of Formosa last June. There is no doubt that it hit the Chinese hard. Formosa had not only been promised to China at Cairo and Potsdam. The Chinese regard it as their own territory, taken from them by foreigners — Japanese — at a time of Chinese weakness and humiliation fifty-five years ago. Moreover, it is the last stronghold of the little-loved Chiang Kai-shek, the base from which a damaging blockade of the Chinese coast was being operated, and from which Chinese coastal cities were being wantonly bombed. It is fairly certain that the Chinese were actively preparing to invade and take

Formosa, and that they felt wholly within their rights in doing so. The American interdiction of this, however reasonable and justified it seemed to the Americans, could appear to most Chinese only as a hostile act."

The Future

But supposing the present international tension is relieved by 'concessions' on both sides ("wiser counsels have prevailed", etc., etc.) is the situation basically altered? American concessions in Formosa only increase the military importance of Japan, while Chinese withdrawals in Korea will not stop the Asiatic struggle to drive the British out of Malaya. The Chinese and Russians (in the context of the present world, these terms mean their governments) cannot ignore military threats, potential or otherwise. Nor can the Americans ignore threats to their pacific outposts, or the British forget the importance of Singapore to the defence of Australia. The pattern of international rivalry which underlies it all remains unchanged. When it comes to an issue, the headlines only obscure the reality. If active intervention, as in Korea, is embarked upon, a "much-needed demonstration of resolution and solidarity by the freedom-loving peoples" has taken place; if a retreat is sounded, "the voice of moderation has at last prevailed among the nations". But all that has really happened is that the point of attrition has changed. When settlement is reached in Korea, the Formosans or the Malayans had better look out.

The situation is actually worse than this even: for the last twelve years since Munich have shown us that the pattern of international rivalry is independent even of its principal actors. How often were we told that Germany was the aggressor in Europe, Japan the aggressor in Asia? Yet the total elimination of these major factors in the international scene has found worthy understudies immediately ready to take the footlights. What an irony that one of them is the war-stricken China for which collections and Red Cross work were such a feature of the pre-war Left!

Can one escape the conclusion of the anarchists that the existence of States not only affronts the natural solidarity of mankind, but provides actively the cause for internecine strife?

But to leave the matter on this abstract level would be to ignore another question, which involves the atomic bomb, but which ought to be discussed in a more fundamental and analytical way. When Mr Peter Roberts, Conservative MP for Keeley, asked in Parliament on June 27th whether the government would advise the use of the atomic bomb on the North Korean capital if the North

Korean Government ignored the UN resolution on Korea, he was greeted with shocked cries from the Government benches, and was finally ruled politely out of order by the Speaker. The impression conveyed was that 'of course' the Western governments had never even dreamed of using the atom bomb.

It now appears that in fact the whole question was thoroughly considered at the time, for the *Manchester Guardian* (27th November 1950) reports that, "authoritative sources in Washington" say that the United States Joint Chiefs of Staff considered — but voted against — dropping atomic bombs on North Korean troops early in the campaign.

The proposal is said to have been made almost simultaneously, but independently, by army and air force officers when the bulk of the North Korean army was concentrated in a small area near the town of Suwon, south of Seoul, the South Korean capital. Because the approval of the President is required before atomic weapons can be used in war, the question was put first to the Joint Chiefs of Staff, who apparently decided on their own that it would be unwise and did not refer the matter to President Truman." As might be expected, the decision not to use the bomb was tactical rather than moral, for the report continues: "At that time the United States was seeking wide support for the stand against aggression in Korea, and it was feared that world sympathy might be alienated by what might have been considered a hasty resort to atomic warfare."

The military situation, however, now offers many good tactical reasons in the opposite direction. The Chinese armies are far less well equipped than the Americans and British, but they achieve success by an overwhelming expenditure of the one factor in which they have vast superiority — manpower. Their 'human sea' tactics involve a fantastic toll of human life. "We are killing them by the thousand", one correspondent was told, "but they just come marching on". He goes on to say that this tactic "has emphasised as never before the grave handicap confronting a Western country, where human life rates higher than anything else, in fighting the fatalistic Asiatic armies where men are the cheapest and most expendable commodity".

We will pass over here the demoralising effect on men who to save their own lives have to inflict a ghastly carnage on less well equipped, less educated, altogether poorer fellow-men. Long may human life rate higher than anything else in the West. Progress demands that the same respect should be extended to the coolie workers in the East, but this kind of war clearly does not favour progress there.

Now the United Nations' reverses show that the Chinese superiority in expendable manpower is greater than the American superiority in arms. Since the UN Forces can only with difficulty be increased and relieved, the military problem is clearly to increase still further the technical power of the troops in the field to inflict even greater slaughter on the advancing 'human seas'. It does not need very much imagination to see that to use the atomic bomb would achieve this result to some extent, and could be justified on the grounds that not to use it would be to sacrifice unnecessarily 'our boys' lives'. It will also be seen that there will always be a strong temptation — and strong military arguments — for using it against the limitless armies of the peasant countries.

It is a grave prospect.

But underlying it there remains the world pattern of sovereign states — handfuls of men ruling over millions and all drawing daggers on each other. This is not a necessary form of human organisation, but an arbitrary one. It can be changed. But only if men of good will give up struggling for alleviations of present 'pressing' problems, and give themselves to the revolutionary problem of changing the pattern of social and economic life.

9th December 1950

THE WAR IN KOREA

Korea — A Phoney War

"Taegu is accepting tragedy and disaster with the expressionless calm of a people well adjusted to despair. One gets the impression, irresistibly, that for total victory, whichever way it went, Taegu would put out no flags and shed no tears."
War report in *The Observer*, 27th August 1950

If you went to the cinema the week before last, you probably saw the newsreel of war planes and ships being taken out of storage and refitted "after long years of peace", as the commentator put it without a trace of irony in his plummy voice. You saw too, the bombing of Korean villages and towns in the name of 'freedom and democracy'. The newsreels, the radio, the press and the politicians are all preparing us for the idea that the Korean war is the first stage of the Third World War.

While a rational and calm approach will show that neither the Russian nor the American government is prepared technologically for a full-scale war, and that Russia will not be for a long time, it is obvious that they may well have created a situation from which they cannot withdraw. The American government in particular is so deeply committed, that, no matter what the cost in soldiers' lives, it must continue to defend what its own advisors considered last year to be strategically undefendable. Defeat in Korea would be so disastrous to American *prestige* that, however great the losses, the government whose prestige is at stake dare not end the war. Men may die, the country (which was once called *Chao Hsien* — Land of the Morning Calm) may be utterly ruined, but prestige must not be lost.

The manner in which the 'values of the free world' are being defended should be enlightening to those who imagine that the Korean war is being fought 'for civilisation'.

The war correspondent of the American paper *Time* (21st August 1950) writes that the war in Korea is forcing upon the American troops "acts and attitudes of the utmost savagery, not the usual inevitable savagery of combat in the field, but savagery in detail — the blotting out of villages where the enemy *may* be hiding, the shooting and shelling of refugees who may include North Koreans . . . And there is savagery by proxy . . . The South Korean police and the South Korean marines whom I observed in front lines are brutal. They murder to save themselves the trouble of escorting prisoners to the rear; they murder civilians simply to get them out of the way, or simply to avoid the trouble of searching and cross-examining them. And they extort information — information our forces need and require of the South Korean interrogators — by means so brutal that they cannot be described."

We may be sure that whether the victory in Korea should go to America and its puppets or to the Soviet Union and its, the people of the country will be the losers. C. P. Fitzgerald, an anthropologist of the Australian National University, writing in *The Listener* (24th August 1950) says:

"The Korean people wanted independence and unity — liberty from the Japanese yoke. Instead they were given a country divided by a preposterous artificial parallel, a frontier conforming to no natural feature, cutting off the towns from their electric power, the harbours from their hinterland, the rice fields from the head waters of the fertilising streams. One half of the country had thrust upon it a Russian-inspired Communist regime, the other received, under American protection, a feeble government of former exiles, men who had spent their lives abroad, wholly out of touch with the Korean generation which had grown up under the Japanese. It can safely be said that the great mass of the Korean people would never willingly have chosen the one or the other, and least of all a division between the two."

And another authority, Mary Linley Taylor, who has known the country for over thirty years, tells us in *The Listener* (17th August 1950) that:

"Even today the Koreans sing a little shanty when they see us coming:
      Foreigner, foreigner,
      From the Western Seas,
      What is your business here?
      Go away, go away,
      Foreigner from the Western Seas."

Mary Taylor's article is entitled 'What do the Koreans themselves want?' Her Korean street song supplies the answer. *The New Statesman* remarks that "the war in Korea will settle nothing, and will degenerate into an increasingly bestial and savage butchery on both sides unless it is made clear that its conclusion is to be followed by a political settlement acceptable to Asia." But what do the silent anonymous Asiatic millions want? Not the half-baked commissar, the ruthless idealists or the ambitious Westernised smart-alecs. Not the decrepit imperial-commercialism of the white sahibs and planters. Not the hard-boiled civilisation of juke boxes, pin-ups and Coca Cola. Surely what Asia wants is freedom to live, freedom from sudden death and from slow death from famine and avoidable disease. Freedom to live its own life in its own way.

2nd September 1950   W

Can Peace Be Enforced?

Is Korea a New Spain?

Even before the tide of events turned in favour of America and the 'United' Nations, the question was being asked 'Is Korea a new Spain?' It is a question which serves as a focussing point for left-wingers and progressives to discuss their attitude towards the post-war power rivalries. Since left-wingers and progressives are now the most important intellectual current which provides justification for wars, this discussion has an importance far beyond immediate appearances.

In 1914 it was the H. G. Wellses who provided rallying cries sufficiently cogent to bring in those who might otherwise have followed the instinct which intuitively recognises that wars between major powers have nothing to do with ethical considerations. The post-1918 'no-more-wars' feeling was more effectively swept away by the anti-fascists of the Left Book Club, literary figures like Spenser and Auden — and we must not except Orwell and Koestler — than by frank warmongers. It was these rather than reactionaries who provided the arguments which enabled the anti-fascist left to line up behind (of all people) Chamberlain and Churchill.

Do Wars Achieve Progress?

H. G. Wells was personally disillusioned after 1918 about the part he played in the manufacture of propaganda during the preceding four years. But however much revolutionists may have seen that the post-war world differed but slightly from pre-1914, the League of Nations provided a seeming achievement for the progressives and gave justification of their support for the war. H. G. Wells could not undo his war work. It was, of course, impossible to argue whether the price of so many million dead was 'worth' the apparent gains in progress at that time; it only became a dead loss with the development of the new war. But here the feeling of a new crusade again had the effect of stilling doubts.

From an objective standpoint it seems clear that the world of today is more totalitarian than the world of 1939. Yet the fascist régimes of Italy and Germany were terminated, and this seems a sufficient gain to many; especially if they can persuade themselves that the Russian system is somehow less bad than those overthrown. The point which emerges is that for progressives and left-wingers the last war can still be represented as having been 'worthwhile'. Hence they approach the question, 'is Korea a new Spain?' without having learned anything from the past.

Appeasement or Firm Stand?

Anarchists have to adjust their minds somewhat in considering the question. For those who ask it, Spain represented principally a trial of strength between the fascist countries against the democracies. The Spanish people were just one more among those sacrifices to Fascist aggression which began with Abyssinia and ended with Austria and Czechoslovakia and Albania.

Anarchists (and a very few other revolutionary thinkers) see Spain rather differently; the Spanish revolution has a special and enormous significance to them. That George Orwell saw this aspect of Spain is clear from his *Homage to Catalonia*, and he was by far the most perceptive and sensitive thinker on the pro-war left. But even for Orwell the main difference of Spain lay in the conflict which he imagined existed between the fascist and the democratic systems. For more humdrum anti-fascists the issue was the simple one of 'standing up to aggression', or of failing to do so.

The left have for years blamed the last war on the policy of appeasement culminating in Munich. They are joined by Churchill and they say that the 1939 war would not have been 'necessary' if the democracies had shown strength instead of weakness. The same argument obtains today. 'Russia will not dare to go to war if we show her that we are not afraid to stand up to her.' The success of the United Nations in Korea is hailed with great enthusiasm by those who take this view, not unnaturally.

In *Freedom* we have consistently advanced the view that wars are not caused by ideological rivalries (as Churchill and the lefties claim) but are necessary to the continuance of the system of market economy called capitalism. Unhappily, time will almost certainly show that this view is the more correct one, even if the democracies 'stand up' to Russia with the same determination elsewhere as they have shown in Korea.

Where the Real Struggle Lies

The importance of this question of Korea and Spain lies in this: that for simple anti-appeasers the main question is being stronger than Russia. If this is the main consideration, all other problems are secondary — and such secondary problems include the defence of civil liberty, the struggle for better living conditions, against the encroachments of the militarised state. In short, the secondary considerations include even the struggle between the democratic state and the fully developed totalitarian tyranny exemplified by Russia.

For anarchists, the main problem is elsewhere. War is not merely an evil in itself — it is that for everyone who is sane; it is also a process which is ineffectual to stem tyranny, but rather advances the spread of totalitarian patterns. Moreover, we see the mentality of war acceptance and war preparedness as being a precursor of the totalitarian mentality. Since we see this mentality already firmly entrenched not only in frankly totalitarian régimes but also in our own country and America, acceptance of war only hastens the advances of the very thing which the honest left wing or progressive war acceptors seek to prevent.

For us therefore the real struggle is against the principles for which Russia stands as a symbol, but which are by no means confined to the Iron Curtain. For this struggle to be effective it must be absolutely thoroughgoing, and must seek completely to

transform the thought and outlook of society. To do so it must not simply react against totalitarian trends in their separate manifestations, but must have a positive outlook on life and towards the living, alive forces in human society. Such an outlook is very much wider than that of the democratic war acceptors like Koestler and his proposed 'Legion of Liberty'; but it is more difficult to explain, to reduce to slogans, to 'get across'. Nevertheless, it is possible that such a viewpoint is more acceptable to peace-hungry people than might appear at first sight.
14th October 1950

The 38th Parallel

Power politics has its ludicrous moments. The jockeying for a 'correct' position over the 38th Parallel provided such a one, when American (United Nations) troops paused at the frontier between North and South Korea in order, it was said, to await the directions of the United Nations. With the legalistic blessing they resumed their advance.

One wonders how much the man in the street is impressed by this respect for 'law'? If the war in Korea can be made to have any moral justification at all, it can only be that a totalitarian régime (in the North) is overthrown, and the corrupt régime (of the South) replaced by something better. Such an aim is not incompatible with the fundamental power question — that of Korea as an American base on the mainland, which if in Russian hands constituted a grave threat to American Japan. It seems likely that the American administration will have absorbed the lessons of the South Korean collapse and instituted some kind of land reform which will enable their kind of régime to hold both the North and the South. The expressed aim of free elections over the whole country may well give them the chance to drop Syngman Rhee and so get clear of the unsavoury aspects of his rule which have been given such prominent publicity.

None of these aims conflicts with an ideological gloss in the shape of an anti-totalitarian crusade. Yet the Anglo-American

ruling class seems curiously unwilling to take up such a line. Even
during the last war, Anthony Eden saw nothing wrong in his
declaration to the effect that we had no quarrel with the German
(Nazi) régime inside Germany; it was only when they began to
export it that we became interested. For ordinary people who are
concerned with right and wrong, and who instinctively react in a
hostile manner to tyranny, such a position is hideously immoral.
Yet it is the same attitude which informs the legalistic rectitude of
the USA posing as dutiful UN member.

We have made our position on Korea plain. We are sickened by
these wars between great powers fought on other peoples'
territory, and largely with other peoples' lives. Vicarious wars
which provide the war offices with 'valuable technical data' and
the opportunity to experiment with new weapons and young lives.
That is the basic aspect of Korea that we can never forget.
Nevertheless, granted that Korea has fallen between the jaws of
rival powers, we would not be human if we did not wish that some
social progress may result, though only as a by-product.

The democratic powers utilise the man-in-the-street's desire for
freedom, and paint an ideological gloss with it. One would respect
them more if they paid as much attention to giving some slight
reality to this gloss rather than striking pious attitudes of rectitude
at the United Nations.

Trading with the Enemy
In past wars it has always — and not unnaturally — aroused great
indignation when it has been found that 'our boys' have often been
killed with weapons made at home. That such should happen
causes no surprise to those who look upon war with an objective
eye. But it is very shocking to those bred on the history book tripe
about just wars, defending right causes, and the rest.

After Hitler's rape of Czechoslovakia in the spring of 1939, it
was perfectly clear that war was a likely event. Yet trade in war
materials between Britain and Germany became increasingly brisk
right up to September 3rd itself.

On 23rd September this year, the BBC Home Service News
declared that Russian exports to America had increased by two
million dollars' worth in the last six months, and that the principal
exports from Russia were furs, chrome and manganese. American
exports to Russia had increased by one-and-a-half times.

Churchill has recently been complaining about the sale of 'vital
war material to Russia', and the government, not without a certain

unwillingness, has agreed to hold all material necessary to the defence of Britain even if it means breaking trade agreements.

It appears that the great Czech armaments firm of Skoda have also been exporting arms to South Africa, even though the amounts involved are small.

Now, in *Freedom*, we have consistently pressed the view that war is an economic activity as market contracts and 'normal' trade are tied up in various tortuous ways. Trading with the enemy therefore is quite a natural proceeding, as armaments manufacturers have always clearly seen. We, therefore, don't raise out hands in scandalised horror like those who support and glamorise war, but don't want to see its ugly side. We know that trading with the enemy doesn't even stop with the outbreak of war, for it is one of the functions of neutral countries to act as brokers between the contestants, as in the case of the submarine nets sold to Sweden during the last war.

Tortuous Thinking

What interests us now that the matter is being rather more openly ventilated is the extraordinarily tortuous thinking displayed. The main principle is clear enough. It is obviously outrageous to supply your enemy with the means to kill your sons, and perhaps yourself also. But the strange thing about our distracted civilisation is that one doesn't accept obvious propositions. The manufacture and sale of armaments is obviously a much more immoral and destructive traffic than, say, the traffic in narcotic drugs or prostitution. Yet the United Nations and the League of Nations busy themselves with these, but not with armaments. Bernard Shaw, who is one of the ablest apologists for a twisted civilisation, also defended armaments manufacturers in the character of Undershaft in *Major Barbara*.

Shaw is to be commended for his honesty. Most 'realists' are content to support detestable causes without admitting it, and to make use of the most ludicrous circumlocutions to justify themselves. Here is the *Times Educational Supplement* for 22nd September 1950:

". . . the member who said it would be a scandal if a single British soldier were killed by a weapon made out of materials exported by Britain summed-up most people's first reaction. It is, however, a fallacy to suggest that anyone who makes or authorises the export of potential war materials must be held responsible for the purposes for which they are used. Moral responsibility only enters when the manufacturer or the government department authorising export could have foreseen the use to which the material would be put. Even then it has to be proved that the disadvantages of introducing political discrimination into peacetime commerce are less than the disadvantages of slightly increasing the war potential of a probable enemy. The question is really one of expediency, not morals."

Such arguments require little comment, and we will confine ourselves to pointing out that the lighthearted irresponsibility which the writer permits to the governments would never be tolerated in an engineer charged with building a bridge, or a physician treating a patient. Governments, it seems, are immune from professional responsibility.

A Touchstone

Such arguments may, however, be used as a kind of touchstone. On the one hand are people (regrettably a minority) who think so simply because they think wars are bad, that one should not even then trade with the enemy; who think that the homeless should be housed, the sick attended to, and the hungry fed. Who think, moreover, that it is not beyond the organising capacity of man to arrange that where there is plenty, goods should be transported to where there is a scarcity or famine even. The more radical among these people think it unnatural that the needs of everyone for love and for sexual happiness should be obstructed.

On the other hand are those who, when confronted with simple, self-evident propositions, react by a slight shrinking away, and then by arguments of the 'yes, but . . .' type. These are the practical folk. Their practical hard-headedness acts as a cushion between simple indignation and getting things done; and it preserves the world for us as it is, instead of as it ought to be. Their practical arguments dissipate the power of thought and prevent it from being transformed into action. Be on your guard against them.

14th October 1950   J. H.

Background to the Korean War

Report by Korean Anarchist Federation

In earlier issues of Freedom we have drawn attention to the strength and influence of the anarchist movement in Korea, and have pointed out that, like ourselves and anarchists all over the world, they support neither American nor Stalinist imperialism, but struggle for the freedom and independence of all peoples from governmental control of any kind. The following report from W. Karim, the general secretary of the Korean Anarchist Federation, was written before the outbreak of frank hostilities in Korea; it provides an informative and interesting background to the present struggle.

The following report was submitted by the Korean Anarchist Federation to the International Anarchist Congress held recently. In this critical situation, the Anarchist Federation of all countries is the only body which reaffirms its complete independence of both imperialist camps. It supports neither the Yankee nor the Stalinist variety. In Korea there is a strong anarchist movement which has a long and honourable tradition in the fight against exploitation.

The Pacific war put to an end the cruel Japanese oppression in Korea. In December 1945, the Moscow Conference gave to the country a provisional government accredited by Russia, the United States, Britain and China. But Russo-American antagonism and above all the movement of opposition by the Korean people (a movement initiated and sustained by the anarchists) defeated this attempt. A series of Russo-American Conferences failed to solve the problem and in 1947 the United Nations authorised South Korea to elect an autonomous government.

North Korea, ruled by a government of the 'People's Republic' type is a satellite of Russia. In Southern Korea the democratic government is economically and militarily dependent on the United States.

The frontier dividing these two parts is the scene of what has been baptised as 'the battle of the 38th parallel'. Every night, the Bolshevik groups attack, burn, murder and sack.

This state of affairs allows the Southern Government to bombard the people with decrees and under the pretext of anti-Bolshevik struggle to extend its authority.

In spite of this state of nascent war and permanent insecurity, life in Southern Korea is infinitely better than north of the 38th Parallel. The following figures speak for themselves.

Population of the South, 1944: 16,545,370 Koreans, 462,508 Japanese and 12,648 other nationalities. In 1946: 19,369,270 Koreans, no Japanese or other nationalities. In 1947: 21,800,800 Koreans, no Japanese or other nationalities.

The reason for this rapid growth of the native population between 1944 and 1947 was the return of about 100,000 workers and soldiers and, above all, the flight of some five million Koreans from the Bolshevik terror of the North.

Working conditions: as a result of the rise in prices, due to monetary disorganisation, wages are very low and cover barely two-thirds of one's strictly necessary expenses. There is, moreover, great unemployment. In November 1946 there were 1,050,937 workless according to official figures, and to these must be added more than ten million people who receive periodic assistance.

Northern Korea is mainly an agricultural region, although its soil is not very fertile (22 per cent arable land). After the Japanese withdrawal many big landowners, fearing agrarian reform, sold their estates. But these transfers brought about no great changes and the land continues to be very little divided out.

Anarchists in the Forefront

Struggle of Anarchists: after the defeat of the Korean revolution, the anarchists fought on and killed many of the leaders of Japanese imperialism. The Emperor himself was attacked several times by our comrades, who destroyed the means of invasion and sabotaged Japanese exploitation, organising at the same time working class unity.

The police decimated our groups repeatedly. When action became impossible inside the country, the militants went to China, Manchuria and Japan itself, to carry on the struggle. The sacrifices they made were enormous and this stimulated fervour and desire for justice and freedom among the survivors.

The Japanese authorities were obsessed with fear and the police became even more severe. The terrorised people had great admiration and sincere .respect for those who in such great numbers died for their cause. At last when the terrorist régime was defeated, the General Federation of Korean Anarchists (GFKA) resumed its struggle openly.

In Spite of Them All . . .

Since the war: in September and October 1945 the majority of the workers and peasants joined the Workers' Union, sustained and led by the anarchists. Heavily aided by the USSR the Bolsheviks succeeded in using the union as a means of action for their political ends, lesening the strength of our comrades. Soon another 'union' was formed, of American inspiration, and in short time it supplanted the other. Undismayed, our comrades carried on the struggle on all fronts.

In May 1946 our comrades created the Agricultural Workers' Party and the movement of Independent Workers, together with the General Conference of Korean Anarchists, the General Workers and the General Students' Federation.

Some figures show the influence of Korean anarchists. The GFKA has 3,000 militants who by means of the above mentioned movements influence 600,000 perfectly organised Koreans. The GFKA has two daily papers and one weekly printed on its own presses. The GFKA has created a University where young workers can study in the evenings and has founded two schools in the country.

28th October 1950

PROBLEMS OF ATOMIC ENERGY

Aspects of Atomic Energy

The BBC recently gave a series of some twelve talks, spread over eight evenings, on various aspects of the atomic bomb and atomic energy, and, since the series was arranged elaborately, was given publicity, and included among its speakers all the leading scientific experts on the question in England, as well as such writers as J. B. Priestley and Bertrand Russell, it was quite evidently intended to give to the public as comprehensive a survey as possible of the various problems connected with atomic energy. It may therefore be profitable to make a survey of some of the salient features of the talks and also to draw some general conclusions from an anarchist point of view.

One interesting aspect of the talks was the precision with which the scientific experts described the effects of the bomb, and the balancing imprecision with which the other experts discussed what should be done about the social problems produced by the atom bomb. It was quite clear that the situation has got them into a state of puzzled fear from which their acceptance of current social ideas can give them no satisfactory way out.

Scientists Enslaved

The series began with an introductory talk by Priestley which made an unremarkable and pessimistic opening on a general line. Then followed two wholly objective accounts of the research into the atomic bomb, the first, by Professor Cockcroft, showing no apparent concern for the results of the work, the second, by Professor Oliphant, recognising in a very frank way the kind of slavery into which the scientists have precipitated themselves by their unthinking failure to recognise their social responsibility. He remarks:

"The very success of the work of the nuclear physicists had created the most horrible of weapons in the hands of man. The first explosion in the desert destroyed the traditional freedom of the scientist, for his work now menaced the security of the world. The first military use of the bomb on Hiroshima came as a complete surprise to all nations. The security restrictions and secrecy, so hateful to the scientists, had been extremely successful. It is the fear of every man of science that these same restrictions will surround his work for evermore."

The fact, of course, is that the scientists have been led into this slavery because they followed their research without any consideration for their debt to others; they did not realise that their own freedom of research was conditional on the attainment of freedom for all men, and that in a society based on tyranny and war their discoveries would be turned to those ends. The scientists are beginning to awake to these facts, but whether they will use their new consciousness to any positive purpose is another question.

The Intoxication of Power

One of the most terrifying facts about the atomic bomb has been that many people who took an active part in its construction were actually ignorant of the object of their endeavours. But, more than this, almost every one of the people who actually knew went about their work with a lack of imagination and a detachment which failed to take into account the results. How many would have started on it if they had themselves had some actual prevision of the consequences? One of the men who was actually concerned in the dropping of the bomb on Hiroshima described very frankly this mood of indifference in which the bomb was actualy thrown; and, moreover, the corroding sense of power which helped to destroy any consciousness of the suffering likely to be involved. His statement stands out as sufficiently important to be quoted at length:

"The few weeks I spent on Tinian, the island in the middle of the Pacific from where the two attacks were launched, stand out in my life not so much for the sight of the bomb itself, as for the effect on myself and the others of what we were doing. Of all worldly attractions, the most vicious is that of power, and atomic energy spelt power. It spelt power of destruction, power of delving into the realm of the unknown, power of being able to achieve our objective. On every one of us it had its own personal significance, and inevitably it had its effect. We, who hitherto had been occupied with ordinary affairs, became transformed temporarily into kings, as it were, of the new realm. We found ourselves in sole possession of a weapon with which an entire empire, even were it in the ascendent and not, as happened, on the verge of surrender, could be defeated overnight, by one lone aeroplane and without the least danger to ourselves. We were not soldiers waging war, for there was no opposition to stop us, but rather a research team conducting an experiment, and like all researchers, we were cold and detached. As we lay on the beach sunbathing, or sat at table eating, or even as we flew across the Japanese coast under a faultless, sunlit sky, we gave, I am afraid, little thought to the human life that we were to cut so abruptly short. The end was too overpowering for us to pause and consider the means.

"You will probably say that the novelty has now worn off. We have had time for sober reflection, Even if you believe my account of what happened inside us on Tinian you will argue that it was born of the heat of battle, that it will not happen again, that we have learned our lesson. I doubt it. I lived through those fateful weeks, and I know that if the weapon is powerful enough, the stakes sufficiently high, and the attainment of the goal is within grasp, human nature can lose its sense of values and not even know that it has done so."

This piece of honest description of how men feel when they are in possession of such a monstrous weapon as the atomic bomb illustrates both the corrupting nature of power which the anarchists have always stressed, and also the dangers of the kind of objectivity unillumined with social consciousness which makes the research worker so careless of the ultimate results of his action.

Risk of War Greater

At least two of the talkers exploded convincingly the idea which some sentimentalists have expounded that the very horror of the atomic bomb would put an end to war. Their conclusions were to the contrary. Professor Cyril Falls said:

"But now the risk of the mobilisation period and of the large-scale moves of forces and material to battle stations are greater than ever. A much bigger margin of safety is gained when they have got to their battle stations and organised them. So the time factor gets more important, and the urge to set things in motion in a period of tension grows more insistent. And that in itself is a danger to peace. Mobilisation and preliminary strategic moves might tend to bring on a war because when one nation takes precautionary action another is likely to keep step, and the series of events set in train may go to the point where a clash of forces occurs."

And Bertrand Russell shows that even the attempt to guard against a major disaster in an atomic war may breed war itself:

"To guard against the possibility of this disaster, there would be great restrictions on the admission of alien travellers, and new restraints upon native citizens whose political loyalty might be open to suspicion. Nationalism would be stimulated to a continually increasing intensity. Fear of the horrors of war, so far from promoting peace, as some optimists have imagined ever since Nobel invented dynamite, would promote hatred of possibly hostile nations and generate the states of mind that lead to war. Sooner or later the tension would become unbearable and war break out."

Against these possibilities what had the speakers to offer? Very little. Mere inspection, even if it were efficient, would be useless, since, as Sir George Thompson points out, the process of converting atomic energy to industrial purposes involves the preparation of materials which can be used in bombs.

Bertrand Russell comes out with the old chestnut of an international police force possessing all the atomic bombs. But this would not be any guarantee of peace. For what is to prevent the international police, intoxicated with the power in their hands, deciding to set themselves up as a new world ruling class, and attempting to terrorise the world into submission by the use of atomic bombs?

Prerequisite of Peace

It becomes steadily more clear that, while government exists and ruling class rivalries are allowed to continue, we shall be less rather than more safe from a violently destructive war than we have been in the past. Peace will only come about when capitalism and the state are ended, and when the uses of industry are subordinated to the interests of the workers and the production of useful instead of destructive articles.

It might be argued that eventually a series of atomic wars will bring the end of states and governments and the rise of a series of small self-subsistent free communes. But we do not want to start again from scratch if we can avoid it. The workers should themselves enjoy the benefits of civilisation, or at least have the chance to choose; and to gain this, the only means is to end the kind of society that encourages and even needs the atomic bomb. The workers, even in the days of atomic energy, have the last say, in that the withdrawal of their labour can still cripple any system that oppresses them. Large-scale direct action of the workers is still a force which the governments fear more than their national enemies, and which only can bring about the era of peace when we shall be exempt from the fear of man-made disasters.

22nd March 1947   GEORGE WOODCOCK

Working with Death

Disease for Atom Workers

A few weeks back, we made mention in *Freedom* (14th June 1947), of the government's latest scheme of recruiting new workers to its atomic energy plant at Springfields, near Preston, Lancs. The Ministry of Supply is to open a training school for boys and girls of 15 years and over with the promise of salaries which must seem quite attractive at that age.

The salaries offered for older, qualified chemists, however, are not considered particularly good for the industry, and we rather cynically thought at the time that this lowness of reward was the reason why there was a shortage of workers at the plant. Now, however, it seems that another reason may be the more important one — that the effects upon health of working on atomic research are becoming known, and health is, rightly, considered before wealth.

We have to thank Bob Edwards, assistant general secretary of the Chemical Workers' Union, for bringing forward to public notice (in a report to the TUC) what is happening to workers at the Risley research station, near Warrington, where, he says, the ill-effects of atom work include sterility.

News Review, 17th April 1947, described Bob Edwards' report thus:

"The CWU claimed that members engaged on atomic research are suffering from the effects of atomic energy radiation.

Of 250 men employed on research at a Northern atomic station, more than 20 men are ill. They claim they have . . . become sterile, that they are breaking out in rashes, and falling asleep in 'buses. Their home lives are being disrupted.

Complained CWU Assistant Secretary Bob Edwards: 'The men are human guinea pigs. The scandal is that nobody seems to know the toxic effect on the men's future health and well-being . . .'

Most surprised were atomic scientists. To Birmingham University's Professor C. P. Moon. the charges came as a complete shock.

Responsible for atomic research in Britain, the Ministry of Supply announced: 'There are no grounds for supposing that precautions so far taken are inadequate. There is no evidence of lassitude or sterility. There has been one case of dermatitis. This is a good record.'

But the CWU's Edwards was not satisfied. 'Twelve months from now', he challenged, 'all my statements will be vindicated'."

Secrecy Demanded

Shortly after Edwards' statement to the TUC, a more sinister incident occurred. The vice-president of the Chemical Workers' Union, George Turton, was due to speak at a conference on industrial health in Manchester, and intended to deal with the illnesses which are said to be attacking workers near radio-active plants. He received a letter, however, just before he went, warning him "to use the utmost discretion in dealing with this matter. It is still on the secret list." Turton said that the letter implied "that any detailed disclosures might constitute a breach of the Official Secrets Act and I am not going to do that.

What I had to say would have been in the interests of the community and not of an alien country . . . A number of men are suffering from atomic sickness and I do not know how long they will last."

Since then the British and American governments openly banned the discussion of atomic energy at the International Congress of Pure and Allied Chemistry which met in London on July 17th.

The horrible thing about all this is that not only are workers already in atomic research open to danger from radio-active substances, but that the curtain of secrecy over the whole business means that new entrants into the industry — including boys and girls just leaving school at 15 — will take up the work in complete — and one can only believe *deliberately* fostered — ignorance of the possible consequences to their health.

Security Measures

The tightening up of secrecy on atomic matters had led to the Home Secretary declaring the atomic research development station at Harwell, Berkshire, the Department of Atomic Research at Risley, Lancashire, and the Ministry of Supply Factory at Springfield, to be regarded as prohibited areas under the Official Secrets Act of 1911.

In America, the 'atom bomb town' of Los Alamos, New Mexico, is being transformed from a township of huts and trailers clustered round the atom plant into a permanent institution under a multi-million dollar programme.

The 7,000 workers are to be provided with 1,000 new houses, six new blocks of flats, schools, cinemas and shops — and the population is strictly limited to workers on the atom plant and their families who all live behind an intense security curtain.

At a new base at Sandia, New Mexico, according to the *News Chronicle*, 17th July 1947, "New forms of warfare are being planned by a 'superblitz board' of young Army officers working, with scientists, under the orders of General Eisenhower, Chief of Staff. They are answerable only to him."

Workers' Protection
All of which adds up, one way or another, to misery for the common man. If he works in an atomic plant, he lays himself open to horrible disease. Even if he lives near such a plant, there seems to be no guarantee that he cannot be affected by radio-action in the neighbourhood. And the fate of the peoples of the world when these 'new forms of warfare' break out needs no stressing.

Is it retrogressive to wonder if any of it is worthwhile?

Is it reactionary to suggest that maybe we could get on quite well without atomic energy?

Only one thing seems certain. That workers *everywhere* should refuse to work in their State's atomic research plants. That workers should boycott these filthy activities as long as they are controlled by maniacs whose first thought is for their own power, and whose only use for such power is destructive.

We can wait for the possible benefits of atomic energy until all industries are under the decentralised control of the workers in them. For only then can we be certain that those industries are being used for the common good; that workers will not be asked or forced to sacrifice their health or their lives on behalf of a larger lunacy; and that the benefits to a community of any product are weighed against the cost of production in terms of humanity, not in terms of cash or national pride.

26th July 1947

Channel Tunnel and Atomic War

During the middle of January, an old plan, raised and rejected time and again during the last century, came up once again for discussion. It was the Channel Tunnel, which at last seems to have gained some kind of general official blessing, in that it was the subject of discussions of a presumably serious character which involved two representatives of the British government and also the former French Minister of Reconstruction, Dautry.

The Channel Tunnel is a perfectly practicable project. It involves problems which are greater in magnitude but no different in kind from such works of engineering as the Severn Tunnel. At any time during this century it could have been built, provided competent engineers and the necessary capital were available. Even to-day, when costs have risen, the price of £100,000,000 suggested is little more than a week's expenditure of the British Government during the last war.

Yet the fact remains that in time of peace this project was not put into operation and that it only appears as a 'practicable' venture at a time when the British and American governments are seeking closer political and strategic relationships with Western Europe. The real significance of the present proposal seems to be that, in an atomic war, transport of troops to France by sea may be easily interrupted, while a tunnel under the Channel would perhaps provide a safer method. This, of course, is conjecture, but it is significant that the project should come forward for serious discussion at this particular time.

Inventions and War

It is, of course, merely one illustration of the way in which, under the capitalist system, efforts are made for destructive purposes where they cannot be made for constructive ones. While the Channel Tunnel was merely an idea of great social value, a means of making it more convenient for people to travel between England and France, continual objections were raised to it on financial and other grounds. Now that it becomes a matter of strategic value, the air seems immediately to have cleared. Money can be spent freely where it was grudged before.

It is not difficult to find other instances of the kind; indeed, they abound. Before the 1914-18 war, the original development of aircraft was left in the hands of derided amateurs; as soon, however, as it became evident that aeroplanes could be used for military purposes, their development was taken in hand by the governments and went on at a greatly accelerated pace, because money was no longer grudged for their development.

Similar developments have been carried out in all branches of industry, in chemicals, in medicine. Such products as synthetic oil and rubber, such processes as the extraction of aluminium from clay and magnesium from sea-water, all of vast importance in creating an economy of abundance, were deliberately held up, and their development sabotaged by capitalist vested interests in time of peace. As soon, however, as they became useful in time of war, they were immediately developed, armies of scientists were set to work on them, money was lavished so that they could be brought into operation on a full scale.

In the same way, such medical discoveries as penicillin, which would have been carried on by neglected individual research workers in time of peace, were heavily subsidised, so that they could be rapidly brought into general use. And, most obvious of all, there is the question of atomic power. Before the war, the idea of atomic power was little more than a vision, but the needs of war brought about its development, not in a beneficial manner, but as the most destructive kind of military weapon the world has yet known.

Fallacy of Progress in War

These facts, the apparent stagnation of scientific and industrial development of the amenities of life during peacetime, and their sudden blossoming under the impetus of war, have led many people to say, unthinkingly, that war is the great medium of progress. Nothing could be farther from the truth.

In fact, as we have seen, almost every discovery which has been developed in war has in fact been originated in peacetime and could not be developed then for lack of support. Atomic energy, the aeroplane, a host of chemical and medical discoveries, and our old friend, the Channel Tunnel, all are the ideas of independent men, originated and neglected in peacetime, developed and perverted in time of war.

It is, as has often been observed, one of the essential contradictions of imperialist capitalism that, in order to preserve the class inequality necessary for its maintenance, it cannot give back to the workers in its own society the benefits of their productive effort. Where possible, the excess of production is used for export to dependent and colonial countries; when imperialist competition has saturated the world markets, war is the inevitable result, and then, not only is the surplus production absorbed in destructive activity, but the needs of the conflict force the seizure and perversion of discoveries beneficial in their original intention, to destructive ends.

The progress of war is in fact quite illusory. It represents one step forward, two back; it gives us civil aeroplanes, but it also gives us supersonic bombers and atom bombs for them to carry. It gives us penicillin, but it also gives us bacteriological warfare. It is, in fact, a phenomenon of a system by which natural scientific and industrial progress are continually halted and diverted from their course.

Real Progress
Logically, since the original discoveries are almost always made by individual scientists or engineers working on their own lines, or in small, neglected groups, during time of peace, it should be possible to develop them for popular benefit without war. Instead, except for destructive purposes, capitalism deliberately hinders them. True progress, by which the results of scientific progress are used immediately and beneficially for the improvement and broadening of life, can only be achieved in a society where a privileged system, with all its contradictions, has been ended, and where production is adapted to use rather than gain.
7th February 1948

Atom Bomb Statistics

Peace News (22nd July 1949) quotes from a lecture given in Bristol by Dr Daniel Posin, Professor of Physics at North Dakota State College in which he stated that it is now estimated that the atom bomb dropped on Hiroshima accounted for 35,000 men, women and children who perished leaving no trace; 25,000 whose bodies were found a mile off; 75,000 who died of flash-burn three miles off, and a further 20,000 affected by Gama rays who died of fever and sickness lasting not longer than 10 days.

That is a total of 155,000 compared with the figure of 60,000 given by John Hersey in that memorable piece of journalism, *Hiroshima* (Penguin Books).

But Hiroshima was an example of the atom bomb in its infancy, for as Dr Posin pointed out, "Since then the Bikini Mushroom has been produced and now it was known that a body of water could be made to ascend 20,000 feet from its river bed and to disappear as a cloud in the sky. But it was an atomic cloud that perhaps 75 miles away would shed its fine spray, contaminating man, woman and child and food and water with the merciless Gama rays."

And having taken in the full significance of this we cannot repress the somewhat sad reflection that the average person thinks of an anarchist as a desperate individual with a smoking bomb in his right hand and of the Government as a peace-loving father protecting him from the anarchist's home-made bomb!

More Political Death Sentences

One day it is Greek rebels being sentenced to death. Another day it is the Spanish underground fighters. Now from Beirut comes the news that twelve alleged members of the National Syrian party have been sentenced to death by a military tribunal for participating in a revolt against the state.

Fifty-three others were sentenced to prison terms ranging from three years to life in a mass trial which was one of the biggest ever to be held in Lebanon.

It appears that the party advocated a greater Syria, under the leadership of its head, Antoun Saadeh, who was captured on July 7, tried secretly and executed within twenty-four hours.

Those sentenced were charged with participating in raids early this month on five police stations in an attempt to capture arms and ammunition.

6th August 1949

The Bomb

The *Russia Has The Bomb* story exploded at just the right psychological moment for the Western bloc. American steel, aircraft and ship-building shares went up on Wall Street "in the belief that America will now build up its armaments, increasing employment and preventing any return of the near-slump". The *Daily Mirror* reports that, "There was great excitement in America. Radio network announcers broke into musical programmes. Newsboys shouting, 'The Russians have the Bomb', quickly sold out to people queuing for special editions of the newspapers. Telephone switchboards in newspaper offices were swamped with calls from people who had heard distorted versions of the radio announcements. The head of the US Senate Atomic Commission, Senator McMahon, heralding a race in bomb-production said: "America will rely on an overwhelming stockpile of atomic weapons as a warning against aggression". On the other hand, Dr Brock Chisholm, chairman of the World Health Organisation, had the cheerful comment: "Germ warfare weapons have been developed so much that the atomic bomb does not count any longer".

In Britain the bomb story served to take the public mind off the devaluation troubles, and has been followed by reports of an agreement with Fascist Portugal, 'Britain's Oldest Ally', under which this country will receive the entire output of a vital radioactive by-product of the Portuguese tin mines, and so achieve a world lead in atom experiments. The *Sunday Empire News* states that "Dr Salazar, Portuguese Dictator, took a personal interest in the negotiations", and goes on to say that "another important development is a decision to provide the British Navy with a flotilla of aircraft carriers for bombers capable of dropping atom bombs".

How nice for you, British taxpayer. We feel sure you will agree with the conclusion of the editorial on Devaluation in last *Sunday's Observer*: "In the prospect before us there are many uncertainties; but this one thing is quite certain: we must be ready now to work harder and live less well, or presently we shall be hard put to live at all".

1st October 1949

After Ten Years

They have made a desert and call it peace . . .

It is ten years since the war began, and we are as far from peace as ever. The whole course of the war and the post-war years has brought to fulfilment all the gloomy, but completely justified prognostications of the anarchist press, and as we survey the world of today, how can we avoid asking: "What else could you expect?".

Not one of the objects for which the war was supposedly fought, has been achieved; not one of the sacrifices of life, comfort, or material happiness has been made fruitful. In the words used by Herbert Read at the end of the war: "Our statesmen have made a chaos and call it victory. Millions of men are dead, and their silence is called peace."

Germany

Has the war succeeded in destroying German nationalism? Last week's elections give the answer. The victorious right-wing, campaigning under the flag of Imperial Germany, with brass bands, and a pastoral letter giving the support of the Catholic Church, will open the path for neo-Nazi groups like the German Right Party and the Economic Reconstruction Association of Loritz, the 'Blond Hitler'. An even more sinister prospect, reminding us of the secret alliance of the 1920s, between Moscow and the Junkers, the industrialists and the High Command, is given in the report that Herr Nadolny, formerly German Ambassador to Moscow has summoned his Right-wing circle to meet at Bad Godesberg. Among those invited are a number of prominent politicians from the satellite parties of the Soviet zone.

Meanwhile, the printer of the pornographic Jew-baiting paper *Der Stuermer* is to begin a new paper in Nuremberg, and the editor of the *Neuer Kurier*, published by a group of large industrialists, states that "My newspaper will show the German people what they lost in Hitler".

Who are responsible for this rebirth of reaction? In the words of a German correspondent of *Freedom*, "The new nationalist development has been furthered by the victorious and occupation powers not only indirectly by their brutal suppression and exploitation, but also directly by favouring Nazi officials, officers and politicians in the new State apparatus. The new German reaction has the political, financial and moral support of the authoritarian powers of the whole world."

Genocide

Was the war fought to end the massacre of whole populations, the concentration camps and the pogroms? As Lewis Mumford wrote:

"By our concentration on atomic weapons and similar airborne agents, we have publicly announced, in effect, that in any large struggle with an enemy power we shall abandon the methods of war and resort to the wholesale extermination of enemy populations.

The exact term for this method of attack is genocide: a crime against humanity which in the United Nations we piously profess to abhor."[1]

Nagasaki and Hiroshima cancelled out any Allied claim to moral superiority over their enemies. "If evil is to be retaliated by equal evil, what should prevent us from imitating the practises of the German extermination camps? For every rule of war the Japanese broke against us on the scale of hundreds, we have broken on the scale of thousands."[2]

To-day, the concentration camps still exist, run by our former allies. Sometimes even the occupants are the same.

Numerically, the biggest victims of the Nazis were the Jews. Can we claim that Britain fought to save them? The answer is that, outside Germany, no government did more than the British *before, during and after* the war, to prevent their escape from the Continent. We do not need to be reminded of Bevin's campaign against the post-war immigrants, which only ceased because of the requirements of Anglo-American foreign policy and the armed strength of Jewish nationalism (a phenomenon for which we bear a large share of responsibility); but it is as well to recall the British government's White Paper of May 17th, 1939, which planned to end Jewish immigration to Palestine. It never became law because it was never endorsed by the League Permanent Mandates. Commission, but, despite this:

"Its' provisions were implemented point by point: the sale of land to Jews was prohibited in 94.8 per cent of their homeland, access to it was refused to survivors of the great massacre, and shiploadsful of them drowned in 1941 and '42 in the waters of the Mediterranean and the Black Sea. Those who succeeded in getting ashore were sent to prison or deported to Eritrea, the Sudan or the Island of Mauritius; helpers in the work of rescue were treated as criminals and given long sentences of imprisonment."[3]

1. *Freedom* 6th August 1949.
2. Mumford's Programme for Survival.
3. Koestler, *Thieves in the Night.*

Has the war preserved the territorial independence of Britain? The answer is that this island has now become a bombing base for America. It was recently announced by the US General Vandenburg that the American Air Force in Britain, which was recently increased in size, was to be maintained after the end of the Air-Lift (although it had been stated when the first planes and men arrived that "There is no question of the USAAF establishing or reopening United States air bases in England").

General Bradley, Chief of Staff of the US Army, who recently visited this country for strategic discussions, stated to the Foreign Affairs Committee of the House of Representatives that the collective strategy of the North Atlantic Powers was being built on certain 'assumed factors'. These assumptions included the following:

That the United States would be charged with strategic bombing;

That the hard core of the ground power would come from Europe, aided by other nations as they were able to mobilise;

That Britain, France and the closer countries would be charged with the bulk of the short-range air attack and defence, while the United States would maintain a Tactical Air Force for its own ground and naval forces and the defence of the United States.

This amounts to an official confirmation of the recent brutally frank remarks by Senator Cannon, who said:

"In the next war, as in the last, let us equip soldiers from other nations, and let them send their boys into the holocaust, instead of sending our own boys. That is what long-range bombing means.

We will blast at centres of operation, and then let our allies send the army in, other boys, not our boys, to hold the ground we win."

Our contemporary, *Peace News*, drawing attention to the war fever which is being whipped up in the American press, reprints from an American magazine, a 'War Map' with the title *Battle Areas of the Next War: The Opening Campaigns*. One of the captions to the map explains that "Britain would be a base of great value, although Russian attacks would make it hazardous and might limit its use".

Here, then, is the pattern of the future, as planned for us from the other side of the Atlantic. Britain is to be an aircraft-carrier anchored off the continent, our homes are to be a 'legitimate' target for Soviet attack, while our men are doing the dirty work overseas.

Satisfied?

Now the question we would put to everyone this paper reaches is this: What are you going to do about it? *Will you make war again?*
3rd September 1949

War's Living Victims

It is a not insignificant paradox of what a Cambridge historian has grimly and not unjustly termed 'The Era of Violence', that a generation suicidally preparing for a third world war is concerning itself increasingly with the welfare of the disabled of the two great conflicts that disfigured the first half of the twentieth century.

Symptomatic of the spirit of the age was the recent visit of the Rt. Hon. H. A. Marquand MP, Britain's Minister of Pensions, to France to study pension problems there. This laudable initiative, in perfect keeping with the Government's policy of transforming a grudged service into one gladly given, followed immediately on the visit to Queen Mary's Hospital, Roehampton, of M Etienne Nouveau, President-General of the Fédération des Amputés de Guerre de France, and M Edouard Besnard, Secretary-General of the South West Region of the Fédération.

A feature of this inspection of Roehampton was the party's introduction to three teenage French boys there for artificial arm fitting, and the presence of a Parisian girl student of Roehampton's uniquely diversiform service for the disabled. Not long ago, four German ex-servicemen — on two of whom the Krukenberg operation had been performed, and two with Cineplastic operated arms — visited this country and demonstrated the results of these operations before British ex-servicemen and women and our most famous surgeons.

Infirmity, disease and disablement know no frontiers. It is remarkable how long the majority of thinking people have remained indifferent to this manifest truth. The professional healers have long recognised the gain to be made from a co-operative tackling of the universal problems of the disabled, by combined research and the pooling of invention. But it is only after the second instalment of large-scale war in our time, and with a third instalment feared, that people generally have become thoroughly alive to — and apprehensive of — the totality of the situation.

Hitherto public memory has been notoriously short and spasmodic. When we had finished crying in public each November over the lads who had been killed — an exhibition reinforced by the wearing of an artificial poppy whose size was held to denote the extent of sympathy with those of us who were only half killed — the artificially-limbed victims of artificially-inflicted injuries had

'had it' once more. But today's concern cannot be ascribed to any spontaneous rush of ephemeral and emotional pity. It arises from a sober realisation of the all-in quality of modern war, and a growing conviction that war and disablement are inseparable from the civilisation we have no intention of renouncing.

The historian may cite The Disabled Persons (Employment) Act of 1944. I will offer only two personal experiences, as an individual who travels around on harnessed crutches, minus one arm and one leg, in illustration of the general change of viewpoint.

In 1937 I was hailed by an elderly and apparently near-sighted woman in my Lancashire home town. She evidently thought she had known me at some time or other and said: "Eee, I hardly knew you. Have you been to the war then? And this is what it did to you? Don't answer! I know very well. Here, have a nice peppermint!"

In 1942 in London, another lady similar in age and class to the first, and a perfect stranger, asked me: "Did that happen in the blitz?" On my answering, "Oh no, I was wounded in the *last* war", the lady's interest faded immediately, and she left me without another word to, I must confess, my great amusement.

The significance of these incidents is that they are representative of a staggering transformation. The old Lancashire woman's vaguely comprehending interest was typical of those pre-1939 days. Had I in 1937 still been the slim youth in khaki, probably the good dame would have kissed me as one kisses a child who has fallen and hurt himself on the hard pavement. But the abrupt turning away of the Londoner reflected the view that nowadays war is no distant thing of deceiving enchantment inflicting disillusion and disablement upon young warriors in foreign fields, but something that has literally come home to us.

The ending of the 1939-1945 shooting war with the freeing of atomic energy was the final factor in a consistent swing of public opinion which has come down heavily on the side of pessimism. Thus since 1939 has been bred a spirit of doing one's duty by the disabled, illumined only by the dangerous notion that as we certainly cannot be assured of immunity against disablement our policy must necessarily be one of monetary and rehabilitatory insurance.

If it is objected that our thoroughly representative legislators, in decreeing thus that disablement, 'natural' or 'acquired', is an inevitable feature of the civilisation to which man clings more desperately than he clings to life itself, were moved only by the generous desire of the community to guarantee compensation to the unfortunately handicapped, I can only assert that this is beside my point. I am concerned with the peculiar quality of the despairing spirit behind such otherwise excellent legislation.

We may measure the stumps of limbs and assess the value of eyes by the timid method of tape measure and the relative gauge of any remaining range of vision. But to insure these at the price of the complete renunciation of hope is to begin at the wrong end. Can it be denied that so long as society prefers war to the sharing of privilege, that the corollory of industrial and military disablement will be as inevitable as death? When the hydrogen bombs have been dropped and the survivors among us sorted as between the disabled and the non-disabled, we may very well be faced with the situation in which the present percentages of pensionable and otherwise are reversed.

How ironical if the new Poppy Day must needs be for the benefit of the few *not* in receipt of a Government pension!

2nd September 1950   SAM WALSH

[Sam Walsh was a frequent writer to Freedom Press up to the time of his death (in the early 1970s). He was a living victim of World War One, having lost his right arm and right leg completely, so that he could not even be fitted with artificial limbs — Editor]

WHICH FUTURE?

The Western Powers are Following in Russia's Footsteps

That the post-war epoch would see a continuation of the general trend towards totalitarian forms has long been obvious to those anti-fascists who were not blinded by support of war. But the pace has hitherto been slow. Now, however, that pace has been enormously speeded up during the last few months. We had already noted with disquiet the anti-Communist proceedings in Australia and South Africa — not that we have even the smallest sympathy with the Red Fascists themselves, but are very much concerned with the rapid abandonment of liberal principles of civil liberty. Thirty years ago these principles, whose general acceptance was the fruit of centuries of hard struggle, seemed to have been achieved for good. Today we see them not only officially abrogated, but witness the extraordinary spectacle of a flight from liberal conceptions both light-hearted and seemingly unaware of the issues involved.

In the past we have often had to point to governmental measures which are in fact quite unworkable; that measures designed to 'test' a citizen's relationship with Communist activity in any sort of equitable way are quite impossible has been recognised by many people of all shades of political belief. In America, the Dies Committee and Senator McCarthy survive general ridicule and contempt only because of the general hysteria; such a situation is just part of the sinister paradox of our times.

The McCarran Act

The same verdict of unworkability has now overtaken the Communist Control Bill which Senator McCarran pushed through in the United States in spite of the President's veto. It is now being said that Truman will now have his revenge, but the irony of the situation (for Liberals) is that this means not that Truman will be able to throw out a piece of totalitarian legislation, but that he will be able to make it workable, that is, practicable.

This piece of legislation exemplifies some of the ludicrous, yet sinister, aspects of the legal cold war. Put forward as a Bill to protect democratic institutions from totalitarian enemies, it was aimed at Communists and Fascists. But Senator McCarran is himself known to be a friend of General Franco. So the chief promoter of an allegedly anti-totalitarian measure is himself a friend of fascism. Accordingly, Falangists were at first exempt from the attentions of the Bill. Now, presumably because of the manifest absurdity, they are brought within its scope.

We have already protested against the depriving of many Americans with Communist affiliations (or suspected of them) of their passports, a bureaucratic manoeuvre which, in effect, forbids them to leave the country. Now the reverse process is piling up queues of suspected foreigners on Ellis Island, while many applications for entry visas are being refused on the grounds of an applicant's association (at any time during the past thirty years) with Communism.

Such legislation is, however, commonplace in contemporary America. An occasional voice is raised against it, like that of Mr Dubridge, the president of the California Institute of Technology, who observed that in defending liberty we may very easily lose it. But there are others, like an Illinois professor who opposes such doubters and urge that one has to trust the government to do the right thing.

Continued Trend in Britain

All aliens in America are to be investigated for loyalty — a sufficiently formidable undertaking which will certainly involve considerable hardship to some and no doubt much injustice as well.

Now the same manoeuvre is to be undertaken in Britain also, for it is announced that 200 aliens are to be interviewed by officials of the alien office. Such investigations are not bound by the rules of evidence, are frequently influenced by statements not made upon oath, and which provide no facilities for the victim to cross-question informers who may, indeed, be unknown to him. Nor is it easy to provide a satisfactory avenue of appeal from any decisions the investigators may reach. Hence these aliens are not even protected by the ordinary processes which the law provides. When one remembers that they are already, often enough, victims of anxiety who sought asylum in this country from repression abroad, one can begin to envisage the kind of cruelties which such an investigation will perpetrate.

Now, too, it is reported that a new department of the Special Branch is to be set up to investigate the infiltration of the Communist Party into industry, to probe into industrial unrest and strikes, and so to imply that such are of a criminal character. This new branch will be headed by Superintendent Wilkinson, who speaks Russian and was Molotov's bodyguard during his visit to England.

Just how far we have slipped down the totalitarian path is shown by a recent question in Parliament. Concerning the disappearance of Professor Pontecorvo, Mr Peter MacDonald (Conservative, Isle of Wight) wanted to know how it was that Professor Pontecorvo was allowed to leave this country, *and take his family with him*, when his sister was the wife of a Communist? Pontecorvo has been naturalised for several years, and is therefore a British citizen. The implication of this question is clearly that a man's family can justifiably be held as hostages for his good behaviour and return. It is unfortunate that this system of family hostages is a feature of Soviet life which has received the most searing criticism in this country. Further comment is scarcely required.

The Observer's Position
If one has embraced a revolutionary conception, and has recoiled from existing society, one no longer finds oneself automatically involved in the judgements of society. Hence it is possible to see clearly the extraordinary capers of the legalistic struggle against Russian sympathisers and the vicarious patriots of the Communist Party. But if one accepts present day society, feels oneself to some extent part of it, it is difficult to take so objective a viewpoint. Embroiled in the social problems of governmental society, such people fail to recognise the pattern of affairs, fail to understand them. Arguments about the details of legalistic anti-Communism is likely to be completely sterile, so that meeting those who differ from us halfway (a course beloved of the realists) offers very little chance of success. The strength of the revolutionary anarchist position derives just from its uncompromising nature, its rejection of bargaining, and in its insistence on moral values. Such an uncompromising attitude is very much needed to stiffen what feeling there is for the older liberal principles.
28th October 1950

Peace and the Wolves

On the Eve of the Sheffield 'Peace Congress'

The Sheffield Peace Congress and the discussions going on in the United Nations serve to direct attention not merely to the desirability of peace but to the means necessary to achieve it. We would like to stress the idea of *achieving* peace, rather than that of 'preserving' it. The people of the great powers are too apt to congratulate themselves on enjoying peace (even if in ever briefer intervals) when they themselves are not directly involved in a declared war. They too often forget that war has been continuous in some parts of the world for the past forty or more years. They do not even consider it a state of war when a government wages continuous war on its people by means of a secret police, forced labour, concentration camps and the like. This situation may be termed 'peace' by some, but it is certainly not a condition which anarchists desire to preserve. Nor do we think that any honest, humane persons would regard our feelings as destructive of desirable conditions.

We have often enough indicated our hostility towards war. We have sufficiently stressed, too, our disbelief in the possibility of destroying totalitarian tyranny by going to war. And, finally, we have also made clear our attitude towards totalitarian regimes, such as those of the Cominform Empire; for we do not focus our attention on the struggle between the Russian government and its satellites, on the one hand, and the Anglo-American group on the other. For us the main struggle here is the struggle between the totalitarian governments and the populations they oppress. In a less acute form this same struggle exists between democratic governments and their subjects. Our sympathies lie with the ruled against the rulers. Whatever the political rivalries of the powers, we stress the common interest of the peoples of the world against all who exploit them and deprive them of the opportunity to organise their own lives.

The Disarmament Issue

This bald statement must serve as a background for our attitude towards the Sheffield Peace Congress. First and foremost, of course, is the fact that it is a Communist outfit. This means that whatever ends it seems to serve, its real purpose is to advance the foreign policy of Russia. It is only necessary to recall the 'People's Convention' which the British Communist Party organised in the winter of 1940-41 when Russia was allied to Nazi Germany and the British Communist Party was consequently opposed to the war. The People's Convention demanded a negotiated peace, sought to mobilise all sentimental anti-war opinion, with all the familiar trappings of petitions and public statements by prominent intellectuals, preferably non-Communists. Six months later Hitler invaded Russia, the British Communists became pro-war overnight and the People's Convention was dropped, leaving its sentimental pacifist adherents looking, and perhaps feeling, very foolish.

It is needless to indicate that the same purpose underlies the Sheffield outfit.

Attlee's Broadside

In the circumstances, most that Attlee had to say about the Congress was perfectly justified. He stressed the obvious fact that the Cominform countries which represent themselves as peaceful, are in fact about as peaceful as Hitler and Goebbels. He might have been more modest about the peace-loving intentions of the Democratic powers — we have often stressed that all governmental regimes resort to war, and derive certain important benefits from war. For he could have gone on to point out that the Democracies are not able to recognise Peace Congresses inside the Cominform countries and denounce their rulers as warmongers.

The *Daily Worker*'s reply to Attlee was interesting. They sought to give the impression of a point by point examination of his speech. But they wholly omitted to mention or discuss Silone's anecdote of the open contempt for truthfulness expressed by the old Comintern, which Attlee tellingly recounted. He also punctured the democratic façade of elected delegates. "It was announced in a Viennese paper that the Austrian delegates would be elected at a meeting to be held on Oct. 21st. Sounds alright, doesn't it? However, as early as Oct. 5th application was made for visas for sixteen named delegates. The results of the 'election' were known sixteen days before." The *Daily Worker* made no mention of this.

'Humanising War'

They scored a point over Attlee's statement that "You cannot humanise war, you cannot draw up a set of 'Queensberry rules' which will rid it of its horrors. The only answer is to root out war itself, war and the causes which make it." The *Daily Worker* rightly points out that this contradicts the Hague Convention, which seeks to humanise war, and the Nuremburg Trials which condemned many Germans for waging war in complete disregard of the laws and customs of war."

On the other hand it could be said that Attlee was truthful, and merely let the cat out of the bag; for the fact is that in war, it is not rules, but policy and expediency which determines the choice of military method. This was the basis for our denunciation of the Nuremburg trials — which Russia and the Communists, be it remembered, declared to be altogether too mild.

Mr Attlee said of the Sheffield Congress that it was "an appeal by the wolves to get the sheep to demonstrate against the use of shepherds and sheepdogs". In this he gets near the knuckle, perhaps nearer than he intended, for though we regard the Communists and their dupes as properly compared to wolves and sheep, we find the rest apt in a sense he did not intend. For if the sheep should avoid the wolves, they also have much to gain by freeing themselves from shepherds who fleece them and sell them as mutton.

The Reality Behind the Battle of Words

Let us, however, pierce to the core of the matter. The fact is that the Western Powers have decided to re-arm against Russia. The purpose of the Stockholm Peace Petition and its offshoot at Sheffield is explicitly to limit armaments. Such congresses are held, however, exclusively outside Russia and the Cominform countries. Attlee and Truman seek to strengthen the armed power of Democracies; Stalin and the Peace Congresses seek to weaken it. Stated thus blankly it is clear that the Congress has nothing to do with peace — and, let us state, Anglo-American re-armament has nothing to do with it either.

Realism in Peace

Once again we face the question of the past fifty years — how does it come about that no-one desires war, yet it has been an almost continuous shadow over our generation? It is obvious, as Attlee pointed out, that one does not need a petition to know that men and women desire peace. And to anarchists, at least, it is obvious that one does not get what one wants by signing on a dotted line, still less when it is such a crooked line as the Communists provide.

Those who oppose war used to think that it was as simple as just acting out one's desire for peace and refusing to support war or its preparation. But new problems appeared after the first world war. There was not much difference between the political structure of Imperial Germany of the Kaiser and the British Empire. But there was an undoubted difference between the democracies and the Nazis, sufficient to puzzle the one-time anti-militarist left into support for the second war. Now difference between the Russian type of dictatorship and the democracies is still enough to complicate the anti-war question.

Hence opposition to Allied re-armament, by itself, manifestly strengthens the 'other side', and is repugnant to all but irresponsibles and religious cranks. Especially so since the same opposition cannot be openly canvassed behind the Iron Curtain. It is clear, therefore, that something more is needed. The difficulty lies in the fact that initiative does not lie with the people whose interests are at one — the common people all the world over. Instead it lies with governments, who know of no other way than that of building up armies and bombs. Whose interests demand that initiative should remain with an oligarchy whether socialist or capitalist, and not with the people at large.

Is it necessary to remind our readers once more how the various wars are fought between different line-ups among the powers; even that Russia can start on one side and end up on the other? Is it not clear that such temporary and mutable alliances do not safeguard peace. The underlying reality is that war and peace alike, governments and people are locked in permanent struggle, even if it is not conscious and open.

If therefore the peoples of the West wish to demonstrate their desire for peace they must do so in a way which will win them the support of the people of the Iron Curtain countries. If they do not do so, they will merely weaken themselves without avoiding war. Such support is not to be won through the intermediaries of governments. And since the capitalist system cannot now continue to exist without war — whether the State Capitalism of Russia or the so-called 'free' capitalism of America — the way to peace does not lie through the continuance of such a system.

Hence the practical problems of securing peace involve the problems of bringing about that revolution which will place initiative, with both freedom and responsibility, in the hands of the people at large. Which will terminate the conception of government as a necessary tutelage and usher in an anarchist society.

The Hidden Factors
But to express the matter thus simply is to neglect a most serious difficulty of operating a free society without government. It is much more serious than that for it saps the very desire for peace which everyone takes so readily for granted. The fact is that many men and women, however much they desire peace on the surface, actually secure greater fulfilment and self-realisation from war. It is not simply that wages are higher, that the material rewards are higher than those of peace. It is the emotional rewards, the heightened excitement, the sense of purpose, the need to live in the moment which may be our last, the relaxation of sexual prohibitions. In short, the realisation of these psychological factors favouring war, is yet another indictment of the 'peace' which we earlier stated to be not fit to preserve. It makes the need for a form of society which brings fulfilment to its members even more necessary, even more certainly the practical prerequisite for real peace.
11th September 1950

Secret Police at Work

Home Secretary Reveals unlimited power of Special Branch

The questions put to the Home Secretary about the methods used for allowing or refusing entry to foreign delegates who wished to attend the 'Peace Congress' in Sheffield have aroused strong feelings and revealed the sinister role played by MI5 and the Special Branch. For it is quite clear, as we shall attempt to show, that these organisations are a law to themselves: they need give no explanation for their actions, either to their victims or to any government department answerable to the public.

In a letter to the Secretary of the organising committee of the 'Peace' Congress, the Home Office gave a list of 43 people who "were likely to be refused leave to land" if they came to the congress. But the Home Office added that "those whose names are not on the list can still not be sure that they will be allowed to land. It will be for the immigration officers to decide."

The *Manchester Guardian* (11th November 1950) points out that the "immigration officers act under general instructions from the Home Office with, in these cases, presumably, detailed information from MI5". But in fact their powers transcend any instructions from government departments. For instance, Mr Ede stated in the House (November 14th) that of 82 foreigners to whom visas had been granted, and who presented themselves at the ports, 75 were given leave to land. Thus, seven were turned back by our Secret Police against the instructions of the government department which granted them visas. And no explanations are given. So that if the immigration officers or the Home Secretary have been given false information about a person, there is no redress. And what are the Minister's sources of information? That is also a mystery. When he was asked how he could assess the individual merits of various Soviet delegates, Mr Ede replied: "*You* would be surprised how much I know about them and about other people of alien origin." On another occasion, when asked where he obtained his information, his reply was "from various sources. I would not like to be too precise because it might hinder us from getting information on another occasion."

A further example of procedure was given to the House by Sir Richard Ackland (17th November 1950) when referring to the experiences of members of the American delegation. They were not allowed to get in touch with him by phone from the airport and later, in a letter from Paris, their treatment is described:

"We were severely grilled. I came through the questioning easily. I told of my previous visit and my connection with the National Religion and Labour Foundation. We all thought in the long interval of waiting that the British authorities were in touch with our State Department, and that the long finger of America was in the pie. We were kept waiting for more than five hours under strict surveillance and the American delegation was ordered to leave for Paris immediately, and not to return. Although asked for, no reason was given for this drastic and tragic action."

In a letter to the *Manchester Guardian* Victor Gollancz sums-up the position very frankly:

"Any refusal of free assembly is deplorable, but what is really fatal is that we, in the present state of the world, should have taken even half a step on the road to a secret police. When, to use your own words, 'minor Foreign Office clerks or immigration officers whose speciality is smugglers and criminals' are given the job of investigating just how dangerous it might be to allow A to express his opinions, just how influential B is in the Cominform, and just how much contamination C might spread during a few days in this country, this is not yet, not nearly, the GPU, or the Gestapo, or whatever body it was that looked out for 'dangerous thoughts' in Japan. But a faint stench begins to arise, nevertheless, from these drains, and to pollute our air. For God's sake do not let us allow it."

We would, however, add that the 'faint stench' to which Gollancz refers has long been in our nostrils, for the Sheffield scandal has only brought to the public's notice a scandal which has existed for a long time.

We recall that two years ago, the *Freedom Defence Committee* issued a fourteen foolscap page document dealing with the treatment of aliens landing and embarking at ports, and making a number of recommendations for safeguarding the rights of travellers. It includes the correspondence that passed between the Committee and the Home Office which reveals in black and white the unlimited powers conferred on immigration officials. It also reveals the way port officials can abuse their powers as a result of travellers' ignorance of their rights — very much in the same way as the police obtain statements from people, or enter houses without search warrants, simply because their victims are ignorant of the law.

As a first step, Mr Gollancz might publish a pamphlet telling the man in the street what rights he still has. And then might it not be possible for socially conscious men and women, above party politics, to come together to publicly agitate for an awakening of the people in defence of freedom, before all human values are thrown overboard in the name of 'freedom'?

25th November 1950

Neither Sheffield Nor Berlin

In June of this year, a Congress for Cultural Freedom was held in Berlin. It turned out to be as bogus as the Sheffield 'Peace' Congress for, if the latter were engineered by the Communists the former was simply a counter blast by those committed to the 'democratic' cause. And just as the delegates to Sheffield could be divided into the sheep and the wolves, so the Berlin show succeeded, by falsely representing its real motives, in drawing many independent intellectuals who must now regret their association with that body. The document issued last month by the Executive Committee of the Congress for Cultural Freedom with the title 'We Put Freedom First' should leave them in no doubt as to its true nature.

The document we are examining consists in the main of a series of questions and answers: the questions being 'typical' of those they have received from people throughout the world since the Berlin Congress launched its Manifesto.

In the introductory note the Executive Committee (which includes such names as David Rousset, Arthur Koestler and Ignazio Silone) declare that "we want our civilisation to survive" and two conditions are essential, "freedom and peace". For them freedom is the more important "since peace is a function of freedom. A nation enslaved can at any time be whipped by its leaders into war hysteria and aggression."

That wars are an inevitable concomitant of Capitalism is not even considered by these gentlemen of "the educated classes who determine the intellectual climate of the nation", or is it that such a point of view would obviously drive them out of both camps — into the third camp where Ignazio Silone once stood? Yet they also tell us that the task they have set themselves is "to change the present confused and poisoned intellectual climate". When they baldly state that "the threat to peace came successively from countries in various degrees of enslavement: militarist Prussia, Fascist Italy, Nazi Germany, Japan, Soviet Russia" by such a half-truth they are simply adding to the confusion which they so deplore.

The limitations of the Congress for Cultural Freedom (we shall in future refer to it as the CCF) are revealed in the first Answer: "We do not pretend that our democracies are anywhere approaching an ideal State. We are defending our relative freedoms against the total unfreedom of dictatorial regimes." With such a starting point it is inevitable that this CCF should become simply a tool of the Americans (and their satellites) and a recruiting sergeant for the next war. We suggest that they adopt Mr Churchill's high moral slogan of the last war: that anyone prepared to kill a Nazi was an ally, with of course the substitution of Russian for Prussian, as the Nazis will be our allies this time.

Let us see to what depths this 'lesser evil' policy can drag these men of the 'educated classes'. To the question whether a real collaboration between "Socialists and right-wing parties is possible or even desirable" our brains trust answers "We believe such a collaboration to be both possible and desirable — with certain reservations." It is desirable "if its objectives are limited to the task of uniting each free nation against threats to its freedom from within and without and thus acting as a deterrent against aggression. It is *undesirable* if the slogan of unity serves as a cloak for attempts to suppress the democratic rivalry between political parties and groups". But this is exactly what all 'democratic' governments tell us and since we have been living in the shadow of aggression — first it was Germany, now Russia — for the past twelve years and this seems to have become a permanent state, the CCF may as well 'come clean' and forget about the long-term policy altogether.

To the question "What about Spain?" they answer that they abhor Franco's regime but as it is "unlikely that fifteen million Spaniards will start a war of aggression against the world", whereas Russia will continue the "war of aggression they started in Korea", we can forget about Spain for the time being. Actually these are not their words. Theirs is a much more responsible and diplomatic language; the language of strategists and men who "determine the intellectual climate of a nation". "Therefore our emphasis" — they answer — "is on the immediate and principal danger from the East, and we refuse to fall into the trap of Cominform propagandists who want to divert our attention and energies from the real threat into a crusade against Francisco Franco."

Another questioner asks: "Your Manifesto protests against totalitarian slavery, but is silent on matters like racial discrimination against Negroes in the United States. Why?" Once more the Communist bogey is the excuse for their silence. "Communist propaganda deliberately plays up the Negro question to divert attention from the totalitarian threat and to spread confusion in the progressive camp."

The 'lesser evil' philosophy is well summed-up in a footnote to their answer to the above question:

"Incidentally during the last decade the number of negroes lynched in the United States has never exceeded two a year. However horrifying even two such crimes are, they only represent a fraction of one per cent of the number of crimes against humanity committed annually by the totalitarian regimes."

We have said enough, we believe, to expose the Congress for Cultural Freedom as yet another phoney organisation from which we can hope for nothing. Their ineffectualness is only matched by their vanity and their impertinence.

"Tolerance of mental aberrations cannot be extended to members of the professional intelligentsia. Farmhands and factory workers labour under the handicap of a fragmentary education, and often it is physically impossible for them to get at the facts. *The professional intelligentsia has no such excuses*. Refusal to acknowledge facts, conscious or unconscious distortion of facts, frivolity and foolishness on the part of those who influence public opinion, are crimes against the spirit even if rarely definable by law.

"Before the last war, intellectuals who supported Hitler's policy of concentration camps, or refused to admit that German concentration camps existed, were ostracised by progressive intellectuals. The writers and scientists who to-day support Russian concentration camps and mass deportations, or refuse to admit the facts concerning them, are still regarded as 'progressive', 'idealistic', and so on. We are opposed to the persecution of the ignorant and the innocent. We are opposed to the toleration of the totalitarian creed in the professional intelligentsia. *We refuse to grant intellectual respectability to the active or passive accomplices of tyranny, terror and defamation.*"

Silone and Koestler were for many years active members of the Communist Party. Of the other members' political pasts we know nothing. But to Silone and Koestler we must put this question: As prominent Communist Party members for many years, were you aware that concentration camps and a secret police existed in Russia long before you left the Party?

As we have repeatedly pointed out in *Freedom*, there is room for an international Manifesto drawn up by men and women above party politics, and whose concern is not as to which is the lesser or the greater evil, but between what is good and what is evil. For this they must have the courage to concentrate on the long-term struggle. The CCF condemns such an approach, "A nation is doomed to perish if a considerable part of its population refuses to fight against an immediate threat unless and until an ideal state of social justice is achieved." It must be pointed out that what is becoming a permanent struggle against an 'immediate threat' — and today every country is declaring that it is being threatened by a potential aggressor — is the most potent weapon for the ultimate destruction of *all* values.

Koestler and Silone to-day support expediency, and all the somersaults it implies, against those 'highbrow French intellectuals' who maintain that what is most important in our political conduct is that "our revolutionary conscience should be kept clean". What now separates Silone from the Ilya Ehrenburgs and other Soviet writers, is only *time*. As admirers of Silone's works we write these words with a deep feeling of regret.

The CCF will in fact, if successful, tie the writers of the 'West' hand and foot to the American military machine in the name of 'relative freedom against total unfreedom'. Their slogan is: "Who is not with *us* is with the Stalinists". They must be challenged by those men and women with the courage to say: "We stand alone, against both American and Russian imperialism, for what we consider to be the truth and man's real social aspirations".
9th December 1950

Re-arming Germany

How soon the fine phrases of the Allies can be forgotten is a perfect example of the technique of making people forget what the politicians *want* them to forget. We were told that never again would Germany be allowed to arm, and that we, the Allies (US, France, Britain and Russia) would occupy Germany for fifty years, if necessary, to ensure that Germans were not allowed to plunge the world into another conflict (or words to that effect). Only six years, since these noble words were uttered, we know that the Russians have armed the police in their zone and trained them as a military formation, and now the Americans are doing likewise. The alleged purpose of this measure is to relieve American forces from the duty of guarding American dumps in their zone. A further message from the American zone states that the US Army there has "ordered 21,000 of its German and displaced persons guards to receive small arms training and to live in 'barracks' ".

It's the thin edge of the wedge.
19th August 1950   LIBERTARIAN

Do You Accept Permanent War?

This issue of *Freedom* will be in the hands of its readers in time for an anniversary — the eleventh since the outbreak of the Second World War on 3rd September 1939. For many, these eleven years represent a substantial fraction of their lives; for younger people, almost the whole of their adult lives. The conditions of war have been the main external factors pressing on the existence of our generation; the events of recent months make it nearly certain that war conditions, if not war itself, are likely to remain the dominant social factor.

For English people, war has hitherto only been acceptable as a temporary expedient to meet an apparently pressing political situation. That it was losing this temporary, improvised character began to suggest itself when, after 'the ending of hostilities', permanent conscription was retained instead of being repealed with relief, as the politicians promised. Now it is 'peace' which has a partial, temporary character. The permanent war preparedness of Leninist-Stalinist Russia, of Fascist Italy and Nazi Germany is now the lot of the Western Democracies also. Just as they were ahead of us in the trend towards permanent war, so Britain is slightly ahead of America. Eleven years ago, there were many in this country who deluded themselves that the so-called 'anti-Fascist' war was necessary for the safeguarding of peace; but there are few so naive as to find acceptable the American wishful illusion of 'Let's get World War Three over and done with'.

This is the world we live in. Those who find it an acceptable world may also be able to accept its permanent war. But for those who find the social structure of our society so faulty that they wish to alter it, the growing dominance of war appears as a ghastly symptom requiring analysis and explanation.

The 'Anniversary'
First of all, it is apparent that to consider 3rd September as a starting point, 'eleven years from then . . .' is illogical and absurd. A better, though still by no means an initial date, is 1931, the outbreak of the war of China and Japan. Besides making clearer that the war has longer roots in our lives than our 'anniversary' suggests, consideration of some aspects of the 1931 war helps to clarify the general problems of war for us.

In those days there were many statesmen and captains of

industry who supported or apologised for Japan, whose colonial war seemed to them to be no different from the ventures of the British for two hundred years before. With Sir John Simon and Mr L. S. Amery as their spokesmen, they formed a tactless group of the Right. The Left had for many years denounced imperialism and colonial methods of rule. That the British had got away with it in less enlightened times seemed to them no reason at all for letting Japan get away with it in the mid-twentieth century. The Left therefore supported China ('Arms for China', etc.) — and also Chiang Kai-Shek. They laid the foundation for that wartime build-up of the Chinese leader as a champion of the 'free' nations. This is a significant point, because it illustrates the necessity which war lays upon its supporters of 'adjusting' the truth to suit political requirements — as much or more for the Left as for the Right. To support Chiang Kai-Shek the Left has to forget that only a few years before he had been the 'Butcher of the Chinese Revolution' who had fought his way to power through an appalling political slaughter of Chinese workers. As WAR COMMENTARY pointed out during the time of the Churchill-Roosevelt-Chiang conversations at Cairo, he has more blood on his hands than any other successful politician with the exception of Stalin. Political fashions have now stripped the veneer from this particular leader. The truth, however, has always been there, however much the Left tried to gloss over or conceal it. It is perhaps unnecessary to do more than point to the glorification of Churchill by the pro-war Left.

The important matter here is that the claims of truth are largely incompatible with the waging of war or with acceptance of the war-pressed social structure. The more one adheres to the truth — both for moral reasons and in order to understand the modern dilemma — the less one can put up with the half-truths and downright lies of war propaganda.

Why is it Acceptable?
To turn from those who manipulate the facts of history for the purposes of propaganda to those at the receiving end is equally disillusioning, perhaps more so. For soon it becomes apparent that however flimsy the propaganda pretexts, and however much 'we all hate war', there is something about war which is highly acceptable to modern men and women. Even before 1939 there were those who were prepared to admit that the only time they had ever been really happy was in 1914 to 1918, and who were

frank enough to say that they would welcome the outbreak of hostilities.

Psychologists have somewhat diffidently explained satisfaction in war by reference to 'release of aggressive drives in a socially acceptable form'. The layman is often aware that the pulse beats quicker in wartime, that the sense (one should say the illusion) of purpose lends point to life. Many are able to recognise that army life with all its squalor has something to offer which wage-labour on a clerk's stool cannot.

That this is so — and who can deny it? — is a formidable criticism of peacetime society. Students of militaristic totalitarianism know the dictators make political use of this pseudo-corporate spirit, and can feel that there is something severely wrong with a social structure that gives such psychological handles to reaction. Radical psychologists like Reich have been courageous enough to state outright that war provides sexual gratifications which peace denies, and that such a perversion of natural sexual desire itself stems from the sexual repression of our society. Th 'drift to war' is not a *drift* at all, it is a *drive*, all the more uncontrolled because its motivating forces — the need for an outlet (a socially tolerated outlet) for repressed sexual urges — are unconscious. That they are unconscious is again due to the structure and *mores* of our society.

Sexual repression has an answer to all this — it is simply nonsense, say those whose training forces them to be blind to everything which an anti-sexual training has dubbed taboo. But the band of those who say this with 'sincerity' (that is, complete self-deception in this case) is a diminishing one. The army and the forces generally are careful not to diminish the appeal of their known opportunities for sexual licence, though they do not openly offer such.

An article in *Picture Post* (26th August 1950) on why recruits volunteered for Korean service is remarkably frank within the repressive framework of our times. Almost all the men interviewed found civvy street unsatisfactory. One, aged 25, "went all over the Far East in the war, wants to go back. Says he's a freelance, has no relations and . . . '*well, it's not the army, actually, I'm going in for* . . .'" (our italics). Another, aged 27, "admits there are also unspecified possibilities in the Far East, like those he found in Hamburg. But if you press him too closely, again draws your attention to the news." That there are reasons which most are unwilling to put into words (still less into print) is clearly implied in this article, and *Picture Post* are to be congratulated on avoidance of the hypocrisy of stressing patriotic motives whose superficial character is only too apparent.

What is one to think of a society whose sexual mores are such that war is a necessity to provide an outlet for them? How trifling is the sexual 'delinquency' of adolescents in the *News of the World* compared with this vast delinquency of the social structure?

The Economic War . . .

Who shall say what is the fundamental, the underlying factor which makes war inevitable in our society? Sexual repression is necessary to make war acceptable — in army ideology licence goes hand in hand with chastity for 'decent' women, and all that revolting farrago abour 'honour' in sexual affairs of an open character. But it seems unlikely that sexual repression, or any other psychological factor, is a *cause* of war; they only operate within the framework provided by war, and in its absence find other outlets. But they do not create the form of such outlets.

For this reason it seems to us that a more fundamental (though not necessarily more important) cause is the economic system of competition made necessary by the inherent expansionist demands of the capitalist mode of production, with its demand to 'export or burst'. Eight years ago, WAR COMMENTARY published an article with the significant title 'War Without End'. It pointed to the economic causes of war, and described how a war, far from relieving (still less removing) those causes, only exacerbated them. Hence the 'end' of the war would see the foundations of a 'new' conflict. And all this at the expense of the living standards of the workers of the world.

. . . In Sum

An analysis such as the above — and we believe it to be truthful, and not a merely partisan account — shows that every aspect of war, if viewed without hypocrisy or idle gesturing, exhibits the social structure in a discreditable light. And our analysis has done this without once referring to another side — the actual horrors, miseries, bereavements, psychological deformities, which individuals suffer in the course of war. Politicians are either cynical, like the imperialists Simon and Amery; or, like the Left, willing to travesty the truth for the sake of 'progressive' propaganda. We could have added those pacifists who seek to whitewash the other side, or who delude themselves that 'goodwill' on both sides is all that's necessary. Briefly, they can all be described as either shameless or lying, cynical or wishful.

The individuals who accept war with open reluctance, but secret anticipation — and it is important not to shy away from this truth which is becoming more and more manifest — are also seen to be driven to the immortality of war by the frustration of natural and human urges.

Finally, war is itself the product of an economic and psychological defeat for millions of men and women the world over.

It does not require much logic to see that war and our society are intimately tied up with one another; that criticism of war leads to basic criticism of society. Nor is it a long step from war-reluctance to war-resistance to the desire to alter the basics of society in a radical fashion — to take up, in short, a revolutionary position.

But it is also clear that to arrive at such a position requires that one has some idea of what life is for, some conception of a better life. The revolutionary urge is not mere blind destruction; it seeks to destroy something foul and life-destructive, in order to permit human life to expand in a life-giving manner. Effective resistance to war arises out of a hopeful attitude to *life*, with a willingness to see the rottenness (there is no other word) of contemporary social structures.

. . . In Practice

When we have said all this, there still remains the fact of an increasing trend towards totalitarian denial of all life-giving activities. There is no use burking the effects of Russian expansionism, nor is it effectively answered by pointing to the defects of western imperialism — or of denying that they exist as the war-supporting socialists and, doubtless, anarchists of the coming war will claim. We are concerned with life, and with individual fulfillment in life. Our movement knows better than any other, perhaps, the effects of Bolshevik dictatorship. But, as our analysis shows, we also know what the actual, as distinct from the wishfully hoped-for, effects of war are. It is for this reason that our anti-militarism is only a part of our general revolutionary outlook and activity.

The coming war will accentuate the totalitarian trends in society. The revolution will uproot them and at the same time provide the basis for a satisfactory organisation of life. We were against the last war because we were anti-Fascist; our anti-totalitarianism makes us anti-war in the coming struggle.

At the beginning of our analysis we glanced at recent history in the Sino-Japanese war. In the war that began in 1931 and is still going on, the one bright page has been the revolutionary struggle of the Spanish workers against Fascism — against all that way of life which still menaces us. We know that the Spanish workers were crushed not merely by Franco and the 'Non-Interventionists', but also by the counter-revolutionary Stalinists and the help they received from Russia. We also know that with all that arrayed against them, the Spanish workers' revolutionary struggle achieved more, and struck more hope in the hearts of workers in other parts of the world than all the truth suppressing propaganda of the left.

For those who see the war with an unwavering eye, who do not crush down the contempt which contemplation of society arouses in them, the revolutionary struggle will be the most practical activity for our times, and the most life-giving one.

2nd September 1950

Mankind is One

declare UNESCO Biologists in Statement on Race Problems

"Biological studies lend support to the ethic of universal brotherhood; for man is born with drives towards co-operation, and unless these drives are satisfied, men and nations alike fall ill. Man is born a social being who can reach his fullest development only through interaction with his fellows. The denial at any point of this social bond between men and men brings with it disintegration. In this sense, every man is his brother's keeper. For every man is a piece of the continent, a part of the main, because he is involved in mankind."

The idea that man is inherently social, that a co-operative commonwealth based on universal brotherhood, lies at the root of all anarchist teachings. Yet the passage above is not quoted from anarchist writings: it is the concluding paragraph from the remarkable UNESCO 'Statement by Experts on Race Problems', issued in Paris on 20th July 1950.

This succinct statement — it covers three and a half mimeographed pages of typescript — contains matters which are of tremendous importance to a world hovering between one war and the next. It touches a number of current problems in an authoritative manner, and therefore is of exceptional interest to all who are concerned with the future welfare of man. To anarchists it gives added scientific support to the basic conception of anarchism.

Eminent Scientists of Many Nations

The original statement drafted at Unesco House, Paris, by the following experts: Professor Ernest Beaglehole (New Zealand); Professor Juan Comas (Mexico); Professor L. A. Costa Pinto (Brazil); Professor Franklin Frazier (USA); Professor Morris Ginsberg (UK); Dr Humayan Babir (India); Professor Claude Levi-Strauss (France); Professor Ashley Montagu (USA). The text was revised by Professor Ashley Montagu, after criticism submitted by Professor Hadley Cantril, E. G. Conklin, Gunnar Dahlberg, Theodosino Dobzhansky, L. C. Dunn, Donald Hager, Julian S. Huxley, Otto Kineberg, Wilbert Moore, H. J. Muller, Gunnar Myrdal, Joseph Needham. We print the names in full to show how representative the list is, and to indicate that the view expressed is general among leading biological scientists, and therefore cannot be dismissed as the idealist conception of a small group.

They stress at the outset that "scientists have reached general agreement in recognising that mankind is one; that all men belong to the same species, *homo sapiens*. . . . The likenesses among men are far greater than their differences." They go on to make an important definition: "A race, from the biological standpoint, may therefore be defined as one of the group of populations constituting the species *homo sapiens*. These populations are capable of interbreeding with one another but, by virtue of the isolating barriers which in the past kept them more or less separated, exhibit certain physical differences as a result of their somewhat different biological histories. These represent variations, as it were, on a common theme."

After specifically indicating that the English, the Americans, the Jews, the Indians or the Chinese are not races, the statement declares: "National, religious, geographic, linguistic and cultural groups do not necessarily coincide with racial groups: and the cultural traits of such groups have no demonstrative genetic connection with racial traits, because serious errors of this kind are habitually committed when the term 'race' is used in popular parlance, it would be better when speaking of the human races to drop the term 'race' altogether and speak of *'ethnic groups'*."

The importance of this paragraph is very great: for it means that the basic unity of all men transcends these "national, religious, geographic, linguistic and cultural groups". One's first loyalty is to the brotherhood of mankind, and not to one's government or one's religion or to any mere group loyalty.

Three Main Divisions

Men may be divided into three major divisions: the Mongoloid, the Negroid and the Caucasoid divisions. But the UNESCO statement is careful to point out that just as these divisions arose from the separation of mankind geographically, so they are not static "and there is every reason to believe that they will change in the future."

There is no scientific ground for one division regarding itself as superior to any other. "Given similar degrees of cultural opportunity to realise their potentialities, the average achievement of the members of each ethnic group is about the same. The scientific investigations of recent years fully support the dictum of Confucius (551-478 BC): 'Men's natures are alike: it is their habits that carry them apart'."

And they drive the lesson home: "As for personality and character, these may be considered raceless. In every human group a rich variety of personality and character types will be found, and there is no reason for believing that any human group is richer than any other in these respects."

Now, the bearing of all this on the colour bar is obvious. It also bears on war propaganda about the 'sub-human' Japanese, or about the Russians). The UNESCO scientists are not afraid to direct the light of science on such dark places as Malan's laws against mixed marriages in South Africa, or similar laws in some States in the USA, or the Nuremberg laws of Hitler. As their statement is absolutely direct, we reproduce their passage in full:

"With respect to race mixture, the evidence points unequivocally to the fact that this has been going on from the earliest times. Indeed, one of the chief processes of race-formation and race-extinction or absorption is by means of hybridisation between races or ethnic groups. Furthermore, no convincing evidence has been adduced that race mixture of itself produces biologically bad effects. Statements that human hybrids frequently show undesirable traits, both physically and mentally, physical disharmonies and mental degeneracies, are not supported by the facts. There is, therefore, no *biological* justification for prohibiting inter-marriage between persons of different ethnic groups."

Later on they repeat this: "There is no evidence that race mixture as such produces bad results from the biological point of view. *The social results of race mixture, whether for good or for ill, are to be traced to social factors.*" (Our italics.)

The apologists for the colour bar are thus deprived of their chief arguments. If they fall back on social difficulties of 'race-mixture', then it is incumbent on them to seek to dispel the causes of these difficulties — ignorance and segregation of communities. Their real motives — the attempt to maintain a difference of social status — are thus exposed. "All normal human beings are capable of learning to share in a common life, to understand the nature of mutual service and reciprocity, and to respect social obligations and contracts. *Such biological differences as exist between members of different ethnic groups have no relevance to problems of social and political organisation, moral life and communication between human beings.*" (Our italics.)

Imperialism and War
The implications of these statements are very far-reaching. They condemn as impertinent and superfluous the pretensions of imperialism whereby one group of men impose their domination on another, *even when they claim to do so for the good of the colonial people.* They condemn utterly the arrogance of the white (caucasoid) peoples towards the coloured (Negroid and Mongoloid). And they do so from no merely negative attitude. The statement of the UNESCO scientists rests on the solid positive fact of the biological unity of mankind.

The stressing of this unity could not be more timely, coming as it does at a moment when the menace of yet another global war seems more or less imminent. In the face of scientific knowledge the responsibility for continued war lies clearly on the social institutions of mankind, political, rational, economic and religious. Anarchists have long denounced these institutions which *divide* mankind and have insisted on internationalism, on the essential brotherhood of man. Now the scientists have explicitly endorsed this teaching.

Co-operation a Biological Tendency

Let us not fail to note the importance of the UNESCO statement from another point of view. The development of the atom bomb, of projects for bacterial warfare, show the irresponsibility not of science but of scientists in our present society. The UNESCO experts are to be warmly extolled for their courage and their sense of responsibility which men of science owe to their fellows in the promotion of social progress and the dispelling of the results of error and ignorance. Our final quotation requires no comment:

"The biological fact of race and the myth of 'race' should be distinguished. For all practical social purposes, 'race' is not so much a biological phenomenon as a social myth. The myth of 'race' has created an enormous amount of human and social damage. In recent years it has taken a heavy toll in human lives and caused untold suffering. It still prevents the normal development of millions of human beings and deprives civilisations of the effective co-operation of productive minds. The biological differences between ethnic groups should be disregarded from the standpoint of social acceptance and social action. The unity of mankind from both the biological and social viewpoints is the main thing. To recognise this and to act accordingly is the first requirement of modern man. It is but to recognise what a great biologist wrote in 1875: 'As man advances in civilisation, and small tribes are united into larger, the simplest reason would tell each individual that he ought to extend his social instincts and sympathies to all the members of the same nation, though personally unknown to him. This point being once reached, there is only an artificial barrier to prevent his sympathies extending to the men of all nations and races.' These are the words of Charles Darwin in *The Descent of Man* (2nd edition, 1875, pages 178-188). And, indeed, the whole of human history shows that a co-operative spirit is not only natural to men, but more deeply rooted than self-seeking tendencies. If this were not so we should not see the growth of integration and organisation of his communities which the centuries and the millennia plainly exhibit."

19th August 1950

NEITHER EAST NOR WEST
Selected Writings by
Marie Louise Berneri

Marie Louise Berneri (1918-1949) was a leading member of the Freedom Press Group for twelve years and an active editor of and frequent contributor to its periodicals throughout that period. This collection of her articles which were published in *War Commentary* and *Freedom* between 1939 and 1948, is one of the four supplementary volumes to Volume 3 *World War — Cold War* in the Freedom Press Centenary Series. It includes sixteen pages of anti-war cartoons by John Olday which were published in *War Commentary* in 1943 and 1944.

The 52 items included are divided into three sections — 'Defenders of Democracy', which mercilessly exposes the democratic pretensions of the communist and capitalist allies during the Second World War; 'The Price of War and of Liberation', which starkly reports the terrible effects of the war on the people who suffered them in Europe; and 'United Nations', which takes the sad story on after the end of the Second World War into the Cold War between the former allies. The title of the book is taken from an article in 1947 insisting on opposition to state oppression wherever it exists.

Here is a critic who was wise during the events, whose judgement has been borne out by subsequent developments, and whose warm humanism and intellectual honesty shine through everything she wrote.

John Olday (1905-1977) was a militant anarchist in Germany and Britain before he went to Australia in 1950, and his caustic cartoons were a notable feature of *War Commentary* and *Freedom* from 1942 to 1949.

208 pages   ISBN 0 900384 42 5   £4.50

FREEDOM PRESS

A DECADE OF ANARCHY: 1961-1970
Selections from the monthly journal
Anarchy

Anarchy was published by Freedom Press for the first ten years of its existence, and during that period it became known as the leading voice of reflective anarchism in the English-speaking world. No fewer than 118 32-page issues were published under the editorship of Colin Ward, and the present volume contains a representative selection of less than 10 per cent of all that material chosen, arranged and introduced by him.

The thirty items included are classified under seven headings: 'Restatements', in which a number of anarchists seek to link anarchist thought to the contemporary scene; 'Experiences', which are descriptions of the human condition in different parts of the world as witnessed by the writers; 'Work', consisting of four detailed essays ranging from the practical experience of the Gang System in Coventry to the theoretical future of work; 'Education', the ever-topical subject with contributions from, among others, Paul Goodman and Harold Drasdo; 'Deviance', yet another burning topic of the day, with contributions from Tony Gibson and Stan Cohen; 'Environments', a topic which has assumed increasing urgency ever since; and 'Retrospects', which gives Colin Ward's contemporary discussion of *Anarchy* in *Freedom* and Rufus Segar's account of doing his famous covers.

Colin Ward's introduction describes the conception and creation of the paper and reflects on its relevance two decades later.

283 pages   ISBN 0 900384 37 9   £5.00

FREEDOM PRESS